Liszt and Virtuosity

Eastman Studies in Music

Ralph P. Locke, Senior Editor
Eastman School of Music

Additional Titles of Interest

Analyzing Wagner's Operas: Alfred Lorenz and German Nationalist Ideology
Stephen McClatchie

Bach to Brahms: Essays on Musical Design and Structure
Edited by David Beach and Yosef Goldenberg

Beyond "The Art of Finger Dexterity": Reassessing Carl Czerny
Edited by David Gramit

Brahms and the Shaping of Time
Edited by Scott Murphy

*Brahms's "A German Requiem":
Reconsidering Its Biblical, Historical, and Musical Contexts*
R. Allen Lott

Busoni as Pianist
Grigory Kogan
Translated and annotated by Svetlana Belsky

Heinrich Neuhaus: A Life beyond Music
Maria Razumovskaya

John Kirkpatrick, American Music, and the Printed Page
Drew Massey

Liszt's Final Decade
Dolores Pesce

*Liszt's Representation of Instrumental Sounds on the Piano:
Colors in Black and White*
Hyun Joo Kim

Liszt's Transcultural Modernism and the Hungarian-Gypsy Tradition
Shay Loya

A complete list of titles in the Eastman Studies in Music series
may be found on our website, www.urpress.com.

Liszt and Virtuosity

Edited by
Robert Doran

UNIVERSITY OF ROCHESTER PRESS

Copyright © 2020 by the Editors and Contributors

All rights reserved. Except as permitted under current legislation, no part of this work may be photocopied, stored in a retrieval system, published, performed in public, adapted, broadcast, transmitted, recorded, or reproduced in any form or by any means, without the prior permission of the copyright owner.

First published 2020
Reprinted in paperback 2025

University of Rochester Press
668 Mt. Hope Avenue, Rochester, NY 14620, USA
www.urpress.com
and Boydell & Brewer Limited
PO Box 9, Woodbridge, Suffolk IP12 3DF, UK
www.boydellandbrewer.com

ISBN-13: 978-1-58046-939-5 (hardcover)
ISBN-13: 978-1-64825-114-6 (paperback)

ISSN: 1071-9989; v. 168

Cataloging-in-Publication data available from the Library of Congress.

Cover image: Henri Lehmann, Portrait of Franz Liszt, 1839. Musée Carnavalet/Wikimedia Commons, CC-PD-Mark.

Cover design: riverdesignbooks.com

Contents

Preface vii
Robert Doran

Acknowledgments xi

Introduction: Virtuosity and Liszt 1
Robert Doran

Part One: Liszt, Virtuosity, and Performance

1 *Après une Lecture de Czerny?* Liszt's Creative Virtuosity 41
  Kenneth Hamilton

2 Transforming Virtuosity: Liszt and Nineteenth-Century Pianos 93
  Olivia Sham

3 Spirit and Mechanism: Liszt's Early Piano Technique and Teaching 109
  Nicolas Dufetel

4 Paths through the Lisztian Ossia 148
  Jonathan Kregor

5 Brahms "versus" Liszt: The Internalization of Virtuosity 186
  David Keep

Part Two: Lisztian Virtuosity: Theoretical Approaches

6 The Practice of Pianism: Virtuosity and Oral History 221
  Jim Samson

7 Liszt's Symbiosis: The Question of Virtuosity and the Concerto
  Arrangement of Schubert's *Wanderer* Fantasy 238
  Jonathan Dunsby

8 From the Brilliant Style to the Bravura Style: Reconceptualizing
  Lisztian Virtuosity 267
  Robert Doran

Part Three: Virtuosity and Anti-virtuosity in "Late Liszt"

9 Harmony, Gesture, and Virtuosity in Liszt's Revisions:
  Shaping the Affective Journeys of the Cypress Pieces from
  Années de pèlerinage 3 311
  Dolores Pesce

10 Anti-virtuosity and Musical Experimentalism: Liszt, Marie Jaëll,
   Debussy, and Others 346
   Ralph P. Locke

11 Virtuosity in Liszt's Late Piano Works 387
   Shay Loya

   List of Contributors 415

   Index of Liszt's Musical Works 417

   General Index 423

Preface

The present volume derives in large part from a conference held at the Eastman School of Music (University of Rochester) on March 2–4, 2017, entitled "Liszt and Virtuosity—an International Symposium," organized by Jonathan Dunsby, Ralph P. Locke, and me. All of the essays contained herein have been rewritten or extensively revised and lengthened; a few were newly commissioned specifically for this volume. Unfortunately, Alexander Stefaniak's and Dana Gooley's papers were unable to be included due to their having been promised elsewhere.[1] Rena Charnin Mueller, another participant, was unable to revise and submit her paper due to illness.

The book's division into three parts reflects the contributors' principal areas of interest with respect to Lisztian virtuosity and to virtuosity more generally: (1) how Lisztian virtuosity relates to performance practices, (2) the theoretical or conceptual aspects of virtuosity as manifested in Liszt's example, and (3) the role of virtuosity or anti-virtuosity in Liszt's late works. My editor's introduction offers a broad overview of the subject of virtuosity and of Liszt's essential relation to it, along with some consideration of the major questions and problems involved in its treatment. Although it does not summarize the individual contributions made in each of the book's chapters, it refers to all of them in passing, thereby setting them in the context of larger trends within the fields of historical musicology, music theory and analysis, intellectual history, and performance studies.

The idea of virtuosity has become topical in music studies only relatively recently, reflecting a broad reappraisal of this long-undervalued aspect of music. Volumes devoted to it during just the past few years include the collection *Exploring Virtuosities: Heinrich Wilhelm Ernst, Nineteenth-Century Musical Practices and Beyond* (2018), a special issue of the journal *Musicae Scientiae* titled "Virtuosity" (2018),[2] and several monographs: Hyun Joo Kim, *Liszt's Representation of Instrumental Sounds on the Piano: Colors in Black and White* (University of Rochester Press, 2019); Alexander Stefaniak, *Schumann's Virtuosity: Criticism, Composition, and Performance in*

Nineteenth-Century Germany (2016); Žarko Cvejić, *The Virtuoso as Subject: The Reception of Instrumental Virtuosity, c. 1815–c. 1850* (2016); and Mai Kawabata, *Paganini: The "Demonic" Virtuoso* (2013).[3] The now-classic study that set in motion many recent interventions is certainly Jim Samson's *Virtuosity and the Musical Work: The "Transcendental Studies" of Liszt* (2003), a book that lies at the frontier of music history, music theory, and performance studies—a mix of disciplinary perspectives that, as Samson notes, is precisely what the idea of virtuosity in music requires: "It is not obvious to me that existing methods can easily accommodate the concept of virtuosity that is so clearly prescribed by [Liszt's] etudes."[4] Indeed, the contributions to this volume represent an effort to develop new, more holistic approaches to account for virtuosity in its specificity.

Following Samson's lead, the present volume aims to treat virtuosity as a musical *concept*, rather than the *image* of Liszt-as-virtuoso, that is, as a touring concert pianist and salon favorite. The latter has received a great deal of attention from biographical (Alan Walker's seminal *Franz Liszt: The Virtuoso Years, 1811–1847* [1983]) and cultural-historical (Dana Gooley's more recent *The Virtuoso Liszt* [2004]) accounts, even if these also deal to some extent with Liszt's technical innovations.[5] Heinz von Loesch notes that "in the wake of post-structuralism, cultural studies and the performance turn, an abundance of studies have emerged, interested above all in virtuosity as a socio-cultural phenomenon and as a performative act. The virtuoso appeared as a deeply exciting subject matter: his appearance, his body, his gender, his effect on the public as well as the discourse that surrounded him."[6] Although it is the idea of Liszt as an unparalleled stage performer that most captures the popular imagination, this volume demonstrates that Liszt's more essential contribution to the history of virtuosity is *compositional*: it is based on his published body of work and is therefore an integral part of the work concept, even if it often challenges the propriety of this concept. The essays that follow thus seek to understand, as Carl Dahlhaus puts it, "the musicohistorical significance of the virtuosity that culminated in Paganini and Liszt, a significance at first cultural but which later affected the history of composition."[7]

In sum, the present volume offers a reevaluation of the concept and practices of virtuosity as they are defined and shaped by Liszt's multifaceted oeuvre, including reconsiderations of Liszt's relations to other major and lesser-known musical figures, such as Czerny, Schubert, Chopin, Brahms, Debussy, and Marie Jaëll (a recently rediscovered pianist-composer who was a member of Liszt's circle). Although it has often been treated with opprobrium, Liszt's legacy in the realm of virtuosity is essential and productive: it represents a singular contribution to music history that continues to influence the music world today.

Robert Doran,
March 2020

Notes

1. Alexander Stefaniak, "Clara Schumann's Interiorities and the Cutting Edge of Popular Pianism," *Journal of the American Musicological Society* 70, no. 3 (2017): 697–765; Dana Gooley, "Liszt and the Romantic Rhetoric of Improvisation," in Gooley, *Fantasies of Improvisation: Free Playing in Nineteenth-Century Music* (Oxford: Oxford University Press, 2018), 198–242.
2. The essays in the special issue of *Musicae Scientiae* derive from the conference "Virtuosity—an Interdisciplinary Symposium," held at the Liszt Ferenc Academy of Music, Budapest, on March 3–6, 2016 (my paper for this conference was folded into my editor's introduction).
3. One could also mention Olivia Sham's doctoral dissertation in this group: "Performing the Unperformable: Notions of Virtuosity in Liszt's Solo Piano Music," PhD Dissertation (Royal Academy of Music, 2014), as well as Cécile Reynaud, *Liszt et le virtuose romantique* (Paris: Honoré Champion, 2006), and Susan Bernstein, *Virtuosity of the Nineteenth Century: Performing Music and Language in Heine, Liszt, and Baudelaire* (Stanford, CA: Stanford University Press, 1998).
4. Jim Samson, *Virtuosity and the Musical Work: The "Transcendental Studies" of Liszt* (Cambridge: Cambridge University Press, 2003), 2. Samson's book echoes in some important respects Charles Rosen's *The Romantic Generation* (Cambridge, MA: Harvard University Press, 1995) in its rehabilitation of the virtuosity of the early Liszt. Compare, for example, Rosen's chapter entitled "Liszt: On Creation as Performance" (472–541), to Samson's entitled "Composing the Performance" (66–102). See also Kenneth Hamilton's *After the Golden Age: Romantic Pianism and Modern Performance* (Oxford: Oxford University Press, 2007), which is exemplary in its effort to examine virtuosity from the perspective of performance studies.
5. See, in particular, the chapter entitled "Liszt and the Keyboard" in Alan Walker, *Franz Liszt, Volume 1: The Virtuoso Years, 1811–1847* (New York: Alfred A. Knopf, 1983), 285–318.
6. Heinz von Loesch, "Mapping Virtuosity 2015," in *Exploring Virtuosities: Heinrich Wilhelm Ernst, Nineteenth-Century Musical Practices and Beyond*, ed. Christine Hoppe, Melanie von Goldbeck, and Maiko Kawabata (Hildesheim, Zurich, New York: Georg Olms Verlag, 2018), 17.

7. Carl Dahlhaus, *Nineteenth-Century Music*, trans. J. Bradford Robinson (Berkeley and Los Angeles: University of California Press, 1989), 134. Although Samson in his contribution to this volume claims that he will reflect "on virtuosity as a dimension of performance rather than of composition" it is really the *theory of performance*, or as he calls it, the "practice of performance" that interests him, rather than its cultural-historical aspect per se. Samson has been influenced in this regard by French sociologist Pierre Bourdieu, especially his seminal *Outline of a Theory of Practice*.

Acknowledgments

I would like to thank the University of Rochester for its generous sponsorship, through a Humanities Project grant, of the 2017 conference "Liszt and Virtuosity—an International Symposium," from which most of the contributions of this volume are derived. I would also like to thank my co-organizers, Jonathan Dunsby and Ralph P. Locke, who also contributed to this volume, for their assistance with the conference. Finally, I would like to express my gratitude to the editorial staff at the University of Rochester Press, to its director Sonia Kane, and to the editor of its series, Eastman Studies in Music, Ralph P. Locke, for their enthusiasm for and careful attention to this volume.

Robert Doran,
March 2020

Introduction

Virtuosity and Liszt

Robert Doran

It would not be quite right to say that in [Liszt's] work the technical aspect stands in the foreground, much less that it was in any sense its own excuse for being. It is inseparable from the creative—from the creative in the service of Romantic ideas and feelings.

—Alfred Einstein[1]

Virtuosity ought to be a subject for today.

—Jim Samson[2]

In many ways Franz Liszt has come to define or incarnate piano virtuosity, even virtuosity tout court. Liszt is certainly the archetypal virtuoso: a flamboyant performer whose hair-raising technical feats at the piano created a sense of awe-inspiring excitement and an icon whose star power radiated far beyond the realm of music. While Liszt's early model, the Italian violinist Niccolò Paganini, may have been the first instrumentalist to define himself principally by virtuosity, Liszt transformed it into a revolutionary musical force, one that pushed the piano aesthetic to the limits of sound and poetic meaning. Lisztian virtuosity did not, however, arise in a vacuum but coincided with a number of interrelated historical phenomena: the rise of the middle-class consumer of concerts and lessons, the emerging centrality of the piano in musical culture, the popularity of opera, and the political shifts that led to a decline in aristocratic influence over music making and the concomitant valorization of the individual artist-genius. Moreover, Liszt forged this virtuoso image not alone but in the company of a host of dazzling pianists who brought keyboard virtuosity to heights not previously imagined: Friedrich Kalkbrenner, Alexander Dreyschock, Henri Herz, Adolf von

Henselt, Clara Schumann, and especially Sigismond Thalberg, Liszt's only real rival. But Liszt alone among this group of composer-pianists—which notably does not include Fryderyk Chopin,[3] who performed rarely in public and assiduously avoided the trappings of the virtuoso—was able to rescue this surfeit of virtuosity from its superficial, banal, and time-bound aspects,[4] projecting a brand of romantic virtuosity that would become a wellspring for late nineteenth- and early twentieth-century piano writing, most spectacularly in the concertos of Grieg, Anton Rubinstein, Saint-Saëns, Tchaikovsky, Rachmaninoff, Prokofiev, and even Brahms (see David Keep's contribution to this volume on the Brahms-Liszt relation).[5]

As noted in the preface, we insist, in our investigations, on a distinction between the *image* of Liszt as a virtuoso performer—the child prodigy of the 1820s, the salon favorite of the 1830s, the touring artist of the 1840s—and Liszt the *creator* of seminal virtuosic works and arrangements. The idea that Liszt is a "model" for today's young superstar pianists (e.g., Lang Lang on his 2011 Sony Classical CD entitled *Liszt—My Piano Hero*) is based on a misapprehension. For, despite the fact that Liszt invented the solo piano recital ("le concert c'est moi," as he proclaimed), codifying many innovations that are now taken for granted—such as playing from memory and consistently placing the piano at a horizontal angle on stage, thereby showing the performer's profile and his/her facial expressions—we must nevertheless not forget that much of Liszt's legend as a performer is rooted in practices that have little or nothing to do with what goes on in today's concert halls: the spontaneous improvisation based on themes provided by the audience, the preference for the performance of one's own works, the ubiquity of fantasies or variations based on popular operatic themes, not to mention the pianistic stunts and ostentatious showmanship that would certainly shock contemporary audiences.[6] Little of this has survived. However, the loss of these nineteenth-century virtuosic traditions inspires little nostalgia: they are considered excesses of which we have fortunately rid ourselves. In fact, modern pianistic practice would appear to owe more to the example of Clara Schumann than to Liszt, given her scrupulous attention to the musical text, subservience of virtuosity to the musical idea, and consistent programming of serious works by earlier composers, such as Beethoven's "Appassionata," one of her mainstays.[7] But she nevertheless continued, well into the 1840s, to program operatic fantasies and variations by Henselt, Thalberg, and Liszt, as was expected of virtuosos of the time.

It should also be noted that the works of Liszt that are now considered the pinnacle of today's virtuoso repertoire—the B-Minor Sonata, the First Mephisto Waltz, the Spanish Rhapsody, the Hungarian Rhapsodies—were all composed or completed *after* Liszt had retired from the concert stage and thus could not have contributed to Liszt's legend as a performer. Among Liszt's (fully) original compositions, only the brief (and now rarely played) *Grand galop chromatique* (S. 219 / LW A43, 1838) was featured with regularity in his concerts (it was in fact his most programed piece overall; see my analysis of this piece in my chapter in this volume). According to Michael Saffle's exhaustive catalog of Liszt's performing repertoire during his German tours, Liszt "rarely played what critics would today would consider his most interesting pre-1845 works: early versions of the pieces that eventually comprised the first volume of the *Années de pèlerinage*, for instance, or the early versions of the 'Transcendental Études.'"[8] Liszt's appeal rested for the most part on his opera fantasies and transcriptions of others' works—his arrangement of Schubert's song "Erlkönig" (S. 558/4 / LW A42/4, 1838) and his fantasies on the waltz from Meyerbeer's opera *Robert le diable* (S. 413 / LW A78, 1841) and themes from Mozart's *Don Giovanni* (S. 418 / LW A80, 1841) were especially popular.[9] Similarly, Thalberg, although he composed a sizable number of original works (including the Piano Concerto in F Minor, op. 5, 1831), earned his virtuoso reputation primarily through showpieces such as his *Fantasia on Rossini's "Moses,"* op. 33 (1839).

Perhaps most unfortunately, the virtuosic art of improvisation is all but lost in "classical" music (surviving only in jazz and some popular-music genres), cast aside by the preference for the programming of historical works (1700–1950) of the standard repertoire, with perhaps a few contemporary pieces thrown in (most often not composed by the performer him- or herself). Virtuosity persists, but the spontaneous virtuosity of improvisation and of loosely constructed fantasies and variations, the norm for much of the nineteenth century, is replaced in the twentieth by tightly constructed, compositional virtuosity; the performer becomes an "interpreter."[10] (However, Jim Samson contests what he calls the "paradigm of interpretation" in his contribution to this volume.) That Liszt attempted to some extent to combine the two—that is, that he endeavored in his works to preserve an element of spontaneity—is no doubt one of the sources of the antipathy that some critics feel toward the Hungarian-born composer. Indeed, Liszt often displays a keen sensitivity toward the variability of performance, making what should appear as necessary (the composition as written, its idealized *concept*) appear as contingent (the vagaries of *actual* performance), thereby putting him at odds with the more recent, pseudo-Platonic conception of the artwork as possessing an inviolable ontological purity or integrity—a notion that invariably restrains the performance choices of today's musicians.[11] The plethora of ossia passages, alternate cadenzas, and optional cuts, not to mention the sheer number of *versions* of most of Liszt's works, give the performer of Liszt far more choices than do those of any other composer.[12] Does this mean that Liszt is an exception, out of step with musical norms?[13] This is a difficult question to answer, for many composers simply destroy earlier versions of their works, giving the false impression of a unitary creative process. Liszt's zeal for transcription and arrangement, although uncommon among major composers, is certainly matched by J. S. Bach. And Friedrich Kalkbrenner no doubt inspired Liszt with his transcriptions of Beethoven's nine symphonies for solo piano in 1838. Liszt writes that "the recent publication of the same Symphonies, *arranged* by Mr. Kalkbrenner, makes me anxious that mine should not remain any longer in a portfolio."[14] Liszt no doubt saw himself not as an outlier but as carrying out urgent projects in music.[15] This being said, and as a general rule, virtuosity produces contingency, and, in the realm of compositional contingency, Liszt is clearly in a class by himself.

As Jonathan Kregor's contribution on Liszt's ossia aptly shows, these contingencies challenge the very concept of the "work." Indeed, twentieth-century Lisztians such as Vladimir Horowitz,[16] Earl Wild, György Cziffra, and Jorge Bolet have often taken a more nineteenth-century—which is to say, liberal—view of the Lisztian score, modifying it according to their needs and preferences, particularly in the virtuosic passages.[17] But more classically oriented pianists have generally deplored the perceived need for creative license in performances of Liszt's works. Thus Alfred Brendel, while admiring Liszt's achievements, tended to apply a more idealist concept of the musical work to the Lisztian corpus, insisting that Liszt's "optional variants (*ossias*) testify to restlessness and indecision."[18] Specifically taking Horowitz's 1966 recording of *Vallée d'Obermann* to task, Brendel confidently asserts that "Liszt would surely have been the first to object to others meddling with his texts, unless he had given the player *ad libitum* authorization."[19]

Despite the anachronism of Brendel's views—Liszt himself had written that "virtuosity is not a submissive handmaid to the composition"[20]—they nevertheless point up an important tension in music history. For there was an inevitable clash between Liszt the performer and Liszt the composer, between the performance virtuosity developed during Liszt's touring years (1838–47) and the compositional virtuosity on which his current musical reputation is built (after his retirement and establishment in Weimar, especially 1847–61), revealing an artist at pains to fuse or reconcile two divergent parts of his being, reflecting two different moments of his career. More broadly, Liszt can also be said to be navigating between two opposed but interconnected strands of nineteenth-century musical culture: the one bound up with spontaneity, ephemerality, and publicness, and the other with inertia, accumulated history, and ideality. This dichotomy has also presented a challenge to contemporary music studies. As Samson avers:

> Virtuosity brings into sharp focus the relationship between music's object-status and its event-status. It marks out a relational field in which text, instrument, performer, and audience are all indispensable to defining significance. It draws the performer right into the heart of the work, foregrounding presentational strategies that are hard to illuminate through the familiar, pedigreed methods of music analysis. And it spotlights the instrument, elevating the idiomatic (the figure), a category much less amenable to analysis than theme, harmony and form.[21]

Indeed, virtuosity has an *irreducible* character, and any investigation into this subject will thus require the kind of multifaceted approach that characterizes the contributions to this volume. In view of the fact that virtuosity "spotlights the instrument," it is with the instrument that we shall begin.

Virtuosity and the Evolution of the "Piano"

Unfortunately, the question of the piano is vastly underappreciated in musical education and in conservatories in particular,[22] where pianists are trained exclusively on modern instruments, relegating the study of the harpsichord and the fortepiano to specialists in historical performance.[23] We tend to forget that what we now take for granted as the instrument called "piano"—from the living-room upright to the nine-foot concert grand—underwent constant and often radical development during much of Liszt's lifetime, so much so that it is difficult to say whether we are talking about the same instrument—a point eloquently elaborated in Olivia Sham's contribution to this volume. This development was not only in the realm of sound or timbre—the qualities most in evidence in recordings of historical instruments—but, and more importantly, from a compositional and performance perspective, in that of volume, register balance, sustaining capacity (including the damper pedal), keyboard action, and keyboard compass. No comparable evolution can be observed in the violin, the only other acoustic instrument that can rival piano virtuosity.[24] Today's violin virtuosos are still using, and in most cases much prefer, instruments made two to three hundred years ago (in particular those built by Antonio Stradivari).[25] Thus, violin virtuosity evolved without any corresponding developments in manufacturing. The development of the keyboard, on the contrary, is constant and unidirectional: during this period of rapid evolution, one could play on a given keyboard instrument all the music composed before its manufacture but little of the music composed after it (i.e., after the next major "improvement"). Thus one cannot play a late Beethoven sonata on Bach's clavichord or Chopin's études on Mozart's fortepiano (for one thing, many of the notes could not be played at all, since the keyboard range is simply too small on these earlier instruments). But Liszt could play anything by Bach, Mozart, Clementi, or Beethoven on all his pianos, even though these composers had in mind a very different instrument and sound. It is not merely a question of "authenticity" (or "authenticism," as Richard Taruskin puts it—a debate that would take us too far afield); it is a matter of understanding the possibilities and limitations of the instruments that composers had at their disposal and of how "piano" manufacturers (who were often composers and performers themselves) were pushed to modify their products in response to creative and performance exigencies.

This is especially true with regard to virtuosity. One could even argue that the lure of virtuosity itself was the prime mover behind many of the most important modifications of piano design: the double-escapement mechanism making possible the rapid repetition of notes, the expansion of the keyboard compass permitting spectacular runs and arpeggios from one end to the other, the significant increase in volume (especially the booming bass) that allows the pianist to overwhelm the audience in large spaces and to play above the din of the increasingly large orchestras in concerto performances. Starting in the 1820s and 1830s, the piano becomes an instrument of startling virtuosity and a vehicle of individual—and even egotistical—self-expression, such as it had never been before. This movement toward an extroverted and hyperbolic virtuosity also marks the decisive break between what is known as the "classical" and "Romantic" eras, even if virtuosity obviously existed and flourished previously.[26] (I explore this transition from the postclassical "brilliant style" to early Romantic virtuosity in my contribution to this volume.)

Prior to the 1830s, the most important shift in piano manufacturing was that from the Viennese fortepiano used by Mozart to the English Broadwood piano favored by Haydn (in his late keyboard works composed just after Mozart's death), Clementi, and the later Beethoven.[27] This also marked a shift in piano touch, from the detached style of Mozart to the legato technique of the English school, represented by Clementi and Cramer (originally from Rome and Mannheim, respectively, but brought to England at a young age) and embraced by Beethoven. Beethoven reportedly told his student Czerny that Mozart "had a fine but choppy (*zerhacktes*) way of playing, no *ligato*."[28] And Czerny recalls that Beethoven was "particularly aware of the Legato, of which he had such an unrivalled command, and which all other pianists at that time considered unfeasible at the pianoforte."[29] As Hummel (who had lived and studied with Mozart but who had also taken lessons with Clementi in London) observes in his 1828 manual, *A Complete Theoretical and Practical Course of Instructions on the Art of Playing the Pianoforte*:

> The German piano may be played upon with ease by the weakest hand. It allows the performer to impart to his execution every possible degree of light and shade, speaks clearly and promptly, has a round, flute-like tone, which, in a large room, contrasts well with the accompanying orchestra, and does not impede rapidity of execution by requiring too great an effort. . . . The English piano also has much to offer. Among other things, it must be praised for its durability and fullness of tone. Nevertheless this instrument does not admit of the same facility of execution as the German. The touch is much heavier, the keys sink much deeper, and consequently, the return of the hammer on the repetition of a note cannot take place so quickly. . . . As a counterpoise of this, however, through the fullness of tone in the English Piano-Forte, the melody receives a peculiar charm and harmonious sweetness.[30]

Hummel describes nothing less than two very different "piano" aesthetics, with attendant differences in keyboard technique and creative possibilities. But there are important trade-offs between the desire for virtuosity and the style of sound. In short, ease of execution is sacrificed for other virtues. We often do not realize that the piano has become a much more difficult instrument to play than it was in Mozart's time (particularly for children), whereas the difficulty level for most other instruments has remained constant (and, unlike the piano, many instruments are available in child sizes).

As Hummel notes in the passage above, the English (Broadwood) piano allowed for a rich, legato sonority. It was in fact the first keyboard instrument to feature a divided bridge between treble and bass, "which allowed for an equalization of tension and created an equalization of tone."[31] The hammers were covered with a soft material (now felt), resulting in a fuller and louder tone, with subtle gradations. In addition, and no less importantly, with the English piano the keyboard compass was increased from the five-octave keyboard that marked the limit of all of Mozart's piano works and approximately half of Beethoven's, to a five-and-a-half- and then a six-octave keyboard.

Thus, up to and including the opus 31 set (featuring the "Tempest" Sonata, op. 31, no. 2), composed in 1801–2, Beethoven was restricted to just five octaves, from F1 to F6.

Recent attention has been given to the influence of French piano building at this time;[32] for it was Beethoven's acquisition of a five-and-a-half-octave Érard piano in 1803 (extending the treble to C6) that made a world of difference,[33] allowing for the titanic virtuosity of the groundbreaking "Waldstein," op. 53 (1804), and "Appassionata," op. 57 (1804–6), Sonatas, as well as the Fourth Piano Concerto, op. 58 (1805–6). These works took great advantage of the slightly expanded upper register as well as of novel effects with the Érard's sustaining pedal. In the "Appassionata" in particular, keyboard virtuosity makes a quantum leap.[34] One can hear this work played alongside those by Rachmaninoff on a modern grand piano and not think that they were written for different instruments. One reason for this is the regular, almost constant use of the sustaining pedal implied (although only sparingly notated) throughout the three movements of opus 57, enabling an astonishing array of new virtuosic effects, colors, and greater emphasis on the extreme treble and bass. (It is surely no coincidence that this sonata, along with the first movement of the "Moonlight" Sonata, which calls for the damper pedal to be employed for the entire movement [*sempre pianissimo e senza sordini*], were the most popular of Beethoven's piano works during the Romantic era.) Whereas in the classical period the sustaining pedal is considered a special effect and a dry (and often non-legato) sound the norm (Kalkbrenner observes, incredibly, that as late as 1831 "in Germany the use of the pedals is scarcely known"),[35] for the Romantics the use of the sustaining pedal becomes the default and its nonuse a special effect.[36] However, we should also note that early nineteenth-century pianos often had as many as four or five pedals (Beethoven's Érard had four), enabling, organ-like, a wide range of mechanically produced colors.[37] In addition, the sustaining capacity of the damper pedal on these pianos is much less effective than on a modern piano (post-1850), hence the unfeasibility of many pedal markings by Liszt and his contemporaries.

In 1817, a carefully selected new Broadwood was gifted to Beethoven by the manufacturer, resulting in the mighty "Hammerklavier" Sonata, op. 106, which, as the moniker indicates (Beethoven called it *Große Sonate für das Hammerklavier*), excludes performance on the fortepiano. It was thus the first true "piano sonata," in the full sense of the term, and it remained the most innovative solo piano work in terms of sound, sonority, and structure until Liszt's own Sonata in B Minor, of 1853, the first major composition to take full advantage of the modern, seven-octave piano (A0 to A7 or C8). (Recall that the revision of the *Transcendental Études* in 1851 retained the restricted range of the six-and-a-half-octave piano, not employing the three notes below the low C1, and with several ossia passages in the upper registers for use with a smaller piano.)[38] Today we strive as much as possible to respect the limits of the instruments of the composer's time, even if this means "imitating" or at least creating a sonic field similar to that of the original instrument, which typically has the effect of restraining the virtuosity, although not always: Glenn Gould's idiosyncratic approach to performance (extreme tempos and detached, ultra-clear articulation) transformed Bach's harpsichord/clavichord works into exhibitions of startling, piano-specific virtuosity.

Between 1820 and 1830 the standard keyboard was extended to six and a half octaves. Chopin's first Étude, op. 10, no. 1, celebrates this new range, from C1 in the bass to F7 in the treble. (Liszt repeats this gesture in his *Preludio* to his *Transcendental Études*, also in C major, which sounds out the entire keyboard range that was standard in the late 1830s, from C1 to A7, with an ossia to accommodate a piano that stops at F7.) The additional bass notes (C1–E1) gave the piano a much richer and more powerful sonority (amplified by the sustaining pedal), particularly in climactic and virtuosic passages, making it the functional equivalent of the orchestra (at least in terms of richness of sonority, since a double bass without an extension stops at E1). Indeed, the expanded range made for much more effective transcriptions of orchestral works, of which Liszt would of course be the undisputed champion. Although the seven-octave piano was available during his lifetime, Chopin remained faithful to the six-and-a-half-octave range of his youth, which for the most part did not disturb his compositions, save for one instance: the climactic double octaves of the Fantasy in F Minor, op. 49 (mm. 109–16), which in their first iteration require the low B-flat (as is clear from the recapitulation); Chopin opts for E-flat instead, which sounds quite unsatisfactory.[39] Chopin also preferred the lighter Pleyel piano, which fit his classically oriented, post-brilliant-style piano aesthetic. Liszt, on the other hand, favored the much more powerful and technologically advanced Érard (with its recently introduced double-escapement technology), a choice that reflects Liszt's modernist approach to virtuosity.[40]

The rapid evolution of the piano both contributed and responded to an exponential increase in virtuosity. But it could also make virtuosity more difficult to attain. One of the main impediments to virtuosity, as noted above by Hummel, was the increasingly stiff action. The action of a modern piano requires nearly four times the force, and the depression of the key is nearly twice the distance, of Mozart's fortepiano. Thus, complicated ornaments, executed with relative ease on a fortepiano, pose significant challenges for the modern pianist.[41] The action of the pianos of the 1830s was somewhere in the midrange between these two extremes. In terms of pure virtuosity—velocity, ease, and accuracy of execution, combined with a good deal of power—the Érard that Liszt played in the 1830s and 1840s, the principal years of his touring career, may have been the ultimate virtuoso keyboard instrument. Many of Liszt's achievements in the realm of virtuosity during his touring years may be literally unattainable today on modern instruments, rendering pointless the comparative judgments we sometimes hear about Liszt's exploits versus those of contemporary pianists or even late nineteenth-century pianists. Lisztian virtuosity was a function of the specific instrument for which it was intended.

Indeed, in response to the standardization of the seven-octave piano in the 1850s, with its heavier action and enriched sonority, Liszt was obliged to reconfigure his approach to virtuosity.[42] As Olivia Sham notes in her chapter, "The effect of these new instruments can also be seen in Liszt's compositions during his Weimar years. Liszt's virtuosity became more economical: he relied much less on finger facility, which created large quantities of small notes in order to fill the sonority, but rather more on the power of the instrument in larger chords and octave passages." The revisions of the *Paganini* and *Transcendental Études* in the 1850s can therefore be seen, at least in part, as a way of responding to significant changes in piano manufacturing and design.[43] Indeed, many of Chopin's études have become more difficult than they were originally intended to be (especially op. 10, no. 2, which is now quite a hand breaker and a competition tour de force, not to mention Chopin's metronome markings, which are blazingly fast). But Chopin died in 1849, just prior to the standardization of the iron-framed, modern piano.[44] Stories of pianists of the 1830s (including Liszt) spending ten, twelve, or even fourteen hours a day hunched over the keyboard now seem quaint in the age of carpal-tunnel syndrome.[45]

Virtuosity and the Question of "Difficulty"

Almost every definition of virtuosity points to the idea of *great skill* or *difficulties overcome* in performance.[46] The relation between difficulty and virtuosity is hardly straightforward, however (as David Keep explores in his contribution). The presence of virtuosity in the work would appear to imply that the composer intended the work to be difficult to play or, in certain "showpieces," to at least give the *impression* of difficulty, as if difficulty were itself an aesthetic quality and even if the "difficulties" are both highlighted and negated by virtuosic ease. There are, however, many types of difficulty. An intricate five-part fugue from Bach's *Well-Tempered Clavier* is difficult in a very different way than the ostentatious virtuosity of the "friska" section in one of Liszt's Hungarian Rhapsodies. And interpretative difficulty is typically separated from technical difficulty—even if it is not always quite clear where one stops and the other starts. (See Nicolas Dufetel's contribution to this volume for an exploration of this question in relation to Liszt's early teaching.) Virtuosity is, then, a specific *kind* of difficulty, requiring a special kind of skill, understood as digital/technical in nature and typically involving speed, accuracy, and power; but as Sham notes, it can also include "subtler aspects of a superior technical command of the piano, such as the control of colors, volume, pedal, articulation."[47] We might further distinguish between the digital/technical difficulty that is perceivable by the non-pianist listener and that which is not, with the former earning the public designation of virtuosity and the latter only under certain prescribed circumstances, such as the piano competition or the conservatory examination. Hence the preference in competitions for the quiet but difficult Chopin études, namely, opus 10, number 2 (chromatic) and opus 25, number 6 (thirds), which are considered to be much more difficult than the ostentatiously virtuosic "Revolutionary" Étude (op. 10, no. 12). (The "Winter Wind" Étude, op. 25, no. 11, is perhaps the only Chopin étude that fulfills the twin requirements of extreme difficulty and surface virtuosity.) The typical audience will thus enthusiastically applaud the "Revolutionary" Étude but will show only a muted reaction to even a brilliant execution of opus 10, number 2, whereas the competition or conservatory jury will react in just the opposite manner. Volume is surely one of the most important factors in perceived virtuosity. It is certainly no accident that concerts almost always end with a bang. Among Liszt's *Transcendental Études*, the ethereal *Feux follets* (no. 5) will not create the same audience furor as the ferocious endings of *Wilde Jagd* (no. 8) or no. 10 in F Minor, even though it is a more technically difficult étude. On the phenomenological level, at least, audience perception is inextricable from the way in which virtuosity shows itself.

 As a rule, then, not all virtuosic piano writing is as difficult as it sounds; but all virtuosic piano writing *appears* to be difficult, that is, it appears under the *sign* of difficulty whether or not, from the executant's perspective, the writing is in fact difficult. Playing Liszt's *La campanella* Étude in G-sharp Minor is challenging enough; playing it a half step lower or higher would be nearly impossible at the same tempo (large leaps to raised back keys are easier to execute). One can say the same for Chopin's aforementioned Étude op. 25, no. 6, coincidentally in the same key of G-sharp minor: the piece is designed to be played in that key and no other; this is not a musical but a technical necessity (relating to the position of the hand with respect to the black keys when playing thirds).

The question of the level of difficulty and its relation to virtuosity and aesthetic value is an essential if overlooked part of the creative process. The notion that the wings of a musical idea might have to be clipped by practical or commercial concerns is surely anathema to the ideology of aesthetic autonomy. Nevertheless, is will not come as a surprise that the level of difficulty should be a determining aspect of the work. Mozart was often asked by his aristocratic patrons to write for the "amateur" (a somewhat different notion from the pejorative sense that now often attaches to the term), namely the moderately but competently skilled nonprofessional.[48] Both Mozart and Beethoven wrote some of their most beautiful sonatas with students in mind. Chopin's livelihood depended in no small part on the sale of the rights to his compositions (published simultaneously in France, England, and Germany), which for commercial reasons could not be too difficult—hence the abundance of smaller, less dramatic works (mazurka, waltzes, nocturnes, etc.) that could be played by the student or intermediate pianist. Thus one assumes that Chopin simply excised, during the creative process (namely, his improvisations), those passages that appeared to be too far above the general level of difficulty of the rest of the piece, rather than provide ossias for simplified passages or compose alternative, simpler versions of his works—something that Liszt did with regularity in the first instance and on occasion in the second.[49] The wide gap that separates the difficulty of many, if not most, of Chopin's études (obviously intended to be difficult, though not always, as mentioned above, in the standard virtuosic sense) from the vast majority of his other compositions is certainly suggestive of such a practice. Perhaps even the mighty Chopin Ballades are somewhat simplified versions of the improvisations on which they were based.

However, when aiming for the very highest musical attainment, a composer will not want to be limited by players of lesser skill. In practice, then, virtuosity and difficulty are highly correlated with aesthetic value. The greatest solo piano works of a given composer tend also to be the most virtuosic and technically challenging that that composer produced. If we exclude the étude genre, the following brief list of eighteenth- and nineteenth-century masterworks is instructive: Bach's *Goldberg Variations*, Haydn's Sonata in E-flat Major (Hob. XVI: 52, L. 62), Beethoven's "Hammerklavier" Sonata and "Diabelli" Variations, Schubert's *Wanderer* Fantasy, Schumann's Fantasy in C Major, op. 17, Chopin's F-Minor Ballade, op. 52 (or his Second or Third Piano Sonatas), Mendelssohn's *Variations sérieuses*, op. 54, Liszt's B-Minor Sonata, and Brahms's *Variations and Fugue on a Theme by Handel*, op. 24.[50] (Counting the Chopin ballade as a kind of fantasy, all of these fit neatly into three distinct genres: variations, sonatas, and fantasies—two of which are often derided as less than serious . . .) Each of these works is arguably the greatest that its composer produced for solo piano, and in each case there is a very high level of virtuosity and technical difficulty relative to other piano works by the same composer.[51] The presence of virtuosic difficulty is thus simply a by-product of the composer's unfettered creative impulse: the composer-pianist uses *all* of his or her skill, not allowing the exigencies of execution to impede those of expression when it comes to reaching for the musical heights.[52] Paradoxically, then, it is the most virtuosic works that come closest to the musical ideal.[53]

Of course, in the case of epoch-making virtuosos such as Paganini and Liszt, the fetishization of difficulty could place severe limits on who could play their works. As Samson notes, they "effectively narrow down the availability of the music—its use value—to a single location."[54] This gives rise to the trope of *unplayability*, which was something new in the history of music performance.[55] The Liszt of the 1830s certainly pursued difficulty in a way that Chopin or even Thalberg never did, particularly in his "Clochette" Fantasy on a theme by Paganini (*Grande fantaisie de bravoure sur "La clochette" de Paganini*, S. 420 / LW A15) of 1831–32, in some of his more elaborate opera fantasies, and above all in the two sets of études in their 1837–38 version. At this time Liszt wished to become the "Paganini of the piano," to set an example of *uniqueness* in virtuosity. The ideal of these two supervirtuosos was not simply virtuosity but the exhibition of superhuman, transcendental skills of which no other performer on their respective instruments was capable. Regarding the "Clochette" Fantasy, Jonathan Kregor observes in his contribution to this volume that "it is the only piece in Liszt's oeuvre to include an easier and more practical alternative that Liszt himself took in performance."[56] Similarly Liszt's 1830s études are perhaps less designed for performance than they are a *pianistic statement* about the virtuosic possibilities of the instrument as it existed at that time.[57]

Such was his revolutionary approach to piano technique that Liszt often underestimated the degree of skill required for the proper realization of his virtuosic works, even when we exclude the études. Indeed, many prominent pianists to whom he had dedicated works were unable to play the piece themselves. After a performance of the *Norma* Fantasy (S. 394 / LW A77, 1841) by Emil von Sauer in one of his master classes, Liszt remarked that "Madame Pleyel wanted 'Thalberg passages' in a piece I was supposed to write for her [the *Norma* Fantasy]. . . . But she never managed a credible performance of this fantasy."[58] After a master class performance of the *Grosses Konzertsolo*, Liszt stated that "I had no luck with my two dedications to Henselt [the *Grosses Konzertsolo*, S. 176 / LW A167, 1849–50] and Kullak [*Scherzo und Marsch*, S. 177 / LW A174, 1851]. No, said both of them, 'Listen, you, no one is able to play that, that goes beyond the possible.'"[59] And these works are not nearly as difficult as the études. Referring to the left-hand octave accompaniment at the end of *La campanella* (*Paganini Étude*, no. 3, 1851 version), Liszt notes that it might be simplified, remarking that "when I wrote that I did not teach as much as I did now."[60]

For perspective, let us recall that such technically formidable and revolutionary compositions as Beethoven's "Waldstein" and "Appassionata" Sonatas had been performed at sight in the presence of the composer, the first by Czerny and the second as a soggy manuscript by noted pianist Marie Bigot. Beethoven was so gobsmacked by Bigot's sight reading of the "Appassionata" that he gave her the manuscript as a gift.[61] Clearly even the most difficult of Beethoven's compositions (with the possible exception of the "Hammerklavier" Sonata) did not present a problem for the leading virtuosi of the day. But it was different with Liszt. Those who had been trained in the classical manner found themselves completely outmatched by Liszt's "transcendental" virtuosity, which was based on a new approach to the keyboard, one requiring a much higher level of bodily coordination and force (arm/shoulder versus wrist/forearm), as well as a keener sense of keyboard topography than had hitherto been necessary. Looking back on his youth, Camille Saint-Saëns recalls that Liszt's compositions "seemed impossible to play, except by him, and such they were if you recall the old method which prescribed complete immobility, elbows tucked into the body and all action of the muscles limited to fingers and forearm."[62] It was only when piano pedagogy had fully absorbed the Lisztian challenge that a new generation of pianists could competently grapple with Lisztian virtuosity.

For the Liszt of the 1850s, difficulty is effectively detached from virtuosity as a guiding principle; it is now a matter of what one could call a *musical virtuosity*: virtuosity that creates new *musical* possibilities, especially musico-poetic possibilities, as the addition of descriptive titles to the revised *Transcendental Études* attests. Generally speaking, beginning in this period Liszt is interested in writing music that is more difficult than it sounds; that is, given that excessive difficulty can impede virtuosity, especially for those not as spectacularly talented as Liszt, he seeks the most effective and economical way—one without *unnecessary* difficulty—to achieve the greatest virtuosic effect. The 1851 revision of his two sets of études is certainly a case in point.

Lisztian virtuosity also became more economical in the way it was called on to develop the musical motifs of a piece; his vaunted technique of "thematic transformation," achieved by means of virtuoso elaboration, becomes the very basis for the construction of larger-scale forms (in particular, in the B-Minor Sonata). In this sense there is less "virtuosity for its own sake" in Liszt's major original compositions than, say, in the written-out cadenzas of Mozart's and Beethoven's piano concertos, which often feature stock and otherwise unremarkable passagework derived from the conventions of improvisation. The three rather banal transitional cadenzas in the third movement of Beethoven's Third Piano Concerto in C Minor, op. 37, are a good example of this; Liszt no doubt substituted something more interesting in his own performances of the work. (For a subtle discussion of Liszt's reworkings of other composers' compositions, see Jonathan Dunsby's contribution to this volume on Liszt's concerto version of Schubert's *Wanderer* Fantasy.) Carl Dahlhaus surmises that it was in fact the very economy of Lisztian virtuosity that marked the end of the age of improvisation: "Once the dialectic of predefined continuity and improvised or quasi-improvised, momentary effects gave way to thematic manipulation as the principal arbiter in the evolution of instrumental music, any form of virtuosity nourished on the legacy of improvisation was threatened in its very essence, regardless of whether it remained intact for decades as an institution."[63] In other words, Lisztian virtuosity became so completely intertwined with compositional elaboration (the creative principle) that its status as improvisation (conventional virtuosic forms) no longer made sense: *virtuosity killed improvisation*. Liszt's retirement from the concert stage in 1847, then, should not be seen merely as a sign of world-weariness and of a desire to make more time for composing; it also represented a "historiological insight."[64]

This said, despite their increased economy and musical sophistication, the difficulty of Liszt's virtuoso works, even after "revision," is still immense; and yet all agree that his piano writing is some of the most idiomatic, effective, and comfortable (at least for fairly large-sized hands) in the repertory. Thus difficulty in (post-1850) Liszt never stems from awkwardness but from the peculiar and unprecedented demands he makes in his virtuoso piano writing. This has created a situation in which the perceived shortcomings of Liszt's works in performance are typically ascribed to the composer rather than to the performer. (I shall return to this idea below.)

The reduction in difficulty of the revised two sets of études effectively removed them from the apex of the étude genre; nevertheless, they remained (and remain) close to its summit. In his 1868 preface to his edition of Cramer's *Fifty Studies*, Hans von Bülow (Liszt's son-in-law for a time and, along with Carl Tausig, his greatest student),[65] offers a list of étude sets of ascending difficulty—Heller, Cramer, Czerny, Clementi, Moscheles, Henselt—the final three of which are listed as follows:

> V. Chopin: op. 10 and 25, with which may be associated the study of the single Preludes (of a special mechanical tendency) from his op. 28.
>
> VI. Liszt: Six Etudes after Paganini; three Concert-Etudes; twelve grand Etudes, "exécution transcendante."
>
> VII. *a*. Rubinstein: Selected Etudes and Preludes.
>
> *b.* C. Alkan: Selections from his twelve grand Etudes; for the most part more difficult than the aforementioned.

Bülow is most definitely referring to the 1851 revision of Liszt's two large sets of études here; Liszt had stipulated that these were the only authorized versions and therefore supersede the 1830s efforts. No doubt the 1830s version would be placed after Alkan's études on the list. Today, of course, only the Chopin and Liszt études are widely used for advanced students and piano competitions, and the top spots on the difficulty list would no doubt go to the études of Ligeti, Godowsky, and Hamelin (the last two of which often feature more difficult arrangements of études of Chopin and Liszt).[66] While the pedagogical import of Chopin's études is readily apparent from the single-figure focus common to the genre, Liszt's are thought to *reveal* great skill more than to teach it. What Charles Rosen says of Chopin's études can certainly, and with even greater insistence, also be said of Liszt's: "They quickly became concert display pieces."[67]

But Bülow's emphasis on the *pedagogical* import of Liszt's études (which, after all, appear on a list with Cramer and Clementi exercises) is instructive. One is reminded of Ferruccio Busoni's statement: "I discerned such gaps and errors in my own playing that, with an energetic decisiveness, I began to work on the piano on a thoroughly new basis. Liszt's works were my teachers, and opened for me the door to an intimate understanding of his special art; from his 'texture' I created my technique."[68] Like Chopin, Liszt also effectively teaches us how to play the piano in a new way; as noted above, he introduces a new physicality into piano technique that, generally speaking, goes far beyond what Chopin had required. And it was not simply a matter of playing loud, fast, or both for long stretches, but also of the creation of new piano textures (as Busoni notes), often through novel fingering, which, unfortunately, is not always respected, to the obvious detriment of Lisztian virtuosity.

Before Liszt and Chopin, fingering was utterly conventional; it was a matter for piano methods, and composers did not indicate fingering in the score. Indeed, with the influence of the "finger equalization" school then in vogue, it would have been quite superfluous, given that fingers were supposedly interchangeable and ease of execution the only concern. But Liszt and Chopin saw each finger as having its own character, saw that fingering itself could produce novel and virtuosic effects: "there are as many different sounds as there are fingers," Chopin wrote.[69] On many occasions fingering is part of the work itself; that is, a passage may have been conceived with a specific fingering in mind and thus is no more optional than an expressive marking—for it is in some sense an expressive marking. See, for example, the very unorthodox use of 3–3–3 in the right hand for successive, legato melody notes in measure 6 of Chopin's Nocturne in G Minor, op. 37, no. 1. (Liszt makes the same gesture with the thumb 1–1–1 in measures 81 and 83 of *Funérailles*, S. 173/7 / LW A158/7, 1849, a work that coincides with Chopin's death). The right-hand ossia in Liszt's Second Concert Étude, *La leggierezza* (S. 144/2 / LW A118/2, 1845–49, mm. 60–66), which is always preferred over the main text, was conceived for a particular fingering, which, while it goes contrary to the standard fingering for minor chromatic thirds, offers the cleanest and most effective execution; in fact, the traditional fingering would be somewhat awkward given the peculiarities of the passage and would thus hamper the aesthetic aims of the piece.

On occasion, Liszt prescribes a more technically difficult fingering to achieve an aesthetic effect that would otherwise be more difficult or impossible to achieve. The best example of this is certainly the opening figure (after the introduction) of the 1851 version of *Mazeppa* (*Transcendental Étude* no. 4), where Liszt indicates the use of 2–4/2–4, 2–4/2–4, 2–4/2–4 in alternating hands as they cross over each other in a chopping movement, suggesting the galloping of a horse. Nevertheless, many if not most professional pianists employ 4–2/3–1, 1–3/2–4, 4–2/3–1 (left-right-left) to facilitate speed of execution, creating a whirlwind. But this is to misunderstand the character of the piece. Emil von Sauer (called "the legitimate heir of Liszt" by Martin Krause, another Liszt pupil),[70] published an edition of Liszt's *Transcendental Études* that contains only five editorial notes, one of which refers to this passage: "It is absolutely inadmissible to facilitate the fingering here, as contrary to Liszt's ideas."[71] Similarly, Rosen observes, "It should be clear that any attempt to play the martellato figure with four fingers, 2–4, 1–3 instead of only 2–4, 2–4 (as pianists often do to avoid strain on wrist and arm), is an inexcusable betrayal of Liszt's intentions."[72] Such martellato passages are in fact found in many of Liszt's works (e.g., the opening cadenza of *Totentanz*, the left-hand "forked" finger martellato in the Sixth Variation of the Sixth Paganini Étude, 1851 version, mm. 116–19).[73] Emphasizing the percussive aspect of the piano that composers and performers usually strive to avoid (indeed, this effect is completely missing in Chopin), these violent, martellato passages contribute significantly to Liszt's modernist bravura aesthetic.[74]

The Ethics of Virtuosity

The main complaints against virtuosity are twofold: (1) that virtuosity is inessential to music and thus distracts from the purity or true nature of music; and (2) that due to music's status as a performing art, there is an unavoidable tendency toward virtuosic display, a tendency that corrupts the nobler aims of music. The first is a priori conceptual, the second empirical; both positions see virtuosity as having a supplementary character, subjecting it to a specifically moral critique. Hence Samson's observation that "the opprobrium that has so often clung to virtuosity extends beyond the occlusion of reference and surrender to mechanism. Virtuosity can also wear the stigma of the gratuitous. It is a surplus or supplement, a surplus of technique over expression, detail over substance, even (implicitly) facility over quality."[75] Indeed, vulgarity, superficiality, and bombast are among the most habitual of virtuosity's sins. Virtuosity is thereby opposed to so-called serious music, a dichotomy that has a specific geographical and historico-stylistic underpinning—eastern European Romanticism (Chopin, Liszt, the Russian composers) versus central European classicism (German, Austrian)—one that continues to the present day.

Perhaps no canonical composer has been more maligned than Liszt for indulging in the sins of virtuosity. This has probably been the greatest impediment to Liszt's acceptance as a "great composer" in the traditional sense.[76] Liszt himself discusses virtuosity in moral terms in his obituary for Paganini (1840):

> May the artist of the future gladly and readily decline to play the conceited and egotistical role which we hope has had in Paganini its last brilliant representative. May he set his goal within, and not outside, himself, and be the means of virtuosity, and not its end. May he constantly keep in mind that, though the saying is "Noblesse oblige!," in a far higher degree than nobility—GÉNIE OBLIGE![77]

In other words, although virtuosity itself can be considered kind of temptation—and its defense a moral quicksand—the problem posed by the figure of Paganini is not virtuosity per se but rather its purpose and provenance: virtuosity should always serve a musical end, and it should spring from the inner being of the "artist" rather than from an extrinsic source, namely, the desire to please the public and bask in its adulation.[78] Of course, this statement sounds wildly idealistic—and even unbelievable, given what we know about Liszt's performing career. One will certainly be inclined to read a bit of self-criticism (if not self-irony) into this famous statement. Yet Liszt meant it sincerely, and there are several reasons to take it seriously.

First, it perfectly corresponds to the ideal of Romantic subjectivity as self-expression, drawing on a revolution in early nineteenth-century thinking about the "cause" or origin of art (previously understood, since Aristotle, as a mimetic act with the artist as efficient cause).[79] The Romantic virtuoso wears his self on his sleeve. Second, Liszt is implying that the virtuoso is not a mere pianist or violinist, or even a musician, but is first and foremost an "artist" (*artiste* in French). (Liszt had in fact previewed this use of the word in an earlier article, "De la situation des artistes," 1835.)[80] In other words, the performer-composer is part of an ideal community of art adepts, one that includes poets, painters, and sculptors. Creative geniuses such as Dante, Michelangelo, and Beethoven therefore inhabit the same rarefied plane of creativity; through their devotion to the ideals of their respective arts, they contribute equally to the well-being and betterment of humanity.[81] This brings us to the third, and most important point, which is the coining and adoption of the motto *génie oblige*, an artistic equivalent to the moral imperative of the aristocratic *noblesse oblige*. The natural gift of talent or genius is compared to the privilege of aristocratic birth. Liberated from aristocratic sponsorship and beholden only to the public and society as a whole, the artist assumes a similar role of responsibility vis-à-vis society. This also means transcending or at least resisting the commercial or egotistical impulse associated with virtuosity. As Ralph Locke observes in his book on the Saint-Simonians:

> Liszt was filled with a sense of mission, an urge to find a fulfilling new role for the artist in a society that had come to treat art as a consumer good and status symbol. This mission had been first and most plainly articulated by the Saint-Simonians. [Among the musicians who came into significant contact with the Saint-Simonians,] it was Liszt in whom the ideas of the Saint-Simonians echoed loudest and longest.[82]

In sum, one can say that Liszt effectively marries the Romantic ideal of self-expression to the ethico-social commitment of the Saint-Simonians.

Liszt's high-mindedness certainly did not silence his critics—nor those of virtuosity, particularly in the first half of the twentieth century, a time when an often pedantic and classicizing ideal, no doubt inspired in part by an esoteric modernism, prevailed over a discredited Romanticism. An anti-virtuoso attitude thus emerges in the United States and Europe in reaction to the perceived excesses of nineteenth-century performance practices, an attitude that obviously did not bode well for Liszt's legacy. According to the German pianist Artur Schnabel, although he performed them, "Chopin pieces were superficial, only virtuoso, not important."[83] (Recall that Chopin was long thought of as a mere "salon composer.") And Schnabel could take pride in saying that, unlike many of his colleagues, "when I build a program, the second half is as boring as the first!"[84] It is thus not surprising that a "Chopin-and-Liszt" virtuoso such as Ukrainian-born Vladimir Horowitz expressed disdain for the concert scene of interwar Berlin: "I hated them all! I would go to a concert and one artist would play only five Haydn sonatas for the program."[85]

Referring to the 1940s and 1950s, Alfred Brendel (Austrian) remarks in an interview that "the word 'virtuosity' was mistrusted, not only in Vienna but also in Amsterdam or Stockholm at that time, and Liszt was seen as mainly a virtuoso, a bravura player. Early on I noticed that this was a misreading, a misunderstanding, and [I] wanted to counteract it."[86] Brendel goes on to note that, unlike, say, Chopin and Schumann, Liszt's greatness "depends very much on the performance; he can be completely ruined by a performance which only follows the fingers."[87] This is a recurrent theme in the literature: that the perception of the aesthetic value of Liszt's works is more highly dependent on the qualities of a specific performance than that of other composers. (This is most surely the case with Thalberg, who was able to impress the likes of Robert Schumann and Felix Mendelssohn with striking renditions of his own works, works that all now agree are insipid and fully deserving of the oblivion to which they have been consigned.)[88] But Brendel is also criticizing the *use* to which Liszt was put, namely a one-dimensional "bravura" reading of his works that neglected other, more "serious" aspects of Liszt's art.

Brendel was also advocating and drawing on a reappraisal of the minimalist, non-virtuosic virtue and forward-looking nature of Liszt's late works, what Shay Loya calls in his contribution (which discusses this issue at length) Liszt's "modernist rehabilitation." (On the relation of Liszt's late work to virtuosity, see also Dolores Pesce's and Ralph Locke's contributions to this volume, which explore different aspects of this question.) This rehabilitation began in the 1930s with fellow Hungarian composer Béla Bartók and English composer and Liszt scholar Humphrey Searle (the first to create a numbering system for Liszt's works), and picked up steam midcentury with pianists Louis Kentner and Brendel. This focus on the late works from the 1870s and 1880s, coupled with an emphasis on the greatness of the B-Minor Sonata—in particular its structural, thematic, and harmonic innovations—shifted attention away from the "virtuoso Liszt" and toward the "virtuous Liszt," an ascetic and "modernist" Liszt who could more easily be accepted by musicologists, music theorists, and classically oriented performers such as Brendel.

In his magisterial *The Romantic Generation* (1995), Charles Rosen undertook a second rehabilitation, one intended to undo the first. Mocking the piety of Brendel and others, Rosen endeavors to counter the stereotype of Liszt's earlier compositions as "empty" or "tasteless," his image as a composer redeemed only by the restraint and harmonic experimentation of the late works. Against the grain, Rosen argues that it was in fact virtuosity that "gave Liszt his stature":

> Liszt may be compared to an old ancestor who built up the family fortune by disreputable and shameful transactions in his youth and spent his last years in works of charity. Recent criticism reads like an official family biography that glosses over the early life and dwells lovingly on the years of respectability.... [Liszt's] invention of novel keyboard effects and his mastery of musical gesture have always been undervalued, especially by pianists of the German school who prefer the kind of music that can be executed while soulfully regarding the ceiling.[89]

Rosen thus summarily dismisses the valorization of the "virtuous" over the "virtuoso" Liszt that had infected his mid-twentieth-century reception. This subtle jab at Brendel was in fact the culmination of a long-running feud. Brendel had responded to Rosen's essay "The New Sound of Liszt" (*New York Review of Books*, April 12, 1984, an essay containing many of the ideas later expressed in *The Romantic Generation*) in an article in the same publication entitled "The Noble Liszt" (November 20, 1986). Commenting on the debate between the two pianist-critics, Richard Taruskin gives the nod to Rosen: "While sympathizing with his reaction to Rosen's deliberately annoying formulations, I find Brendel's fastidiousness insufficiently generous toward Liszt and the impulses that his work embodies, which, though not always noble, are undoubtedly great. Rosen came closer than Brendel did to pinpointing the fascination that Liszt exerted over his times, and continues to exert over us."[90]

Indeed, Rosen sees the Liszt of the 1830s and early 1840s, the Liszt that is most often disparaged and neglected, as the key to understanding his distinctive contribution to music. This despite the fact that Liszt himself seemingly took a rather critical view of most of the works of this period, as evidenced by his extensive revisions of them, and many of those he did not revise—e.g., *Apparitions* (S. 155 / LW A19, 1834) and *Lyon* (S. 156/1 / LW A40a/1, 1837–38)—were left to languish in obscurity. Rosen turns the conventional wisdom on its head, observing that "most of the piano works by Liszt that have remained in the repertory today were written, at least in their initial form, before 1850."[91] The extent to which a work owes more to the inspiration of a later rather than an earlier moment of its creation is certainly open to debate. (For a different take on this question, see Kenneth Hamilton's chapter on Liszt's creative process in the present volume.) But Rosen does examine—and extensively praise—the unrevised 1830s versions of the études and 1840s-era virtuoso showpieces such as the *Don Juan* Fantasy, which Rosen counts as "one of Liszt's most personal achievements,"[92] to support his contention that "Liszt was the first composer in history to understand fully the musical significance—dramatic and emotional as well as aural—of new techniques of execution. . . . Liszt's feeling for sound was the greatest of any keyboard composer's between Scarlatti and Debussy, and he surpassed them in boldness."[93] Thus, Rosen can be said to reinterpret Lisztian boldness—Lisztian *bravura*—as modernist in a very different way than the "modernist rehabilitation" referred to above (a point I explore in my contribution to this volume on the "bravura style").

But what of the accusation, leveled even by contemporaries such as Mendelssohn, that Liszt's opera fantasies were frivolous and beneath his genius? According to R. Larry Todd's account, "In [Liszt's] colorful fantasies and transcriptions, all based on other composers' works, Felix [Mendelssohn] detected a lack of original ideas. Liszt's performance was 'as unpremeditated, as wild and impetuous, as you would expect of a genius, but then I miss those genuinely original ideas [that] I naturally expect from a genius.'"[94] (This performance was in 1840; Mendelssohn died in 1847, years before any of Liszt's mature masterworks came to light.) Rosen sees such critiques as beside the point, observing that in the *Don Juan* Fantasy "Liszt displayed almost every facet of his invention as a composer for the piano. That the tunes are by Mozart is largely irrelevant."[95] What is important to Rosen is that "[Liszt] taught the composers who followed him how aspects of music like texture and intensity of sound, violence and delicacy of gesture, could replace pitch and rhythm as organizing principles in the development of new forms."[96] This is of course not something Mendelssohn could have perceived, given his limited historical vantage point.

To be sure, Liszt's greatest breakthroughs in virtuosity occurred in the mid- to late 1830s and early 1840s. Nevertheless, it is telling that none of the 1830s versions of those two sets of études (the six *Paganini Études* and twelve *Transcendental Études*) is played in concert today, and only a handful of the innumerable opera paraphrases/fantasies/transcriptions Liszt composed and featured in his early concert career are performed or recorded with any regularity.[97] (Indeed, many contemporary performers shun these as too ostentatiously virtuosic, unserious, or unoriginal.) To give more perspective and nuance to Rosen's pronouncements, with which I generally agree, I propose the following tripartite, and roughly chronological, division of Liszt's virtuoso period.

The first phase, 1832–37, begins with the sudden inspiration of Paganini's 1832 concert in Paris, the most immediate result of which was the "Clochette" Fantasy (1832–34), and culminates in the two sets of études (1837–38): the reworked *Étude en douze exercices* as the *Grandes études* (S. 137 / LW A39) and the *Études d'exécution transcendante d'après Paganini* (S. 140 / LW A52). In the first phase, it was a matter of completely overhauling and recalibrating piano technique on Paganini's example. This is what is typically referred to as Liszt's "transcendental virtuosity," that is, a virtuosity that tests the limits of what is technically possible and sonorously acceptable. Rosen notes that, with the early Liszt, "the piano was taught to make new sounds" and calls the *Grandes études* "one of the greatest revolutions of keyboard *style* in history."[98] *Style*, not simply technique: technical innovation implies stylistic innovation. However, despite their extreme virtuosity, these études were hardly crowd-pleasers. Their modernism and textural complexity were at odds with the lighter fare expected in the concert halls of the time. Indeed, Liszt rarely played the *Grandes études* in public and never as a set.[99] In addition, both sets of études were far beyond the ability of virtually any contemporary pianist aside from Liszt himself, thus making their dissemination especially difficult. Robert Schumann may have been overestimating when he wrote in a review of the *Grandes études* that they were "for at most ten to twelve [pianists] in the world; weaker players will only raise a laugh at them."[100] One might call this an *abstract virtuosity*, one that exists more to prove a point (a "pianistic statement," as I noted above) than to elicit the typical rewards of performance. (Indeed, as mentioned above, Liszt had written a separate "performance version" of the "Clochette" Fantasy—the later revision of the two étude sets can be seen in a similar light.)

In the second phase, 1838–47, we find the opposite: an extroverted virtuosity, a *performance virtuosity* specifically designed for the concert stage and for the taste of contemporary audiences. This type of virtuosity coincides with Liszt's world tours and fame as a mature virtuoso, and it is this virtuosity that has typically attracted the most censure. It includes Liszt's habit of embellishing the works of other composers when he performed them, which apparently went well beyond even the liberal standards of the time (as can be seen in Liszt's later editions of works he performed during this period).[101] Compositionally, it flourishes in the rollicking *Grand galop chromatique* (1838, see my chapter for an analysis of it), Liszt's Schubert transcriptions, especially the dazzling *Erlkönig* (1837–38, see Jonathan Dunsby's chapter), and, most spectacularly, in Liszt's elaborate opera fantasies of the early 1840s, in particular those based on themes from Mozart's *Don Giovanni*, Bellini's *Norma*, and Meyerbeer's *Robert le diable*, which represent a great advance in that once-dominant genre, both in terms of their bravura virtuosity and in their musical and compositional sophistication, over the "salon virtuosity" of Liszt's earlier efforts and those of other contemporary composer-virtuosos.[102] In a letter to Marie d'Agoult (his romantic partner at that time), Liszt remarked, "As to effect, these latest works [the opera fantasies of the early 1840s] are incomparably superior to my earlier things."[103] Brahms in fact cites these works as having exercised a great influence on his own conception of keyboard virtuosity, remarking to (pianist and Liszt pupil) Arthur Friedheim that "whoever really wants to know what Liszt has done for the piano should study the old operatic fantasies. They represent the classicism of piano technique."[104] Just as he had revolutionized the étude genre in the 1830s, removing it from the single-figure, pedagogical realm, in these virtuoso elaborations Liszt revolutionizes the opera fantasy/variation genre. In both cases, it was a matter of transforming the meaning and purpose of virtuosity.[105]

In the third phase, 1848–59, Liszt endeavors to reconsider his legacy in terms of his artistic creations rather than his concert career. The musicality, efficaciousness, durability, and playability of his works is now uppermost in his mind as he returns to his études and other works of the 1830s, essentially reimagining their virtuosity, reconceptualizing what virtuosity can and should mean in light of the work concept and of his signature technique of thematic transformation. Although tensions remained with the performance-style conception of many of Liszt's works, Liszt nevertheless sees his revisions, his *work-virtuosity*, as vital to his legacy as a composer, thereby avoiding the fate of his close rival Thalberg, who was forgotten the moment he retired from the concert stage.

One might also distinguish a brief late-middle, or early-late phase of virtuoso composition, namely the years 1859–63, which straddles the Weimar and Rome periods. Unlike the first decade of Liszt's retirement, consumed as it was with revision and recomposition, this short span saw both the original conception and completion of many of Liszt's finest and most often-performed piano works, including the *Weinen, Klagen, Sorgen, Zagen* (S. 179 / LW A198, 1859), the First Mephisto Waltz (S. 514 / LW A189/1, 1859–61), the Two Concert Études (S. 145 / LW A218, 1862), the Two Legends (S. 175 / LW A219, 1862–63), and the "Paraphrases" of a scene from Verdi's *Rigoletto* (S. 434 / LW A187, 1859) and the waltz from Gounod's *Faust* (S. 407 / LW A208, 1861). While the virtuosity of these works is largely continuous with that of the 1850s, the late works (1865–86), no doubt influenced by an infusion of religiosity (Liszt took up minor orders in the Catholic Church in 1865), feature their own distinctive styles of virtuosity and anti-virtuosity, which are discussed at length in the third part of this volume.

☙ ☙ ☙

In today's media-driven and celebrity-obsessed culture, virtuosity is no longer disparaged as a moral failing or as antithetical to true music. One of the most notable trends in recent years confirms this. For it is only during the past two decades or so that it has become fashionable to play as a set, both in concert and on disc, the epitome of Lisztian virtuosity, the *Transcendental Études*. Indeed, recordings or performances of the complete set were quite rare prior to 1980. While Lisztians such as Lazar Berman (in 1959 on BMG/Melodya, the first commercially available recording of the entire set) and Jorge Bolet (in a live broadcast recital, Tanglewood, 1964, available on YouTube)[106] made a name for themselves with their pioneering renditions of the set, the two most famous and most widely recorded pianists of the twentieth century, Arthur Rubinstein and Vladimir Horowitz, never recorded a single *Transcendental Étude*, and Horowitz played only two of them in public and only during his early years: *Mazeppa* (no. 4) and *Feux follets* (no. 5).[107] The first known public performance of the entire *Transcendental Études* was by Busoni, who programmed both the 1837 and the 1851 versions in a single marathon concert on February 7, 1903, in Berlin.[108]

While no pianist today may be looking to replicate Busoni's feat, the 1851 version of the set has become something of a rite of passage for today's young virtuoso pianists. Recordings of the complete *Transcendental Études* have spiked threefold since the turn of the century,[109] a trend that has only intensified in recent years: 2019 saw the release of *Liszt: Études d'exécution transcendante* (Naxos), by Russian/Israeli pianist Boris Giltburg (first prize, Queen Elisabeth Competition, Brussels); there were at least four recordings of the set in 2018; 2016 saw two major traversals, those of the young Russian phenomenon Daniil Trifonov (first-prize winner of the International Tchaikovsky Competition, Moscow), *Transcendental—Daniil Trifonov Plays Franz Liszt* (Deutsche Grammophon); and the Russian-American Kirill Gerstein (winner of the $300,000 Gilmore Artist Award), *Transcendental Études* (Myrios Classics). Trifonov also performed the set in a video-recorded concert in Lyon in 2014.[110] Boris Berezovsky (a previous winner of the Tchaikovsky Competition) released a well-regarded DVD of his 2002 performance at La Roque d'Anthéron.[111] Leslie Howard is the only pianist to have recorded all three versions of the *Transcendental Études* (1826, 1837, 1851), and I would be remiss if I did not mention in this context Howard's monumental ninety-nine-CD traversal of all of Liszt's piano music (*The Complete Liszt Piano Music*, Hyperion, 2011), the first such undertaking (one doubts that it will ever be repeated).

Lisztian virtuosity is thus by all accounts experiencing a kind of revival in the new millennium, both in performance and in scholarship, as the present volume attests.

Notes

1. Alfred Einstein, *Music in the Romantic Era* (New York: W. W. Norton, 1947), 210.
2. Jim Samson, *Virtuosity and the Musical Work: The "Transcendental Studies" of Liszt* (Cambridge: Cambridge University Press, 2003), 4.
3. There is of course an abundance of overt virtuosity in Chopin, but it is qualitatively different. He wrote no operatic fantasies for solo piano, which were de rigueur for performers at the time, although he did compose a youthful set of variations for piano and orchestra on Mozart's "Là ci darem la mano," op. 2—a theme Liszt took up in his own fantasy for piano solo, *Réminiscences de Don Juan* (S. 418 / LW A80), which is actually more often played than Chopin's effort. As I discuss in my chapter in this volume, Chopin's virtuosity, while certainly innovative, was nevertheless "classical" in orientation, avoiding most of the technical novelties of 1830s virtuoso pianism.
4. It should be noted that Henselt's F-Minor Piano Concerto, op. 16 (1847), certainly influenced by Chopin and Liszt, was quite popular throughout the latter half of the nineteenth century. While it quickly fell out of favor in the twentieth, it has been recorded a number of times. One work of Henselt's survives: the brief study "Si oiseau j'étais, à toi je volerais" (*Études caractéristiques*, op. 2, no. 6). It has been recorded by Sergei Rachmaninoff and Leopold Godowsky.
5. Vladimir Horowitz, the pianist with the greatest virtuoso reputation post-Liszt (with the possible exception of Horowitz's idol, Josef Hofmann, and Ferruccio Busoni), had only seven concertos in his active repertoire for much of his touring career: Beethoven's Fifth, Liszt's First and Second, Tchaikovsky's First, Rachmaninoff's Third, and Brahms's First and Second. See Glenn Plaskin, *Horowitz: A Biography* (New York: William Morrow & Co., 1983), 246.
6. In this category one could put Alexander Dreyschock's performance of Chopin's "Revolutionary" Étude (op. 10, no. 12), with the left hand in octaves rather than single notes as written; Thalberg's patented "three-hand" effect; and Liszt's string-breaking performances (mimicking Paganini's own string-breaking performances), which necessitated having two pianos on stage so that Liszt could switch when the need arose. Nowadays only the minor gesture is tolerated: "[Daniil] Trifonov even allowed himself a bit of showmanship: at the beginning of the second movement [of Stravinsky's *Petrushka*], in honor of the titular puppet, he let his right arm dangle limply for a moment" (from a *New Yorker* review of Carnegie Hall recital, https://www.newyorker.com/magazine/2017/01/09/daniil-trifonovs-sleight-of-hand, accessed September 24, 2019).
7. Franz Grillparzer, who wrote Beethoven's funeral oration, composed a poem inspired by Clara Schumann's performance of the "Appassionata," entitled

"Clara Wieck and Beethoven" and published it in the *Wiener Zeitschrift* in 1838. See Joan Chissell, *Clara Schumann: A Dedicated Spirit, a Study of Her Life and Work* (London: Hamish Hamilton, 1983), 54. Chissell describes Liszt (in 1838) as having been deeply impressed by Clara's playing, "especially praising her performance of Beethoven's 'Appassionata'" (ibid., 57).

8. Michael Saffle, *Liszt in Germany, 1840–1845: A Study in Sources, Documents, and the History of Reception* (Stuyvesant, NY: Pendragon Press, 1994), 206.
9. According to Michael Saffle's calculations, these three works and the *Galop* were the only ones to receive more than fifty performances during Liszt's tours of Germany in 1840–45. See "Table 2: Liszt's Primary German Repertory" (ibid., 187).
10. Carl Dahlhaus proclaims that "around mid-century, the primacy of virtuosity was gradually undermined by the principle of interpretation" (Dahlhaus, *Nineteenth-Century Music*, trans. J. Bradford Robinson [Berkeley and Los Angeles: University of California Press, 1989], 138).
11. For example, the unwritten prohibition on performing movements of sonatas independently, as was common in the nineteenth century. Today's performers prefer to err on the other extreme: "sets" published out of expediency are now often played as if they were integral works, e.g., Chopin's four Ballades or four Scherzos, Schubert's four Impromptus (op. 90 or op. 142), and so on. (The recording industry may have also influenced the fashion for performing "sets.") Whether Chopin prescribed integral performances of his preludes and études is more debatable (there is an "*attaca il presto con fuoco*" at the end of Étude, op. 10, no. 3, referring to op. 10, no. 4).
12. With the possible exception of the field of opera, e.g., Verdi's *Don Carlos* and Mussorgsky's *Boris Godunov*.
13. When Mozart and Beethoven composed cadenzas for their piano concertos, they typically included more than one possibility, leaving the choice up to the performer. Many of Mozart's slow movements were expected to be extensively embellished by the performer (see the two versions, one embellished, one simple, of the andante movement of the Sonata in F Major, K. 332). But the extent of the expected embellishment has only recently come to light, with the discovery circa 2000 by Robert Levin of a manuscript of the Piano Concerto no. 23 in A Major (K. 488), annotated in a pupil's hand, about which Levin observes: "Barbara Ployer goes mad with the spray can. Her solo part is brimful of notes. It was written by her, but as Mozart's pupil she would have known how much he would have wanted her to write in, and no one today would play their solo with so many frills and flourishes" (https://www.theguardian.com/music/2011/sep/30/embellished-mozart-manuscript-uncovered, accessed September 23, 2019). The minor variants that appear across Chopin's works appear to give the performer some scope for choice, and these are being more

explicitly revealed in the new Peters Edition of Chopin's works, overseen by John Rink, Jim Samson, Jean-Jacques Eigeldinger, and Christophe Grabowski.

14. *Letters of Franz Liszt: Vol. 1 From Paris to Rome*, ed. La Mara, trans. Constance Bache (Covent Garden: H. Grevel & Co., 1894), 22.

15. See Jonathan Kregor, *Liszt as Transcriber* (Cambridge: Cambridge University Press, 2012).

16. Although Horowitz is not as closely identified with Liszt as the other pianists mentioned, the following anecdote is instructive: backstage on the night of his American debut, "Horowitz pulled off his hat and coat, took a photograph of Liszt from his pocket, glanced at it peacefully, and then began pacing back and forth, rubbing his hands to keep them warm" (Plaskin, *Horowitz*, 109).

17. See Earl Wild's "Great Performers Editions" of Liszt (*Piano Music of Franz Liszt: Volume 1* and *Volume 2*, G. Schirmer, 1988), which contains a great number of variants by Wild and other famous pianists (Busoni, Leschetizky). Horowitz even saw fit to produce his own versions of other composers' works—which depart quite radically from the original—as in his reformulations of Liszt's Second Legend and the Second Hungarian Rhapsody (but not only Liszt: he also undertook a revision of Rachmaninoff's Second Piano Sonata, op. 36, combining elements of Rachmaninoff's 1913 and 1931 versions of the work).

18. Alfred Brendel, *Music, Sense and Nonsense: Collected Essays and Lectures* (London: The Robson Press: 2015), 232.

19. Ibid., 233. Glenn Plaskin notes in his biography (Plaskin, *Horowitz*, 365–66) that Horowitz was "especially happy" about programming *Vallée d'Obermann* as the last piece in his 1966 fall recitals, a work he had never before performed and was rarely heard at the time: "Some of the passages, he found, did not lie well in his hand, so he had retouched it, filling in octaves, rewriting some of the cadenzas and adding reinforcements—all of which he considered justifiable within the improvisatory tradition of Liszt as long as the changes were in good taste." Plaskin also quotes music critic Harold Schonberg's reaction to the performance: "At the end, he not only resurrected a noble work. He had also brought an age to life."

20. Quoted in Jim Samson's chapter in this volume. Original source: *Franz Liszt: Gesammelte Schriften*, ed. Lina Ramann (Leipzig: Brietkopf & Härtel, 1881–99), vol. 4 (1882), 193.

21. Samson, *Virtuosity and the Musical Work*, 2. Samson's problematic has been taken up in the volume on violin virtuosity mentioned in the preface to this volume. As one of the editors of this volume writes, "The traditional, classical opposition of work and performance does not allow for a viable understanding of the complex subject of virtuosity. Instead, we must explore the 'Werk' and the 'Event' in relation to one another, thereby effectively combining the processes of creation and presentation in our examination of virtuosity"

(Christiane Hoppe, "Ernst's Concepts of Virtuosity," in *Exploring Virtuosities: Heinrich Wilhelm Ernst, Nineteenth-Century Musical Practices and Beyond*, ed. Christine Hoppe, Melanie von Goldbeck, and Maiko Kawabata Kawabata [Hildesheim, Zurich, New York: Georg Olms Verlag, 2018], 33).

22. But there has been a great deal of recent scholarly interest in the question of the piano. See especially Eva Badura-Skoda, *The Eighteenth-Century Fortepiano Grand and Its Patrons: From Scarlatti to Beethoven* (Bloomington: Indiana University Press, 2017), and Paul Kildea, *Chopin's Piano: In Search of the Instrument that Transformed Music* (New York: W. W. Norton & Company, 2018).

23. Robert Levin notes that "performers playing on later instruments must make adjustments that will be easier if they have had the experience of playing, however briefly, on a good quality period piano (original or copy)" (Levin, "Mozart and the Keyboard Culture of His Time," https://www.biu.ac.il/hu/mu/minad04/LevinMOZART.pdf, accessed September 24, 2019). Even the Steinway piano can be considered in the context of historical performance. Stephen Hough argues that Josef Hofmann was the first pianist to truly understand the virtuosic and sonic possibilities of the Steinway. See Stephen Hough's article, "Why Was Josef Hofmann Considered the Greatest Pianist of All?" (*The Daily Telegraph*, September 17, 2009).

24. The electric guitar of the latter half of the twentieth century comes closest.

25. Even the very best concert grand pianos built today are "retired" after ten to twenty years of service, although there is a lively market for vintage instruments, especially Steinways.

26. Samson notes that "[Vladimir] Jankélévitch is right to remind us that virtuosity is 'as old as music'" (*Virtuosity and the Musical Work*, 68). Indeed, in many ways virtuosity is inseparable from music: qua *technê*, music involves high-level digital, breathing, or vocal skills honed over the course of many years, usually from childhood. Scarlatti's Sonatas and Bach's organ works in particular offer spectacular examples of early keyboard virtuosity (hence Liszt's interest in transcribing Bach's organ works for piano).

27. Specifically his proto-Romantic Variations in F Minor (Hob. XVII: 6, 1793) and his last Piano Sonatas in C Major (Hob. XVI: 50, 1794) and E-flat Major (Hob. XVI: 52, 1794).

28. Quoted in *Thayer's Life of Beethoven*, volume 1, rev. and ed. Eliot Forbes (Princeton, NJ: Princeton University Press, 1967), 88. There is, of course, legato in Mozart—in cantabile passages, for example, and where expressly marked—but the default touch is non-legato. In Beethoven the primacy is reversed. Paul and Eva Badura-Skoda (*Interpreting Mozart on the Keyboard*, trans. Leo Black [New York: St. Martin's Press, 1962], 54–55) note that "according to the practice of Mozart's time, absence of any articulation sign meant 'non-legato'.... For whatever instrument, [Mozart] almost always wanted passage-work played

'non-legato.' At least we have never come across any extended passage of triplets or semiquavers that should be played legato. There is only one type of virtuoso passage for which Mozart favored long legato slurs—rising chromatic scales in quick tempo, of the kind that frequently occur in cadenzas."

29. Carl Czerny, *On the Proper Performance of All Beethoven's Works for Piano*, ed. Paul Badura-Skoda (Vienna: Universal Edition, 1970), 5.
30. Johann Nepomuk Hummel, *A Complete Theoretical and Practical Course of Instructions on the Art of Playing the Pianoforte* (London, 1828), III, 64.
31. Andrea Botticelli, "'Creating Tone': The Relationship Between Beethoven's Piano Sonority and Evolving Instrument Designs, 1800–1810," PhD Dissertation (University of Toronto, 2014), 24.
32. See Christopher Clarke, "Érard and Broadwood in the Classical Era: Two Schools of Piano Making," *Musique, images, instruments: Revue française d'organologie et d'iconographie musicale* 11 (2009): 98–125; and chapter 4, "The 1803 Érard Grand Piano," of Tilman Skowroneck's monograph, *Beethoven the Pianist* (Cambridge: Cambridge University Press, 2010), 85–115. According to Botticelli ("'Creating Tone,'" 39–40), "In the historical literature, the English and French pianos have largely been seen as part of one tradition, despite certain tangible differences in construction and sound between the Érard and Broadwood pianos. It took the insight and experience of [Christopher] Clarke, an historical keyboard builder working in France, to flesh out this simplified picture in significant ways, calling attention to the crucial distinctions between French and English instruments at this time. Thus, Clarke points to the idiomatic soundboards of Érard pianos, which in the treble were less than half as thick as Broadwood's. Furthermore, Érard's scaling was slightly longer than Broadwood's except for in the low bass register. The strings in the treble and middle registers of the Érard were slightly thinner, and there were also significant differences in interior construction and soundboard ribbing between the pianos. All of these features have an influence on the tone."
33. Here is a detailed description: "The instrument has a range of 5.5 octaves (FF–c4) and is triple-strung throughout, without wound strings. It is fitted with the English type of arched iron gap-stretchers between the pin block and the belly rail. From FF–g♯ the strings are in brass; from a–c4 the strings are made of iron. Consequently, the instrument is an example of the named 'English grand action' model, but it displays strong roots in the French keyboard building tradition" (ibid., 43).
34. For the first time, a solo keyboard work could rival Bach's *Goldberg Variations* in depth, profundity of conception, emotional range, and virtuosic energy. Liszt was reportedly an enthusiast for the *Goldberg Variations* when it was rare to be one: "I appeased [Liszt] the next lesson with a performance of Bach's *Goldberg Variations*, which he had brought to our attention and which in those days was completely overlooked by pianists" ("Liszt as Teacher: A Sketch by José Vianna

de Motta," in August Göllerich, *The Piano Master Classes of Franz Liszt, 1884–1886,* ed. Wilhelm Jerger, trans., ed., and enlarged by Richard Louis Zimdars [Bloomington: Indiana University Press, 1996], 167).
35. "On ne connait presque pas l'usage des pédales en Allemagne" (Friedrich Kalkbrenner, *Méthode pour apprendre le pianoforte* [Paris: Schlesinger, 1831], 10). Although David Rowland sees Kalkbrenner as "exaggerating heavily" in this statement, he nevertheless observes that "Kalkbrenner is correct in pointing out the general differences between performers on 'Viennese' and 'London' pianos; and these differences, if considered carefully, provide a useful framework for a study of pedaling" (Rowland, *A History of Pianoforte Pedaling* [Cambridge: Cambridge University Press, 1993], 35).
36. This practice is then projected backward, so that Mozart's keyboards works are played, in the mid- to late nineteenth century, with a great deal of legato phrasing to "update" their sound according to the new capacities of the piano. This is readily apparent in the heavily edited G. Schirmer edition of 1893, still in print and widely used for students.
37. "These pedals were the *una corda, forte* (damping mechanism), *céleste* (in which tongues of leather are inserted between the hammer and strings), and *jeu de luth* (equivalent of the English buff or harp stop, with which a soft leather strip is pressed against the end of the strings to partially damp them). . . . These pianos also included a knee pedal for the *jeu de bassoon* (bassoon stop), in which a roll of fine paper was brought to bear against the bass strings to create a buzzing effect" (Botticelli, "'Creating Tone,'" 39).
38. The passages occur in *Preludio* at measures 7–8, in *Mazeppa* at measures 28 and 113, and in *Wilde Jagd* at measures 192–93. The B-Minor Sonata employs the low A0 (mm. 83, 87, 88) and B0 (m. 760) and contains no such ossia, or any ossia at all, for that matter. But Liszt uses these low pitches below C1 sparingly in the B-Minor Sonata, as if to preserve their value as a special effect. Contemporary pianists tend to add the lower-octave notes at moments of high tension, such as the lower B-flat octave (B♭0–B♭1) at measure 286, or adding an octave doubling in the recapitulation at measure 532 (last four notes). In the First Ballade (1845–49), Liszt marks "*(con 8ve bassa)*" at measures 135 and 138 for the low B0–B♭0–A0 descending notes, but these are clearly optional; the piece otherwise does not require a piano with a bass range lower than C1. The Second Ballade, in B Minor (1854), although written during the same time as the B-Minor Sonata, does not employ B0 in the published version; the two conclusions that were discarded in favor of a quiet ending do, however, use the notes below C1, with an optional "*(con 8ve bassa).*"
39. Modern pianists simply play the sub-C1 notes where they seem warranted or implied, adding octave doublings, for example, in Chopin's Sonata no. 2 in B-flat Minor, op. 35. The final measure of the first movement would seem to call out for the low B-flat octave. See Kenneth Hamilton's CD *Preludes to*

Chopin (Prima Facie Records, 2019), where the octave doubling of the low B-flat is used to great effect in the first section of the "Funeral March" movement of the sonata.
40. See Olivia Sham's contribution to this volume for an explanation of this technology.
41. See, for example, the right-hand ornament in the midst of an upward scalar figure in the recapitulation of the first movement of Mozart's Piano Sonata in C Major, K. 330, mm. 129–30.
42. However, even a composition as late as the First Mephisto Waltz (1861) does not use any notes below C1, although contemporary pianists typically add A0 in a few spots, in particular the final measure.
43. In this regard, see especially Sham's analysis of the opening measures of the 1838 *Grande étude* no. 8 (titled *Wilde Jagd* in the 1851 revision).
44. That there are many recordings of Chopin on period Pleyel instruments but relatively few of Liszt on a period Érard (Olivia Sham is one of the few to have done this: https://oliviasham.com/listen/liszt/, accessed September 24, 2019) is no doubt due to the fact that Liszt revised the majority of his original works composed or conceived before 1850. Nevertheless, a great deal is missed by not attempting to understand Lisztian virtuosity on the instrument that made it possible.
45. At first glance one might think that Liszt was perhaps overdoing his practicing (he had been a prodigy and could already play anything that had been written for the piano at sight), when he wrote in a famous letter, "Here is a whole fortnight that my mind and fingers have been working like two lost spirits—Homer, the Bible, Plato, Locke, Byron, Hugo, Lamartine, Chateaubriand, Beethoven, Bach, Hummel, Mozart, Weber, are all around me. I study them, meditate on them, devour them with fury; besides this I practice four to five hours of exercises (3rds, 6ths, 9ths, tremolos, repetition of notes, cadences, etc. etc.)" (quoted in Alan Walker, *Franz Liszt, Volume 1: The Virtuoso Years, 1811–1847* [New York: Alfred A. Knopf, 1983], 174). Perhaps Liszt meant that he was developing new ways of approaching traditional techniques. But a more plausible interpretation is that he simply needed to maintain a high level of fluency in all areas of piano technique, so that he could draw on them "spontaneously" in his public improvisations. Today's pianists need only to learn prepared pieces and to be familiar only with the particular techniques contained therein.
46. In today's music scene this invariably means a virtuosity that is prescribed by the canonical works that make up the standard repertory.
47. Olivia Sham, "Performing the Unperformable: Notions of Virtuosity in Liszt's Solo Piano Music," PhD Dissertation (Royal Academy of Music, 2014), 8.
48. In a letter dated July 12–14, 1789, Mozart writes, "Meanwhile I am working on six easy clavier sonatas for Princess Friederike [the King's eldest daughter]

and six quartets for the King [Friedrich Wilhelm II of Prussia]" (quoted in Alan Tyson, *Mozart: Studies of the Autograph Scores* [Cambridge, MA: Harvard University Press], 36). Mozart's final Piano Sonata in D Major (K. 576), supposedly one of these "easy sonatas" (the only one he completed of the projected set), is actually considered to be the most technically difficult of his sonatas.

49. Given his very lucrative performing career, Liszt did not depend on the sale of works of moderate difficulty to earn a living; it is therefore no wonder that there are fewer such works, proportionally speaking, in Liszt's oeuvre.

50. I deliberately exclude Mozart from this list, since his piano works are generally of the same level of difficulty, which is to say, quite difficult—not in the traditional "virtuoso" sense but in the sense that the highly transparent textures and sensitivity of touch required to make the comparatively clunky modern grand effectively translate the sonic world and subtlety of Mozart's fortepiano is a feat achieved by few pianists.

51. Mozart may be the only exception to this rule. Some of his greatest achievements—Piano Concerto no. 17 in G Major (K. 453), Piano Sonata in A Major (K. 331)—are available to the intermediate player (with the caveat expressed in the previous note).

52. To be sure, the composer-pianists among this group knew well the limits of what was technically possible on the piano and, more importantly, how to write *idiomatically* for their instrument (so that the difficulties do not stem from mere awkwardness).

53. A more mundane reason would be that large-scale works, which are more apt to achieve greatness, require virtuosity to sustain interest over the length of the composition. But this of course goes as well for lesser great, large-scale works.

54. Samson, *Virtuosity and the Musical Work*, 86.

55. Hence the title of Sham's PhD dissertation: "Performing the Unperformable." In another sense, Liszt's works were also retroactively unplayable, given the developments in piano technology noted above. This was undoubtedly one of the rationales for the revision of the two sets of études in 1851.

56. Liszt indicates "Exécuté par l'Auteur" in the score. See Jonathan Kregor's chapter in this volume.

57. Presumably, Liszt had been improvising around his youthful *Étude en douze exercices* for many years before the appearance of the *Grandes études* (which would explain why he used these slight works as models) and continued to so after their publication, until he produced the "definitive" version in 1851. The *Grandes études* of 1837 can thus be thought of as a snapshot in time, rather than as "compositions" in the traditional sense.

58. Göllerich, *The Piano Master Classes of Franz Liszt*, 38.

59. Ibid., 25.

60. Quoted in Carl Lachmund, *Living With Liszt: From the Diary of Carl Lachmund, an American Pupil of Liszt, 1882–1884*, ed. Alan Walker (Hillsdale, NY: Pendragon Press, 1995), 33.

61. Beethoven once remarked of the twenty-two-year-old Bigot's playing of a newly composed sonata, "That is not exactly the character I intended to give the piece; but go on, if it is not mine, it is better than mine" (quoted in Ludwig Nohl, *Beethoven Depicted by His Contemporaries*, trans. Emil Hill [London: W. Reeves, 1880], 64). Haydn similarly praised her: "Oh my dear child, I never made this music; it is you who compose it" (ibid.).
62. Quoted in Cyril Ehrlich, *The Piano: A History* (Oxford: Clarendon Press, 1976/1990), 23.
63. Dahlhaus, *Nineteenth-Century Music*, 138.
64. Ibid.
65. Tausig died at age thirty, the promise of his life as a piano virtuoso largely unfulfilled. See Alan Walker, *Hans Von Bülow: A Life and Times* (Oxford: Oxford University Press, 2009), for a perceptive account of this figure's contribution to the history of virtuosity.
66. The only étude of Rubinstein that is still (occasionally) played is the one in C Major, op. 23, no. 2—quite awkward unless one has very large hands.
67. Charles Rosen, *The Romantic Generation* (Cambridge, MA: Harvard University Press, 1995), 385.
68. Quoted in Grigoriĭ Kogan, *Busoni as Pianist*, trans. Svetlana Belsky (Rochester, NY: University of Rochester Press, 2010), 16.
69. Quoted in Jean-Jacques Eigeldinger, *Chopin: Pianist and Teacher: As Seen by His Pupils*, trans. Naomi Shohet, Krysia Osostowicz, Roy Howat (Cambridge: Cambridge University Press, 1987), 17.
70. Emil von Sauer, quoted in Steven Heliotes, CD Notes for *Scharwenka: Piano Concerto no. 4; Sauer: Piano Concerto no. 1*, Stephen Hough, pianist, City of Birmingham Symphony Orchestra conducted by Lawrence Foster (London: Hyperion, 1995).
71. Emil von Sauer, *Liszt Transcendental Études* (Edition Peters, 1913–17), 17.
72. Rosen, *The Romantic Generation*, 498. Rosen does not refer to Sauer's note, however.
73. By imitating the violin martellato, the piano comes closest to its actual condition as a percussion instrument (striking hammers).
74. Unless one counts the triple *forte* chords in the coda to the B-Minor Scherzo, op. 20, measures 594–600.
75. Samson, *Virtuosity and the Musical Work*, 85.
76. Arthur Friedheim, Liszt's student and secretary in the 1880s, spoke of "the continuous failure of Liszt's works" (Friedheim, *Life and Liszt*, ed. Theodore L. Bullock [New York: Dover Publications, 1961/2012], 48).
77. Quoted in Walker, *Franz Liszt, Volume 1: The Virtuoso Years*, 177.
78. For a discussion of the anti-virtuosity attitude of many of Liszt's contemporaries, see Dana Gooley, "The Battle against Instrumental Virtuosity in the Early Nineteenth Century," in *Franz Liszt and His World*, ed. Christopher H.

Gibbs and Dana Gooley (Princeton, NJ: Princeton University Press, 2006), 75–111.
79. The Ancient Greeks considered music to be a mimetic art. See Stephen Halliwell, *The Aesthetics of Mimesis: Ancient Texts and Modern Problems* (Princeton, NY: Princeton University Press), 2002.
80. Ralph Locke introduced and translated this article in the chapter "Liszt on the Artist in Society," in *Franz Liszt and His World*, 291–96.
81. The inclusion of musicians in the pantheon of artistic greatness reveals the recent revaluation that the musical arts had undergone in the wake of Beethoven's revolutionary example but also in philosophy, specifically in Schopenhauer's 1818 tome *The World as Will and Representation*, which would exercise a great influence over nineteenth-century conceptions of music.
82. Ralph P. Locke, *Music, Musicians, and the Saint-Simonians* (Chicago: University of Chicago Press, 1986), 106.
83. Quoted in Plaskin, *Horowitz*, 73.
84. Quoted in ibid.
85. Ibid., 72.
86. From a video interview: https://www.youtube.com/watch?v=M97rQCdIbTU, accessed September 24, 2019.
87. Ibid.
88. Mendelssohn observes, "Thalberg gave a concert yesterday evening and pleased me extraordinarily. He restores one's desire for playing and studying as everything really perfect does. A fantasia by him (such as, in particular, the one of *La donna del lago*) is a piling up of the choicest, finest effects, and an astounding climax of difficulties and elegances. Everything is so thought-out, refined, with such sureness and knowledge, and full of the finest taste. Moreover, the man has incredible strength of hand, and yet such practiced light fingers" (Letter to Fanny Mendelssohn, December 29, 1838, quoted in Douglas Bomberger, "The Thalberg Effect: Playing the Violin on the Piano," *The Musical Quarterly* 75, no. 2 [1991], 201).
89. Rosen, *The Romantic Generation*, 474, 540.
90. Richard Taruskin, "Liszt and Bad Taste," *Studia musicologica* 54, no. 1 (2013): 88.
91. Rosen, *The Romantic Generation*, 473.
92. Ibid., 539.
93. Ibid, 496, 508.
94. R. Larry Todd, *Mendelssohn: A Life in Music* (Oxford: Oxford University Press, 2003), 393.
95. Rosen, *The Romantic Generation*, 539.
96. Ibid., 541.

97. A few of the 1837 versions of the *Transcendental Études* were on the repertoire list for the Eighth International Franz Liszt Competition held in Utrecht, the Netherlands, in 2017.
98. Ibid., 492, 491, my emphasis. I should mention in this context the new monograph by Hyun Joo Kim, *Liszt's Representation of Instrumental Sounds on the Piano: Colors in Black and White* (University of Rochester Press, 2019).
99. It would appear that Liszt played only no. 4 (*Mazeppa*), no. 6 (*Vision*), and no. 11 (*Harmonies du Soir*) in his public concerts of the 1840s. The programs featured in Saffle's *Liszt in Germany* contain the descriptive titles that were not officially given until the 1851 revision of the Études.
100. Quoted in Alexander Stefaniak, *Schumann's Virtuosity: Criticism, Composition, and Performance in Nineteenth-Century Germany* (Bloomington: Indiana University Press, 2016), 131.
101. "The reviewer also noted Liszt's habit of introducing novelties into Weber's score [of the *Konzertstück*], including doublings to render relatively easy passages more difficult, and a superabundance of ornaments to give the work a more brilliant veneer" (Todd, *Mendelssohn*, 393). See Jonathan Dunsby's chapter in this volume.
102. The first public performance of *Grand galop chromatique* was on November 25, 1839. See also "Table 2: Liszt's Primary German Repertory," in Michael Saffle, *Liszt in Germany, 1840–1845*, 187.
103. Quoted in Charles Suttoni, Introduction to Franz Liszt, *Complete Piano Transcriptions from Wagner's Operas* (New York: Dover Publications, 1981).
104. Quoted in Arthur Friedheim, *Life and Liszt*, 138.
105. But there is also the practical aspect of Lisztian virtuosity that these showpieces bring to the fore. It is little noticed that the *Don Juan* Fantasy, for all its hair-raising virtuosity, studiously avoids the employment of any notes below F1 (there is one ossia in the bass at the beginning of the piece that goes down to the low C♯1 and one E1 at the beginning of the optional middle section, which can be easily dropped), presumably because many of the pianos Liszt was going to encounter on tour had a smaller keyboard compass—certainly, prior to the era of standardization, their quality and type varied greatly, and one had no idea what kind of piano would be available in the next town. Thus perhaps the most famous and greatest of all bravura piano showpieces was composed for a bass range that was, incredibly, the same as Mozart's fortepiano! The same year as the composition of the *Don Juan* Fantasy (1841), Chopin, with no such practical performance concerns to constrain him, completed his Fantasy in F Minor, op. 49, which makes extensive and evocative use of the bass notes from C1 to E1 (the piece is in fact impossible to play without these notes). The difference between Chopin's and Liszt's approaches to the piano could not be clearer from a comparison of these two fantasies.

106. https://www.youtube.com/watch?v=FvJo1ciAq3M, accessed September 24, 2019. While Bolet does play the entire set, he completely rearranges the order, something that would be considered eccentric or even somewhat taboo today.
107. See Horowitz's "concertography" at http://vladimirhorowitz.com/1_4_Concertography.html, accessed November 3, 2019.
108. Kenneth Hamilton (*After the Golden Age: Romantic Pianism and Modern Performance* [Oxford: Oxford University Press, 2007], 66) has remarked upon Busoni's "monumental approach" to the recital.
109. There is a Website that endeavors to list all of the recordings of the *Transcendental Études*: http://www.cnk.dk/Liszt%20etudes%20dexecution%20transcendante%20discography.htm, accessed September 24, 2019.
110. Https://www.bing.com/videos/search?q=trifonov+lyon+liszt&&view=detail&mid=3D89B0D400D3FD0E48D13D89B0D400D3FD0E48D1&&FORM=VRDGAR, accessed September 24, 2019.
111. https://www.medici.tv/en/concerts/boris-berezovsky-liszt/, accessed September 24, 2019.

Part One

Liszt, Virtuosity, and Performance

Chapter One

Après une Lecture de Czerny?
Liszt's Creative Virtuosity

Kenneth Hamilton

And as imagination bodies forth
The forms of things unknown, the poet's pen
Turns them to shapes, and gives to airy nothing
A local habitation and a name.

—Shakespeare, *A Midsummer Night's Dream*

In recent decades several scholars have convincingly located elements of Liszt's compositional technique in the training in improvisation that he undertook with Carl Czerny.[1] Carrying on from this, we might now ask, What did Liszt actually improvise on when his subject was not a musical motif handed to him by his teacher for practice or a selection of tunes suggested by his audience, picked out from a vase with a flourish as the climax to a concert? Was he inspired to initial extemporization, and subsequently to written composition, by "airy nothing," by potent yet nebulous "poetic ideas" stimulated by recollections of lakes (*Au lac de Wallenstadt*) or streams (*Au bord d'une source*) and masterpieces of poetry or prose (Dante's *Divine Comedy*, Senancour's *Obermann*)? Or was his starting point occasionally more down to earth: preexisting music tailored, adapted, and transformed to suit the subject in hand?

Liszt himself understandably insisted upon the former, although I am here proposing the latter. In the preface (1842) to his *Album d'un voyageur*, his most ambitious collection of music to date, he emphasized the inspiration of life lived, of nature, of places and peoples. This was his own musical travelogue, recollected in tranquility: "As I soon as I started to work my memories intensified." His aim was to heighten expression to such an extent that music "became a poetic language perhaps more appropriate than poetry itself to express those things within our souls that transcend the common horizon."[2]

I doubt neither Liszt's sincerity nor the multifarious nature of the influences upon him, nor the really startling originality of much of his music. Nevertheless, I do argue here that several aspects of major works from the 1830s were clearly inspired by pieces from Liszt's public or private performance repertoire, that there was a direct line from his virtuoso recreations in concert—his outrageously extensive modernizing, updating, and transforming of other composers' music—to his own original works. Just as, according to Dryden, "great wits are to madness near allied, and thin partitions do their bounds divide," Liszt's practice of virtuosity was closer than one might think to his process of composition. In fact, the distance between one and the other was occasionally well-nigh invisible. Accordingly, I attempt to identify in the pages that follow specific pieces that appear to have sparked his interest both as performer and composer. The creative process discussed here, however, was hardly confined to the 1830s: it provides a new, and hopefully convincing, context for the striking similarities between the *Quasi Faust* movement from Charles-Valentin Alkan's *Grande sonate: Les quatre âges* and Liszt's own Sonata in B Minor a decade later.[3] To summarize in advance: the so-called *Malédiction* Concerto is neither a concerto nor based entirely on original themes. It is rather a sextet "after Schubert," inspired by the song "Du bist die Ruh." Compelling structural and thematic similarities show that *Vallée d'Obermann* from the *Album d'un voyageur* was originally built upon the scaffolding of the first movement of Carl Maria von Weber's Sonata no. 4 in E Minor, op. 70; while lurking in the background of the "Fantasia quasi Sonata," *Après une lecture du Dante* is the surprisingly powerful scherzo from Carl Czerny's Piano Sonata in A-flat Major, op. 7, a piece performed by Liszt with markedly demonic flair in Vienna just before he turned his thoughts toward his own depiction of Dante's *Inferno*. But whereas in *Vallée d'Obermann* the modeling on Weber is deftly disguised in the extensive revision published in the Swiss volume of *Années de pèlerinage*, in the case of *Après une lecture du Dante*, Czerny's fingerprints remain obvious, even in the final version of the piece. They are, in effect, hiding in plain sight.

That they have not, as far as I am aware, been noticed before can be attributed to posterity's lack of interest in the hapless Czerny's creative endeavors and to the preposterous unlikelihood that one of the most glaringly radical examples of the "music of the future," should, whether consciously or not, have been inspired by a composer pigeon holed as a filing clerk of classical music, as a pedantic codifier of piano performance practices—as a mere molehill between the mountains of Beethoven and Liszt. Even in the oft-reproduced lithograph by Josef Kriehuber, Czerny shyly averts his eyes with amiable modesty, a perfect portrait of industry without inspiration.[4] The contrast could hardly be more intense with the images of his teacher, the truculent, tormented Beethoven, or of his most famous student, the visionary Liszt. Czerny, in other words, looked like we expect him to have looked—a Viennese Charles Pooter, applying himself assiduously to a musical "diary of a nobody"—and few have bothered to search beyond the stereotype. It does, after all, fulfill a useful function when presenting music history as a glorious procession of great composers. Czerny is the ideal anti-genius, a warning that in art, toil without talent is ultimately a waste of time.[5]

Nevertheless, while Czerny may have been mocked and belittled, he was not entirely cast aside. As consolation for the muses' lack of enthusiasm for his artistic endeavors, he enjoyed a fame that would have been the envy of many a more ambitious composer, underpinned by the ostentatious presence of volumes like *The School of Velocity* on parlor pianos. Czerny's brand may have been underwhelming, but it was at least one with excellent name recognition. As early as the 1830s, Robert Schumann was making catty comments about the apparently endless flow of brilliant but not-too-difficult piano pieces for well brought-up young ladies issuing from Czerny's indefatigably fertile pen. By the mid-1860s, an anonymous critic from the London *Musical World* characterized his music, in preposterously Victorian terms, as "namby-pamby" and pronounced his entire oeuvre "of little value."[6] And Friedrich Nietzsche knew exactly the effect an association with the distinctly unglamorous Czerny would have when he satirized Liszt as "*Die Schule der Geläufigkeit*—nach Weibern" (the School of velocity—toward women).[7] Nearly twenty years later, in her magisterially verbose "official" biography, *Franz Liszt as Artist and Man*, Lina Ramann summarily dismissed her idol's teacher as "Der Mann der Mechanik und Form" (the man of mechanics and form)—a blanket condemnation that drew from Liszt himself the wry annotation "nicht ganz richtig" (not quite right) scrawled into a copy of the offending page.[8]

Hell and *Hexaméron*

For Ramann, Liszt's early studies with Czerny were useful in establishing a bona fide connection with Beethoven and consequently with Viennese classicism. As a supposed creative nonentity, Czerny was cited not for his own sake but as a drab yet necessary link in the chain of quasi-apostolic succession from the great man himself. Liszt had received the blessing of Beethoven from Czerny's hands just as Haydn had channeled "the spirit of Mozart" to Beethoven, his own overachieving but recalcitrant pupil.[9] Echoes of Ramann's narrative still resound even in recent scholarship.

But alas for her attempt to fashion a German classical Liszt, complete with Beethovenian shield and Wagnerian spear, ready to be "cast into the boundless realms of the future," relatively little trace of Beethoven can be found in Liszt's adolescent music, with the questionable exception of a Sonata in F Minor (S. 692b / LW S22), surviving only in a fragment copied out from memory many decades later by the elderly composer at Ramann's request.[10] This begins with harmonies and figuration palely reminiscent of the opening of Beethoven's "Moonlight" Sonata. Liszt (or more likely his father) did not think enough of this piece to publish it, or indeed any of the other more "serious" compositions of this period, including two further piano sonatas, the opera *Don Sanche*, and at least one piano concerto, described in 1827 by Moscheles as containing "chaotic beauties" (so much for the strict Viennese classical training).[11] There is, in fact, no shadow at all of Beethoven in the music that Liszt did commit to print, including the *Étude en douze exercices* of 1826, but instead a close kinship with the "brilliant style" of the contemporary virtuoso school, as seen also in Czerny's numerous studies and in the widely promulgated *Éxercices et préludes*, op. 21, by the equally maligned Henri Herz.[12]

Liszt was, however, closely connected in public with both Czerny and Herz, participating in the concerts of the latter and playing the music of both. During his visits to England in 1824 and 1825, his repertoire largely centered on pieces by Czerny, including the Piano Concerto in F Major, op. 28, dedicated to him, the *Reichstadt Waltz with Brilliant Variations*, op. 14, and the *Variations on a Theme by Rode "La Ricordanza,"* op. 33, famously disinterred by Vladimir Horowitz over a century later.[13] Liszt not only played but also praised Czerny's music—this was no reluctant concession to popular taste. And the personal connection remained strong. In 1830, he wrote to Czerny entreating him to come to Paris, where he would "do for you what I would do for my father." Liszt had, moreover, become an evangelist for Czerny's serious music, not just for his crowd-pleasers. He had been "making a special study of your admirable Sonata (op. 7), and [had] since played it at several gatherings of connoisseurs (or would-be connoisseurs): you cannot imagine what an effect it made; I was quite overcome by it."[14]

Liszt obviously thought there was more to Czerny than initially met the eye—or ear. His motivation for defending him was not just "the gratitude and reverence of a student" with which he later dedicated his *Transcendental Studies* to his master, but genuine admiration for his "many-sided musical experience."[15] He even absorbed some of his aesthetic preferences, not least Czerny's enthusiastic advocacy of an eclectic musical style.[16] In 1856, when Liszt's own student Dionys Pruckner was planning a trip to Vienna, Liszt advised him to seek out Czerny. He hailed him, in complete contrast to the by then established image, as a progressive:

> In the twenties, when a great portion of Beethoven's creations was a kind of Sphinx, Czerny was playing Beethoven *exclusively*, with an understanding as excellent as his technique was efficient and effective; and later on, he did not set himself up against some of the progress that had been made in technique, but contributed materially to it by his own teaching and works. It is only a pity that, by a too superabundant productiveness, he has necessarily weakened himself, and has not gone further on the road of his First Sonata (op. 6 [actually 7], A-flat Major) and of other works of that period, which I rate very highly as compositions of importance, beautifully formed and having the noblest tendency. In those days, unfortunately, societal and publishing influences were of a damaging kind, and Czerny did not possess the necessary abrasiveness to withdraw from them and preserve his better self.[17]

It is not surprising that Liszt's comments on Czerny's music center on the opus 7 Sonata. It appears to have remained in his repertoire throughout the 1830s, although played more often in private circles than in public. Nevertheless, it assumed a notable role in Liszt's triumphant return to Vienna in 1838 for a series of concerts that effectively marked the start of his mature career as a touring virtuoso.

Czerny was one of the first musicians Liszt visited on his arrival in the city on April 10 of that year. Two days later he gave a private performance of the first two movements (the Andante and Scherzo) of Czerny's opus 7, along with some studies of his own and his fantasy on Bellini's *I puritani*.[18] On April 29, Czerny's pieces appeared again, in a prominent place as the opening numbers of Liszt's packed public concert at the Musikverein. They featured equally prominently in the review by Heinrich Adami in the *Allgemeine Theaterzeitung*:

> He began with and Andante and Scherzo from a Sonata by his former teacher Carl Czerny. With this choice he wished to demonstrate his respect and

gratitude. Liszt achieved a beautiful result, and that it at the same time was such a splendid one speaks no less to the magnificence of his talent. He mastered his given material with all the spirited liveliness that characterizes his particular style of playing and developed the most brilliant effects from it.[19]

But this was not achieved by scrupulous fidelity to Czerny's score—nor would Czerny likely have expected it to be so. According to Adami, it was the "original and bold manner" of playing the Scherzo that created a special sensation. Liszt offered a modernized performance using his latest battery of virtuoso techniques—blind octaves, coloristic pedaling, extended figuration, and the like.[20] In a wider-ranging article published a few days later in the *Wiener Zeitschrift für Kunst*, entitled "Liszt and French Romanticism" and signed "Carlo" (actually a pseudonym of Liszt's own publisher Pietro Mechetti—such was the unimpeachable objectivity of music criticism), the demonic effect of Liszt's pianism was delineated in equally diabolical prose: "He wants to go beyond current bounds, and utilizes the piano, like a *Faust*, as a hellish force to summon up the spirits of the underworld in the service of wonderful artistic goals. . . . He even plays pieces by other composers as if they were his own improvisations—and what improvisations they are!"[21] No doubt Liszt's habit of playing much of his repertoire from memory—an uncommon approach at the time—enhanced the extempore effect, but nevertheless, his performance style remained both highly original and extreme in its liberties, even taking into account the more relaxed aesthetics of the day. Mechetti admittedly had some qualms about the artistic acceptability of some of the techniques used—"frequent employment of the sustaining pedal, leading to blurring . . . an over-heroic treatment of the instrument, not taking into account the weakness of the piano frame . . . augmentation of the original [score] by doubling and filling out [of chords and passages]"—but he seemed to be of two minds about whether they constituted genuine "flaws." In typically Romantic fashion, he argued that if the piano cannot cope with such virtuosity, manufacturers should simply build sturdier pianos; and if composers had known Liszt's technical talents, they would have written their scores differently in the first place.[22] The Early Music movement would have received short shrift in the 1830s.

Liszt's next Viennese concert, on May 2, 1838, also began with the Sonata in A-flat, this time not by Czerny but by Beethoven (op. 26). Ever the canny self-publicist, Liszt intended to make his status as heir apparent to the great classical tradition as clear as possible. Nevertheless, having made his gracious tribute to Czerny at the earlier concert, he seems to have committed a minor diplomatic gaffe when he gave the Viennese premiere of the solo version of the collaborative "monster piece" (his own description) *Hexaméron* on May 8 in the hall of the Musikverein. This is an entertainingly trashy set of variations on a theme from Bellini's *I puritani*, composed, one variation apiece, by an unlikely committee of six artists, consisting of Chopin, Czerny, Pixis, Herz, Thalberg, as well as Liszt—the whole then cobbled together by the latter, who added an introduction, interludes, and a finale. The bombastic title refers (jokingly, one hopes) to the "six days of creation" in the Bible.

Hexaméron was originally commissioned by Princess Cristina Belgiojoso as the main attraction of a charity concert in her Parisian salon on March 31, 1837. As is often, alas, the way with such symposia, the individual contributions were not delivered on time, with Chopin the worst laggard. The princess did nevertheless persevere. All parts eventually having been obtained and assembled, *Hexaméron* was belatedly unveiled by Liszt on February 18, 1838, in La Scala in Milan. But his rendition was not entirely complete. No doubt owing to the sheer length of the piece, more than twenty minutes in its longest version, Liszt omitted the Czerny variation and proceeded to do the same at the Viennese premiere a few months later. *Hexaméron* was a massive hit, but the absence of Czerny's contribution was inevitably noted in the latter's hometown. Liszt quickly made amends, repeating *Hexaméron* at his next Viennese concert on May 14, this time with all six variations. Heinrich Adami insisted—probably after a conversation with Liszt himself—that the previous omission had been "by accident," but it does seem more likely that Liszt had merely replicated his cuts for the Milan premiere.[23]

When the solo version of *Hexaméron* was published in 1839, six variations were indeed included, but Liszt rarely waded through all of them. He had, in fact, already made a much shorter version for piano and orchestra (orchestrated in San Rossore, Italy, in September 1839, premiered in Leipzig on March 30, 1840) wholly omitting the Czerny and the Chopin variations and including a section of the Pixis variation only as part of a significantly cut finale.[24] It is worth noting here that the *Hexaméron* score published in 1839 also includes a piano reduction of an orchestral part, with tutti sections in a different typeface (to be omitted if the piece is played solo) and in one case an alternative reading of the solo part, to be used if an orchestra is available. This is not the same as the (unpublished) cut version for piano and orchestra finished in San Rossore, and it was the latter that Liszt featured in his own concerts. Owing no doubt to a modern "completist" philosophy of the type aptly illustrated by the lyrics of the song "All, or Nothing at All," every solo recording of *Hexaméron* known to me has failed to omit the tutti sections as instructed.[25] Listeners have suffered accordingly: in this inflated form, the piece is more to be endured than enjoyed.

Liszt followed the structure of the shorter orchestral version in a reworking for two pianos premiered in London (with Louise Dulcken) on May 31 the following year, advertised with admirable hyperbole as "a grand duet for two pianos arranged from his stupendous *Hexaméron*." An extensive, unpublished revision of this version from the mid-1840s—entitled "Grand Bravura Variations from *Hexaméron*," hence neatly explaining the fact that there are fewer than six—includes a new slow section based on an additional theme from *I puritani* ("Credeasi, misera! da mi tradita"). Nevertheless, neither the Czerny nor the Chopin reappear.[26] Liszt changed his mind yet again in the final version for two pianos published in 1870. Here he now removed the "Credeasi, misera!" section and further shortened the finale, completely excising Pixis's contribution, along with Czerny's and Chopin's. Like photographs of Stalin's Politburo, successive versions of *Hexaméron* catalog a series of unexplained disappearances.

And as with the Politburo, it was not necessarily the good that survived. In one of several ironies associated with the work, Chopin's wonderfully graceful and touching variation does not appear in any of the later published versions, although Liszt did occasionally play it.[27] Perhaps he thought it showed the others up? Like his own contribution, it is lyrical rather than brilliant—and if there was room to retain only one lyrical variation, Liszt could rarely bring himself to discard his own. In ironic contrast, Herz's pitifully vacuous variation survives in every reworking of *Hexaméron*, even though it had been sharply satirized in the first version of the finale. To explain this, we should expand a little on Liszt's love-hate musical relationship with Herz.

"I would," the aged Liszt once reminisced to his student August Göllerich, "have been happy to take second or third place after Herz."[28] Liszt was talking about his early years in Paris. In the Paris of the late 1820s, Henri Herz was fashionable, popular, and commercially successful both as pianist and composer. Liszt played his music, participated in his concerts, and in the Fantasy on Auber's *La fiancée* even attempted to out-Herz Herz in outrageous imitation. But, as the 1830s progressed, Herz's reputation began to suffer a steep decline, and Liszt became keener to demonstrate some distance. Herz had become the whipping boy for Maurice Schlesinger's *Gazette musicale* (from 1835, when it merged with Fétis's *Revue musicale*, the *Revue et gazette musicale de Paris*) in several issues of which his "industrial" production of vapid variations was contrasted with music of true, elevated artistry—Beethoven, Berlioz, and the other usual suspects. But as Katharine

Ellis argues, the attacks on Herz were likely motivated more by Schlesinger's desire for a controversy to whip up sales than by a selfless crusade for all that was noble in art.[29]

Liszt himself was a writer for the *Gazette*. Indeed, he may have personally contributed some of the anonymous anti-Herz polemics that appeared with tedious regularity, although most of them were likely written by François Stoepel.[30] There can be little doubt that Liszt's original piece entitled *Harmonies poétiques et religieuses* (S. 154 / LW A18), published in 1835, not surprisingly also in the *Revue et Gazette Musicale*, was a part of the propaganda war, prefaced as it was by a long extract from Lamartine emphasizing its refinement and exclusivity: "These verses are addressed only to a small number of people." In a wry twist of fate, Stoepel then turned his fire back on Liszt himself, writing a scathing review of the *Harmonies* in the *Allgemeine Musikalische Zeitung*. He complained that it was not a "proper" composition but simply a written-out improvisation.[31] In 1853, when a much-revised version of the piece was republished as *Pensée des morts* (173/4 / LW A158/4), the Lamartine extract reappeared as a preface to the larger collection of works (now itself entitled *Harmonies poétiques et religieuses*) in which *Pensée* was included. But significantly, the first sentence was now omitted, even if some of Steopel's musical criticisms were implicitly addressed.[32] By now, Liszt was courting a wider public than a clique of Herz-hating connoisseurs.

Nevertheless, in 1839 Liszt was too closely associated with the campaign against Herz to give his music an entirely free pass in *Hexaméron*. He obviously considered a certain supercilious distance advisable. In the finale of the original version of the piece, he recapitulated passages from Thalberg's and Pixis's variations in straightforward fashion, but when Herz's inoffensively elegant music dared to step forth, Liszt dismissed it brusquely with a "Mephisthophelean" semitonal sneer, the first example of the barbed humor later to figure in the *Faust* Symphony and the First Mephisto Waltz. One wonders whether he got the basic idea for this from the overture to Weber's *Der Freischütz*, which he knew very well indeed and which he even transcribed for piano. In the development section of the overture, Agathe's blithe theme is similarly menaced by an obtrusive semitone, presumably representing Samiel, the devil of the piece, rather than Mephistopheles. It seems that once you've heard one musical devil, you've heard them all (see ex. 1.1). Herz is thus laughed to scorn, yet his variation survived through every revision. Like a microcosm of the reception history of Liszt's own music, Herz was ridiculed but regularly played.

Example 1.1. Liszt, *Hexaméron*, S. 392 (1839 solo version), Finale, mm. 24–31

Czerny was another obvious candidate for early ejection from *Hexaméron*, perhaps for the opposite reason of that which accounts for Chopin's fate. In the original 1839 edition, Czerny's is simply a third redundant variation in the brilliant style already essayed by Pixis and Herz. As if to say, "that's enough of that," Liszt violently dismisses the Czerny with an abruptly deflected cadence leading directly to a typically Lisztian storm (see ex. 1.2). Such storms were soon established as something of a calling card for Liszt, both as virtuoso and composer. At least three other pieces in his concert repertoire of the period also feature similar scenes: his piano transcriptions of Beethoven's "Pastoral" (Sixth) Symphony (S. 463b / LW A37b/2, 1837), of Rossini's *William Tell* Overture (S. 552 / LW A54, 1838), and of *Un soir dans les montagnes* (S. 156/18 / LW A40c/2, 1837–38).[33] Although the last of these is a lengthy paraphrase of a song by Ernest Knop, the elaborate "storm" is, as in *Hexaméron*, Liszt's own addition. And soon afterward, Liszt was thrilling British audiences with an improvised tempest enthusiastically added to his accompaniment of John Orlando Parry's song "The Inchcape Bell." "Storms," Liszt proudly told Amy Fay, "are my *forte*."[34]

In later versions of *Hexaméron*, Czerny's variation, and consequently the ensuing tempest, are cut completely. But as in an imperfectly cropped photograph, an intriguing shadow of Czerny does in fact remain visible, in the form of a new cadenza added to Liszt's own variation in the revised two-piano version from the 1840s, retained in the 1870 edition (see ex. 1.3). Although modified, modernized, and Lisztified, this is clearly based on the similar cadenza in the Czerny variation (see ex. 1.4).

Thus, a little bit of Czerny lives on through his pupil. His fingerprints, as it were, remain. Was this a conscious tribute? It would be amusing to think so. In a final irony, the Liszt rewriting of Czerny's figuration is actually easier to play, lacking as it does the awkward hand crossings, although more virtuosic in effect. Not just a tribute, then, but a definite improvement.

Example 1.2. Liszt, *Hexaméron*, S. 392 (1839 solo version), conclusion of Czerny variation and beginning of "storm" interlude, p. 19, m. 3 to p. 20, m. 5

Example 1.3. Liszt, *Hexaméron*, Weimar D-WRgs W14, new cadenza in Liszt Variation, pp. 19–20

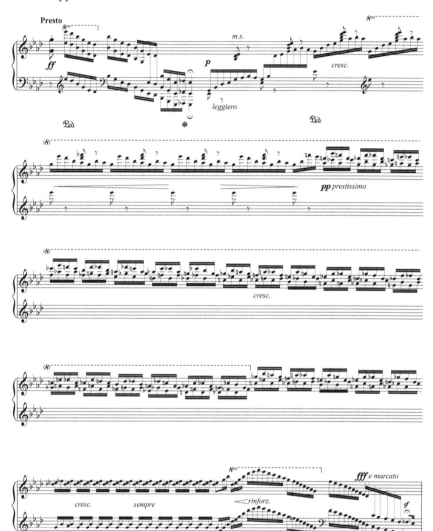

Example 1.4. Liszt, *Hexaméron*, S. 392 (1839 solo version), Cadenza from Czerny's variation, p. 18 and first two mm. of p. 19

And what of Liszt's "serious" Czerny repertoire, namely the opus 7 Sonata? The piece is rarely played today, but the fingerprints of its Scherzo remain identifiable in a masterpiece firmly lodged in the repertoire, Liszt's "Fantasia quasi Sonata," *Après une lecture du Dante.*

Czerny the Progressive

Liszt began composing the first version of this piece, then entitled *Fragment nach Dante*, on the morning of September 26, 1839, in Pisa. This we can pinpoint precisely from a letter written by his partner at the time, the

Countess Marie d'Agoult, who heard him starting work on it at the piano. Even as the first notes emerged, she was obviously skeptical about its potential popularity. She described the piece with prescient cynicism as "destined to remain in his portfolio."[35] The intention to write it had been forming in Liszt's mind since at least the previous February. He had long loved Dante's *Divine Comedy*. Admiring references to it appear throughout his correspondence, and even occasional quotes from the original, although Liszt's command of Italian left much to be desired—he owed his deeper knowledge of the poem to a French translation. As early as 1832, Liszt told his student Valérie Boissier that J. C. Kessler's octave study reminded him of Dante's *Inferno*. He proceeded to play it with "inconceivable vigour" and "a fist of Hercules," producing a tremendous, but ultimately discouraging, effect far beyond the restricted abilities of his dazzled pupil.[36]

Perhaps Liszt was further motivated to composition of the *Fragment nach Dante* by the Mechetti review quoted above, colorfully hailing his playing as a "hellish force summoning up the sprits of the underworld," a description that could have fit the unwritten *Dante Fragment* like a glove, just as it recalls the "fury, horror, anger, vengeance and delirium" supposedly elicited by Kessler's study. A diary entry from the same month shows that Liszt was not just planning a piano piece on Dante but *Dante* and *Faust Symphonies* as well.[37] As Marie d'Agoult predicted, the *Fragment nach Dante* remained unpublished, but it was revised in 1845–48, when the title was changed to the pretentiously unpronounceable *Paralipomènes à la "Divina commedia": Fantaisie symphonique* (S. 158a / LW A55/7) and subsequently, in 1849, to *Prolégomènes à la "Divina commedia"* (S. 158b / LW A55/7). These versions also remained in manuscript during Liszt's lifetime, but the *Paripolemènes* has now been edited by Adrienne Kaczmarczyk and published in the *New Liszt Edition*, along with an intelligently written and informative preface detailing the piece's checkered compositional history.[38] Further revisions were made before its publication in 1858 as *Après une lecture du Dante* in the Italian volume of *Années de pèlerinage*.

Although we do not have a complete score of the *Fragment nach Dante*, we can reconstruct much of it from the underlying and deleted layers of the *Paralipomènes* manuscript.[39] We can also tell that Liszt's revisions were mostly in the nature of cuts and refinements rather than expansions. The *Paralipomènes* is significantly longer than *Après une lecture du Dante*. Indeed, one entire theme was excised from the final version, in addition to the garrulous development passages associated with it. It seems highly likely, however, that all the basic material in the *Paralipomènes* appeared in some form or other in the *Fragment nach Dante*. And although the *Paralipomènes* manuscript divides the piece into two parts, it is clear that these parts are not independent but instead are simply the exposition and development/recapitulation of a sonata form exhibiting Reicha's celebrated "grande coupe binaire."[40] In other words, the piece always consisted of a single continuous movement.

All surviving versions display the same general structure: an initial introduction of themes (a tritonal trumpet call, waking the dead) followed by a clamorous minor-key first group—a wailing procession of the damned.[41] Long-held pedals produce the requisite swell of lamentation (again echoing the Mechetti review) and of course the material is in the "demonic" key of D minor, as featured in Mozart's *Don Giovanni* and Liszt's own *Totentanz*. This eventually culminates in a plainchant/chorale second group in the raised mediant major (F-sharp major), a tonal relationship relatively uncommon for the time but frequently found in Liszt's symphonic poems.

Of course, all this is far beyond anything Czerny (or Kessler) could have achieved, or would have wanted to achieve, but nevertheless there remain some startling similarities between fundamental features of the *Paralipomènes* (and by inference the *Fragment nach Dante*) and of the Scherzo from Czerny's opus 7 Sonata, namely, the rhythm, shape, and character of the principal theme (especially at measures 93–109) (see exx. 1.5–1.6) and the use of a grand chorale melody in block chords as the contrasting material (see exx. 1.7–1.8).

Both of these resemblances remain in *Après une lecture du Dante*, although the notation is slightly altered from example 1.6 and the keyboard setting from example 1.8. Moreover, the octave flourish at the end of the Czerny example 1.7, although not appearing in the *Paralipomènes*, will surely ring a bell with those who know the development section of *Après une lecture du Dante*.

Conversely, a part of the development later cut from the *Paralipomènes* also has a clear counterpart in the Czerny (see exx. 1.9–1.10). The resemblances are compelling, although it is impossible to say whether Liszt was conscious of them. Moreover, the piano writing itself is exactly what one might expect if one were to update Czerny according to Mechetti's description of Liszt's playing: "frequent employment of the sustaining pedal, leading to blurring . . . augmentation of the original [score] by doubling and filling out [of chords and passages]." One might reasonably also assume that Liszt's "original and bold manner" (according to Heinrich Adami) of playing the Czerny would have encompassed the use of alternating octaves in furious passages such as the lead-in to the chorale melody in example 1.7.

Example 1.5. Czerny, Scherzo from Piano Sonata, op. 7, p. 12, *Prestissimo agitato*, mm. 1–16

An imaginary Lisztian version of the Czerny might therefore come very close to the world of the Dante. The virtuosic performance of the one seems to have led to composition of the other. Of course, the overall effect of the Czerny is only a fraction of that of the Liszt, even if the former is an unexpectedly vigorous and effective piece. I am not questioning the greater range of Liszt's genius here, simply suggesting that his inspiration had more than merely poetic roots. Indeed, the transformation of the Czerny into the Dante distinctly recalls the similar wholesale transformation of Liszt's Czerny-like *Étude en douze exercices* into the *Grandes études* at around the same time. And the influences on the Dante were not restricted to Czerny's Scherzo. Another prominent *Dante* theme—perhaps signifying the hope of redemption—is conspicuously derived from a melody in the last movement of Weber's Piano Sonata no. 2 in A-flat Major, op. 39, a further piece from Liszt's repertoire, which he later edited (see exx. 1.11–1.12).

The *Fragment nach Dante* was greeted with distaste and incomprehension at its first and only public performance in Vienna on December 5, 1839. Liszt did play it privately on a number of other occasions but was hesitant to inflict it again on a paying audience. Czerny's influence passed unnoticed amid widespread stupefaction. For Heinrich Adami (unconsciously echoing

Example 1.6. Liszt, *Paralipomènes*, S. 158a, *Allegro agitato assai*, mm. 57–109

Example 1.7: Czerny, Scherzo from op. 7, p. 14, *Risoluto*, mm. 7–23

Example 1.8. Liszt, *Paralipomènes*, S. 158a, *Con entusiasmo*, mm. 304–18

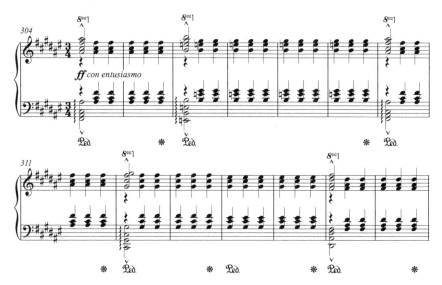

Example 1.9. Czerny, Scherzo from op. 7, p.16, mm. 1–20

Example 1.10. Liszt: *Paralipomènes*, S. 158a, *Presto agitato assai*, mm. 526–42

Example 1.11. Weber, Sonata in A-flat Major, op. 39, last movement, Rondo, p. 33, mm. 14–20

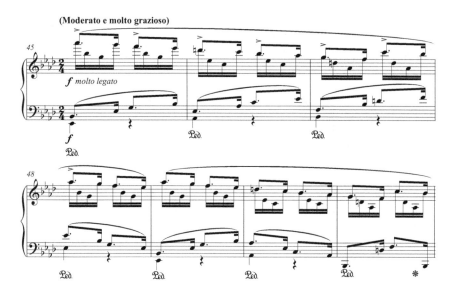

Example 1.12. Liszt: *Paralipomènes*, S. 158a, mm. 810–14

Stoepel's criticism of the *Harmonies poétiques*) the piece seemed like an "improvisation . . . a collection of colorfully varied ideas chasing each other . . . the whole in the character of the French New Romantic School." Only a tiny minority of listeners in France like this sort of stuff, he assured his readers, and no one at all in Germany.[42] Writing in the *Allgemeine Theaterzeitung*, Karl Tausenau, normally a fervent admirer of Liszt, was even more damning: "I can't deny my prejudice against the tendencies of this [the French Romantic] School, which perhaps go beyond the boundaries of music." He had, however, talked to Liszt after the performance. The composer explained the conception behind the piece and pointed out some of its novel harmonic effects. Tausenau acknowledged that "an entire future" was contained in the "rich and original" modulations. But in sum, he would far rather have heard a repeat of Liszt's wonderful performance of Beethoven's Third Piano Concerto in C Minor than the premiere of the *Dante*. If this was the future, then Tausenau wanted no part of it.[43]

From Dante's Inferno to Obermann's Valley

Just as *Après une lecture du Dante* is the climax of the Italian year of *Années de pèlerinage*, *Vallée d'Obermann* is the most ambitious of the Swiss set. It also had a literary inspiration: the 1804 epistolary novel *Obermann* by Etienne Pivert de Senancour. The book features an angst-ridden central character seeking, Parsifal-like, an ill-defined self-fulfillment amid the sublime beauty of the Alps. This appealed tremendously to young, equally angst-ridden Romantics like Liszt. Moreover, given his overly complicated personal life, which to some extent was hampering his professional career and thwarting his own self-fulfillment (more on this below), Liszt identified especially strongly with Obermann. He was accordingly inspired to a composition titled not simply "Obermann," but "Obermann's Valley."

The reference to a specific spot was especially appropriate for the *Album d'un voyageur*, in which the first version of *Vallée d'Obermann* was first published. The album abounds in evocative illustrations (*The Chapel of William Tell*, *The Bells of Geneva*, *The Lake of Wallenstadt*), but the "valley" in question also has metaphorical meaning: it refers to Obermann's psychological state—like a "trough of despair," or the "slough of despond" from Bunyan's *Pilgrim's Progress*. Lest this not be explicit enough, Liszt prefaced the score with extensive quotations both from the novel itself ("What do I want? Who am I? What do I ask from nature?" gives something of their flavor) and from Byron's equally self-absorbed *Childe Harold's Pilgrimage*.

However, Liszt's musical material was, again, less metaphysical and much more down to earth. The first version of the piece contains striking reminiscences of the aforementioned Fourth Piano Sonata by Weber, in the same key of E minor. Both themes and structure follow Weber very closely, perhaps too closely, with the exception of some added instrumental recitatives and yet another Swiss "storm scene" along the lines of Liszt's almost exactly contemporaneous *Un soir dans les montagnes*, which acts as a substitute for Weber's central development section.

The original *Vallée d'Obermann* is also a sonata form—a monothematic movement with a rhapsodic recitative-like introduction based on three descending notes, G–F♯–E. The entire piece is developed from this figure, which is expanded to create the Weberian first subject theme (see exx. 1.13–1.14).

It is easy to see here how Liszt's theme could have resulted from an improvisation on the Weber: a rhythmically varied version of the tune in the bass register, as in its second statement in Weber's sonata. Liszt's contrasting material in the relative major consists of a *dolcissimo con amore* transformation of the theme, again with more than a hint of Weber's elegant transformation of his own theme (see exx. 1.15–1.16).

Example 1.13. Liszt, *Vallée d'Obermann*, first version, S. 156/5, opening

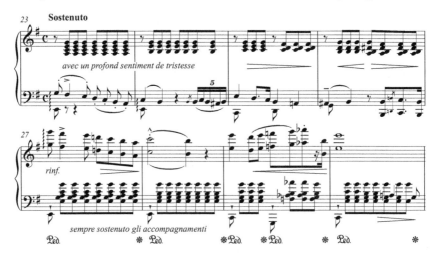

Example 1.14. Weber, Piano Sonata no. 4 in E Minor, op. 70, opening

A tempestuous development elaborates music from the introduction with a torrent of tremolos and tempest of octaves, leading into a generously extended, dare one say somewhat tedious, recapitulation in E minor/major.

Liszt extensively recast *Vallée d'Obermann* in the 1850s, turning one of his most disappointingly rigid large-scale works into one of his most sublime. Many of the problems with the earlier version can be traced to its almost textbook sonata structure—decidedly music of the past rather than music of the future. In the revision, the recapitulation of the main theme in the minor is ruthlessly jettisoned; the major mode appears like an angelic consolation immediately after the central development section, and to incomparably greater effect. The exposition too is radically recomposed. The new *Vallée d'Obermann* is no longer a painting-by-numbers sonata *"nach"* Weber" but a massively more mature production: subtle in construction and stamped with a sophisticated chromatic harmony that appears to have cast its spell even on Amfortas in Wagner's *Parsifal*.[44] There is no clearer illustration of the great

Example 1.15. Liszt, *Vallée d'Obermann*, first version, S. 156/5, second group

Example 1.16. Weber, Sonata no. 4 in E Minor, second group

strides Liszt made as a composer during his Weimar years nor indeed of the stiffness of some of his earlier attempts at large-scale composition.

And as a secret "word to the wise," as John Rink has perceptively noticed, Liszt introduced something extra, namely a reference to Schubert's song "The Wanderer" (set to a poem by Georg Philipp Schmidt), which features a similarly frustrated traveler, constantly seeking the perfect paradise he can never quite reach.[45] With adept sleight of hand, Liszt slyly quotes Schubert's music for the words "Sighing, I constantly ask 'where am I going?'" The Schubert also offers an explanation for the otherwise puzzling close to the piece: the music mounts up to a glorious virtuoso climax: jubilant chords resonate splendidly; octaves abound. It appears to be a typically Lisztian "apotheosis," concluding with a gargantuan arpeggio in double octaves ascending through the entire length of the keyboard. But the piece is not over. A couple of querulous measures are unexpectedly added, with strikingly deflationary effect. It is another reference to "The Wanderer": "My land so green with hope . . . where are you?" For a character like Obermann, Liszt is subtly telling us, happiness will always be around the corner.

Liszt and Marie Sing Schubert

Can Schubert's fingerprints be found elsewhere in Liszt's music? Indeed they can. A case in point is the so-called *Malédiction* Concerto, otherwise (and correctly) known as the Sextet for Piano and Strings.

This one-movement sextet was written in 1834–35 but remained in manuscript during Liszt's lifetime.[46] An edition by Liszt's pupil Bernhard Stavenhagen finally appeared in 1914 but attracted relatively little attention. There were, after all, more pressing issues to deal with in Europe that year. Stavenhagen assumed that the five string parts in the manuscript referred to orchestral forces, rather than a solo quintet, and therefore called the work "*Malédiction* Concerto," a somewhat misleading designation, for, as Jay Rosenblatt pointed out in a pioneering dissertation in 1995, the piece is obviously not a concerto, nor was it given any title in the manuscript.[47] Liszt had indeed inscribed the word *malédiction* (curse) into the score, but only over the grindingly dissonant opening theme. Subsequent sections of the exposition were marked "orgeuil" (pride), "pleurs—angoisses—songes" (tears—anxieties—dreams), and "raillerie" (mockery). The scoring, for piano, two violins, viola, cello, and double bass, nevertheless makes it highly likely that this single-movement piece in sonata form is the otherwise mysterious "sestetto" mentioned by Liszt in a letter to his mother written in Geneva on July 28, 1835. In it, he asked her to send to him the score of the sestetto from Paris, along with, among many other things, his volume of Schubert lieder.[48]

We do not normally associate Liszt with chamber music (which is probably one of the reasons Stavenhagen—a fine musician—assumed that the untitled manuscript was scored for orchestral strings), but in the early 1830s he seems to have devoted a considerable amount of time to the genre, composing not only the sextet but also a duo for violin and piano on a Mazurka by Chopin and a piece for two pianos on melodies from Mendelssohn's "Songs without Words." The sextet appeared to be the odd one out, given that the published score has hitherto been thought—even by Rosenblatt—to contain only original themes by Liszt himself; but appearances are in this case deceptive, for the source material for the piece is hiding in plain sight.

In the manuscript, a lengthy arrangement of Schubert's song "Du bist die Ruh" turns up in the middle of the recapitulation, just before the coda (figure S in the published score). Liszt crossed this out in his final revision and then abandoned the work completely. Believing that the Schubert had nothing to do with the earlier part of the piece ("musically there is no antecedent to it in the work"), Rosenblatt was understandably puzzled by what he described as this "interpolation."[49] But it is far from an interpolation—rather, it is both the musical and emotional goal of the work. Much of the preceding music is based on fragments of the song. The sextet, in other words, is a tortured meditation upon a melody by Schubert, a "Sextet nach Schubert"—in this respect a fitting companion to its sister pieces based on Chopin and Mendelssohn and also sharing certain features with the Third *Apparition*, an equally unsettling *Fantaisie sur une valse de François Schubert*.

We do not have to look far to find a possible explanation for Liszt's fondness for this particular Schubert song. The emotional tumult suggested by the verbal descriptions in the sextet's manuscript is borne out by its restless— at times hysterical—character, and by the soap opera that constituted Liszt's private life during the 1830s, the period of its composition.

As mentioned above, Liszt had for some time been involved in a passionate and illicit relationship with the Countess d'Agoult, a woman of exactly the type he tended to go for—titled, talented, and married to someone else. The lovers shared many passions, including one for Schubert's music: Marie often sang Schubert lieder in her salon to Liszt's piano accompaniment. It is highly likely, therefore, that the inclusion of "Du bist die Ruh" in the sextet represented for Liszt and d'Agoult the equivalent of "they're playing our song." And that for Liszt himself, Marie was the *Ruh* (rest) spoken of.[50] On top of this, the sextet was composed during a period of profound crisis in their relationship. Toward the end of 1834, Marie's infant daughter Louise died. In March 1835, she again became pregnant; but this time the father was obviously not her husband (the child was Blandine, the first of three she would have with Liszt). She eloped with Liszt in May to Geneva in Switzerland. It is hardly surprising, then, that many of the letters Liszt wrote to the countess just before their elopement are couched in the same tone of fervent anguish as the almost hysterical jottings in the sextet manuscript, nor that Liszt should have wanted both the score of the sextet and his volume of Schubert songs sent to him so urgently after the couple arrived in Geneva.

With the biographical background in mind, mapping Schubert's music for the first stanza of the text (by Friedrich Rückert) onto Liszt's sextet yields intriguing results (see ex. 1.17). The song's opening music ("You are rest / Gentle peace") first appears in a fraught minor-key variant as a transition theme in the sextet's exposition (see ex. 1.18). This eventually leads to Liszt's second group material, *teneramente amoroso*, based on the music for the lines "I dedicate to you, full of joy and sorrow . . . my whole heart" (see ex. 1.19). It was this section that Liszt inscribed with the words "pleures—angoisses—songes" (tears—anxieties—dreams) in the score. The jauntily acidic music following this (the close of the sonata exposition) has no counterpart in the song, but Liszt describes it as "raillerie" (mockery). One might guess that it refers to the social reaction to Liszt and Marie's relationship. Her social status was, after all, distressingly far above his. After a hectically picturesque development section and the customary recapitulation, the full version of the piece finally reaches the goal of all its yearning with a complete unveiling of the song that provides its source material.

Why, then, did Liszt consider eliminating the naked statement of "Du bist die Ruh"? We can only speculate. The last revisions to the manuscript seem to have taken place in Geneva in 1835. Liszt probably asked his mother to send him the score of the sextet and of Schubert's songs partly for this purpose. But perhaps the message contained in this particular lied was just too personal (although that sort of thing does not seem to have worried Liszt elsewhere), and he therefore decided that by removing the full statement of the Schubert, the biographical key to the piece, the sextet would become a safer, more "abstract" piece of chamber music. But simply cutting the song outright, as he perhaps belatedly realized, is not an ideal solution, for the result is frustratingly incomprehensible. It turns the sextet into *Hamlet* without the prince, or even, to continue the Shakespearian analogy, into *Much*

Example 1.17. Schubert, "Du bist die Ruh," D. 776 (op. 59, no. 3)

Ado about Nothing. Faced, then, with a choice between the devil and the deep blue sea, between musical incoherence and autobiographical exposure, Liszt simply abandoned the piece. He proceeded to cannibalize its best ideas. The arresting opening (the *Malédiction* itself) was reworked three times: in the symphonic poem *Prometheus*, in *Totentanz* for piano and orchestra, and in *Orage* for piano (from the Swiss set of the *Années de pèlerinage*—a further storm with shades of *Un soir dans les montagnes*), while the theme marked "orgeuil" (pride) was used in the "Mephistopheles" movement of the *Faust Symphony*, no doubt with the same signification, although this is neither indicated in the score nor likely to be guessed at by audiences. And in 1838 Liszt published a solo piano transcription of "Du bist die Ruh" with similarities to the version in the sextet. This publication probably marked his consignment of the sextet to the realm of musical might-have-beens. But unbothered by painful personal resonances, we ourselves might simply listen to the piece—to its uncut version, which is by far the most coherent—as a

Example 1.18. Liszt, *Malédiction*, S. 121, p. 5, *molto agitato*, figure C in published score, mm. 1–6

Example 1.19. Liszt, *Malédiction*, S. 121, p. 7, m. 12 to page 8, m. 5

musical confession by a young composer in his early twenties whose private life has suddenly turned out to be much livelier than he expected or even wanted.[51]

"Yes! Yes!—The Sonata Is All Stolen!"

The reception history of Liszt's music has been stamped by the persistent claim that he was more imaginative as an arranger than as an original composer. The common ways of countering this have been to argue that his bolder transcriptions really are original works (a position first staked out by Schumann in his review of the Berlioz-Liszt *Symphonie fantastique*), to emphasize unceasingly the novel aspects of his oeuvre as a whole, and to overlook his fairly frequent creative allusions to other composers' music.[52] The last is most amusingly seen in the strident attempts of many musicologists, from Liszt's "official" biographer, Lina Ramann, onward, to wish away the blatant reference to Chopin's A-flat Major Polonaise (op. 53) in *Funérailles*. In this piece, according to Ramann, "The similarity . . . with the octave figure in Chopin's A-Flat Polonaise can mislead one to the assumption that the former is based on it. This, however, results only from the family resemblance that all diatonically constructed ground basses have from Bach to the present day."[53] Nearly a century later, Alan Walker continued to dismiss claims of an intentional allusion as "little more than a romantic fabrication"[54] However—if probably unknown to Ramann and Walker—when *Funérailles* was played at a master class in Weimar in 1885, Liszt was entirely open about the inspiration of the passage in question, telling the pianist, Conrad Ansorge, "That is essentially an imitation of Chopin's famous Polonaise; but here I have done it somewhat differently."[55] In fact, the reference to Chopin is not simply a casual aside.[56] Its recognition extends and enriches the multiplicity of emotional resonances.

A more nuanced approach to Liszt's output would consider his creativity as a continuum stretching from performance to original composition via improvisation and transcription—the categories are far from independent. Few composers had as profound a knowledge of the then-developing standard repertoire of piano music as did Liszt, and few had internalized so much of it. As the contemporary critic François-Joseph Fétis observed, "All music of any value whatsoever is stored away in Liszt's mind in such a way as he is able instantaneously to perform whatever piece by whatever celebrated composer that one might care to name."[57] Liszt was, after all, a pioneer of playing from memory and fond of improvising for hours not just on specific themes but on whole pieces.[58] Some of his performances of notated music were so free as to verge upon improvisations, and, as we have seen, some of his original compositions sounded merely like written-out improvisations to his critics. For Liszt, simply playing a piece often involved refashioning or re-creation.[59] As Wagner aptly commented, his virtuosity was not just reproductive but actively productive.[60]

On visiting the elderly Liszt in Weimar, the Russian composer Alexander Borodin observed him being exactly that: "He improvised new arrangements like Balakireff, sometimes altering the bass, sometimes the treble notes. By degrees there flowed from this improvisation one of those marvelous transcriptions in which the arrangement for piano surpasses the composition itself."[61] It is therefore hardly surprising that several aspects of the pieces Liszt played should have seeped into his own music, whether consciously or not. Sometimes references and allusions to a musical model were obviously intended to be heard, at least by a select audience who could identify the "quieter tone for those who listen in secret" (to quote the aphorism by Schlegel that prefaces Schumann's op. 17 Fantasy). *Funérailles* and the Schubert references discussed above are suggestive examples.

Liszt could have been completely unaware that he was aping aspects of Czerny and Weber in his *Fragment nach Dante* and *Vallée d'Obermann*. I do, however, think it is as least as likely that the creative work for these pieces began by improvisation on the initial models, in the manner described above by Borodin, and proceeded apace to develop its own distinctive character. In the case of *Vallée d'Obermann*, Liszt even required a second major revision before he distanced the piece sufficiently from Weber to make the similarities implicit rather than explicit. This does not call into question the originality or the profundity of the final version; but simply charts its evolution. Creation often begins with recreation; this is simply how composers tend to compose. As Bartók aptly put it, "All composers, even the greatest, must start from something that already exists. . . . From such foundation, one composer—the innovator—gradually reaches new points, from which it is hardly possible to remember the start."[62]

With this in mind, we might finally circle back to the vexed issue of influences upon Liszt's great Sonata in B Minor (1853): Did the same process of creative adaptation that led from the Czerny Scherzo to *Après une lecture du Dante* also lead from the cinematic *Quasi Faust* movement of the Alkan *Grand Sonata* (*The Four Ages*) to the Liszt Sonata? The resemblances are difficult to ignore and suspiciously similar to those argued for *Dante* and *Obermann* above. We cannot definitely prove that Liszt knew the Alkan Sonata, but it is more than probable that he was either sent or sought out a copy soon after the piece's publication in Paris in 1848. Liszt was a friend of Alkan. He regarded him, just like Czerny, as a serious artist who had been unfairly overlooked and undervalued ("a composer far too little known, who has many good things") and as a musical radical whose output chimed with the artistic ideals he sought to promote during his residency as Kapellmeister in Weimar.[63] He even encouraged his student Hans von Bülow to review Alkan's Twelve Studies in the Major Keys to assist in promoting them to German audiences. It would therefore have been strange if news of the appearance of a major Alkan opus such as the *Grande Sonate* had not excited his curiosity. It has now been convincingly demonstrated by Gerard Carter and Martin Adler that an initial draft of Liszt's sonata was finished in 1849—earlier than usually thought. The closeness of that date to the publication of the Alkan, as Carter and Adler also argue, makes direct inspiration even more likely.[64] Moreover, Liszt would have been one of the few pianists actually able to play and appreciate Alkan's dauntingly difficult sonata. Many would have been able to read it silently or clatter chaotically through it at the keyboard, but Liszt could have brought the dead score to living musical life.

Did Liszt's playing through of the Alkan catalyze creative work on his own sonata? The case for the prosecution follows (see exx. 1.20–1.22).

Both pieces feature at the start (exx. 1.20 and 1.21) a clipped unison theme followed by "hammer-blows" (Liszt's own term). Alkan's attention-grabbing performance indication "satanically" is later supplemented by the inscription "The Devil," which appears underneath a crudely pompous inversion of the opening theme (ex. 1.22). No doubt the inversion is intended to illustrate Goethe's "spirit that always negates" (Der Geist, der stets verneint), but it also happens to bring Alkan's melody even closer to the shape of Liszt's. Liszt's unison theme can itself be considered as a partial inversion: of the rising seventh and subsequent falling second of the bass line of the sonata's opening lento assai (also in ex. 1.20). In addition to all this, the unison theme has a family resemblance to one of the main motives in Liszt's *Faust* Symphony (see ex. 1.23).

This thematic shape was strongly associated in Liszt's mind with the character of *Faust*. He later noted the coincidence that Wagner had independently come up with a similar tune for his own *Faust* Overture, telling his student August Göllerich, "Wagner and I adopted the same theme for *Faust* before we even knew each other—I give you my word on this."[65] The first version of Wagner's overture was written in 1840, while the initial sketches of

Example 1.20. Liszt, Sonata in B Minor, S. 178, opening

Liszt's symphony seem to date from the middle of that decade.[66] But Wagner sent Liszt a score of his *Faust* Overture only in 1849, well after the first *Faust* Symphony sketches but around the time Liszt was working on an initial version of his sonata.[67]

As we proceed to play through the Alkan and Liszt pieces, connections begin to multiply. In both *Quasi Faust* and the sonata, the hammer-blow theme undergoes a remarkable lyrical transformation (see exx. 1.24–1.25). On top of this, the grandioso second subject of the Sonata in B Minor (see ex. 1.26) has its counterpart in the Alkan. Liszt's theme constitutes an early instance of his use of the "cross motif," based on the Gregorian chant *crux fidelis*—it also features prominently in *Invocation* (S. 173/1 / LW A158/1) from *Harmonies poétiques et religieuses* and in his oratorio *St. Elisabeth* (S. 2 / LW I4).[68] It is paralleled in *Quasi Faust*, both in melody and keyboard texture, by Alkan's theme *Le seigneur* (The lord) (see ex. 1.27).

Example 1.21. Alkan, *Grande sonate: Les quatre âges*, second movement, *Quasi Faust*, opening themes, *Sataniquement*

Example 1.22. Alkan, *Grande sonate: Les quatre âges*, second movement, *Quasi Faust, Le Diable*

Example 1.23. Liszt, *Faust* Symphony, S. 108, first movement

Example 1.24. Alkan, *Grande sonate: Les quatre âges*, second movement, *Quasi Faust*, lyrical transformation

Example 1.25. Liszt, Sonata in B Minor, S. 178, lyrical transformation

Example 1.26. Liszt, Sonata in B Minor, S. 178, *Grandioso*

Example 1.27. Alkan, *Grande sonate: Les quatre âges*, second movement, *Quasi Faust, Le seigneur*

An anticipation of *The Lord*'s theme forms the Bachian subject of a fugue (with a distinctly un-Bachian countersubject) ushering in the final section of *Quasi Faust*. Correspondingly, a fugue acts as a transition to the recapitulation in Liszt's sonata, a section that, according to his student August Stradal, Liszt wanted performed "ironically and sarcastically," for the theme is here depicted in a "Mephistophelean" manner.[69] There is no parallel in the Liszt piece to Alkan's coda, which contrapuntally combines two of the movement's main themes against a triplet rhythm. But intriguingly, a very similar conclusion does appear in the revised version of Liszt's *Invocation* (S. 173/1 / LW A158/1), published in 1853. Significantly, this passage does not occur in the initial (1847) version of *Invocation* (S. 172c / LW A61/1) and therefore was composed after Liszt's possible acquaintance with *Quasi Faust* (see exx. 1.28–1.29). Similar perorations later conclude both *St. Elizabeth* and the Second Legend, *St. Francis Walking on the Waves*.

It thus seems more than possible that Liszt's sonata was extensively inspired by *Quasi Faust*. Yet there is an alternative "case for the defense." This does not completely negate, in a Mephistophelean manner, the allegation of Alkanesque influence but clearly complicates the issue. I noted in a much earlier publication that Liszt's *allegro energico* unison theme (ex. 1.20) is akin to the opening of Hummel's once well-known Piano Sonata no. 5 in F-sharp Minor, op. 81 (1819), a piece in Liszt's repertoire. It shares an additional kinship, especially noticeable in its later fugal treatment, with the main theme of the first movement of Beethoven's Piano Sonata in C Minor, op. 111. Similar family resemblances occur in works by Liszt with no apparent connection to *Faust*: for example, in the Symphonic Poem *Ce qu'on entend sur la montagne* (S. 95 / LW G1), after a poem by Victor Hugo, or in the *Grand Concert Solo* (*Grosses Konzertsolo*, S. 176 / LW A167). One could at least argue that the program of *Ce qu'on entend* is illustrative of a similar metaphysical struggle to that of *Faust*, but the *Concert Solo*, on the contrary, appears to have no program at all. On a larger scale, the tonal structure of the Liszt sonata owes something to Hummel's F-sharp Minor Sonata and something to the first movement of Chopin's Sonata no. 3 in B Minor, op. 58, but little to the Alkan. Finally, the only other apposite comment of Liszt's concerning the Sonata related its opening page to "the mood of the beginning of Beethoven's *Coriolan* Overture," not to Goethe's *Faust* or Alkan's *Quasi Faust*.[70] We can, accordingly, assume that there were multiple influences on the sonata. Just as *Après une lecture du Dante* was probably catalyzed by the Czerny but also borrows from Weber, the sonata was possibly catalyzed by the Alkan but encompasses influences from Beethoven, Hummel, and Chopin.

Example 1.28. Alkan, *Grande sonate: Les quatre âges*, second movement, *Quasi Faust*, coda

Example 1.29. Liszt, *Invocation*, S. 173/1 (1853), coda

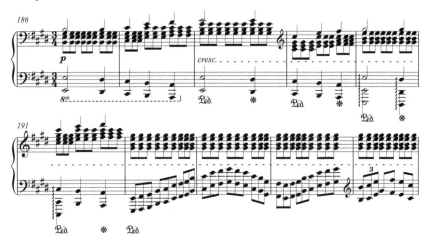

key to their significance, as does the Wagner *Faust* Overture / Liszt *Faust* Symphony thematic link.[71] I have changed my mind to and fro about this over the years, but now I think it more than likely that the sonata is indeed the symphony's incognito twin. However, we have no proof sufficient for complete conviction, for we have only a circumstantial argument that Liszt knew Alkan's Grand Sonata.

Scots law, unlike English law, allows a third verdict beyond "innocent" or "guilty": "not proven." It signifies that there is not enough evidence to convict Does that mean the Liszt sonata is a pianistic twin of the *Faust* Symphony, just as *Après une lecture du Dante* is to the *Dante* Symphony? There is certainly something diabolical and divine about the nature of its themes. If we accept the likelihood of Alkanesque influence, then *Quasi Faust* gives us a beyond reasonable doubt but enough evidence to seriously doubt innocence. It also allows the possibility of a retrial. This verdict seems appropriate here, with a musicological retrial to be scheduled if new sources ever come to light.

Liszt, contrary to his usual custom, never supplied a program, nor even a programmatic title, for the Sonata in B Minor. It was presented as a successor to Beethoven's and Chopin's sonatas, not to "characteristic" sonatas like Dussek's *Sufferings of the Queen of France*. The Hungarian composer Ferenc Erkel once waspishly amused himself by pointing out to Liszt the incidental resemblance of the prestissimo to a figure in Beethoven's third *Leonora* Overture. Liszt responded sarcastically with, "Yes! Yes! The Sonata is all stolen."[72] But he was not to be drawn on its ancestry. He thought of the sonata as his "masterpiece," not only in the figurative sense but in the literal: his proof of compositional mastery. He would frequently play it to visitors in Weimar, but always from the music, to show that it was no improvisation. Consequently, the score was soon falling apart.[73]

It is perhaps improbable that Liszt intended the sonata's musical resemblances to *Quasi Faust* to be recognized, even if he himself had been actively aware of them—unless, of course, one wishes to speculate that the sonata's dedication to Schumann was intended to lead listeners to seek a "quieter tone" underlying the music, in exact parallel to the echoes of Beethoven in Schumann's opus 17 Fantasy. The situation is dissimilar to that of the *Malédiction* Sextet—with its detective-novel unmasking of a Schubert song—different from the blatant salute to Chopin in *Funérailles* and different even from the case of the *Faust* Symphony. The start of the symphony's *Mephistopheles* movement graciously doffs its hat to the opening of the *Witches' Sabbath* from Berlioz's *Symphonie fantastique*. Berlioz, of course, was the *Faust* Symphony's dedicatee. Thus, the dedication is both inscribed above the score and within it. Had Liszt dedicated the Sonata in B Minor to Charles Valentin Alkan, we would have had a nearly identical story. But there is an obvious parallel to the generative process already demonstrated in *Dante* and *Obermann*: from performance to composition. Or, as Wagner put it, from reproduction to production. Liszt's outstanding virtuosity was not a demeaning, if lucrative, distraction from his "better self" as a composer; it was a crucial creative catalyst.

Notes

1. See Kenneth Hamilton, *The Opera Fantasias and Transcriptions of Franz Liszt: A Critical Study*, PhD Dissertation (Balliol College, Oxford, 1989), 4–8; Zsuzsanna Domokos, *Carl Czernys Einfluss auf Franz Liszt: Die Kunst des Fantasierens*, in *Liszt Studien* 4, ed. Serge Gut (Munich: E. Katzbichler, 1993), 19–28; Michael Saffle, "Czerny and the Keyboard Fantasy: Traditions, Innovations, Legacy," in *Beyond The Art of Finger Dexterity: Reassessing Carl Czerny*, ed. David Gramit (Rochester, NY: University of Rochester Press, 2008), 202–28; David Trippett, "*Après une Lecture de Liszt:* Virtuosity and *Werktreue* in the 'Dante' Sonata," *19th-Century Music* 32, no. 1 (2008): 52–93; and Dana Gooley, *Fantasies of Improvisation: Free Playing in Nineteenth-Century Music* (Oxford: Oxford University Press, 2018), 200–201.
2. The original reads, "Une fois le travail commencé les souvenirs se sont pressés . . . à devenir non plus une simple combinaison des sons, mais un langage poétique plus apte peut-être que la poésie elle-même à exprimer tout ce qui en nous franchit les horizons accoutumés."
3. See Kenneth Hamilton, *Liszt: Sonata in B Minor* (Cambridge: Cambridge University Press, 1996), 40–41.
4. Dated 1833. See: https://commons.wikimedia.org/wiki/File:Czerny_2.jpg, accessed September 21, 2019.
5. Czerny was fond of working on four scores quasi-simultaneously, each on a separate desk in the respective corners of his study. While the ink dried on a page of one of them, he would move to another, and so on—like the production line of a factory. See John Ella, *Musical Sketches Abroad, and at Home*, vol. 1 (London: Ridgeway, 1869), 241. "Such," wrote Ella, "was the mechanical labor of this musician's life."
6. *The Musical World*, May 9, 1863, 295.
7. In *Götzen-Dämmerung (Twilight of the Idols)* of 1888. *Geläufigkeit* is more properly rendered here as "fluency"; but as the mistranslation "velocity" has been firmly established for the best part of two centuries, and as it possibly makes Nietzsche's joke work even better, it would be pointless pedantry to battle against it.
8. Lina Ramann, *Franz Liszt als Künstler und Mensch*, vol. 1 (Leipzig: Breitkopf & Härtel, 1880), 37. Liszt's annotations to Ramann's volume are held by the Goethe- und Schiller-Archiv, Weimar, *Liszt Nachlass*, 59/350, 1.
9. According to Count Waldstein, Beethoven, on arriving in Vienna to complete his studies, was to "receive the spirit of Mozart from Haydn's hands" (Barry Cooper, *Beethoven* [Oxford: Oxford University Press, 2008], 42). I am leaving aside here the much-disputed topic of the *Weihekuss* Liszt allegedly received from Beethoven.

10. "Cast into the boundless realms of the future" was Liszt's own characterization of his "only ambition as a musician." From a letter to Princess Wittgenstein, 9 February 1874, in La Mara, *Franz Liszts Briefe an die Fürstin Carolyne Sayn-Wittgenstein*, Band 7, Theil 4 (Leipzig: Breitkopf & Härtel, 1902), 58. Sonata in F Minor was first published in Lina Ramann's *Lisztiana*, ed. Arthur Seidl (Mainz: Schott, 1984), it has recently been included in the *New Liszt Edition, Supplements to Works for Piano Solo*, vol. 13, ed. Adrienne Kaczmarczyk.
11. Charlotte Moscheles, *Life of Moscheles with Selections from His Diaries*, vol. 1 (London: Hurst and Blackett, 1873), 143.
12. [Ed.] On Liszt's relation to the "brilliant style," see Robert Doran's chapter in this volume.
13. For more detail, see William Wright, *Liszt and England* (Hillsville, NY: Pendragon Press, 2016), 77–82.
14. Both quotes from a letter of August 26, 1830, in *The Letters of Franz Liszt*, ed. La Mara, trans. Constance Bache (New York: Scribner's, 1894), vol. 1, 6.
15. Letter of March 17, 1856, in ibid., 266.
16. "For the young composer should never entertain such a predilection for any particular school or manner, as to suffer it to exercise too great an influence upon his labors, and lead him to despise and neglect what is meritorious in other schools and nations. This highly reprehensible partiality has already ruined many young composers" (Carl Czerny, *The School of Practical Composition*, vol. 2 [London: Robert Cocks, 1848; original German edition 1839], 45–46).
17. Letter of March 17, 1856, in *The Letters of Franz Liszt*, 266. Translation slightly modified. Original version: *Franz Liszts Briefe*, ed. La Mara, vol. 1 (Leipzig: Breitkopf und Härtel, 1893), 219: "In den zwanziger Jahren, wo ein großer Theil der Beethoven'schen Schöpfungen für die meisten Musiker eine Art von Sphynx war, spielte Czerny *ausschließlich* Beethoven mit ebenso vortrefflichem Verständnis als ausreichender, wirksamer Technik; und späterhin hatte er sich auch nicht gegen einige gethane Fortschritte verschlossen, sondern wesentlich durch seiner Lehre und seine Werke dazu beizutragen. Schade nur, dass er sich durch eine zu übermäßige Productivität hat schwächen müssen und nicht auf dem Wege seiner ersten Sonata (op. 6, As dur) und einigen anderen Werken dieser Periode, welche ich als bedeutsame, der edelsten Richtungen angehörige und schön geformte Compositionen hochschätze, weiter fortgeschritten ist. Leider waren damals die Wiener gesellschaftlichen und verlegerischen Einflüsse schädlicher Art, und Czerny besaß nicht die nothwendige Dosis von Schroffheit, um sich ihnen zu entziehen und sein besseres *Ich* zu wahren." For more on Czerny in general, see the aforementioned *Beyond the Art of Finger Dexterity: Reassessing Carl Czerny*, ed. David Gramit, and Levi Keith Larson, "An Underestimated Master: A Critical Analysis of Carl Czerny's Eleven Piano Sonatas and his Contribution to the Genre," PhD Dissertation (University of Nebraska–Lincoln, 2015).

18. Christopher Gibbs, "'Just Two Words.' Enormous Success': Liszt's 1838 Vienna Concerts" in *Franz Liszt and his World*, ed. Christopher Gibbs and Dana Gooley (Princeton, NJ: Princeton University Press, 2006), 183.
19. Dezsô Legány, *Unbekannte Presse und Briefe aus Wien 1822–1886* (Vienna: Boehlau, 1984), 31: "Er begann mit einem Andante und Scherzo aus einer Sonate von Carl Czerny, seinem ehemaligen Lehrer, welchem er durch die Wahl dieser Komposition einen Beweis seiner Achtung und Dankbarkeit geben wollte. Ein schönes Resultat hat Liszt mit der Czernyschen Sonata erzielt, und dass es sogleich ein so glänzendes war, spricht wohl nicht minder für die Herrlichkeit seines Talentes. Mit all der geistigen Lebhaftigkeit, welche seinem Spiele eigen ist, und es charakterisiert, hatte er sich des gegebenen Stoffes bemeistert, und aus demselben die brillantesten Effekte entwickelt. Nach dieser Nummer, bei welcher namentlich der Vortrag des Scherzos durch die originelle und kühne Behandlungsweise Sensation erregt hatte, sang Herr Titze. . . ." My translation here and elsewhere, except when otherwise noted.
20. Blind (otherwise known as alternating or interlocking) chromatic octaves make their first appearance in Liszt's Fantasy on Halévy's *La juive*, published in 1836. Liszt likely invented the technique—at least, I know of no earlier printed occurrence.
21. For more on the strangely intense debate over the "French Romantic" elements of Liszt's art, see Kenneth Hamilton, "The Embarrassment of Influence: Liszt, Paris, and Posterity," in *Liszt et la France: Musique, culture et société dans l'Europe du XIXe siècle*, ed. Malou Haine, Nicolas Dufetel, Dana Gooley, and Jonathan Kregor (Paris: Vrin, 2012), 33–54.
22. Legány, *Unbekannte Presse und Briefe aus Wien*, 38–40: "Er will über die Grenzen des Bestehenden hinaus, und gebraucht wie ein *Faust* das Clavier als Höllenzwang, um sich die Geister der Unterwelt zur Erreichung wunderbarer Kunstzwecke dienstbar zu machen . . . selbst fremde Tonstücke, die er spielt, als seine eigenen Improvisationen erscheinen lassen, und als *welche*! . . . Häufiger Pedalzug—zur Verwischung führend. . . . Heroische zu großartige Behandlung—nicht immer ganz übereinstimmend mit der Schwächlichkeit des Clavierkörpers: Nun gut, *so bauet stärkere*!—Augmentierung des Originals—durch Verdopplung und Vollgriffigkeit."
23. "Wir hörten sie diesmal sogar noch vollständiger, als das vorige Mal, wo durch Zufall eine von den Variationen, ich glaube, es war die Czernysche, weggeblieben war" (ibid., 44).
24. See Jay Rosenblatt, "Orchestral Transcriptions," in *The Liszt Companion*, ed. Ben Arnold (Westport, CT: Greenwood Press, 2002), 312–13. An unfinished copyist's score of this version is held in the library of the Gesellschaft für Musikfreunde in Vienna. Liszt orchestrated earlier versions of his Piano

Concertos nos. 1 and 2, and the "posthumous" Piano Concerto in E-flat Major (S. 125a / LW Q6), at the same time. According to Alan Walker (*Franz Liszt, Volume 1: The Virtuoso Years, 1811–1847* [Ithaca, NY: Cornell University Press, 1988, rev. ed.], 269), in San Rossore Liszt and Marie d'Agoult "passed their days walking along the beach, watching the fishermen mend their nets, bathing, reading." But Liszt must have been doing a bit more than that.

25. Under the impression that the published 1839 score represents the version of *Hexaméron* used by Liszt when performing with orchestra, Leslie Howard has deftly completed and recorded a piano and orchestra arrangement of it: *Liszt Music for Piano and Orchestra 1* (Hyperion CD B00000G3ZH). But Liszt seems never to have played the piece in this format with orchestra—its length would have sorely tested the patience of the audiences of his day.

26. Goethe- und Schiller-Archiv, Weimar: Score D-WRgs W14, Preface and title page W18a. At one time Liszt evidently intended to publish this score, hence the newly written preface. The first modern performance of this version of *Hexaméron* was given by the present author and Olivia Sham at the Eastman School of Music (Rochester, New York) on March 3, 2017, as part of "Liszt and Virtuosity: An International Symposium," the conference on which the present volume is based.

27. He does, unusually, seem to have added the Chopin Variation, at the expense of his own, to the piano and orchestra version, for a concert in the Weimar Court Theatre on November 29, 1841. The playbill reads: "Hexaméron. Bravour-Variationen, 1ste von Thalberg, 2te von Pixis, 3te von Herz, 4te von Chopin, Introduction und Finale von Franz Liszt über ein Thema aus: *Die Puritaner*, gespielt von Franz Liszt."

28. August Göllerich, *Franz Liszt* (Berlin: Marquardt, 1908), 161: "Ich dachte damals in Paris wahrlich nicht an 'Ruhe,' wie geschrieben ist. Eine zweite oder dritte Stelle nach Herz einzunehmen, wäre mir wünschenswert erschienen."

29. A perceptive summary of the entire story can be found in Katharine Ellis, *Music Criticism in Nineteenth-Century France* (Cambridge: Cambridge University Press, 1995), 143–45. A more detailed treatment, including copious quotes from the relevant journalism, can be found in Christopher Kammertöns, *Chronique Scandaleuse: Henri Herz—ein Enfant terrible in der französischen Musikkritik des 19. Jahrhunderts* (Essen: Die Blaue Eule, 2000), 87–164; and, most recently, in Laure Schnapper, *Henri Herz, Magnat du Piano* (Paris: Editions de l'EHESS, 2011), 82–96. The latter volume is by far the most detailed treatment of Herz's life and work as a whole.

30. Ellis, *Music Criticism*, 145.

31. *Allgemeine Musikalische Zeitung*, September 30, 1835, no. 39, 646–47: "Einige Worte über Franz Liszt bei Gelegenheit der Anzeige seiner neuesten Kompositionen."

32. For a more detailed discussion of this, see Kenneth Hamilton, "Franz Liszt Defended against His Devotees" in *Keyboard Perspectives* X (Ithaca, NY: Cornell University Press, 2017), 119–43.
33. [Ed.] For a further discussion of the storm topos, specifically in regard to the tremolo technique, see Robert Doran's chapter in this volume.
34. Amy Fay, *Music Study in Germany* (London: Macmillan, 1893), 221. See also Kenneth Hamilton, *After the Golden Age: Romantic Pianism and Modern Performance* (New York: Oxford University Press, 2008), 44.
35. Marie d'Agoult, *Correspondance générale*, ed. Charles F. Dupêchez (Paris: Honoré Champion, 2004), vol. II, 389: "Le bravo suonatore commence ce matin un fragment dantesque qui le fait donner au Diable. Il est tout enchanté de ne pas aller à Naples afin de pouvoir terminer cette œuvre (destinée à rester en portefeuille!)."
36. Madame August Boissier, *Liszt Pédagogue: Leçons de piano données par Liszt à Mademoiselle Valérie Boissier à Paris en 1832* (Honoré Champion, Paris, 1993, original edition 1927), 53 (26th Lesson, Wednesday, February 21): "Liszt a fait jouer à ma fille l'exercice d'octaves de Kessler à mon avis fort au-dessus de sa portée. Il compare cet exercice à l'enfer de Dante, la comparaison est juste; pour le mécanisme de l'exercice il veut qu'on le joue avec souplesse et pique; que les octaves soient bien pleines, bien pures et qu'on les attaque la plupart du temps avec une vigueur inconcevable. L'expression de ce morceau est la fureur, l'horreur, l'indignation, la vengeance, le délire; pour rendre tout cela il faut un poignet d'Hercule. Valérie est encore très loin de cela."
37. *Mémoires, souvenirs et journaux de la comtesse d'Agoult*, ed. Charles F. Dupêchez (Paris: Mercure de France, 1990), vol. II, 219: "Si je me sens force et vie, je tenterai une composition symphonique d'après Dante, puis une autre d'après Faust—dans trois ans—d'ici là, je ferai trois esquisses: Le Triomphe de la mort (Orcagna); la Comédie de la mort (Holbein), et un fragment dantesque."
38. *New Liszt Edition*, ed., Adrienne Kaczmarczyk, Supplement, vol. 13.
39. As Kaczmarczyk comments, "the version first performed in 1839 was essentially identical with the version that partially survived as the basic layer of the *Paralipomènes*" (ibid., Preface, LI).
40. See Hamilton, *Liszt: Sonata in B Minor*, 11–12.
41. Liszt offered this description of the opening to August Stradal: "Das Thema soll ein Weck- und Beschwörungsruf an die Geister der Verdammten sein 'Hervor ihr Schatten und Geister aus dem Reich des Jammers und Elends!' Dann erklärt er, dass das chromatische Motiv ... das Herannahen, Auf- und Absteigen der Verdammten darstellen soll" (August Stradal, *Erinnerung an Franz Liszt*, ed. Jens Hagen Wegner [Berlin, 2015; original edition Bern, 1929], 47).
42. Legány, *Unbekannte Presse und Briefe*, 70: "Mir erschien das Ganze ungefähr wie eine Improvisation, zu welcher sich Liszt nach dem Durchlesen der 'göttlichen Komödie' begeistert gefühlt hatte, ein Aggregat von bunt durcheinander

jagenden Ideen, oft schnell abbrechend, eine Gemütsstimmung mit der anderen vertauschend, im Entwurfe kühn, in der Ausführung aphoristisch, im Ganzen dem Charakter der neuromantischen Schule, wie sie sich in Frankreich ausbildete, sehr nahe stehend. Bekannt ist indessen, dass die Tendenzen dieser Schule gerade in Deutschland nirgends rechten Anklang finden wollen, und selbst vom französischen Publikum dürfte auch nur der kleinere Theil denselben einen Geschmack abgewinnen."

43. Legány, *Unbekannte Presse und Briefe*, 72–73: "Rückblick auf Liszts Fragment nach Dante": "Diese seltsame und geistreiche Tongemälde scheint in die Schule der französischen Romantiker einzuschlagen. Ich läugne nicht mein Vorurtheil gegen die Tendenzen dieser Schule, die vielleicht über die Grenzen der Musik hinaus sind . . . in der Entwicklung und Vielfältigen des bedeutenden Hauptsatzes durch reiche und originelle Modulationen einen Fortschritt beweist, in dem eine ganze Zukunft liegt."
44. The dragging theme of lamentation in the cellos that we hear as Amfortas first arrives on stage in *Parsifal* shows the long shade cast by the opening of Liszt's *Vallée d'Obermann*.
45. John Rink, "Translating Musical Meaning: The Nineteenth-Century Performer as Narrator," in *Rethinking Music*, ed. Nicholas Cook and Mark Everist (Oxford: Oxford University Press, 1999), 226–29.
46. The score (D-WRgs H2) and sketches are in the Goethe- und Schiller-Archiv, Weimar.
47. Jay Rosenblatt, "The Concerto as Crucible: Franz Liszt's Early Works for Piano and Orchestra," PhD Dissertation (University of Chicago, 1995), 295.
48. Klara Hamburger, ed. *Franz Liszt: Briefwechsel mit seiner Mutter* (Eisenstadt: Amt der Burgenländischen Regierung, 2000), 65.
49. Rosenblatt, *The Concerto as Crucible*, 324, 311.
50. In another part of the notebook (D-WRgs N6), where Liszt wrote down an initial draft of his sextet, we find the words "inspiration Mariotique." Mariotte was Liszt's pet name for Marie. The sextet is probably an example of such inspiration.
51. The public premiere of the complete version of the sextet, including the full statement of the Schubert song, was given by the present author (piano) with the Philadelphia Classical Symphony, conducted by Karl Middleman, in Philadelphia on November 15, 2009. For reasons of balance, the string parts were doubled on that occasion. Perhaps I should simply have played more quietly.
52. Robert Schumann, *Music and Musicians*, trans. Fanny Raymond Ritter (Berkeley and Los Angeles: University of California Press, 1983), 171.
53. Lina Ramann *Liszt Pädagogium* (Wiesbaden, 1986, reprint of 1902 Edition), II: 5, 6.
54. Alan Walker, *Franz Liszt, Volume 2: The Weimar Years, 1848–1861* (Ithaca, NY: Cornell University Press, 1989), 72–73.

55. August Göllerich, *The Piano Master Classes of Franz Liszt, 1884–1886*, ed. Wilhelm Jerger, trans., ed., and enlarged by Richard Louis Zimdars (Bloomington: Indiana University Press, 1996), 61.
56. See Kenneth Hamilton, "Chopin-Liszt: Paradoxes of Reception and Performance History in the Polonaise op. 53 and *Funérailles*," in *The Integration of a Work: From Miniature to Large Scale*, ed. Jim Samson and Zofia Chechlińska (Warsaw: Narodowy Instytut Fryderyka Chopina, forthcoming, 2020).
57. François-Joseph Fétis, "Études d'exécution transcendante pour le piano, par F. Liszt" (*Revue et Gazette musicale de Paris*, May 9, 1841), introduced and translated by Peter Bloom in the chapter "Fétis's Review of the Transcendental Etudes," in *Franz Liszt and His World*, ed. Christopher H. Gibbs and Dana Gooley (Princeton, NJ: Princeton University Press, 2006), 427–39, here 435.
58. In addition to the works discussed in more detail here, particular favorites seem to have been Weber's *Invitation to the Dance* and the *Valse infernale* from Meyerbeer's *Robert le diable*.
59. The same was true for Ferruccio Busoni, unsurprisingly an enormous admirer of Liszt, who wrote: "An Stücken die ich wiederhole, muss ich fortwährend ändern—Fingersatz, Claviersatz, Aufbau—sonst sterben sie mir unter den Fingern ab. Zum letzten, kommt eine Art definitive Fassung doch zu Stande" (I have to constantly change things in pieces that I play repeatedly—fingering, keyboard setting, structure—otherwise they die under my fingers. Nevertheless, a sort of definitive version emerges at last) (Busoni, *Briefwechsel mit Gottfried Galston*, ed. Martina Weindel [Wilhelmshaven, 1999], 87; letter of January 6, 1920).
60. Richard Wagner, *Ein Brief über Franz Liszts Symphonische Dichtungen* (Leipzig: C.F. Kahnt, 1857), 10: "Wer oft Gelegenheit hatte, Liszt zu hören, wenn er namentlich in vertrautem Kreise z.B. Beethoven spielte, dem muss doch von je aufgegangen sein, dass es sich hier nicht um Reproduktion, sondern um wirkliche Produktion handelte? Den Punkt, der beide Tätigkeiten scheidet, genau anzugeben, ist viel schwerer, als man gemeinhin annimmt." (Was there ever anyone who frequently had the opportunity to hear Liszt, especially when he played, for example, Beethoven in private circles, who was not struck with the thought that here we were dealing not with reproduction, but with real production? It is much more difficult than one commonly assumes to identify the point where both activities diverge.)
61. Alfred Habets, *Borodin and Liszt*, trans. Rosa Newmarch (London: Digby, Long & Co., 1895), 68.
62. Béla Bartók, "Liszt Problems" (originally published in 1936), in *Béla Bartók Essays*, ed. Benjamin Suchoff (Lincoln: University of Nebraska Press, 1976), 501–10.
63. A comment prompted by Arthur Friedheim's performance of Alkan's *Aesop's Feast* at a Weimar master class in 1884. Göllerich, *The Piano Master Classes of Franz Liszt*, 27. Many years before, Liszt had published an enthusiastic but not

completely uncritical review in the *Revue et Gazette Musicale* of Alkan's *Trois Morceaux Pathétiques*. The pieces were, admittedly, dedicated to him—a situation likely to elicit warm feelings in any reviewer.

64. See Gerard Carter and Martin Adler, *Franz Liszt's Precursor Sonata of 1849: A Trial Run in the Master's Inner Circle* (Sydney: Wensleydale Press, 2011).
65. August Göllerich, *Franz Liszt* (Berlin: Marquardt & Co., 1908), 172.
66. Goethe- und Schiller-Archiv, Weimar, MS. N4, a sketchbook from the mid-1840s. An undated separate page of sketches (probably from later in the decade) is the first to show the opening of the symphony in a form that we can recognize as similar to the final version, with the juxtaposition of the two principal themes. See Laszlo Somfai, "Die Musikalische Gestaltwandlungen der 'Faust-Symphonie' von Liszt," *Studia Musicologica* 2 (1962): 87–137, esp. 100 and 113.
67. Kesting, *Liszt-Wagner Briefwechsel*, 60. The situation is somewhat complicated here by Wagner's misdating of his January 30, 1849, letter to Liszt assenting to the dispatch of the *Faust* Overture score. As is so easy to do at the turn of a year, he absent-mindedly scribbled "1848." Both the context and the subsequent course of the correspondence, however, make it clear that 1849 is the correct date.
68. The earliest prominent instance in Liszt oeuvre of the musical figure later identified in the preface to *St. Elizabeth* as the "cross motif" is found in an untitled Klavierstück in F major (S. 695 / LW A100), written in 1843 but unpublished during his lifetime. The piece has since appeared in the *New Liszt Edition*, Supplement, Volume 9, edited by Adrienne Kaczmarczyk and Eszter Mikusi (Editio Musica, Budapest, 2009).
69. August Stradal, *Erinnerung an Franz Liszt*, 50. Liszt's remarks were made as Stradal played the sonata to him in Pest in 1885. The direct reference to Mephistopheles appears to be Stradal's gloss: "Das Fugato wollte Liszt ironisch und sarkastisch dargestellt haben. Es liegt hier dasselbe Kunstprinzip vor, wie bei der Dante-Sonate, da das erwähnte energische Thema, seiner Kampfstimmung entkleidet, mephistophelisch auftritt."
70. August Stradal, *Erinnerungen an Franz Liszt*, 50: "Liszt sagte, dass ihm bei dieser Stelle die Stimmung des Anfanges der Beethovenschen Coriolan-Ouvertüre vorgeschwebt habe (wenn auch die Themen grundverschieden sind), und fügte hinzu: 'Ich soll Euch meine Leiden zeigen? Vor Euch verberge ich sie.'" (Liszt said that at that spot the mood of the opening of Beethoven's *Coriolan* Overture hovered before him [even if the themes are fundamentally different], and added: "Should I show you my sufferings? I conceal them from you.")
71. The ascription to Faust has been widely assumed. Alfred Cortot, in his edition of the sonata (salabert) states in his preface that the sonata has no program, but paradoxically then proceeds to analyze it on the basis of Goethe's *Faust*.

72. August Stradal, *Erinnerungen an Franz Liszt*, 50: "Nachdem ich geendet hatte, trat der Direktor der Akademie Franz Erkel an den Flügel und spielt boshaft lächelnd auf der drittletzten Seite der Sonate eine Octavenstelle und dann den Schluss der grossen Leonoren-Overtüre Beethovens, hiermit andeutend, dass hier eine Reminiszenz Liszts vorliege. Der Meister war aber nicht aus seiner Fassung zu bringen und erwiderte nur 'Ja! Ja! Die ganze Sonate ist gestohlen.'"
73. William Mason, *Memories of a Musical Life* (New York: The Devine Press, 1901), 118–19.

Chapter Two

Transforming Virtuosity

Liszt and Nineteenth-Century Pianos

Olivia Sham

After hearing Liszt in 1841, François-Joseph Fétis wrote, "This is the creation of the piano; until now we had no idea what it was."[1] In forging modern piano virtuosity, Liszt has generally been credited for stimulating the development of the modern piano itself. However, it is often forgotten that the relationship between piano and pianist was rather more symbiotic, for the instrument played its own role in shaping Liszt's virtuosity throughout his entire life and oeuvre.

The piano was the instrument of Liszt's virtuosity, but the nineteenth-century pianos Liszt performed on were very different from the modern piano used today. Liszt's long career spanned a period of rapid piano development. As a boy, he played on Viennese fortepianos, but by the time of his death, he was endorsing massive Steinway grands. During the nineteenth century, the piano continually evolved, usually in quest of greater volume and sonority but without sacrificing quickness of action. This chapter therefore explores the correlation between the development of Liszt's virtuosic and innovative pianism and the developing nineteenth-century piano.

In 1837, Liszt described his close affinity to the piano thus: "My piano is to me what a ship is to the sailor, what a steed is to the Arab, and perhaps more because even now my piano is myself, my speech, and my life. It is the intimate personal depository of everything that stirred wildly in my brain. . . . Its strings quivered under all my passions; its docile keys obeyed my every whim."[2] Despite the poetic embellishments, which could be attributed to the public nature of the statement, Liszt here described quite clearly his acute awareness of the piano's capabilities. Liszt wanted the piano to respond to his "every whim," and to do so, he would have tailored his technique specifically to his instrument. Thus, despite infamous sensational reports of vanquished, wrecked pianos, and popular imagery that portrays Lisztian virtuosity as a Herculean feat, Liszt cannot truly be said to have composed music for performance that was impossible to conquer in live performance—at least for him.[3] It was simply too risky for his unimpeachable reputation; he needed to appear in the best possible light.

However, even a brief survey of Liszt's music reveals a variety of compositional strategies that feature a multiplicity of technical demands—some of which may seem impossibly difficult to modern pianists and, in any case, blatantly "technical" as opposed to "poetic" in effect. This essay therefore suggests, through an overview of the pianos Liszt played during his career, the ways in which the instrument's development correlated to Liszt's changing compositional styles.

The Three Versions of *Wilde Jagd*

To clarify what I mean by Liszt's changing style of pianistic writing, offered here is a brief examination of *Wilde Jagd*, the eighth of the *Transcendental Études*. As with all études in the collection, the piece was published in three versions (1826, 1837, and 1851), and thus it demonstrates three different approaches Liszt took toward the same basic material (even if the differences between the adolescent and second versions can be quite extreme—or in the case of no. 11, completely different) (see exx. 2.1–2.3).[4]

While the basic idea is the same—an evocation of a tumultuous atmosphere around the consistent melodic material in C minor—the texture is created in very different ways. The final version is the one most commonly performed (ex. 2.3) and compared to it, the first version (ex. 2.1) may seem immature and lacking in creativity. However, if we consider the types of pianos Liszt was using in 1826—Viennese fortepianos similar to those played by Beethoven and Schubert at the end of their careers—it is immediately obvious that the latest version would have overpowered those delicate instruments. The 1837 version would have been impossible to even conceive of,

Example 2.1. Liszt, *Étude en douze exercices*, S. 136/8 (op. 6, no. 8), mm. 1–2

Example 2.2. Liszt, *Grandes études* no. 8, *Wilde Jagd*, S. 137/8, mm. 1–3

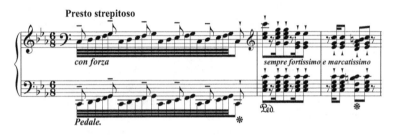

Example 2.3. Liszt, *Études d'exécution transcendante* no. 8, *Wilde Jagd*, S. 139/8, mm. 1–3

for it requires a physicality that was simply not appropriate on the earlier instrument. The middle version (ex. 2.2) is also less unrealistically ambitious than it appears; for while bringing out the melodic notes in the midst of the roiling texture is virtually impossible on a the thick-stringed and textured modern piano, it is, although still challenging, much more feasible on the instrument of the 1830s.

Early Pianos

As a boy, Liszt played on early eighteenth-century Viennese instruments in his hometown of Raiding, and then in Vienna, where he moved to take lessons with Carl Czerny. These Viennese fortepianos, as previously noted, are markedly different from the modern grand piano. The *Prellmechanik* action, perfected between 1777 and 1781 by Johann Andreas Stein, was designed so that the weight of the hammers rested directly on the keys, which was unlike Liszt's later instruments. Mozart wrote a letter praising Stein's piano in 1777:

> This time I shall begin at once with Stein's pianofortes. Before I had seen any of this make, Späth's claviers had always been my favorites. But now I much prefer Stein's, for they damp ever so much better than the Regensburg instruments. When I strike hard, I can keep my finger on the note or raise it, but the sound ceases the moment I have produced it; in whatever way I touch the keys, the tone is always even. It never jars, it is never stronger or weaker or entirely absent; in a word, it is always even. . . . His instruments have this splendid advantage over others, that they are made with escape action. Only one maker in a hundred bothers about this. But without an escapement it is impossible to avoid jangling and vibration after the note is struck. When you touch the keys, the hammers fall back again the moment after they have struck the strings, whether you hold down the keys or release them.[5]

Although this positioning of the hammers resulted in an immediacy between the contact of the pianist's finger on the keys and the hammer on the strings, it also limited hammer weight and size, for to increase them would result in mechanical awkwardness, not to mention the need for greater effort to simply depress the keys.

These mechanical features characterize Viennese fortepianos, and the sound they produce is similar to that suggested by their outward appearance: light, delicate, and precise. This is not to say that they lack energy and strength—the bass register is often surprisingly robust—but the sound they produce does not reach the same level of volume or sonority as it would on later pianos. The physicality required to play them is very different from that required by later instruments. The key depth is much shallower, enabling speed (thus making ornaments much easier to execute than on a modern instrument), and the keys are slightly narrower, enabling greater interval stretches; heavy shoulder and arm strength is not conducive to a pleasant sound quality, since the instrument rapidly reaches its limit when it comes to volume.

Considered in this light, the half-completed *Études pour le piano-forte en quarante-huit exercices dans tous les tons majeurs et mineurs*, op. 6 (S. 136 / LW A8, 1826) seem remarkably well suited to an instrument of this kind, calling for facile finger work to produce brilliant and transparent textures. These brief pieces are hardly groundbreaking. Rather, they follow contemporary virtuoso models effectively. Although the young Liszt no doubt performed with poetic inspiration, as suggested in the critical reviews, his pianism remained of its time—and instrument.

Érard and the Double-Escapement Action

In 1823, Liszt moved to Paris with his father, where they first stayed opposite the Maison Érard. Father and son were impressed with Érard's pianos, and a friendship with the piano maker quickly sprang up. Liszt's father, Adam, wrote to Czerny that

> the new invention of the very clever manufacturer, Érard, stands out in particular . . . To describe it would be beyond me, and so I shall mention only one small feature. It has a soft touch, and yet one can do with the tone (which is very good) what one will. Without lifting the hand from the keys, one can with a single attack make the chord sound soft or loud as often as desired—it is really astonishing.[6]

The new invention Adam referred to was the double-escapement action of 1821.

Prior to Érard's invention, the English action, as found in the pianos by Broadwood and Pleyel, was the most significant alternative to the Viennese *Prellmechanik*. In English-action pianos, the hammers were suspended from a bar, which relieved the burden of their weight from the keys. Hammers could therefore be heavier without causing too much strain for the player, and the heavier hammers used thicker strings and, therefore, produced greater volume. However, there were problematic aspects to this action, as noted by J. N. Hummel: "This instrument does not allow the same facility of execution as the German; the touch is heavier, the key sinks much deeper, and consequently, the return of the hammer upon the repetition of a note cannot take place so quickly. . . . [T]his mechanism is not capable of such numerous modifications."[7] With double escapement, the already-depressed hammer is held closer to the string so that it can restrike immediately. This enables notes to be repeated quickly (a technique Liszt championed in many of his most famous compositions, such as *Totentanz* [S. 126 / LW H8, 1852–59], the *Tarantella* [S. 162/3 / LW A197/3, 1859, from the *Venezia e Napoli* suite], and the Hungarian Rhapsodies); but, more significantly for the development of the piano, it also allowed for greater mass and power, since the heavier parts could move with a newfound facility.

This, together with various other innovations, created a piano sympathetic to Liszt's aims as a pianist of transcendental virtuosity. Liszt was performing for large audiences; thus, he required loud instruments, but at the same time, he wanted a piano capable of subtlety and nuance, with "strings [that] quivered under all my passions" and "docile keys [that] obeyed my every whim." In an 1836 letter to Marie d'Agoult, he wrote to "praise Érard's splendid, aristocratic, candle-lit *salons*, and his piano which brings together two qualities which are generally mutually exclusive: power and mellowness of tone. Mention, if you wish, the effect I made at the Conservatoire and at the Italiens, where with my piano I drowned out the orchestra; say, which is true, that with no other instrument would I have found it possible to produce such an effect."[8] Érard pianos can produce a very sonorous sound yet are still capable of nuance and lightness. The sonority is enhanced, particularly by Érard's unique under-dampening system, which helps to blend sonorities without sacrificing clarity. The instruments were straight strung, as were other pianos of the time, so that the registers on an Érard piano are very clearly defined. Physically, the pianos offer more resistance to the player than do Viennese fortepianos. This is the case both in soft and gentle playing, where the sense of immediacy evident in the Viennese fortepianos is removed because of the more complex action and in louder and more vigorous music, where the Érard pianos can take significant shoulder weight.

Compared to modern grand pianos, however, they are still on a very different scale, and the properties of these mid-nineteenth-century French pianos can make performing Liszt's music from the period revelatory. What might appear in the score as thousands of black notes that produce a clatter of noise on the earlier Viennese instruments or that often sound like an overblown mass on the modern piano fits much more naturally within Liszt's aims of transcendental virtuosity when attempted on an Érard piano. While Liszt's virtuosity still demonstrates impressive technical wizardry, performing his music on an Érard also makes it very clear that exciting poetic effects can be achieved. This is because the flurries of black notes no longer matter so much as the disparate parts; they rather meld together into greater shapes because of the instrument's sonorities. There is also, on a practical level, the greater ease with which the compositions can be played—less struggle allows

Example 2.4. Liszt, *Réminiscences de "Norma,"* S. 394

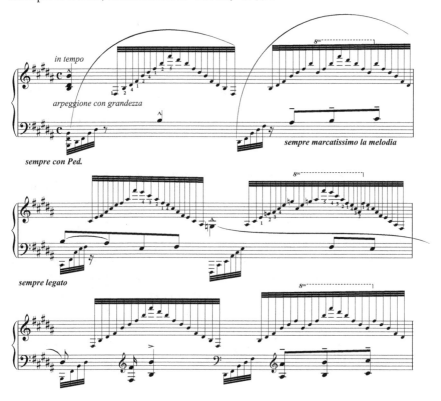

the pianist to remain levelheaded and shape the phrases and lines more effectively. Different voices also sing out more clearly because the instrument was straight strung, as was common at the time. These properties can be seen in the excerpt in example 2.4, from Liszt's *Réminiscences de Norma.*

The connection between Liszt and Érard pianos was synergetic. The piano's development was primarily driven by the popularity of the piano virtuosi of the time—larger audiences required greater volume. Liszt's close relationship with the Érards was important, for it allowed him to provide immediate feedback—and he always begged for flexibility and subtlety not to be compromised in this quest for power, often falling back on comparisons with the Viennese fortepianos that he continued to play on occasion when touring in Europe. After one concert in 1845, he wrote to Pierre Érard:

What an instrument, or rather what a mass of instruments, in this grand piano! ... qualities which seem to be so incompatible ... [were] brought together: extreme lightness of touch with so powerful a volume of sound. ... I am adjusting to it quite marvellously. After three consecutive concerts each containing seven pieces, my fingers have not felt the least bit tired, and if I am not mistaken, I didn't fail in a single passage. It is the first time I have had an experience like that with instruments as magnificent as the Érards; or even with other instruments, cheaper and less magnificent, Parisian or English. Hitherto, in Vienna alone as I told you, have they managed to make pianos which my fingers liked.[9]

In another letter, he wrote to Pierre, "The sole observation I would have to make would again bear on the *touch*, which is a little heavy and above all too *yielding* for me; but this is truly a quarrel about nothing, for I have singularly spoilt myself with these comfortable and agreeable Viennese slippers, as you would gladly call them."[10]

Liszt's repeated comments about not wanting to feel "tired" from playing "heavy" pianos is, from a pianist's perspective, of some significance. It reveals a practical fear that the instrument may impede impressions of his virtuosity and also expresses a real concern regarding physical ease. There is, of course, the possibility that Liszt's vision did not always line up with the instrument that was available to him. But as a composer as well as pianist, he no doubt wrote in a way to best suit the instrument at his disposal—that is, in a way that would minimize the risk of discomfort and therefore allow him to shine on stage.

Pianos in Mid-nineteenth-Century Germany

In the Lisztian literature, remarks concerning Liszt in relation to the piano's development usually conclude with Érard's double-escapement action. In fact, the piano continued to develop substantially year by year; the changes might seem merely incremental technologically, but for a virtuoso pianist always testing the boundaries of possibility, they would have held enormous ramifications. In addition to this development in instrumental technology, Liszt's change of circumstances in 1847 further modified the instruments Liszt himself used. When he retired from the concert platform and took up residence as Kapellmeister in the Weimar court, Liszt acquired new Germanic pianos for regular use. Although an Érard grand piano was always on display at the Altenburg, Liszt's loyalty to the firm did waver: the instruments that sat in the music room, and that he used most during this period, were Viennese instruments by Streicher and Bösendorfer. Liszt also acquired a Bechstein piano for the Altenburg.[11]

The Germanic pianos that emerged midcentury were quite different from Érard pianos; they used a mix of actions—including the Viennese action (Bösendorfer) and new repetition actions (Bechstein and Blüthner). These pianos were heavier and stronger than previous instruments, with increasing numbers of metal parts. Playing these instruments required more effort—even the Viennese actions, which, combined with heavier strings and hammers, created instruments that can seem unwieldy, weighty, and awkward, compared to Érard's smoother double escapement.

Liszt felt the physical effect of these changes. For example, Hans von Bülow wrote in 1849 that "his performance of the Tannhäuser overture [S. 442 / LW A146, composed a couple years earlier] . . . was such a strain upon him that he was obliged to stop for a moment once near the end, and he very seldom plays it because it exhausts him so much."[12] The effect of these new instruments can also be seen in Liszt's compositions during his Weimar years. Liszt's virtuosity became more economical: he relied much less on finger facility, which created large quantities of small notes in order to fill the sonority, but rather more on the power of the instrument in larger chords and octave passages.

This is quite evident in reworkings of pieces such as the *Transcendental Études* or the first book of the *Années de Pèlerinages*. For example, consider the final pages of *Vallée d'Obermann*. The slow, major iteration of the theme in the final version has quite a different texture from the original (exx. 2.5a and 2.5b). Its simplicity relies on a hitherto unavailable depth of sonority to create dramatic effect—quite different from the rippling arpeggiated demisemiquavers of the original. In the same vein, the final measures of the revised version use significantly fewer notes than those of the original, whose repeated chords would be a notable physical strain for any pianist on a later instrument (exx. 2.6a and 2.6b). The stark impact of the final two measures in the revision would never have achieved the same effect on the earlier instrument, relying as it does on the much thicker resonance of the lower register. The piano's changes have in this instance clearly revolutionized Liszt's keyboard writing, intertwining technical economy at the instrument with the older Liszt's honed sense of musical structures and compositional sophistication.

Example 2.5a. Liszt, *Vallée d'Obermann* (*Album d'un voyageur*), S. 156/5, mm. 159–60

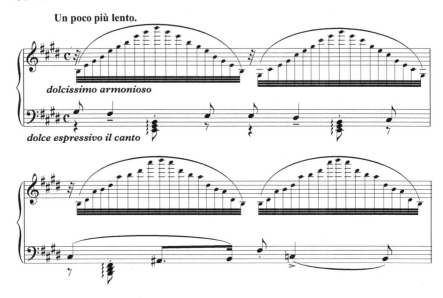

Example 2.5b. Liszt, *Vallée d'Obermann* (*Années de Pèlerinage: Première année, Suisse*), S. 160/6, mm. 170–71

Example 2.6a. Liszt, *Vallée d'Obermann* (*Album d'un voyageur*), S. 156/5, mm. 201–9

Example 2.6b. Liszt, *Vallée d'Obermann* (*Années de pelerinage: Première année, Suisse*), S. 160/6, mm. 208–16

(***sempre animando sin' al fine***)

Late Nineteenth-Century Pianos

Throughout the 1860s and 1870s, piano manufacturing continued its relentless pursuit of greater power and volume. The instruments Liszt mainly played were German, but American instruments also began to feature heavily. In the years he divided among Rome, Weimar, and Budapest giving master classes and composing, Liszt had an assortment of instruments at his disposal including those made by Bechstein, Chickering, Bösendorfer, and even Steinway.

During this time, the instruments grew in size and weight, and sometimes those Liszt played at the end of his life seemed to surpass even today's modern concert models. The pianos were extremely heavy to play, and although they were now cross-strung, the sheer effort required by the later instruments, and their starker clarity of sound, meant that it was much more difficult for notes to meld easily into a warm, sonorous glow. Yet Liszt nevertheless continued to wield his instrument efficiently and in a way that was congenial to his frame of mind at the time. Much of Liszt's music from this period is resoundingly harsh—either in the barely stark textures or in the brash overwhelming noise. This can be fairly easily emulated on the modern piano, but there is an additional level of resonance and heavy strength, and also lack of glossy smoothness, that is quite striking. This is plainly audible in the 1881 Bechstein piano that Liszt had at Weimar.

Indeed, even in Liszt's more technically demonstrative moments, the piano's properties come through in the style of virtuosity. For example, in his *Csárdás macabre* (S. 224 / LW A313, 1881–82, ex. 2.7), his virtuosity stems from having chords or octaves moving relatively swiftly in noisy, blocky leaps. Even Liszt's use of "small" notes is very different from the way they functioned in earlier repertoires, such as in *Les jeux d'eaux à la Villa d'Este* (S. 163/4 / LW A283/4, 1877, ex. 2.8). Instead of providing mere filling in texture, the notes are here precisely crystalline, forming measured harmonic and rhythmic patterns.

&• &• &•

An understanding of the variety of Liszt's pianos can be very helpful for pianists playing Liszt's music today. Although there are many complex factors associated with the condition of historical pianos, they are still a useful source; the experience of playing them offers ways of performing and insights into his music that transcend the modern piano and contemporary interpretative norms. In particular, these pianos offer a fresh perspective on

Example 2.7. Liszt, *Csárdás macabre*, S. 224, mm. 114–42

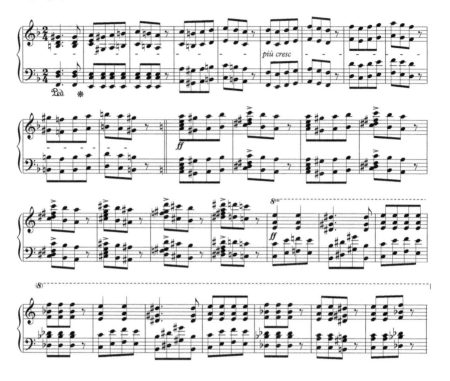

Example 2.8. Liszt, *Les jeux d'eaux à la Villa d'Este*, S. 163/4, mm. 108–13

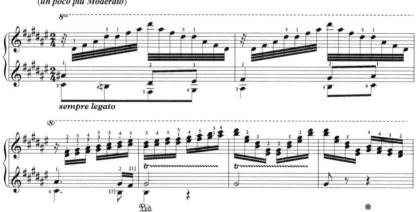

the realization of Liszt's notation and a deeper understanding of Liszt's conception of virtuosity as it developed through his career and in relation to the evolution of his instrument. After all, while the piano was only an instrument, Liszt was so in tune with it that observers like Heinrich Heine could write that compared to Liszt "all other piano players . . . are nothing but piano players, they excel through the skill with which they manipulate the strung wood; whereas with Liszt, one no longer thinks of triumphed-over difficulties—the piano disappears and what is revealed is music."[13]

Notes

1. February 12, 1841. Adrian Williams, *Portrait of Liszt: By Himself and His Contemporaries* (Oxford: Clarendon Press, 1990), 161.
2. Letter to Adolphe Pictet, September 1837. Franz Liszt, *An Artist's Journey*, trans. and ed. Charles Suttoni (Chicago: University of Chicago Press, 1989), 47.
3. One need only glance at Liszt iconography or read the dramatic reports for proof of this, e.g.: "After the concert, Liszt remains like a conqueror on the battlefield, like a hero at his chosen post of honor.—The conquered piano lies at his feet. Broken strings appear here and there like shredded standards. The horrified instruments take cover in their cases" (M. Saphir, *Humorist*, April 21, 1838, quoted in Dana Gooley, *The Virtuoso Liszt* [Cambridge: Cambridge University Press, 2004], 109).
4. See Jim Samson, *Virtuosity and the Musical Work: The "Transcendental Studies" of Liszt* (Cambridge: Cambridge University Press, 2003).
5. http://www.bbc.co.uk/radio3/mozart/piano.shtml, accessed September 21, 2019.
6. Adam Liszt to Carl Czerny, March 17, 1824. Williams, *Portrait of Liszt*, 14.
7. J. N. Hummel, *Ausführlich theoretisch-practische Anweisung zum Piano-forte Speil* [1828] (Vienna, 1929), 462. Robert Winter, "Keyboards," in *Performance Practice: Music after 1600*, ed. Howard Mayer Brown and Stanley Sadie (London: Macmillan, 1989), 357.
8. Letter to Marie d'Agoult, February 20, 1837. Franz Liszt, *Selected Letters*, trans. and ed. Adrian Williams (Oxford: Clarendon Press, 1998), 72–73.
9. Letter to Pierre Érard, December 26, 1845. Liszt, *Selected Letters*, 228.
10. Letter to Pierre Érard, received August 5, 1847, original emphasis. Ibid., 256.
11. Alan Walker, *Franz Liszt, Volume 2: The Weimar Years, 1848–1861* (London: Faber, 1989), 77.
12. Letter from Hans von Bülow to his mother, June 21, 1849. Williams, *Portrait of Liszt*, 254.

13. Heinrich Heine, "Musical Season in Paris," supplement to the *Allgemeine Zeitung* (Augsburg), April 29, 1841. *Franz Liszt and his World*, ed. Christopher H. Gibbs and Dana Gooley (Princeton, NJ: Princeton University Press, 2006), 449.

Chapter Three

Spirit and Mechanism

Liszt's Early Piano Technique and Teaching

Nicolas Dufetel

Yes, yes, methodology, everything is method.[1]

—Liszt, 1884

"Technique is created from the spirit, not from mechanics."[2] This often-quoted precept attributed to Liszt, seemingly cited for the first time by Lina Ramann as one of the pieces of advice he insistently repeated to his pupils in his later years, should not lead one to think that there was something mystical or supernatural about Liszt's legendary mastery of piano technique. As empirical history and documentary evidence show, transcendental piano technique is not magic; it is rather the consequence, at least in Liszt's case, of a balance between musical intelligence, intensive practice, mental rigor and organization, and a mighty but delicate hand. If Liszt verbalized this somewhat vague rule during his lessons, it should be understood in the context of Lina Ramann's introduction to her *Liszt Paedagogium*. There it appears at the end in bold letters, for she insists on the importance of the master's *hand*, described in a somewhat poetic way as the "Organ der Seele" (organ or tool of the soul). Beyond the metaphor always stands an idea: what she wants to emphasize here is that the mastery of technique is due to the complementarity of physical and mental skills. It must also be noted that if this rule does not express word for word what Liszt actually said, it undoubtedly indicates something important about his conception of transcendental piano technique. It is in fact Liszt's conception of the balance between Letter and Spirit that points to a way of clarifying these kinds of declarations.[3]

It is generally assumed that Liszt's teaching, especially the master classes he pioneered later in life, was more about interpretation than about technique. However, this does not mean that Liszt never spoke, especially in his youth, about the latter. Direct and indirect sources can help us understand and illustrate his dictum about spirit and mechanism, which is not, as it has recently been labeled, a "platitude."[4] On the contrary, documented and exemplified, this instruction can illuminate Liszt's conception of piano training in terms of the equation between mechanics and thinking. This chapter will endeavor to go beyond these metaphors and study their empirical basis. Examining Liszt's technical workshop and documenting his piano practice and teaching in the early 1830s, with a view toward comparing these investigations to the more well-known traits of his late teaching, may indeed shed a new light on his relation to technique and teaching. Some rare or hitherto unknown and unexamined documents from the 1830s, such as the exercises written for Valérie Boissier and a few technical fragments scattered in his draftbooks and copied by Henry Maréchal in the early 1870s, offer a unique glimpse into his early technique and teaching as well as his systematic *approche raisonnée* (reasoned approach) to the piano.[5]

Career Transformations: The Example of 1832

Liszt is known for his artistic and personal *transformations*: from wunderkind to dandy and *jeune France* in his youth, to virtuoso and Kapellmeister in his prime, and finally to abbé and old master in his last years. The idea of transformation as a way of managing and invigorating a long artistic career illustrates a strategy of reinvention as the key to maintaining celebrity: transformation is a tool for longevity. A more recent example in the history of artistic celebrity is David Bowie, known by his fans and critics alike for his own artistic as well as physical transformations. As for Liszt, he himself gave clues about his self-conscious career transformations. His declaration to Hiller about the new path he wants to take in composition in 1835 is confirmed by other sources and is illustrated by the new style with which he is experimenting.[6] But the best known of his self-declared transformations may be the 1846 letter he wrote to Grand Duke Carl Alexander, quoting Dante, less than two years before the end of his virtuoso career and his move to Weimar: "The time has come for me ('Nel mezzo del cammin di nostra vita' 35 years!) to break out of my virtuoso's chrysalis and allow my thought unfettered flight—doubtless to flutter about!"[7] Later, in 1874, he would present his life to Lina Ramann as a five-act "classical tragedy," in which he identifies evolutions and transformations.[8]

The year 1832 is often considered in the Lisztian literature as a *transformational* year, as far as his piano technique and musical consciousness are concerned. But in a broader sense, that year may well have been a key year in his overall artistic development and in his private life—at least it encourages the musicologist to gather together many facts and observations concerning it. First, in 1832, as Liszt toured the French provinces (Rouen and Ecorchebeuf in Normandie, Dieppe in the north, Bourges in the center), he mostly stayed in Paris, where he met the woman who would immediately play a decisive role in his personal life. It is indeed at the end of that year, in December, that he met the Countess Marie d'Agoult in the salon of the Marquise de Ferrière le Vayer. Second, earlier in the same year, he had heard two musicians who would immediately influence his artistic development: on February 26, he attended Chopin's debut at the Salle Pleyel, and on April 22, at the Opéra, Paganini's benefit concert for the victims of cholera, an epidemic that would kill thousands that year in Paris. He was also involved, in the first three months of 1832, in a pedagogical relationship that has been widely considered as one of the most important sources for our knowledge of his early piano teaching and ideas about musical style and performance. Through the end of March 1832, he gave some twenty-eight lessons to Valérie Boissier, which are carefully documented in her mother's diary (*Liszt pédagogue*).[9]

After hearing Paganini, Liszt is said to have chosen a new pianistic path. Ten days after the concert, he wrote to his friend Pierre Wolff (later an important professor at the Genève Conservatoire who introduced the Boissiers to Liszt)[10] a famous letter about the impact of the violin virtuoso:

> Here is a whole fortnight that my mind and fingers have been working like two lost spirits—Homer, the Bible, Plato, Locke, Byron, Hugo, Lamartine, Chateaubriand, Beethoven, Bach, Hummel, Mozart, Weber, are all around me. I study them, meditate on them, devour them with fury; besides this I practice four to five hours of exercises (3rds, 6ths, 9ths, tremolos, repetition of notes, cadences, etc. etc.). Ah! provided I don't go mad, you will find an artist in me! Yes, an artist such as you desire, such as is required nowadays!
>
> "And I too am a painter!" cried Michelangelo the first time he beheld a *chef-d'œuvre*. . . . Though insignificant and poor, your friend cannot leave off repeating those words of the great man ever since Paganini's last performance.[11]

It must be noticed that, in this passionate introspection, literature and fine art are mixed with musical and technical elements. Early witnesses, among them Madame Boissier, remarked how Liszt was curious about everything; she observes in her correspondence that his self-taught faculties went beyond pure music, and that he linked and nourished music with everything else: "He brought a few books; he is a *littérateur*, he is well-read, has meditated and thought; his opinions are original; they are *his*, and this education, fruit of talent—even genius— is its most sensational result."[12] "He was his own admirable teacher, and the result of this education, achieved without any regular support, is astonishing. Development of spirit, the habit of delving into everything, individuality, religious feeling, everything is here."[13] "Liszt is a thinker, and while doing his music studies, he found a way to read enormously and deeply."[14]

His own words, "my mind and fingers have been working like two lost spirits," recall Ramann's quote and thus must be linked to the "spirit-mechanic" equation: "Technique should create itself from spirit, not from mechanics," and indeed, in this 1832 letter, the intellect comes before everything. Not only does the mind anticipate the fingers, but the writers precede the composers in his list. At that time, as Madame Boissier, and later Nadine Helbig attested, Liszt used to practice his technical exercises while reading books and dictionaries, to provide himself the general education he felt he lacked because of his exclusively music-focused *Wunderkind* youth.[15] Madame Boissier observed that "he wants Valérie to spend two hours a day on mechanical exercises [*exercises matériels*], in addition to the other assignments," and that he himself does it "while reading to alleviate boredom. In such a way he ponders what he's reading while exercising his fingers."[16] Here the independence of mechanics is clear: pure finger exercises while the mind focuses elsewhere. He then nourishes his interpretation with literature, merging different sources of inspiration.

The finger exercises he recommended were of his own invention as well as from the repertoire. In that respect, he seemed to have claimed for himself the legacy of tradition, especially the Viennese one. As a matter of fact, he wrote in 1877 to Julius Epstein, a piano professor at the Vienna Conservatory, that he considered himself an heir to and maybe an example of the celebrated Viennese school: "With your teaching and example, you educate superbly your students and maintain the tradition of the Viennese piano school. This school starts with Mozart, and goes on with Hummel, Moscheles, Czerny, Thalberg, Döhler, until Liszt."[17] As with his own compositions, Liszt insisted on putting himself in the stream of tradition and historicity. And as far as the piano is concerned, besides being revolutionary, his technique is also encyclopedic and omnivorous. Of course, he invented many new technical features and especially a new relation between body and instrument—Liszt is an important case study in the history of audiotactility, medium-sensitive playing, and psychophysiology.[18] But before he could forge this new path, he studied and absorbed everything he could enthusiastically and exhaustively; thus, his novelty makes sense in the flow of history: for before pure creation there was assimilation. This is no surprise as far as his philosophy of history—somewhat Hegelian—is concerned; this is the way he understood "revolutions," or "evolutions," namely, as palingenesis and regeneration. Although obsessed with modernity, like the double-faced god Janus he always sustained his modernity though an interest in the past and tradition.[19]

The Draftbooks as a Technical and Compositional Laboratory

Liszt's sketchbooks and draftbooks were always within reach when he wanted to write down his thoughts. Hence are they full of music—drafts and sketches of compositions, or of technical and idiomatic keyboard figures—but also quotations from literature and philosophy, even mementos for compositional ideas, lessons, and meetings dates. Two that he used in the early 1830s, the Lord Londonderry draftbook in the Library of Congress (Washington, DC) and the so-called N6 draftbook in the Goethe-und Schiller-Archiv (Weimar), fit this rule insofar as they contain small drafts, fragments from prose literature and poetry, simple and isolated words, and dates.[20] But Liszt also copied down many technical fragments from the piano repertoire, which document his technical workshop.

The Lord Londonderry Draftbook (Washington, DC)

The Lord Londonderry draftbook, entitled "Cahier autographe" on its binding, is, as Rena Mueller writes, Liszt's "usual pot-pourri of ideas—both musical and otherwise."[21] Only 30 of the 159 pages have been written on. The eight literary fragments are either one word, such as "Artiste" (with music, see ex. 3.1), "Werther," or short and longer quotations by Goethe, Madame de Staël, and Ecclesiastes (see table 3.1). The music fragments, none longer than one page, are sometimes disconcerting, such as the three measures for a "Concerto" (piano and "instruments à vent," p. 11) or for a "Duo piano et violon" (p. 33, exx. 3.2 and 3.3). Another type of musical insertion in this draftbook is made up of fragments from Kessler and Czerny.

Example 3.1. Liszt, Lord Londonderry draftbook (Ms. aut., early 1830s), Washington, DC, Library of Congress, Music Division, ML96 .L58 Case (Cahier autographe), 19

Example 3.2. Liszt, Lord Londonderry draftbook (Ms. aut., early 1830s), Washington, DC, Library of Congress, Music Division, ML96 .L58 Case (Cahier autographe), 11

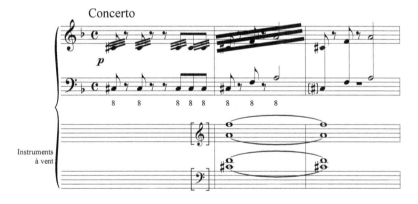

Table 3.1. Literary fragments in the Lord Londonderry sketchbook

Page	Citation	Identification
2	« Lisez la plume à la main »	
19	« Artiste »	
48	« Je ne suis bien nulle part, je suis bien partout. »	Johann Wolfgang von Goethe, Les souffrances du Jeune Werther, trans. Pierre Leroux (1829), in Œuvres de Pierre Leroux (1825–1850), 2 t., Paris, Société typographique, 1850–1851, t. 1, p. 549.
48	« Qu'est-ce que l'homme, ce demi-dieu si vanté ! Les forces ne lui manquent-elles pas précisément à l'heure où elles lui seraient le plus nécessaire[s] ? et lorsqu'il prend l'essor dans la joie, ou qu'il s'enfonce dans la tristesse, n'est-il pas alors même borné, et toujours ramené au sentiment de lui même, au triste sentiment de sa petitesse, quand il espérait se perdre dans l'infini »	Goethe, Les souffrances du Jeune Werther, p. 542 (ibid., II, 6 December). See also the name "Werther," p. 53.
49	« Tous mes jours sont pleins de douleur et de misère, et il n'y a point de repos pour mon ame »	Ecclesiastes, II, 23. Trans. Lemasitre de Sacy, on lit : « Tous ses jours sont pleins de douleur et de misère, et il n'y a point de repos dans son âme . . . ,» La Sainte Bible en latin et en françois (Paris, Lefèvre, 1832)
53	« Werther »	
60	« Celui qui n'a pas souffert, que sait-il ? »	Maybe Ecclesiasticus, XXXIV; 10.
60	« Les fleurs de la vie sont pour toujours jetées derrière moi ! »	Madame de Staël, Corinne ou l'Italie, Œuvres complètes, 17 t. Paris, Treuttel et Würtz, 1820–1821, t. 9 (1820), p. 223 (XV/7).

Example 3.3. Liszt, Lord Londonderry draftbook (Ms. aut., early 1830s), Washington, DC, Library of Congress, Music Division, ML96 .L58 Case (Cahier autographe), 33

Kessler's name appears with a commentary on page 61, associated with one measure in C minor where the two hands play a series of octaves and diminished sevenths (the right one in chords, "en accords"). Actually, as shown by the different inks, Liszt seems to have first written the music, then the following commentary: "(Étude Kessler) / C'est une affreuse pensée . . ." (It's a horrible idea . . .) (ex. 3.4). This comment, emphasized by the series of dots, may correspond to the difficulty of such a figure. Liszt was quite familiar with Kessler's twenty-four Études, op. 20 (c. 1825). More than fifty years later, when they were performed in one of his master classes in May 1886, Göllerich reports that Liszt said that he and Chopin "were very fond of them in the [18]30s. They are very commendable."[22] In 1832 indeed, we know that he played and taught some of these études to Valérie Boissier. During the lesson of February 21, he made a comparison between Dante's *Inferno* and Kessler's Étude no. 8 in C Minor, dedicated to the study of octaves. The one-measure quotation in his draftbook does not correspond to Kessler's étude, but the tonality, the pattern of the fragment, and its difficulty are similar. He may have written his own idea and, afterward, made a comparison to Kessler. Actually, the "horrible idea" could mean that playing this pattern in full chords would be almost impossible.

Czerny's name appears once or twice in the Lord Londonderry draftbook, where Liszt noted down some figurations that caught his eye (pages 1 and 60, see exx. 3.5 and 3.6). The reading of his name on page 1 is uncertain. The two musical quotations (four and one measures respectively) may come

Example 3.4. Liszt, Lord Londonderry draftbook (Ms. aut., early 1830s), Washington, DC, Library of Congress, Music Division, ML96 .L58 Case (Cahier autographe), 61

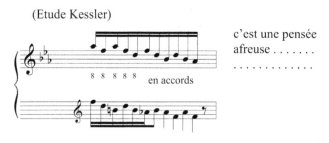

from one of his numerous exercises or études, or from one of his many compositions. They remain unidentified. As Rena Mueller recalls, Liszt kept Czerny at the forefront of his performing repertoire, mentioning him four times in his "Repertoire des Concerts": his first attempt at organizing and cataloging his performing repertory in 1843.[23] In this "Répertoire des concerts," indeed, Czerny's name appears under "Sonatas," "Paraphrases & Transcriptions," "Fugues," and "Variations." The first likely Czerny quotation in the Lord Londonderry draftbook (p. 1) does not seem to be technical in nature and is dated August 13, 1830. Just above it, Liszt wrote at another moment (in a different ink) a pattern based on descending diminished sevenths in thirds (in eighth notes, both hands) and a chromatic movement going in reverse direction (in sixteenth notes, both hands), completed by an "etc." indication. This fragment has an obvious technical aspect. It is very different from the compositional draft at the top of the page. Beneath the Czerny (?) quote, there is also another chromatic scaler figure that may have been written at the same time as the two-handed one.

The second mention of Czerny's name, on page 60, undated, is accompanied by two literary citations. Did Liszt write "Ex." for "Exercise" or "Example"? In any case, it is a digital pattern, a kind of delicate *Fingerübung*, to use Liszt's own word as quoted by Nadine Helbig.[24] The technical and idiomatic nature of the other musical fragments on this page is irrefutable— exercises or transition material—while still other fragments in the draftbook are clearly melodic or harmonic sketches.

Example 3.5. Liszt, Lord Londonderry draftbook (Ms. aut., early 1830s), Washington, DC, Library of Congress, Music Division, ML96 .L58 Case (Cahier autographe), 1

Example 3.6. Liszt, Lord Londonderry draftbook (Ms. aut., early 1830s), Washington, DC, Library of Congress, Music Division, ML96 .L58 Case (Cahier autographe), 60

The N6 Draftbook (Weimar)

The N6 draftbook from Weimar is contemporary with and has a similar profile to the Lord Londonderry draftbook.[25] It contains literary quotations as well as composition drafts, notably the opening motif of the First Piano Concerto in E-flat Major and *Malédiction* (p. 6 and p. 21).[26] On pages 39–40, the eighteen literary fragments about love, religion, and suffering, taken from Edouard Alletz, Byron, Bossuet, de Staël, and *The Imitation of Christ*, are closely interpolated and merged into the music as an example of Liszt's attempt to combine music and poetry.[27]

Example 3.7. Liszt, Draftbook (Ms. aut., early 1830s), Weimar, Goethe- und Schiller-Archiv, 60/N6, 47

Indeed, pages 47 and 48, perhaps written at the same time, contain two series of well-organized short fragments that have nothing to do with composition, with poetic music, but are rather purely piano technical in nature. The three examples on page 47 (ex. 3.7) about articulation and strength, as well as wrist position may have been intended for a pupil (perhaps Valérie Boissier?), also appear to display a pedagogical intention.[28] At the top of the page, Liszt asks that the first exercise (right hand) be continued "in every major key / C sharp. / D major. / E flat." ("Dans tous les tons majeurs / ut ♯. / re majeur. / mib.") The type of the second exercise corresponds to a *Fingerübung* he frequently asked Valérie Boissier to do (see below). The third is in the same spirit as the first, but for both hands.

Page 48 is highly interesting (figure 3.1). First, because the fourteen fragments constitute a synoptic ensemble; second, because Liszt notes down the names of some of the composers he borrows them from: Herz (1), Moscheles (2 and 8), Ries (7), Czerny (9), Clementi (12), and Cramer (13 and 14). They look like the fragments scattered in the Lord Londonberry

Figure 3.1. Franz Liszt, Draftbook (Ms. aut., early 1830s), Weimar, Goethe- und Schiller-Archiv, 60/N6, 48

sketchbook or in other manuscripts, for instance in the "Z" section from the Liszt Bestand in the Goethe- und Schiller-Archiv (D-WRgs 60/Z18). By writing them in a synoptic way, Liszt highlights the similarities of these "formula" patterns and the logic of their juxtaposition: compare Herz (1) to Moscheles (2) for descending scales; Ries (7), Moscheles (8), and Czerny (9) for chromatic symmetrical figurations (also 10 and 11); and Clementi (12) and Cramer (13) for the C-major finger articulation and position of the hand. Like examples 5 (no. 2) and 6, they are idiomatic keyboard figures, an important feature of nineteenth-century piano development, as argued by Jim Samson and more recently by Dana Gooley, who stresses their importance for improvisation and composition.[29] Liszt's draftbooks contain either drafts of compositions, including comments about harmony and rhythm, or excerpts of idiomatic figures. The later are, according to Gooley, "overlooked by musicologists because they do not participate in thematic, harmonic, or formal processes, and are sometimes deemed 'inessential' surface features."[30] Yet, scattered though sources, they are fundamental for our understanding of Liszt's approach to piano playing and teaching.

The "Marie, Poême" Draftbook

A hitherto unknown draftbook from the same period with a similar profile to the Weimar and Washington ones offers new insight into Liszt's piano and composition workshop from the 1830s, including his intentions and projects. Formerly in the collection of Joseph Pierre (1862–1936), who amassed memorabilia from the Berry region of central France (Bourges, Châteauroux, Nohant, etc.), where he was born and lived, the "Marie, Poême" draftbook is now in a private collection. A brief summary of its contents: sixteen pages were written between 1832 and 1836 in black ink (just few words are in pencil), twelve on one side ("A" series pages) and four on the other, upside down ("B" series pages); see table 3.2. The main musical interest lies in the three-page sketch for "Marie, Poême" (twenty-six measures on three pages: B-2–4), hence its name. With a careful study of a facsimile of the first page (thirteen measures) and other sources, Adrienne Kaczmarczyk was able to reconstruct the "Marie, Poême" project, a cycle for piano "en six chants."[31] However, the whole sketchbook, containing thirteen more measures, completes our knowledge of that work. It also gives new insights into Liszt's musical studies and planned works (musical and literary). The rest of the sketchbook is indeed made up of musical examples, as well as comments on Rossini, Mozart, and Field, smaller compositional drafts, and textual fragments (see tables 3.2 and 3.3). These textual inserts, however, are not literary citations, as in the two other draftbooks; they are mainly short comments about rhythm and harmony ("modulation") in Rossini's *Siège de Corinthe*, Mozart's *Requiem*, and Field (with music examples, pp. A-1, A-3, A-8, A-9). Other pages include titles for projected writings or compositions (A-5, A-6, A-7, B-1, see table 3.4. Along with some fantasies for orchestra (and piano?) on national melodies, we find a "Grande Symphonie revolution[n]aire," "La Marseillaise," and an "air revolution[n]aire Polonais" (is it possible that Liszt had been talking to Berlioz, who planned in the early 1830s a symphonic work, *Retour de l'armée d'Italie*, as well as an orchestration of the *Marseillaise?*) For piano solo we find "Harmonies poétiques" and "Études poétiques," "Soirées musicales," "Ressouvenances d'enfance," "Les Djinns," among others. Liszt also planned to include Lützow's "Wild Hunt" in a piano concerto (*Lützows wilde verwegene Jagd*, a poem by Theodor Körner set to music by Franz Schubert and Carl Maria von Weber. Liszt composed his own *Wilde Jagd* as the eighth *Transcendental Étude*). See table 3.4, A-6 and A-7. His plans also include exercises, preludes, and études, all three genres possessing a technical and pedagogical aspect (the prelude was, before Chopin's opus 28, a nonautonomous genre).

A few words, either hastily written or faded, are very difficult to read; until they are clearly identified, one must be cautious in forming conclusions. Yet the list of planned compositions offers an interesting window into Liszt's creative intentions. The chronology of his works and early versions in

Table 3.2. General description of the "Marie Poême" draftbook

Page	Description	
A-1	Rossini, Siège de Corinthe. Music examples with comments	See table 3.3
A-2	Hiller, Études. Music example with comment	
A-3	Mozart, Requiem. Music examples with comments	
A-4	Bach, Suites anglaises. Music examples	
A-5	Text (working plan)	See table 3.4
A-6	Text (working plan)	
A-7	Text (working plan)	
A-8	Field. Music examples with comments	
A-9	Field. Music examples with comments	
A-10	Not by Liszt. Music example ("Worzischez Étude n° 70")	
A-11	Music drafts: "Finale de Septuor," "Valse en fa♯," "Mazurk," "Études"	
A-12	Music draft (no title)	
B-1	Text (working plan)	See table 3.4
B-2	"Marie, Poême." Music sketch	
B-3	"Marie, Poême." Music sketch	
B-4	"Marie, Poême." Music sketch	

his early draftbooks (as in the Lord Londonderry) show that Liszt was almost incapable of completing medium- or large-scale original works during the late 1820s and early 1830s. He was struggling for inspiration. The "Marie, Poême" sketchbook, however, corresponds to the period, in the mid-1830s, when he started to produce his first original works.[32] The "Article à faire sur la situation des artistes" with the list of different categories of artists, clearly corresponds to his essay "De la situation des artistes, et de leur condition dans la société," published in 1835. Some of his later compositions may be the direct result of the plans elaborated in the "Marie, Poême" sketchbook: the *Valse mariotique*, owing its name to Marie d'Agoult, is identified as the *Grande valse di bravura* (S. 209 / LW A32a); the *Lützows wilde Jagd* (after Weber), intended for a concerto rather than for a projected German *Années de pèlerinage*, was eventually included in his piano transcription *Leyer und*

Table 3.3. Description of pages A-1 and A-3 (Rossini and Mozart) of the "Marie, Poême" draftbook

Page	Composer and Work	Music Examples	Liszt's inserts
A-1	Rossini, Siège de Corinthe	4 music examples (Ouverture, "Prophétie", "3eme Acte—Récit de Pamira")	"Siège de Corinthe" "Rhythme" "Combinaison de 2, 3 et même 4 rhythmes" "Union du mode majeur et du mode mineur" "Phrase / maj. Mineur" "Parallelisme des Pedales (dans le genre fugué) et des Crescendos (dans le genre italien rossinien)"
A-3	Mozart, Requiem	4 music examples	"Requiem de Mozart" "Dies irae" "Rhythme" "Modulation"

Schwerdt nach Carl Maria von Weber und Körner (S. 452 / LW A151, 1848), where it concludes the small cycle; the harmonies, études, and rhapsodies were realized, but it is not certain that the "Rhapsodies dramatiques" would have been Hungarian. Could the mention of a "Europe musicale" (p. A-7), if the reading is correct, correspond to the list of countries and nations on p. A-6? This series of fantasies on national melodies, in which the presence of Turkish melodies is noteworthy, may have merged into the idea of a travelling musical diary (the *Album d'un voyageur*, transformed into the *Années de pèlerinage*). More is known about the planned *Symphonie révolutionnaire*, but Liszt never wrote anything called "Exercices" or "Préludes."[33] It is, however, interesting to note that the planned "Méthode" included the group "Exercices-Préludes-Études" according to the traditional model of the time.

Very important in this draftbook are Liszt's thoughts on Rossini's *Le siège de Corinthe* and Mozart's *Requiem* (pp. A-1 and A-3, see table 3.3), two works from which he jotted down harmonies, modulations, and rhythmic patterns that caught his eye and that would inspire him: the first for an *Introduction des variations sur une marche du* "Siège de Corinthe" (S. 421a / LW A13,

Table 3.4. Working plans in the "Marie, Poême" draftbook

Page	Liszt's inserts
A-5	12 Janvier
	Article à faire sur la situation des / Artistes : leurs rapports religieux et sociaux = / Classification (Catégories) = Artistes = [one illegible word] = Artistes grippes-sou - [two illegible words] = artistes exploitants = exploités - artistes invalides = / Artistes et artisans = [these lines crossed out]
	à faire en 1835.
	Marie [?], Poeme.
	(Rhapsodies Dramatiques / <u>Recueil</u> de Morceaux de salon)
	en 1836 et 37—
	Méthode [?] Méthodes [these lines crossed out]
	avec tous les Exemples [a few fadded words]
	avec [?] 24 Exercices, 24 Preludes et 24 nouvelles Etudes / (dans les 24 Preludes, faire mes 1res Etudes [?]
A-6	Grandes Fantaisies avec orchestre sur des airs nationaux / hongrois, espagnols, tyroliens, suisses, russes, anglais, espagnols italiens, espagnols, russes, turques, français (sur des chants de [?])
	Grande Symphonie revolution[n]aire
	La Marseillaise, [one illegible word] et un air revolution[n]aire Polonais[1]
	[the previous lines almost entirely crossed out]
A-7	3 Aout 1836
	Harmonies—poétiques.
	Etudes <u>poétiques</u>
	<u>Marie</u>—
	Juin—Puritani
	3 morceaux pour[one illegible word]
	Douze [corrected « 24 » in pencil] <u>Grandes Etudes</u>
	Ajouter Lutzow / Jagd[2] au Concerto /
	Finale du Sextuor
	Soirées musicales
	Ressouvenances [?] d'enfance
	Dilachante
	Bornetot [the previous line in italics in pencil]

(continued)

Table 3.4.—*(concluded)*

Page	Liszt's inserts
A-7	Novembre 1835 [?] Europe [?] musicale 1. Journal 2. Ecole— 3. Concerti—et poèmes— 4. Airs nationaux 5. Publication (Musée musical) 6. Encyclopedie musicale
B-1	[illegible] 1 2. Valse mariotique 3. Serenade [?][3 illegible words] Prière—Marche fantastique Delire— Les Djinns.

1830), the second for a transcription of Mozart's "Confutatis" and "Lacrymosa."[34] Liszt also copied fragments from Bach's last *Suite anglaise* (p. A-4) and, on two pages (pp. A-8–A-9,), from three pieces by Field: the fantasy *Ah quel dommage* (mm. 84–86), the *Rondo écossais* (mm. 175–77) and the *Rêverie-nocturne* in C Major (mm. 1–2)—one of his favorites, which he would edit twenty-four years later in the 1859 edition of Field's *Nocturnes* for Schuberth in Leipzig. The two pages seem to be organized in four sections: (1) "Modulation," (2) "Passages" (the first from the fantasy *Ah quel dommage*, m. 106), (3) "Extraits et projets [?]," and (4) "Accompagnements et rythmes." Of the *Rêverie-nocturne* in C Major (ex. 3.8) Liszt wrote only the first two measures and only the left hand, which has the melodic pattern (the right hand plays a continuous line of "g"). Just beneath, he drafts a "study to be written" in C minor with a "canto in the basso" (*étude à faire / chant à la basse*) and a long and virtuoso *trait* at the right hand—all of it similar to Chopin's "Revolutionary" Étude, op. 10, no. 12, published in 1833 (op. 10 was dedicated to Liszt) and to Field's example.

The excerpts from Field do not correspond exactly to the published scores, which means that Liszt must almost certainly have copied them from memory. On another page of the draftbook he also wrote approximately two short excerpts from two études by Hiller (op. 15, in E-flat Major and C Minor), which retained his interest for their rhythms, p. A-2 (ex. 3.9). The

Example 3.8. Liszt, "Marie, Poême" draftbook (Ms. aut., c. 1834), private collection, A9

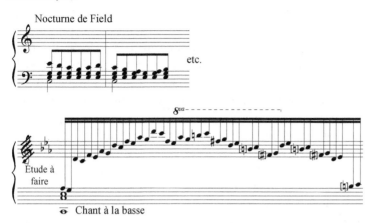

Example 3.9. Liszt, "Marie, Poême" draftbook (Ms. aut., c. 1834), private collection, A-2

"Marie, Poême" sketchbook provides important information about Liszt's thoughts and plans but also, along with the comments and excerpts from Mozart, Rossini, and Field, about his own musical workshop as a composer. Harmony, rhythm, and pianistic formulas that interest him accompany his own sketches, as in the other draftbooks described below or in the sixteen-page manuscript (partially autograph) connected to his lessons to Alfred de Musset's sister (Weber's *Invitation à la valse* and Chopin's *Grande valse brillante*, op. 18).[35]

A Fragmentary Piano Method for Valérie Boissier

The twenty-eight lessons given by Liszt to Valérie Boissier from the end of December 1831 to the March 30, 1832, took place in the composer's own apartment in Paris. The average rhythm of the meetings, which could last two and a half hours, was three times a week. Madame Boissier's diary, published in 1927, does not include the first lessons. Noting that "he has new principles based on reason and on an exquisite sentiment," she decided to take notes only after a lesson on the fugue that made a particularly strong impression on her.[36] However, some description of the early lessons can be found in her correspondence.[37] Valérie's mother, Caroline Butini (1786–1836), was an amateur pianist and composer, hence the intriguing level of detail in her diary, which has attracted scholarly interest.[38] Valérie (1813–94) did not continue her amateur career as her mother did; instead, she devoted herself to literature, beginning, as early as 1833, with the publication of short stories and travelogues. In particular, she wrote about her journeys to Italy and the Levant.[39] Caroline wrote that she was so much impressed by Liszt's playing at the piano that she gave up any hope of becoming a concert pianist. After marrying the Count Agénor de Gasparin in 1837, she started to study religious history, theology, and Protestantism. She was also involved in the construction of a sanatorium for the poor and founded the world's first secular nursing school in Lausanne.

Usually, during her lessons, Valérie played and Liszt listened; but Liszt also played quite often himself and interacted with his pupil not only on purely musical issues. As noted by Madame Boissier, he insisted in his teaching on the importance of literature, poetry, music history, philosophy, and so on (he read excerpts from Pascal and Hugo). John Rink published in 1999 a survey with several tables summarizing the musical content of the lessons.[40] The young piano teacher taught exercises, études, and compositions by Bach, Bertini, Clementi, Czerny, Kalkbrenner, Kessler, Mayer, Moscheles, and Weber. He himself played works by Beethoven, Clementi, Czerny, Haydn, Herz, Hiller, Hummel, Kessler, Mayer, Moscheles, Mozart, and Weber, a piano concerto by Madame Boissier, and maybe his own *Grande fantaisie sur la tyrolienne de l'opéra "La fiancée" d'Auber* (S. 385/1 LW A12a/1, 1829).

Madame Boissier's diary recreates the intimate and intense atmosphere of the lessons with a great many details about the music taught and performed by Liszt. She wrote that he elaborately explained his own way of practicing a new piece as well as his method of sight reading, which enabled him to play immediately anything placed in front of him. She observed that his mind was "remarkably well organized," and she endeavored to describe what one can call a "reasoned" (*raisonnée*) approach to piano playing—in other words, his system. She insisted on the fundamental elements he sought to extract in a very systematic and logical way from the music he was playing:

spirit precedes mechanics. "He goes back to fundamentals in everything he studies."[41] "All musical *traits*, every succession of notes, whatever they might be, can be reduced to a certain number of fundamental figurations [*passages fondamentaux*], which are the key to everything."[42] "He aims to reduce all the possible figurations [*passages*] to certain basic formulas from which are derived all the combinations to be encountered. Once one holds the key to them, not only can the figurations be easily played, but one can also sight read everything."[43]

Unfortunately, no primary sources exist for these lessons, about which Rink writes that "one would be hard pressed to reconstruct a Lisztian 'system' from Madame Boissier's testimonies, not least because an underlying logic is lacking in the succession of topics dealt with during the lessons."[44] What is lacking is a "logical" method, that is, a systematic and organized method with classifications, divisions, and the like. Such a method is perhaps the one Liszt is said to have written for the Genève Conservatoire in 1835–36 and that has never been found, if in fact it ever existed in partial or finished form.[45] Chopin, too, never finished his method; however, the surviving manuscripts have been carefully reconstructed by Jean-Jacques Eigeldinger.[46] A recently discovered letter to Jenny Montgolfier, written in Geneva in 1835 or 1836 (private collection) reveals more about Liszt's projected method and its context. With the reference to preliminary exercises and the études, it complements the working plan from the "Marie, Poême" draftbook (see above and table 3.3). Yet it also shows that Liszt was conscious of being a composer-to-be, and that he conceived his works of the time more as a "stereotype" born out of his improvisations and salon music than as pure creation:

> In the meantime, I am once again (the last time, God willing!) playing the *pedagogue* in Geneva. . . . The introduction and the first installment of the Conservatoire Method will be printed in the next six weeks. You will receive them shortly. You will be able to put them to good use for your pupils. Unfortunately, the preparatory exercises (whose classification is totally new and which cover about a hundred pages) will be published separately just before the 24 original *Grandes études*, that is to say around September 1836. By the way, the introduction of this method at the Geneva Conservatoire is only a *preliminary test*; later we will do better. . . .
>
> Shortly after, I will send a half a dozen of pieces of the same level of quality (or *weakness*). All things considered, these pieces are not worthy; however, I'm not unhappy to see them published, and I also plan to compose more in this genre. They are, in some way, the *stereotyping* (an apt but barbarous term) of

my improvisations and salon successes. It is purely and simply *pianists' music*. The works of the composer (good or bad), inasmuch as there is a composer in my brain, will face the light only a short time after. Two or three things that you know to be part of this series will be completed by the following:
The Harmonies poétiques (original)
The 24 Etudes—
Marie, Poem in 6 Cantos
De profundis, Poem with an overture (dedicated to Mr de Lamennais)
2 Concertos, 2 Sextets, etc. etc.[47]

Liszt's claim about the novelty of the classification of the preparatory exercises is an important new element in his approach (Bruno Moysan makes a similar remark about the later *Technische Studien*).[48] Madame Boissier noted on many occasions the sequence and classification given by Liszt but with no additional detail. On March 6, she wrote that Liszt thought that piano difficulties could be divided into four parts: (1) octaves, (2) tremolos, (3) double and triple notes, and (4) scales. If taken together in a "grand classification" (*grande classification*), all difficulties are less formidable, she wrote.[49]

From the planned works listed in the letter to Jenny Montgolfier, the first part of the twenty-four études are the twelve *Grandes études*, published in 1837. They are derived from his youthful *Étude en douze exercices* of 1826 but never reached the total of twenty-four, as first announced, and would be reworked as the final twelve *Études d'exécution transcendante* (1851). The "preparatory exercises," with a new classification, would have formed the core of Liszt's piano teaching in the 1830s; yet it is possible to reconstruct a partial and plausible *Urfassung*, thanks to a nine-page manuscript written by Liszt for Valérie Boissier (see table 3.5).[50] These exercises, now located in a private collection, are a hitherto unpublished, yet fragmentary, technical vade mecum. Very different from Chopin's sketches for a piano method as edited and studied by Eigeldinger—a general approach to piano playing, including the position of the hand and the fingers, their flexibility, and so on—it may provide a partial "succession of topics" that Rink said was lacking in the description of the 1832 lessons. More than a method, these few pages must be considered a guide that complements the lessons. On page 1 of the manuscript, the title in pencil, not in Liszt's hand, reads, "Exercices écrits par Litz [*sic*] en 1832 Paris." On the binding, however, the engraved title is more precise: "Franz Liszt / Exercices composés pour / Valérie Boissier (1832) / manuscrit."

The first four pages of the manuscript are filled with arpeggios (ex. 3.10); then Liszt writes down two series of chords (pp. 4–5), perhaps in order to train the position of the hand and the fingers (or to provide other patterns

Table 3.5. Short description of Boissier's Vademecum

Page	Content	Comment
1	Arpeggios	Full page See Example 10 (partial)
2	Arpeggios	Full page
3	Arpeggios	Full page
4	Arpeggios Chords (Arpeggio positions?)	Full page
5	Chords (Arpeggios positions?)	Half page
6	"Octaves arpégées et accords"	Full page Three sets of seven exercises (see the first four in Example 11). Short music examples given for the first set, to be repeated in every tonality, nuance, etc. Includes trills
7	Five exercises	Half page Partially similar to music example in Boissier 1927, p. 94
8	Two exercises	One system No music, just text
9	Scales	Full page Partially similar to Boissier 1927, p. 95

for arpeggios?). On page 6, he writes a series of seven exercises for octaves, trills, and chords, which he asks to be played and repeated in every key, with dynamic shadings and "expressions" (ex. 3.11). The tonality table he provides, with every key and its relative (Paris, Bibliothèque nationale de France) may have been intended as an accompanying document for this kind of exercise (figure 3.2).[51] Page 5 shows an obvious attempt to organize and classify the practice: the exercises are numbered with a detailed commentary for each. Liszt's instructions are very clear, and he also suggests an ordered sequence for the repetition of the exercises. A little note at the top right of the page recommends "one hour and a half for the trill and 2 [hours] of holding chords." In the three following pages, Liszt writes other configurations of the seven exercises and other examples. The last one contains scale fragments. None of the exercises is exactly the same as the few published in Madame Boissier's book, but some are similar.

Example 3.10. Liszt, "Exercices composés pour Valérie Boissier" (Ms. aut., 1832), 1 (excerpt)

Example 3.11. Liszt, "Exercices composés pour Valérie Boissier" (Ms. aut., 1832), 6 (excerpt)

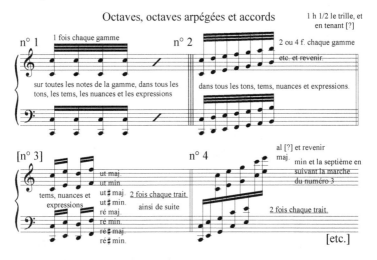

Madame Boissier remarked that "nothing evades his analysis; he goes into things, sounds out as a dreamer-philosopher," and prophesizes about the literary aspect of his legacy: "I would not be surprised to see him attracting attention one day with a profound book."[52] However, toward the end of the lessons, maybe during the spring of 1832 (the Boissiers returned to Geneva in June), she noticed that Liszt had changed: she found him to be dissolute; he practiced little; he frequented high society in the salons, where he encountered many ideas for the development of his art.[53] This change may correspond to Adolphe Crémieux's observation in the early 1830s: Liszt asked the French lawyer, "Tell me everything about French literature!"—to which he replied, "A great confusion reigns in the head of this young man."[54]

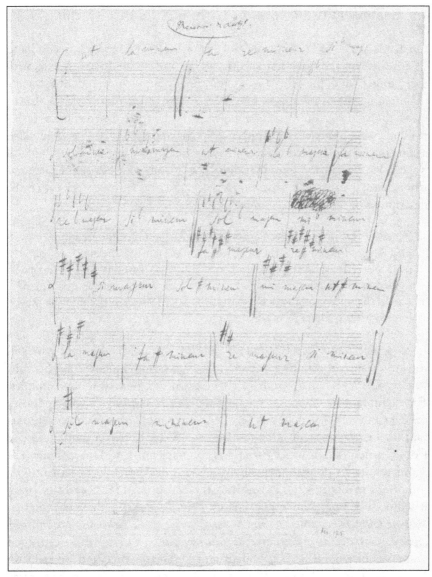

Figure 3.2. Franz Liszt, Table of Tonalities (Ms. aut. early 1830), Paris, Bibliothèque nationale de France, départment de la Musique, Ms 175 (online: https://gallica.bnf.fr/ark:/12148/btv1b550064616)

Continuity between the Early and the Late Teaching

On January 16, 1832, Madame Boissier wrote that Liszt "wants chords to be repeated on the same notes, then simple and broken octaves, trills with every finger while the other fingers rest, finally simple notes, doubled while maintaining the other fingers motionless." She added that "he does that in order to avoid boredom [*se désennuyer*]. It is then that he meditates on his readings while practicing his fingers."[55] On January 31, he "recommended again simple and broken octaves in every tonality, to hit the notes with all fingers, letting rest the ones that don't play, strong and fast scales, then the whole hand gymnastic for two hours a day at least."[56] Three weeks after, the description of the exercise is similar:

> He wants one to put all five fingers on the keys, and then for each in turn to play repeated notes while the others remain motionless. The aim is to make them perfectly equal and independent. He orders that every finger must be trained fifteen minutes continuously, with a high articulation, and putting it not on the tip but on the fleshy part of the finger. This exercise must be performed while reading, to avoid boredom.[57]

In his article about Liszt's *Technische Studien*, Bruno Moysan rightly stresses the importance of this kind of exercise, which he also links to Alois Schmitt (figure 3.3).[58] Yet many sources suggest a direct link to other examples. For example, these exercises for holding chords and fingers correspond to page 47 in the N6 sketchbook (ex. 3.7). They must have been very important for Liszt, since on March 6, he asked Valérie to play a similar exercise from Clementi's *Gradus ad Parnassum* (perhaps no. 1 or 27; see figure 3.4, "pour rendre les doigts indépendants les uns des autres").[59] Clementi was important to Liszt from his youth to the end of his life: as early as 1826, he edited some of Clementi's exercises: *Préludes et exercices doigtés dans tous les tons majeurs et mineurs pour le piano-forté, en 2 livraisons, édition, corrigée et marquée au métronome de Maëlzel par F. Liszt*. This rare printed score was first published by Dufaut and Dubois in Paris and Boisselot in Marseille, in two volumes, followed by Liszt's own *Étude en douze exercices*. It was reissued in 1868 by Sylvain-Saint-Etienne, in Paris, but without the études: by that time they were obsolete and had been replaced by the *Études d'exécution transcendante*.[60]

Fifty years after the Boissier lessons, in 1884, Liszt's pupil Max van der Sandt played various technical studies, after which Liszt himself performed the first and second exercises from Clementi's *Gradus ad Parnassum*. While

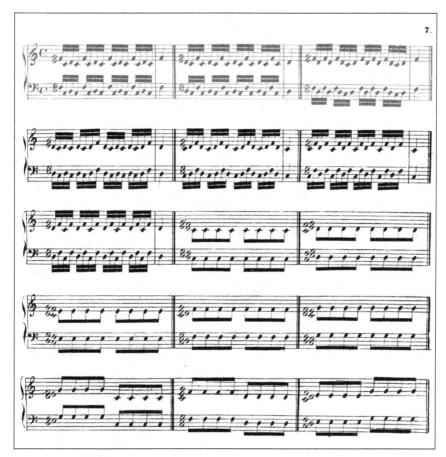

Figure 3.3. Alois Schmitt, *Exercices préparatifs servant à acquérir une indépendance et égalité des doigts possible*, op. 16 (Bonn: N. Simrock, 1834/c. 1850, Plate 1618), 7. Munich, Bayerische Staatsbibliothek/Münchner DigitalisierungsZentrum Digitale Bibliothek, Mus.pr. 56388#Beibd.2 (online: http://mdz-nbn-resolving.de/urn:nbn:de:bvb:12-bsb11150929-9)

doing so he stated, according to Göllerich, "The person is so young and already promotes theory; yes, yes, methodology, everything is method. My old fourth finger already has too little strength."[61] This reported saying is, of course, to be understood in relation to the motto "Technique should create itself from spirit, not mechanics" and to Madame Boissier's observation about his obsession with "systematic" training.

Yet if this kind of exercise for the independence of the fingers can be found throughout Liszt's teaching career, from the lessons of Valérie Boissier,

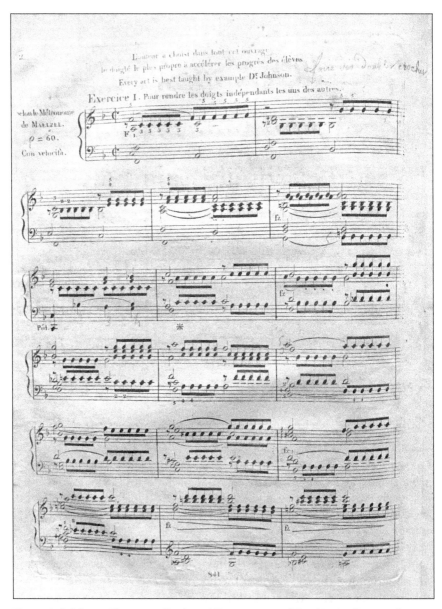

Figure 3.4. Muzio Clementi, *Gradus ad Parnassum, ou l'Art de jouer le piano-forte, démontré par des exercices dans le style sévère et dans le style élégant* (Paris: Mlles Erard, 1817, 1819, 1826), 2. Paris, Bibliothèque nationale de France, départment de la Musique, A782, 1

Example 3.12. Liszt, *Technische Studien*, no. 1, bk. 1 (after *Technische Studien*, S. 146, ed. Mezö Imre, Budapest, Editio Musica Budapest, Neue Liszt Ausgabe, Ser. 1–2 Suppl., Bd. 1–3, 1:2)

Example 3.13. Henry Maréchal, "Exercices pour le piano / par F. Liszt" (Ms., 1871), Paris, Bibliothèque nationale de France, department de la Musique, Ms 12368, 7 (excerpt)

Toutes les notes les unes après les autres dans ce rhytme [sic] et dans tous les tons

the N6 draftbook, Clementi's *Gradus ad Parnassum* in the 1830s, to Liszt's late pedagogy in the 1880s, it also appears in two other sources. First, in the *Technische Studien* composed between 1868 and 1879: the first book opens with a similar "exercises for gaining strength and independence of each individual finger with quiet hand, and chord-studies" (ex. 3.12).[62] Second, at the end of the exercises dictated by Liszt to Henry Maréchal, *pensionnaire* at the Villa Médicis, in June 1871 in Rome ("Exercices pour le piano / par F. Liszt," ex. 3.13).[63]

A comparison of the *Technische Studien*, the Boissier and Maréchal manuscripts, and the other sources mentioned above reveals obvious similarities and nexuses. They are important evidence for the first overarching understanding of Liszt's technical teaching over fifty years. Of course, Liszt, especially in his later years (namely, his master classes), focused his teaching on interpretation, but he also gave technical advice, especially to his many amateur pupils, even as he was reported to have admonished during one of his classes, "Wash your dirty linen at home!" referring to technical issues.[64]

In sum, the sources presented above give an idea of what Liszt's preliminary exercises might have looked like at the beginning of his lost method for the Geneva Conservatoire.

The idea of continuity and coherence is important to understanding the evolution of Liszt's pianism—for instance, through his three sets of *Transcendental Études*. It can also be applied to his late saying about technique, "spirit and mechanics," since, based on the available evidence, the importance of method is clear in his early teaching. Technique, even for Liszt, emerged from hours of mindful training with efficient effort, method, concentration, and logic. This mindful practicing completes—and may precede—the mindless practicing while reading meant to train the bodily reflexes. "My mind and fingers have been working like two lost spirits," Liszt wrote to Pierre Wolff in 1832, presenting a summary of his training method: fingers and the humanities, working together as the two necessary elements of the artist's practice, such "as is required nowadays!" which he differentiated from Paganini.[65]

Madame Boissier was not the only one who admired Liszt's mental organization. In the 1850s in Weimar, Bettina Walker made the same observation about the connection between Liszt's mental faculties and his fingers. She admired the first even more than the later: "What astonished and impressed me most was, not so much that his fingers were responsive to every motion of his mind; I wondered at the *mind*, which one felt instinctively was gifted with the power of grasping in a tiny rapid glance every possible variety of figuration that has ever been written for the pianoforte. His glance seemed to be at once penetrating and all-embracing. He thought it out at once with clearness and rapidity."[66]

It must also be remembered that Liszt's formidable technique was also forged after studying, absorbing, and digesting the tradition. Unlike Wagner, who claimed to have reinvented opera because he considered that it was dead before him, Liszt, drawing on another conception of philosophy of history, always claimed that he thought and created in the flow of history, regenerating as opposed to creating ex nihilo. As far as playing the piano is concerned, he may have tended to do systematic analysis of the digital patterns of the repertoire he knew until the 1830s. As Madame Boissier wrote, and as later observed by Bettina Walker, being able to play every digital pattern he could encounter in every key helped him to sight read anything at the first attempt and master all possible pianistic figurations. In a way, his mental process resembled a kind of mapping of the mechanics of piano technique.

There are other features of piano playing that Liszt may have continued to practice and teach from his early to his late years and that were perhaps, toward the end of the nineteenth century, starting to be forgotten. For example, this is why, as Lina Ramman recalls, he wanted the left-hand arpeggio accompaniment in *Consolation* no. 3 to be played with the old *legatissimo* technique: if the harmony does not change, every finger must keep its note until it plays again. In Czerny's words, "Each finger is suffered to remain on the key for a *longer time* than the note actually prescribes. This kind of touch is applicable only to arpeggiated chords; and great care must be taken to hold down in this way, only such notes belonging to those chords as are consonant or agreeable to the ear."[67] Another tradition that may have been lost when Liszt was teaching at the end of his life was that of rhetoric and declamation. According to Ramann, Liszt insisted on the art of reciting the melodies on the model of poetry (*Periodischer Vortrag*, or periodic performance).[68]

Many witnesses were amazed by Liszt's "declamation" on the piano, suggesting a comparison with oratorical skills. Madame Boissier wrote that "he accentuates as he plays, and his soul expresses itself through words as it does through music."[69] Thirty years later, Émile Ollivier was astonished by the playing of his father-in-law and noted in his diary, "I do not speak about the prodigies of the material performance, but about the poetry, the breath, the elevation, the pathos, and the grace. Often, while listening to him, I felt the same impression as listening to Berryer or reading Mirabeau or Bossuet."[70] And another witness, accustomed to listening to Liszt regularly for more than forty years, Grand Duke Carl Alexander, noted in 1879 in his diary that "in the evening, Liszt deliciously reads some letters by Mérimée published in the *Revue* [*des deux mondes*] on the 15th of August. He reads as he plays, making the spirit flow. He is as lively as Champagne; he ages like an old and good wine."[71]

Additional research into the question of the continuity of Liszt's piano technique and teaching, as well as on the primary sources, will certainly shed new light on his pedagogy and the ways he did or did not teach technique. Sources study and documentary evidence may be a way to interpret the metaphors and precepts of Liszt's teaching. The tension between a seeming distaste for these matters in his teaching and his documented embrace of them is not contradictory. There is nothing to be surprised about concerning his late reputation regarding technique: he was not indifferent to it, but he thought that it was not his job to teach it to his advanced students. Liszt did not want to be perceived as a professor ("Ich bin kein Professor," he is said to have declared), but he never said that technique was not important, nor that it falls from the sky.[72] Before studying with "the master," especially during the open group classes, his disciples had to train properly in private or in the conservatories, as one would prepare the class with an assistant before working with a professor. Was Weimar not, when Liszt and his pupils were there, full of piano practicing up to the point of disturbing the quiet inhabitants?

Notes

1. August Göllerich, *The Piano Master Classes of Franz Liszt, 1884–1886*, ed. Wilhelm Jerger, trans., ed., and enlarged by Richard Louis Zimdars (Bloomington: Indiana University Press, 1996), 21.
2. "Aus dem Geist schaffe sich die Technik, nicht aus der Mechanik," in Lina Ramann, *Liszt-Pädagogium: Klavier-Kompositionen Franz Liszt's nebst noch unedirten Veränderungen, Zusätzen und Kadenzen nach des Meisters Lehren pädagogisch glossirt von L. Ramann. Mit Beiträgen von Aug. Stradal, Berth. Kellermann, Aug. Göllerich, Heinr. Porger, Ida Volkmann, Auguste Rennebaum, u. A* (Leipzig: Breitkopf & Härtel, [1902], facsimile ed. with a preface by Alfred Brendel, 1986), 6.
3. See, for example, Liszt's letter to Richard Pohl, dated November, 5, 1853: "There, as elsewhere, the spirit is killed by the letter, to which I shall never subscribe" (Michael Short, ed., *Liszt Letters in the Library of Congress*, Franz Liszt Studies Series, 10 [Hillsdale: Pendragon, 2003], 295).
4. James Q. Davies, *Romantic Anatomies of Performance* (Berkeley-Los Angeles-London: University of California Press, 2014), 168.
5. The present author is preparing a critical edition of these sources about Liszt's technique for a volume in the Supplements series of the *New Liszt Edition* (Editio Musica Budapest).
6. Gerhard Tischer, "Unbekannte Briefe von Wagner, Liszt, Berlioz, Robert und Clara Schumann, und H. Heine," *Rheinische Musik- und Theater-Zeitung* (June 18, 1910), 455–65. See György Kroó, "'La ligne intérieure,' the Years of Transformation and the 'Album d'un voyageur,'" *Studia Musicologica Academiae Scientiarum Hungaricae* 28, no. 1–4 (1986): 249–60.
7. "Le moment vient pour moi ('*nel mezzo del camin di nostra vita*' 35 ans!) de briser ma chrysalide de virtuosité et de laisser plein vol à ma pensée;—sauf à moins papillonner sans doute!" (Liszt to Carl Alexander, October 6, 1846, in La Mara, ed., *Correspondance entre Franz Liszt et Charles Alexandre* [Leipzig, Breitkopf & Härtel, 1909], 8). See the new edition by the present author: *Correspondance entre Franz Liszt et Carl Alexander, grand-duc de Saxe-Weimar-Eisenach (1845–1886)* (Paris: Société française de musicologie, forthcoming).

English translation from Alan Walker, *Franz Liszt, Volume 2: The Weimar Years, 1848–1861* (Ithaca, NY: Cornell University Press, 1993), 3.

8. Lina Ramann, *Lisztiana: Erinnerungen an Franz Liszt (1873–1887)*, ed. Arthur Seidl (Mainz: Schott, 1983), 36.

9. Madame Auguste Boissier [Caroline Boissier], *Liszt pédagogue: Leçons de piano données par Liszt à Mlle Valérie Boissier à Paris en 1832* (Paris: Champion, 1927 [reprint 1993]). For an English translation, see *The Liszt Studies: essential selections from the original 12-volume set of technical studies for the piano, including the first English ed. of the legendary Liszt pédagogue, a lesson-diary of the master as a teacher, as kept by Mme. Auguste Boissier, 1831–32*, ed. Elyse Mach (New York: Associated Music Publishers, 1973).

10. Caroline Barbey-Boissier, *La comtesse Agénor de Gasparin et sa famille: Correspondance et souvenirs (1813–1894)*, 2 vols. (Paris: Librairie Plon, Plon-Nourrit et Cie, 1902), 1:143.

11. Liszt to Pierre Wolff, May 2 and 8, 1832: "Voici quinze jours que mon esprit et mes doigts travaillent comme deux damnés, == Homère, La Bible, Platon, Locke, Byron, Hugo, Lamartine, Chateaubriand, Beethoven, Bach, Hummel, Mozart, Weber sont tous à l'entour de moi. Je les étudie, les médite, les dévore avec fureur; de plus je travaille 4 à 5 heures d'exercices (3^{ces}, 6tes, 8^{taves}, Trémolos, Notes répétées, Cadences, etc. etc.). Ah! pourvu que je ne devienne pas fou—tu retrouveras un artiste en moi! Oui, un artiste, tel que tu demandes, tel qu'il en faut aujourd'hui! / 'Et moi aussi je suis peintre,' s'écria Michel-Ange la première fois qu'il vit un chef-d'œuvre ... quoique petit et pauvre, ton ami ne cesse de répéter ces paroles du grand homme depuis la dernière représentation de Paganini" (in La Mara, ed., *Franz Liszts Briefe*, vol. 1 [*Von Paris bis Rom*] [Leipzig: Breikopf & Härtel, 1893], 6–7. English translation: *Letters of Franz Liszt*, ed. La Mara and trans. Constance Bache, vol. 1 [London, Grevel & Co., 1894], 7–8).

12. "Il nous apportait quelques livres; c'est un littérateur, il a bien lu, médité, réfléchi; ses opinions sont originales; ce sont *les siennes*, et cette éducation, fruit du talent, du génie même, en est le résultat le plus piquant" (Barbey-Boissier, *La comtesse Agénor de Gasparin et sa famille*, 1:157).

13. "Il a été pour lui-même un admirable précepteur, et le résultat de cette éducation, qui s'est faite sans secours réguliers, est étonnante. Développement de l'esprit, habitude de tout creuser, individualité, sentiment religieux, tout s'y trouve" (ibid., 1:165).

14. "Liszt est un penseur, et tout en faisant ses études musicales, il a trouvé moyen de lire énormément et de bien approfondir" (ibid., 1:179).

15. Nadine Helbig, "Franz Liszt in Rom: Aufzeichnungen" (*Deutsche Revue* [1907]: 71–77; 173–80).

16. "Il exige que Valérie fasse tous les jours deux heures d'exercices matériels sans compter le reste" (9th lesson, January 20, Boissier, *Liszt pédagogue*, 30); "Il fait

tout cela des heures de suite, en lisant pour se désennuyer. C'est alors qu'il médite ses lectures tout en exerçant ses doigts" (8th lesson, January 16, ibid., 22).

17. Liszt to Julius Epstein: "Durch Lehre und Beispiel bilden Sie vortrefflich Ihre meisterhaften Schüler und halten die Tradition der Wiener Klavierschule aufrecht. Dieselbe ist von Mozart auf, mit Hummel, Moscheles, Czerny, Thalberg, Döhler etc. bis auf Liszt herab der Kunst einverleibt" (in *Franz Liszts Briefe*, vol. 8 [*1823–1886: Neue Folge zu Bde. I und II*] ed. La Mara [Leipzig: Breitkopf & Härtel, 1905], 326).

18. Audiotactile theory addresses musical practices such as improvisation, jazz, rock, popular music, etc., not through visual and writing mediation but through sensory mediation. It may also be used to understand nineteenth-century traditions of improvisation and Liszt's physiological approach to piano playing (the piano as an extension of his mind and body). See Vincenzo Caporaletti, *Swing e Groove: Sui fondamenti estetici delle Musiche audiotattili* (Lucca: LIM 2014); CRIJMA, Centre International de Recherche sur le Jazz et les Musiques Audiotactiles, directed by Laurent Cugny and Fabiano Araujo-Costa (http://www.iremus.cnrs.fr). See also Davies's concept of "Handedness," which concerns tactility and bodily sensibility in improvisation: James Q. Davies, *Romantic Anatomies of Performance* (Berkeley: University of California Press, 2014), 51–55, quoted in Dana Gooley, *Fantasies of Improvisation: Free Playing in Nineteenth-Century Music* (London: Oxford University Press, 2018), 165.

19. On Liszt and the philosophy of history applied to his aesthetics, in particular his religious music, see Nicolas Dufetel, "La musique religieuse de Liszt à l'épreuve de la palingénésie de Ballanche: Réforme ou régénération?" *Revue de musicologie* 95, no. 2 (2009): 359–98; Nicolas Dufetel, "Religious Workshop and Gregorian Chant: The Janus Liszt, or How to Make New with the Old," *Liszt's Legacies: Based on Papers Presented at the International Liszt Conference Held at Carleton University, Ottawa, Canada, 28–31 July 2011*, ed. James Deaville and Michael Saffle (Hillsdale, NY: Pendragon Press), 43–71.

20. Rena Charnin Mueller, "Sketches, Drafts and Revisions: Liszt at Work," *Die Projekte der Liszt- Forschung: Bericht über das Internationale Symposion in Eisenstadt 18–21 Oktober 1989*, ed. Detlef Altenburg and Gerhard J. Winkler (Eisenstadt: Burgenländisches Landesmuseum, 1991), 26–34.

21. Rena Charnin Mueller, "Liszt's Indebtedness to Czerny," *Carl Czerny, Komponist, Pianist, Pädagoge*, ed. Heinz von Loesch (Klang und Begriff, vol. 3) (Mainz: Schott, 2009), 147–64.

22. Göllerich, *The Piano Master Classes of Franz Liszt*, 153.

23. [Ed.] See Kenneth Hamilton's chapter in this volume for a discussion of Czerny's compositional influence on Liszt.

24. Helbig, "Franz Liszt in Rom: Aufzeichnungen."

25. Rena Charnin Mueller states that it was used by Liszt from 1829 to 1834 (Rena Charnin Mueller, "Liszt's 'Tasso' Sketchbook: Studies in Sources and Revision," PhD Dissertation [New York University, 1986], 166).
26. [Ed.] For an exploration of the origins and vicissitudes of *Malédiction*, see Kenneth Hamilton's chapter in this volume.
27. For a detailed study of the literary quotes in the Lord Londonderry and N6 sketchbooks (39–40), see Nicolas Dufetel, "Images et citations littéraires dans la musique à programme de Liszt: pour un 'renouvellement de la Musique par son alliance plus intime avec la Poésie,'" *Les colloques de l'Opéra Comique: La modernité française au temps de Berlioz*, ed. Alexandre Dratwicki and Agnès Terrier, http://www.bruzanemediabase.com.
28. Madame Boissier wrote that Liszt once wrote down examples for Valérie, so writing examples is something he apparently did (Boissier, *Liszt pédagogue*, 95).
29. Jim Samson, *Virtuosity and the Musical Work: The "Transcendental Studies" of Liszt* (Cambridge, Cambridge University Press, 2003), 46–47; Gooley, *Fantasies of Improvisation*, 164–65.
30. Ibid., 164.
31. On *Marie-Poème en 6 chants* (inspired by the poetry of Auguste Brizeux), see Adrienne Kaczmarczyk, "Liszt: 'Marie, Poème' (A Planned Piano Cycle)," *Journal of the American Liszt Society* 41 (1997): 88–101. The page from the sketchbook is reproduced in Thérèse Marix-Spire, *Les Romantiques et la musique: Le cas George Sand, 1804–1838* (Paris: Nouvelles éditions latines, 1954), 496–97.
32. Kaczmarczyk, "Liszt: 'Marie, Poème' (A Planned Piano Cycle)."
33. On the *Symphonie révolutionnaire*, see Adrienne Kaczmarczyk "The Genesis of the 'Funérailles': The Connection between Liszt's 'Symphonie révolutionnaire' and the Cycle 'Harmonies poétiques et religieuses,'" *Studia musicologica* 35 (1993–1994): 361–98.
34. In the N8 Sketchbook (D-WRgs 60/N8), Liszt also copied a modulation from Mozart's *Requiem*, which Adrienne Kaczmarczyk links to the *Harmonies poétiques et religieuses*. See Kaczmarczyk, "Liszt: 'Marie, Poème' (A Planned Piano Cycle)."
35. US-NYpm, Mary Flagler Cary Music Coll., L774.S627. The composition sketches and Chopin's and Weber's excerpts are autograph; the other fragments (Mosheles, Weber) are not.
36. "Il a des principes nouveaux, basés sur la raison et sur un sentiment exquis," Caroline Barbey-Boissier, *La comtesse Agénor de Gasparin et sa famille*, 1:160.
37. Ibid., 1:136–99.
38. On Caroline Buttini, see Irène Minder-Jeanneret, "Caroline Boissier-Butini in Paris und London," in *Reiseberichte von Musikerinnen des 19. Jahrhunderts: Quellentexte, Biographien, Kommentare*, ed. Freia Hoffmann (Hildesheim: OMLS, 2011), 37–96, and *"Die beste Musikerin der Stadt": Caroline*

Boissier-Butini (1786–1836) und das Genfer Musikleben zu Beginn des 19. Jahrhundert (Osnabrück, epOS-Verlag, 2013). Irène Minder-Jeanneret also published some of her compositions (Müller & Schade), which have been recorded by pianist Edoardo Torbianelli (Gall).

39. See, for instance, Valérie de Gasparin, *Le mariage du point de vue chrétien* (Paris: Ducloux, 1843); *Journal d'un voyage un Levant: Grèce; l'Égypte et la Nubie; le désert et la Syrie* (Paris: Ducloux, 1848); *Jésus, quelques scènes de sa vie terrestre* (Paris: Calmann Lévy, 1885).

40. John Rink, "Les leçons de Liszt à Valérie Boissier (1832)," *Liszt pédagogue: Actes des Rencontres de Villecroze 15 au 19 septembre 1999*, ed. Claude Viala, http://www.academie-villecroze.com/fr. See also John Rink, "Liszt and the Boissiers: Notes on a Musical Education," *Liszt Society Journal* 31 (2006): 5–36.

41. "Sa tête est remarquablement bien organisée, il remonte aux principes dans tout ce qu'il étudie, ce qui lui donne des notions justes, saines et précises" (16th lesson, February 17, Boissier, *Liszt pédagogue*, 52).

42. "Tous les traits en musique, tous les enchaînements, quels qu'ils soient, se réduisent à un certain nombre de passages fondamentaux qui sont la clef de tout" (16th lesson, February 17, ibid., 49).

43. "Il veut que l'on ramène tous les passages possibles à certaines formules fondamentales d'où découlent toutes les combinaisons que l'on rencontre, et une fois que l'on en a la clef, on les exécute non seulement facilement, mais encore on déchiffre tout à vue" (23rd lesson, March 13, ibid., 78).

44. Rink, "Liszt and the Boissiers: Notes on a Musical Education," 34.

45. On Liszt's teaching in Geneva and his piano method, see Jean Eigeldinger and Jacques Eigeldinger, "Présence et descendance de Liszt au Conservatoire de Genève (1835–1914)," in *Studia Musicologica Academiae Scientiarum Hungaricae* 42, no. 1–2 (*Franz Liszt and Advanced Musical Education in Europe: International Conference*), 2001, 25–46; Alan Walker, *Franz Liszt, Volume 1: The Virtuoso Years, 1811–1847* (Ithaca, NY: Cornell University Press, 1987 rev. ed.), 216–17; Rémy Campos, *Instituer la musique: Les premières années du Conservatoire de Genève (1835–1859)* (Geneva: Éditions Université-Conservatoire de musique, 2003), 241–51; 414–15, especially about Liszt's Piano Method, whose plates may have been destroyed at the Mont-de-Piété in Lyon (Claude Tappolet, *La Vie musicale à Genève au dix-neuvième siècle (1814–1918)* (Geneva: Alex Jullien Libraire, 1972), 44).

46. *Frédéric Chopin: Esquisses pour une méthode de piano*, ed. Jean-Jacques Eigeldinger (Paris: Flammation, 1993).

47. Original in French (private collection): "En attendant, je fais encore une fois (Dieu veuille que ce soit la dernière!) le *pédagogue* à Genève. / . . . L'introduction et la première livraison de la méthode du Conservatoire seront imprimées d'ici à 6 semaines. Elles vous parviendront aussitôt;—Vous pourrez en faire bon usage pour vos élèves. Malheureusement les exercices préparatoires (dont la

classification est entièrement neuve et qui embrassent à peu près une centaine de pages) ne pourront paraître séparément que peu avant les 24 grandes Études originales, c'est à dire vers le mois de septembre 1836. Au reste, pour le dire en passant, l'application de cet ouvrage au Conservatoire de Genève n'est qu'une *épreuve préalable*; plus tard, nous aviserons à mieux. . . . / Peu après, viendront une demi-douzaine de morceaux de la même force ou de la même *faiblesse*. / En somme, ces morceaux ne valent pas grand chose; néanmoins, je ne suis pas fâché de les voir paraître et même, je suis décidé à en écrire un certain nombre dans ce genre. Ils sont pour ainsi dire le *stéréotypage* (passez-moi ce terme correct mais barbare) de mes improvisations et de mes succès de salon. C'est purement et simplement de la *musique de pianiste*. Les œuvres (bonnes ou mauvaises) du compositeur, si tant est qu'il y a un compositeur logé dans ma cervelle, n'affronteront le grand jour qu'un peu plus tard. Deux ou 3 choses que vous connaissez appartiennent à cette série qu'il faudra compléter par / *Les Harmonies poétiques* (inédites) / *Les 24 Études* — / *Marie*, poème en 6 chants / *De Profundis*, Poème avec ouverture (dédié à Mr de Lamennais) / 2 concertos, 2 sextuors, etc., etc."

48. Bruno Moysan, "Les *Technische Studien*, chemin vers la technique de Liszt?" (2012), https://www.jejouedupiano.com/le-mag-du-piano/histoire-documents-les-technische-studien-chemin-vers-la-technique-de-liszt.html#r13.
49. 21st lesson, March 6, Boissier, *Liszt pédagogue*, 68.
50. Private collection. The present author is preparing an edition of this manuscript, together with the other pedagogical sources presented in this chapter.
51. F-Pn, Ms 175.
52. "Rien n'échappe à son analyse; il creuse, il sonde, il étudie en rêveur philosophe, et je ne serais pas surprise de le voir se signaler un jour par un ouvrage profond" (Barbey-Boissier, *La comtesse Agénor de Gasparin et sa famille*, 1:187).
53. Ibid., 199.
54. Walker, *Franz Liszt, Volume 1*, 138. The anecdote is in Lina Ramann, *Franz Liszt als Künstler und Mensch*, vol. 1 (*Die Jahre 1811–1840*) (Leipzig: Breitkopf & Härtel, 1880), 136 (in French).
55. "Il veut aussi des accords frappés sur les mêmes notes, puis les octaves suivies simples et arpégées, des trilles de tous les doigts en maintenant tous les autres appuyés, enfin des notes simples, redoublées, en tenant tous les autres doigts. Il fait tout cela des heures de suite, en lisant pour se désennuyer" (January 16th, Boissie, *Liszt pédagogue*, 22).
56. "Il a encore recommandé des octaves simples et arpégées dans tous les tons, les notes frappées de tous les doigts, en tenant appuyés ceux qui n'entrent pas en action, les gammes rapides et fortes, enfin toute la gymnastique de la main au moins deux heures par jour" (11th lesson, January 31, Boissier, *Liszt pédagogue*, 35).

57. "Il veut qu'on pose les cinq doigts sur les touches, que chacun tour à tour frappe des coups redoublés tandis que les autres sont maintenus immobiles. Ceci pour les rendre parfaitement égaux et indépendants. Le quatrième, le petit, le troisième sont les plus mauvais et ceux sur lesquels on doit fixer son attention; les autres doivent aussi être exercés. Il ordonne donc que chaque jour on exerce chaque doigt un quart d'heure de suite, en le levant très haut et en le posant non sur le bout mais sur le plat du doigt. Cet exercice doit se faire en lisant pour ne pas s'ennuyer" (ibid., 56–57).

58. Alois Schmitt, *Exercices préparatifs servant à acquérir une indépendance et égalité des doigts possible*, op. 16 (Bonn: N. Simrock, 1834). Plate 1618. Bruno Moysan, "Les *Technische Studien*."

59. Muzio Clementi, *Gradus ad Parnassum, ou l'Art de jouer le Piano-Forte, Démontré par des Exercices dans le Style sévère et dans le Style Elégant* (Paris: Mlles Erard, 1817, 1819, 1826), 2 (F-Pn A782, 2). This composite volume entitled "Etudes / Exercices / Préludes" contains on its binding six other titles, all referring to piano technique: Henri Herz, *Exercices et Préludes pour le Piano Forte dans tous les tons majeurs & mineurs* (Paris: Richault) (F-Pn A782, 1); J. Zimmerman, *Collection progressive arrangée et doigtée expressément pour l'étude de ses enfants* (Paris, Chez l'auteur) (F-Pn A782, 4); Henri Herz, *Collection d'Exercices, Passages, Préludes, Sonates, Rondos, Variations, et autres Morceaux d'une difficulté progressive pour le piano* (Paris: Schlesinger) (F-Pn A782, 6). There are also two sets of manuscript exercises: one by Kalkbrenner (F-Pn A782, 5), the other by Liszt (non-autograph): respectively, eleven (repeated and broken chords in twenty-four keys) and three pages (chord and finger positions in twenty-four keys and transitions between all of them), F-Pn A782, 3. The present author is preparing an edition of this manuscript.

60. See F-Pn VM8 S. 146 (Plate Nr J.L.B. 72) and L 6929 (Plate Nr. J.L.B. 72).

61. Göllerich, *The Piano Master Classes of Franz Liszt*, 21.

62. Franz Liszt, *Technische Studien*, ed. Mezö Imre (Budapest, Editio Musica Budapest) *Neue Liszt Ausgabe*, Series 1–2 Suppl., Bd. 1–3), 1:2.

63. F-Pn, Ms 12368. The manuscript is accompanied by a letter by Maréchal on the official paper of the Ministère de l'Instruction Publique et des Beaux-Arts: "*Ministère de l'Instruction Publique et des Beaux-Arts / Beaux-Arts / République Française / Palais Royal, le 7. 2. 1924* / Mon cher M Expert / Je retrouve en de vieux papiers les manuscrits jadis écrits à Rome sous la dictée même de Lisztz [*sic*]! . . . / Ils seront mieux chez vous que chez votre tout dévoué / H. Maréchal / 11bis rue Viète / 17ième." The italics correspond to printed words. The manuscript comprises two series: the first, a folio written on two sides, entitled "Schule des Virtuosenspiels / de Listz (sic)" and dated "Rome—16 Juin 1871" (recto), with sketches; the second, two bifolios (seven written sides) is entitled "Exercices pour le piano / par / F. Liszt" and dated "Rome Juin 1871" and "Roma—24 juin 1871," f. 1r). The later may correspond to a neat copy and

elaboration of the first sketches. It contains chords, scales, thirds, arpeggios, trills (to be played in all twenty-four keys).
64. Alan Walker, *Franz Liszt, Volume 3: The Final Years, 1861–1886* (Ithaca, NY: Cornell University Press, 1997), 229.
65. See above, note 11.
66. Bettina Walker, *My Musical Experiences* (New York: Charles Scribner's Sons, 1892), 108.
67. Ramann, *Liszt-Pädagogium*, II, 6. On the *legatissimo*, See Carl Czerny, *Vollständige theoretisch-praktische Pianoforte-Schule* (Book III, chapter 2), in *Complete Theoretical and Practical Piano Forte School*, 3 Vols., trans. J. A. Hamilton (London: R. Cocks and Co., 1839), vol. 3, 19). For a later definition, see Hugo Riemann, *Vergleichende theoretisch-praktische Klavier-Schule. Eine Anweisung zum Studium der hervorràgendsten Klavier unterrichts Werke* (Leipzig: Kisten, 1883), 12.
68. Ramann, *Liszt-Pädagogium*, II, 6. On the parallel between musical declamation, agogic, and poetry, see Czerny, *Complete Theoretical and Practical Piano Forte School*, 3:6.
69. "Il accentue comme il joue et son âme s'exprime par le verbe comme par la musique" (Boissier, *Liszt pédadogue*, 21 (13th lesson).
70. "Je ne parle pas des prodiges de l'exécution matérielle, mais de la poésie, du souffle, de l'élévation, du pathétique et de la grâce. Souvent en l'entendant, j'éprouvais la même impression qu'en écoutant Berryer ou en lisant Mirabeau ou Bossuet" (Émile Ollivier, *Journal*, vol. 1 [1861–69], ed. Theodore Zeldin and Anne Troisier de Diaz [Paris; R. Julliard, 1961], 21–22 [11 June 1861]). Pierre-Antoine Berryer (1790–1868) was a lawyer and known for being an amazing orator.
71. "Le soir Liszt lit délicieusement des lettres de Mérimée publiées dans la *Revue du 15 août*. Il lit comme il joue en faisant jaillir l'esprit. Il anime comme le vin de Champagne, il fortifie comme du vin bon et vieux" (Carl Alexander, Diary [August 17, 1879], Thüringisches Hauptstaatsarchiv Weimar, Großherzogliches Hausarchiv, A XXVI, 1976 [1879–80], f. 96v–97r).
72. August Göllerich, *Franz Liszt* (Berlin: Marquardt & Co., 1908), 19.

Chapter Four

Paths through the Lisztian Ossia

Jonathan Kregor

About three-quarters of the way through *Vallée d'Obermann*, the anchor of the first book of Franz Liszt's *Années de pèlerinage*, the pianist is confronted with a difficult choice: either play the reading given in normal type at measure 181 and following (ex. 4.1) or select the one above it in slightly smaller print marked "ossia." At first glance, both passages seem to share much in common, including sonorous, open-position right-hand chords and expansive left-hand arpeggios. As each passage develops, however, the differences start to outnumber the similarities. The "ossia" passage introduces accidentals in measure 182 that give the ethereal melody a decidedly melancholic character, while the other remains decidedly in the tonic; only later, at measure 183, does it seem to catch up.

Yet, by that point, the ossia has not only moved much further afield harmonically, but it has also returned to interrogating the piece's main motive, which Liszt has already presented in several clever permutations. Above this primal motivic reprise floats a new arpeggiated figure that seems to have developed out of the preceding left-hand accompaniment and is keen to run through chains of characteristic Lisztian thirds. Meanwhile, the passage in regular type has introduced a hypnotic, oscillating right-hand triplet accompaniment whose high altitude on the keyboard underscores the plaintive features of the melody—another rendition, this time in inversion, of the ubiquitous falling motive—that lies beneath.

Example 4.1. Liszt, *Vallée d'Obermann*, S. 160/6, mm. 180–87

(continued)

Example 4.1.—*(continued)*

(continued)

Example 4.1.—*(concluded)*

To be sure, today it is relatively uncommon to find ossia passages in printed music. Rachmaninoff has a famous one in his Third Piano Concerto, op. 30, as does Beethoven in the first movement of his Fifth, op. 73. Ossia passages can help pianists negotiate some of the thornier spots in Brahms's Piano Sonata in C Major, op. 1, or Glazunov's "Sascha" Suite, op. 2; on the flip side, they can also enhance a performer's virtuosic credentials by providing more difficult or showy readings of shopworn music.[1] Given the hypervirtuosic environment that has grown steadily since Liszt's day, it should come as no surprise that the more difficult alternates have typically become part of a piece's performance tradition: the ossia containing rapid chromatic thirds in the right hand in the climactic middle section of Liszt's Second Concert Étude, *La leggierezza* (mm. 60–65) and the ossia indicating quasi-glissando ascending scales in both hands on the penultimate page of his Second Ballade in B Minor (mm. 292–97) are two famous examples.

The ossia was also a feature of many a nineteenth-century pedagogical edition. Adolph von Henselt routinely employed them in his volumes of Chopin's piano music from the 1870s and 1880s, as did Liszt when he prepared editions of music by Carl Maria von Weber and Franz Schubert about a decade earlier.[2] But since performers and scholars almost unanimously avoid this material—"re-written," as Liszt proudly explained to his editor, "in modern pianoforte form"—the ossia as it was employed by composer-performers in the long nineteenth-century has fallen into near obscurity.[3]

The ossia does endure, however, in the editorial glosses that pepper source-critical editions such as the *Gesamtausgaben* of J. S. Bach, W. A. Mozart, or Chopin (especially the new Peters Edition of the complete works, overseen by John Rink, Jim Samson, Jean-Jacques Eigeldinger, and Christophe Grabowski). Yet, as Theodore Kullak's 1881 edition of Beethoven's First Piano Concerto, op. 15, makes clear (ex. 4.2), in this capacity the ossia occupies a significantly different function than it does in, say, *Vallée d'Obermann*. For Kullak, ossia passages document how the editor arrived at the reading in normal type.[4] The single F with wedge and subsequent slurred sigh figure that appear in Beethoven's autograph manuscript and Breitkopf & Härtel's complete edition from 1862 do not reconcile with the musical context; thus, Kullak elects to follow Tranquillo Mollo's 1801 print that does. Yet, in the very next measure, the editor deems Mollo's reading problematic and presumably follows Beethoven's autograph for the reading of measure 289 in normal type. Rather than present readings of equal status, then, the ossia passages as employed by Kullak indicate a qualitative difference, in which the passages in smaller type are scientifically important but, ultimately, ontologically and practically irrelevant.[5]

Approaching *Vallée d'Obermann*'s only ossia passage as an editorial problem does not solve the performer's dilemma. Simply identifying and cataloging aspects of motive, harmony, and other features mentioned above does not yield a favorite on the basis of authorial "authenticity," since each passage in the aggregate is arguably a textbook case of Liszt's midcentury pianistic and compositional styles. Neither passage can be identified as being composed earlier or later than the other, since both appear in the same manuscript and

Example 4.2. Beethoven, Piano Concerto no. 1 in C Major, op. 15, I, mm. 287–89, ed. Kullak (1881).

same publication. In fact, on the basis of comparison with the earlier version of *Vallée d'Obermann* (S. 156/5 / LW A40a/4), which Liszt published as part of the first book of his *Album d'un voyageur* in 1842 and which contains no ossia passages, it is clear that Liszt composed both the main and ossia readings exclusively for the final version that appeared in the *Années de pèlerinage*.[6]

If neither style nor archaeology can settle the issue, then what about technical difficulty? Both passages in fact require about the same level of skill—and even if one's technique precluded the performance of one passage over the other, Liszt's oeuvre proves conclusively that he did not reserve the small grand staff exclusively for simpler or harder alternative material. Finally, while the upper reading might not draw the eye as easily as its lower neighbor because of its subordinate size, its physical presentation can probably be attributed more to contemporary notational convention than aesthetic privilege. Yet despite the challenges to the orthodoxy that this bifurcated reading presents, today's pianists treat Liszt's ossia for *Vallée d'Obermann* as more informational than actionable—indeed, almost no major recording of the past half century features it, nor do most pianists deign to perform it live.[7]

The questions posed by *Vallée d'Obermann*'s ossia speak to an extraordinarily complex situation that is largely unique to Liszt and his music.[8] First, ossia passages litter his scores, with more than one thousand appearing in the published solo piano music, which will be the focus of this chapter.[9] Second, while "ossia" was characterized as early as 1880 as a term "used *indifferently* to mark a passage . . . which may be substituted for that written in the body or text of the work," many of Liszt's so-called alternatives often strongly affect fundamental components of the composition that in turn significantly reshape its overall profile and attendant effect.[10]

(By extension, their interchangeability should not presume a random or ambivalent deployment.) Third, and related to number two, regards the choice that the performer must make when confronting the ossia: Does he always choose the harder option to show off his virtuosic credentials? Does she select the passage that is better written and thus demonstrates her refined musical taste?[11] In other words, how does the presence or absence of an ossia passage or passages affect musical perception? To what extent, if any, are today's musicians obliged to preserve and present these "supplemental" components of Liszt's music?[12] Finally, if Liszt's ossia passages are considered longitudinally, what can be gleaned about elements of his virtuosity, his ideas on the integrity of the musical work, the ways in which the ossia might operate within the spectrum of spontaneous improvisation and fixed notation, the musical legacy he wished to leave, and the ways in which his musical legacy has been presented?

Supplementing Virtuosity

The ossia played an important role in Liszt's self-fashioned image as a Romantic virtuoso. In fact, ossia passages first show up in works released in the mid-1830s that consciously set out on a path much different from that of his published music from the 1820s and early 1830s, which remains strongly indebted to the pianism of Johann Nepomuk Hummel, the operatic strains of Gioachino Rossini, and the compositional models endorsed and employed by his teacher, Carl Czerny. Indeed, only after Liszt had come into contact with Frédéric Chopin, Hector Berlioz, Niccolò Paganini, Sigismond Thalberg, and other members of Paris's artistic elite did his compositions, playing, and general identity assume characteristics that would define him well beyond his long, multifaceted career.

Liszt's earliest ossia passages appear in his arrangement of Hector Berlioz's *Symphonie fantastique* (S. 470 / LW A16a) and his own *Grande fantaisie de bravoure sur "La clochette" de Paganini* (S. 420 / LW A15), two major works written for public presentation that directly resulted from a series of artistic awakenings Liszt experienced in 1832 and 1833.[13] On the one hand, these two virtuosic solo piano works could not be more different, with the Berlioz arrangement seeking to replicate, to a slavish degree, the beautiful bombast, excesses, and contradictions of one of Romanticism's most iconic compositions. The other seeks to upstage the beautiful bombast, excesses, and contradictions of one of Romanticism's most iconic performers. But both projects are connected by Liszt's urgent need to remedy the self-perceived deficiencies of his artistic identity.

Example 4.3, excerpted from a particularly rich moment of orchestral activity in the first movement of the *Symphonie fantastique*, seems to justify the praise that Liszt's *partitions de piano* of Berlioz's and Beethoven's symphonic works from the 1830s have routinely occasioned. The ossia-like cue staff carefully supplements the grand staff reading of sextuplet violins and, in counterpoint between violas and cellos, the idée fixe—clearly the most thematically important component of the passage—by means of the oboe's obbligato countermelody, under which the winds provide harmonic support at regular but off-beat metrical intervals. Without doubt, Liszt's careful attention to and virtuosic ability at re-presenting the symphony in all its rich detail proved vital to a rational critic like Robert Schumann, who seems to have had no problem conjuring up Berlioz's massive orchestral complex from Liszt's piano score.[14]

Other passages in the *Symphonie fantastique* arrangement provide valuable information about how Liszt prioritized his musical materials and what makes for an appropriate alternative. Take the penultimate page of the *Symphonie fantastique* arrangement (ex. 4.4), which features two out of the work's five ossia passages. Both right-hand readings at measure 486 share the same tremolando figurations, which thus imbue the section with similar characters, but the ossia passage's traversal of three octaves introduces a distinctly pianistic texture into Berlioz's orchestra. At the same time, choosing this ossia passage has important ramifications for how a pianist and listener might process the remainder of the phrase, since the single gesture of Liszt's ossia replaces two distinctly patterned passages (mm. 486–90, 490–92) in the main reading. The ossia passage at measure 496 and following illustrates the opposite case: the main reading's left hand repeats exactly in four-measure phrases (mm. 496–99, 500–503), yet Liszt's alternative left hand is "through-composed," offering different spacings, inversions, and melodic contours from one phrase to the next. Indeed, while pattern-for-pattern replacement is very common among Liszt's ossias, nuances like these suggest that Liszt did not insert them mechanically or carelessly. Finally, both ossia passages also emphasize how the ossia usually affects one hand exclusively or disproportionately privileges one hand over the other and that—at least in Liszt's early music—a sonic ideal was arguably as strong a pursuit as virtuosic showmanship.

Example 4.3. Berlioz/Liszt, *Symphonie fantastique*, S. 470, I, mm. 358–62

Ideals are hard to live up to, of course, and the arrangement of the *Symphonie fantastique* seems to want to have it both ways: it promises a complete "piano score" (*partition de piano*) of Berlioz's original, yet it also consciously qualifies such a claim by presenting alternative options in ossia and cue passages. If the grand staff is the language through which a pianist processes and communicates musical material, then the addition of another staff (or staves) can lead only to ambivalence, misunderstanding, or confusion. Likewise, by introducing supplemental material that challenges, say, the thematic priority of the grand staff's reading (ex. 4.3) or parses it differently (ex. 4.4), Liszt not only ostensibly perverts traditional musical hierarchies but projects a vulnerability—even inadequacy—that is uncharacteristic of the larger-than-life figure that Liszt sought to cultivate during his virtuoso years.

On the other hand, the ossia as presented in Liszt's music seems to challenge the notion that complete communication can truly occur through established conventions of written notation. An admission of incompleteness undergirds the numerous notational supplements that Liszt employs in his contemporaneous works, such as the single-movement *Harmonies poétiques et religieuses* (S. 154 / LW A18, 1833–34) (avoiding key and time signatures), *Apparitions* (S. 155 / LW A 19, 1834) (adding white space between measures to indicate some kind of pause), and his essay *De la situation des artistes et de leur condition dans la société* (1835) (exaggerated ellipses, excessive font variance). Indeed, Liszt's Parisian corpus reverberates strongly with Jacques Derrida's "logic of the supplement" (that which is simultaneously necessary and superfluous, inside and outside the work), in which "substitution and accretion" result from the perennial attempt to incorporate presence and account for absence simultaneously.[15]

Example 4.4. Berlioz/Liszt, *Symphonie fantastique*, S. 470, V, mm. 486–503

(continued)

Example 4.4.—*(concluded)*

If substitution is a foundational feature of the supplemental passages in the *Symphonie fantastique* arrangement, then it is accretion that motivates their use in Liszt's "Clochette" Fantasy, one of the most technically formidable pieces to come from his pen during his Paris years. Even he seems to have been daunted by it—for it is the only piece in Liszt's oeuvre to include an easier and more practical alternative that Liszt himself took in performance. The passage comes at measure 199 (ex. 4.5), where Paganini's ritornello melody inveigles its way into written-out tremolo octaves and chromatic turns. The texture is thick; the spacing, claustrophobic. An alternative passage, printed above with the explanation that it was "performed by the author," alleviates many of the challenges posed by the main reading: the tremolos now follow a consistent down-up pattern, whereas in the main reading they switch direction haphazardly.[16] Likewise, the A♭–G–F♯–G turn that the thumbs must figure out how to juggle has been eliminated to allow the pianist to better realize Liszt's instruction of *marcato il canto*. On the one hand, choosing Liszt's alternative sacrifices a modicum of contrapuntal ingenuity and motivic development. But, on the other, if the pianist can better profile

Example 4.5. Liszt, "Clochette" Fantasy, S. 420, mm. 199–200

the melody, still adhere to the spirit of the original, and even enhance its effect, then it is arguably a worthy sacrifice to make.

While a performer must ultimately select one reading, the presence of an ossia actually removes the onus of choice from the composer: Liszt can have it both ways. Indeed, these two measures of the "Clochette" Fantasy distill a fundamental tension endemic to Liszt's early virtuoso years, in which compositional ideals and performance practicalities collide. For while this example serves as a reminder that Liszt did not always adhere to the letter of the score in the course of performance, it also raises several questions: If the ossia documents how Liszt presented this passage to his public, why did he not just adopt it as the fantasy's main reading? Can pianists assume that they are allowed to play the "Clochette" Fantasy the way he played it, or does Liszt—as the work's author—have an exclusive license to "recompose" the piece however he sees fit? In other words, is the very existence of this type of ossia a concession to or fulfillment of the virtuoso ideal?[17]

That the ossia is intimately tied to this ongoing dialogue on the tenets of his virtuosity is clear in Liszt's next Paganini-inspired work, the *Études d'exécution transcendante d'après Paganini* (S. 140 / LW A52, 1838). Scholars routinely turn to this collection over the "Clochette" Fantasy as Liszt's best transformation of Paganini's art to the piano, a transformation that helped Liszt achieve a half-decade-long goal of becoming "an artist such as you demand, such as is needed these days," as he had deliriously written to Pierre Wolff in 1832, following a concert that the storied violin virtuoso had recently given in Paris.[18] While ossia passages are few in this collection of études, they do in fact support that argument—primarily by militantly establishing a position of superiority. Especially noteworthy in this respect is the forty-nine-measure long ossia passage in the sixty-four-measure-long first étude, which is not of Liszt's making but is rather a slight alteration of Robert Schumann's *Études de concert d'après des Caprices de Paganini*, op. 10, no. 2.[19] Liszt must have become aware of this set of piano studies between November 1837, when he published a generally positive review of Schumann's opp. 5, 11, and 14, and April 1838, when Clara Wieck introduced Liszt to *Carnaval*, the *Fantasiestücke*, and other piano works composed by her clandestine lover that were being overshadowed on concert stages by glitzy, popular virtuosic piano works.[20]

Economically, the republication of Schumann's study in Liszt's is wasteful, since it almost doubles the amount of space needed for publication. Ontologically, it is subversive. Stylistically, it is disruptive. Transcendentally, however, it is ideal. For if transcendence is measured in terms of technical benchmarks—"designed," as Jim Samson observes, "to exclude not just the mediocre performer, but the best performers of the day"—then presenting Schumann's study as an alternative to Liszt's rendition serves to highlight the enormous virtuosic divide that separates him from one of his most thoughtful and creative competitors.[21]

It is worth emphasizing that at this point in his career, Liszt was working hard to establish himself as Europe's preeminent virtuoso. His performance repertory, the choice of melodies for his opera fantasies, the often critical reviews he wrote, and of course his highly publicized feud with Thalberg all contribute to this goal. The ossia passages are more subtle, but nonetheless highly effective, in supporting this mission. Still, while a pianist like Alfred Cortot cited pianistic rivalry as the reason why Schumann's music appeared in Liszt's étude, Liszt himself justified its presence to his publisher Giovanni Pacini on both technical and artistic grounds: "In addition, you had better . . . reprint directly [after my étude] the *Étude facilitée* that I have also sent you.[22] This second arrangement is by M. Schumann, a young composer of very great merit. It is more accessible to the public, and also more exact than my *paraphrase*."[23]

As it happened, Schumann's study—whose authorship is given in a footnote—hovered silently above Liszt's version when the collection appeared in

Example 4.6. Liszt, *Études d'exécution transcendante d'après Paganini*, S. 140/1, mm. 6–7

*) Cette seconde version est celle de M. Robert Schumann

1840 (see ex. 4.6), allowing the public to make direct, measure-for-measure comparisons between the two musicians. Schumann seems to have understood the impetus behind the design, explaining in a review of Liszt's collection that "if the Schumann arrangement tries to bring out the poetic side of [Paganini's] composition, then Liszt—without misjudging them in the least—emphasizes more of the virtuosic."[24] Tellingly, when Liszt revised this collection in the early 1850s, making this distinction seems to have been less important, as Schumann's study is nowhere to be found.

About the same time that he was working through the first version of his Paganini studies, Liszt was preparing three sets of arrangements that would serve him well for his virtuoso years and beyond: *12 Lieder*, *Schwanengesang*, and *Winterreise*. The second collection is particularly germane, since all but one of the fourteen songs contain ossia passages, many significant in terms of length, technical demands, and content. On the one hand, several ossia passages feature facilitated readings, such as in "Liebesbotschaft," where closed-position triads relieve the right hand from playing unbroken dyads of a tenth, or "Die Taubenpost," which replaces the main reading's thick, three-part texture of melody in octaves, jaunty bass, and arpeggiated inner voice with a distribution reminiscent of the nocturnes of Chopin and especially of John Field.[25] On the other hand, Liszt employs a bait-and-switch tactic in "Frühlingssehnsucht," whereby a simplified ossia at measure 62 lulls the pianist into a false sense of technical security, only to continue in measure 112 and following with a main reading sans ossia that is even more difficult than anything that has preceded it. Finally, some ossia passages elsewhere in the collection are not necessarily easier or more difficult but simply offer different ways of rendering Schubert's accompaniments, such as in "Der Atlas" or "Der Doppelgänger."

In all of the examples discussed so far, the performer can move between ossia and main reading on a measure-for-measure—oftentimes even a beat-for-beat—basis. This type of ossia, by far the most common, offers a one-to-one replacement. Recalling example 4.4, for instance, there is no reason that in the *Symphonie fantastique* arrangement—especially given Liszt's proclivity to spontaneous improvisation—a pianist could not opt for measures 486–90 of the ossia and then switch to the main reading in the second half of measure 490. But another type of ossia occurs frequently enough in Liszt's music that the *New Liszt Edition* has christened it the *Entweder/Oder*—the "either/or." Unlike the one-to-one ossia, with the either/or the performer must commit to a chosen reading and see it through to the end. Hence this type might be syntactically styled as a one-not-one ossia.

In "Das Fischermädchen," for instance, what Liszt calls a "second Ritornello" begins at measure 70 as an ossia but replaces the main reading two measures later, while in the famous "Ständchen" a far more complex situation arises. The first two verses of this arrangement include an *ossia più facile* that eliminates the right hand playing two-against-three in verse 1 and the crowded textures of verse 2. The either/or begins at measure 62, where, as example 4.7 illustrates by means of vertical juxtaposition, the two readings are close but often out of alignment. The pianist who

Example 4.7. Schubert/Liszt, "Ständchen," S. 560/7, mm. 62–76

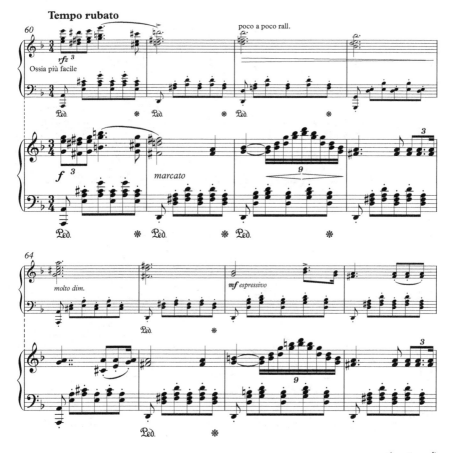

(continued)

Example 4.7.—*(concluded)*

elects for the simpler alternative is obligated to end the piece at measure 76, by which time the main reading has moved on to a third verse that employs a beautiful, dramatically appropriate duet between the lovers, which is followed by a stormy rendition of Ludwig Rellstab's fifth and final stanza at measure 91 and following, a cadenza at measure 106, and an ethereal conclusion that fades out to *quasi niente*—material to which a less gifted or ambitious player does not have access.

Presenting Alternatives

Whether born out of homage, competition, hubris, self-fashioning, or attempts to establish epistemological boundaries, the common denominator across the examples discussed so far has been one of opposition: between Berlioz and Liszt, Paganini and Liszt, Schumann and Liszt, Schubert and Liszt, between piano and orchestra, between musical reactions to the same poem, between compositional design and technical realization, between the ideal and the practical. Recognizing it as a benchmark of mutually opposed categories helps explain another key characteristic of the Lisztian ossia, namely, that it appears far more frequently in Liszt's arrangements or paraphrases than in his works not based on preexisting material. The twenty-four volumes of "free arrangements and transcriptions" that comprise series 2 of the *New Liszt Edition* (*NLE*) include 610 alternative passages spread across 184 works. (For the sake of practicality, a "work" is here defined at the level of the movement; thus Beethoven's "Pastoral" Symphony is treated as five separate works.) Of these, 48 are cue passages, and 27 are student transmissions—which will be discussed below. The label "ossia" is given to 412, of which 64 are designated as easier, 17 as harder; the rest carry no facility designation. The 36 "either/or" passages are either labeled "ossia" or involve cuts. If the three volumes of "Klavier-Versionen Eigener Werke" from series 1 are added to this group of two dozen volumes, then 54 alternative passages, of which 35 are labeled "ossia" and 12 are cue, can be added to the grand total. A summary of these data appears in figure 4.1.

Even though three-quarters of Liszt's ossia passages appear in his arrangements, that still leaves more than 140 alternatives to review in the fifteen volumes of "original" music from series 1, which include pieces like the Hungarian Rhapsodies, the three books of *Années de pèlerinage*, the Ballades, the Sonata in B Minor, and numerous character pieces. As figure 4.2 shows, 112 passages are labeled simply "ossia," 4 are explicitly listed as easier, and 5

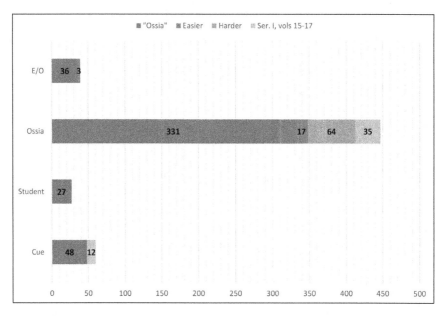

Figure 4.1. Ossia passages in *NLE* 1: 15–17 and 2 (arrangements)

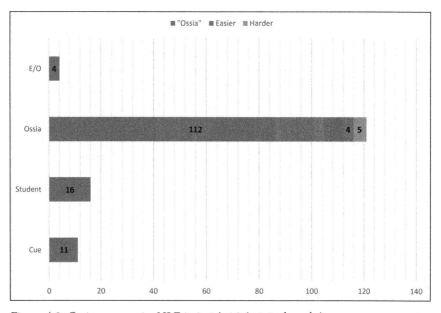

Figure 4.2. Ossia passages in *NLE* 1: 1–14, 18 (original works)

are presented as more difficult. Of those 112 neutrally labeled passages, most are easier to play than their respective main readings, while others require approximately the same skill level. Indeed, although these ossias are attached to "original" works, they generally follow the same precepts as those in Liszt's arrangements, with a greater tendency toward modifying textures and replacing patterns than prioritizing or subordinating melody and altering harmony. However, one notable difference regarding the ossia between the two *NLE* series is location: in series 1, Liszt tends to feature the ossia more frequently at the ends of sections. A typical example comes in the *Cadenza ad libitum* in measures 41 and following and 153 and following of the *Mazurka brillante* (S. 221 / LW A168, 1850) or in the compression of the cadence in measure 24 of *Vexilla regis prodeunt* (S. 185 / LW A226, 1864) from two measures to one. Indeed, such notated additions document an ongoing, improvisation-based performance practice that he had first explicitly set to paper decades earlier in the "Clochette" Fantasy (see ex. 4.5).

At the same time, a handful of ossia passages in series 1 differ substantially from their main reading counterparts. *Vallée d'Obermann*, discussed above, offers one pithy but probing example. The fifteenth Hungarian Rhapsody, a brilliant concert version of the famous Rákóczi March, actually offers two unique ossia passages that begin at measure 171 (ex. 4.8): one simplifies the double stop glissandi in the right hand; the other reimagines that right hand as unmoored, leaping boisterously by tenths, twelfths, even fourteenths, while the left hand subtly introduces some chromatic alterations at measure 174 that result in a half cadence instead of the main reading's closure on the minor subdominant. Differences between the main reading and the ossia occasionally prompt significant editorial explication, such as the assertion in a footnote for the aforementioned ossia passage at measures 60–65 in the second of the three *Études de concert* (*La leggierezza*) that "this *Ossia* is, exceptionally, of equal value to the principal text both as regards technique and range; indeed it adheres even more closely to the preceding material of the piece than does the figurative passage-work of the principal text."[26] The surprise with which the editors characterize the success of this alternative passage speaks volumes about the general ambivalence, even bias, that still plagues the Lisztian ossia.[27]

All of the statistics and almost all of the examples presented up to this point draw on Liszt's piano music as presented in the *NLE*, which to date comprises fifty-five volumes, including thirteen of fifteen planned supplemental volumes. For the most part, data collection has been limited to compositions published during Liszt's lifetime, since he presumably had final

Example 4.8. Liszt, Hungarian Rhapsody no. 15, S. 244/15, mm. 171, 174–75

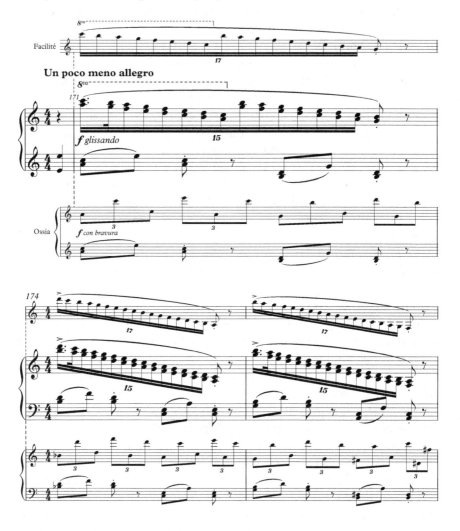

say over the presentation of his music, ossia passages included. For material Liszt did not usher into print, such as the intermediate version of the suite *Harmonies poétiques et religieuses* (S. 172a / LW A61) from the 1840s and early 1850s, one cannot necessarily assume that what appears in manuscript would have made it into the published print.[28]

Besides being comprehensive, the *NLE* is an attractive resource for two practical reasons: First, it would be extraordinarily difficult for one person to collect and adequately assess the myriad contemporary editions of Liszt's compositions, especially those that appeared in the 1830s and 1840s. For instance, many Italian editions published during Liszt's years of pilgrimage and early *Glanzzeit* include substantially different readings than their northern European counterparts, thus frustrating an editor's attempt to establish a definitive "Fassung letzter Hand."[29] Even small differences can have big implications: for instance, three out of the four earliest editions of the *Paganini Études* published in 1840 do not credit Schumann as the composer of the ossia featured in the first étude. Processing this vast cache of material by means of a single, multifaceted resource considerably reduces the overwhelming challenges.[30]

Second, the *NLE* is peerless in its authority. As *the* critical edition of Liszt's music, one assumes that it is complete, accurate, and follows philological and source-critical practices that have been fine-tuned since around the time that Kullak put together his edition of Beethoven's First Piano Concerto, op. 15 (see ex. 4.2). Scholars defer to its readings in their work, faculty refer students to it for research, and piano teachers often encourage their studios to use it over the competition whenever possible. For better or worse, it is the edition through which most scholars and performers communicate Liszt's music.

As the *NLE* celebrates its fiftieth anniversary, it is worth considering how its editorial standards have changed, particularly regarding alternatives like editions, versions, and ossia passages. The preface to series 1, written by Zoltán Gárdonyi and István Szelenyi in the summer of 1969, introduces Liszt's ossia passages as necessary products of their time that have little relevance today: "The variant passages which Liszt indicated with an *ossia* for use with pianos with a limited range could be reduced as the versions for instruments with a range of less than seven octaves are unnecessary in modern practice."[31]

Far more important is the next and final paragraph of the general preface, which states that "the musical text of the *NLE* contains in the form of footnotes all editorial suggestions appropriate to practical considerations and performing technique. The primary aim has always been to proceed as much as possible in the spirit of the 'Liszt Pedagogy.'"[32] As its full title of *Franz Liszt's Piano Compositions, Supplemented by Unedited Changes, Additions, and Cadenzas according to the Master's Teachings, Pedagogically Glossed by Lina Ramann* clunkily explains, the so-called Liszt Pädagogium contains alternatives to Liszt's published music that he composed and in turn authorized his students to adopt in performance.[33] A general preface to series 2 of the

NLE appeared in 1987, and it expanded its coverage to include "Liszt's verbal directions for performance put down by August Göllerich into his diary after his piano classes with Liszt . . . and in other trustworthy sources."[34]

The *Liszt-Pädagogium* supplies the *NLE* with forty-three alternative passages for nine pieces in series 1 and 2; in short, enough material to warrant a separate category of ossia—what tables 4.1 and 4.2 present as "student transmission." Many are cadenzas or cadenza extensions written for Lina Schmalhausen, Toni Raab, Sophie Menter, and Giovanni Sgambati, while the others are transcriptions of Liszt's own emendations, including substantial and significant changes to the *Réminiscences de "Robert le diable"* (S. 413 / LW A78) and the *Tarantelle di bravura d'après la tarantelle de "La muette" de Portici* (S. 386/1 / LW A125, 1846, second version 1869).[35] The most famous is his replacement of the last six measures of the Third Concert Étude, *Un sospiro* (S. 144/3 / LW A118/3), with a seven-measure passage whose bass line descends two octaves via a whole-tone scale, thus producing a nice avant-garde counterpart to the octatonic descent that almost immediately precedes it.[36] Less well known is Liszt's recommendation that the *quasi cadenza* ossia passage at measure 138 of the *Valse-impromptu* (S. 213 / LW A 84c) be extended "ad libitum," and that Liszt often added short extensions to final cadences of three of the *Fünf ungarische Volkslieder* (S. 245 / LW A263)—small but important evidence that he and his circle treated the ossia as a viable option in performance. In fact, there is ample documentation to show that Liszt's comments in the *Pädagogium* are not isolated cases.[37]

Performing Choice

If Liszt wrote it, if he performed it, and if he advocated for its use, then the ossia should be acknowledged—if not treated practically—as a fundamental, inseparable component of his music. By and large, either in scholarship or practice, this has not happened: Peter Szendy has characterized Liszt's use of ossia in his arrangement of Beethoven's "Pastoral" Symphony (1837, revised in 1863–64) as a way to compensate "for the impossible by multiplying the possibilities"—a trenchant observation that admits the limitations and even defects inherent in music's semiotic code but nevertheless still posits the ossia as an emblem of disability, lack, and devaluation.[38]

Performers who have applied the core messages of Kenneth Hamilton's *After the Golden Age* to the ossia have been greeted with critical suspicion.[39] Alfredo Perl was taken to task by *Gramophone* reviewer Bryce Morrison for "surprisingly [using] Liszt's ossia in the final descent from the central fulminating uproar" in *Vision*, from the *Transcendental Études* (no. 6). Perl's infraction presumably begins at measure 56 (ex. 4.9), where Liszt offers the pianist an alternative right hand of chords whose contour mirrors that of the main reading. Morrison considers this ossia—as well as parallel passages at measures 60 and 62—to be "a less glittering alternative."[40] But if glitter is to be equated with keyboard-hopping arpeggios, then *Vision* arguably sparkles too brightly. (On the contrary, the ossia passage that Liszt offers the pianist toward the end of the dreamy slow section in *Mazeppa*, mm. 97–99, is dramatically underwhelming, and in many ways contradicts the "transcendental" nature of the étude.) Liszt, always cognizant of the effect that his music would have in performance, may well have supplied an ossia to offer a welcome new texture to pianist and audience alike. Indeed, many ossia passages strewn about his oeuvre appear at junctures where repetition—of a texture, figuration, or decorative device—becomes too technically or aurally taxing.[41]

While Kirill Gerstein opts for Liszt's ossia passages in his 2016 recording of the *Transcendental Études*, such choices remain rare among professional pianists.[42] The stigma of deviating from the established text—even if the deviation is authoritative—remains great. Leslie Howard has striven to include Liszt's ossia passages as part of his monumental recording project, but these are always carefully presented as subordinate—as opposed to coequal—options. Even the *NLE* is cautious about the potential effect that Liszt's ossia passages might have on a performer's reception. For instance, it includes two replacement passages of 30 and 120 measures, respectively, in its edition of the First Mephisto Waltz, which, if adopted, would be "expedient to mention . . . in concert programmes if they are to be included."[43]

Unfortunately, such a notice is inadequate for most of Liszt's music that contain ossia passages. Take *Schlaflos! Frage und Antwort* (S. 203 / LW A322). A relatively humble piano piece from Liszt's late years, it demonstrates the difficulty involved in establishing a definitive reading when the ossia is added to the interpretive mix. Example 4.10 reprints the complete work as edited by José Vianna da Motta for the so-called *Old Liszt Edition*.[44] The two parts of Liszt's composition presumably follow the structure of the eponymous, lost poem written by his pupil, Antonia "Toni" Raab: the first section an impassioned nocturne with an accompanimental figure that fixates on a couple of mildly dissonant harmonies and a right-hand melody in octaves that rises and falls through a couple of tritone windows; the second section a subdued *andante quieto* that sheds the insomniac's restlessness for the comfort of homophonic chorales and, later, monophonic intimacy. The two sections

Example 4.9. Liszt, *Études d'exécution transcendante* no. 6, *Vision*, S. 139/6, mm. 55–56

are bound by a recitative-like passage that ostensibly helps explain the key signature changing from one sharp to four. (As seen at m. 50, the *Old* and *New Liszt Editions* disagree on where the cut extends.) Each section has one large ossia passage, and the first has two additional short ones. Taken as a whole, then, these passages allow for twelve legitimate versions of *Schlaflos!* to be fashioned. But even if the focus were restricted exclusively to the two major ossias—the passages labelled *B* and *C* in example 4.10, which are of the "either/or" type—four scenarios remain.

By what criteria should the pianist choose the listener's aural adventure? Programmatically, if he wishes to emphasize the neurotic features of Liszt's insomniac, then he might prolong the main reading's harmonically obstinate left hand as long as possible—B2; likewise, if he understands the question's "answer" to be sleep, then the second section's main reading, C2, is arguably more appropriate. On the contrary, if sleep is taken to be more metaphorical

Example 4.10. Liszt, *Schlaflos! Frage und Antwort*, S. 203, complete, ed. José Vianna da Motta (1927), annotated

(continued)

Example 4.10.—*(continued)*

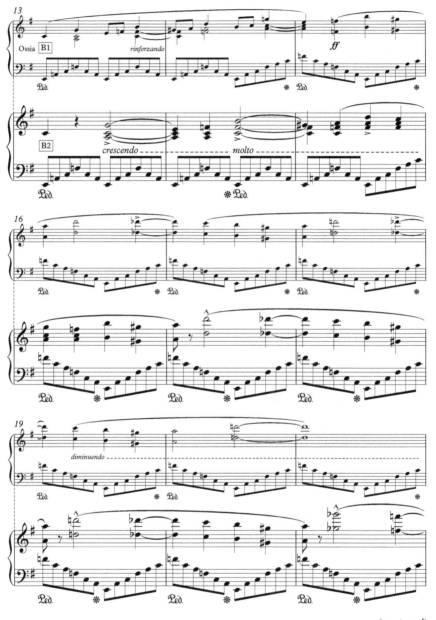

(continued)

Example 4.10.—*(continued)*

(continued)

Example 4.10.—*(continued)*

(continued)

Example 4.10.—*(concluded)*

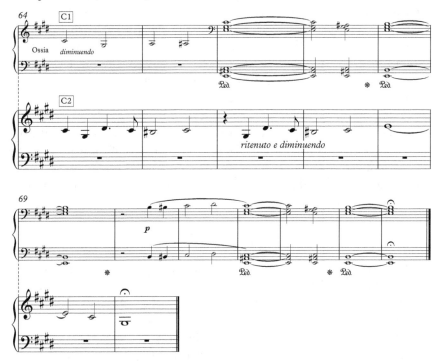

than literal, more definitive than temporary, then the urgency of the first section's ossia—B1, with its compressed content and dramatic, abrupt conclusion on a half-diminished seventh chord—might better reflect the protagonist's death throes, just as the familiar texture, rich harmonies, and similar character of the other ossia, C1, arguably better extends the religious consolations of the second section.

Other considerations materialize if the performer chooses to treat the title like an ossia—that is, by either forgetting it or at least lowering its hermeneutic priority. If she likes the idea of having temporal balance, then the main readings suffice—most recordings of this piece that select ossias B2 and C2 clock in around two and a half minutes, the two sections often being of near equal length. If maintaining motivic consistency is important, then the top ossia in measure 3, A1, is her best bet, since the rhythmic profiles of the other ossia, A2, and the main reading, A3, appear nowhere else in the heavily repetitive composition. If she chooses to exhibit the developmental nature of *Schlaflos!*, then it would behoove the pianist to forgo the ossia at measure 13, since the tritone interval of D–G♯ that bookends the melody at measure 15 and following is widened to G♭–B at measure 21, thus delineating an important structural pillar in the first section. Likewise, adhering to the second section's main reading, C2, enhances the impression of harmonic development by suggesting—but never really committing to—C-sharp minor, a far cry from the E-minor "feel" of the work's opening. Or the ear might be drawn to the non-diatonic A♯ that appears in measure 2 of the left hand and returns sporadically thereafter, and thus one could justify Liszt's alternative conclusion, C1, in which an A♯ plays an important harmonic and melodic role. Or maybe audiences just like the idea of ending on a definitive, diatonic harmony like E major, especially given the harmonic turmoil that preceded it. That alone could form the basis for a legitimate, well-rehearsed musical narrative.[45]

Well-performed music should supply surprise in abundance. In Western classical music, which overwhelmingly favors exclusive repertories and performance traditions, surprise often shows up in the little things: a bold *crescendo*, a pause pregnant with tension, a heretofore unheard inner voice. Such nuances can make a well-known composition seem completely new and consequently imbue its performer with a singular artistic persona. Indeed, for the vast majority of the classical canon, interpreting a composition along these lines is enough to articulate it successfully, to make the familiar familial.

The Lisztian ossia adds a wrinkle to this tidy interpretive system. Easily dismissed, in his hands it becomes a tool for fomenting otherness: by bifurcating the musical reading, ossia passages visually disrupt the tidy linearity of the score. Ossia-like cue notes appearing in his transcriptions highlight the aural gulf between piano and large ensemble. Performing a work's *facilité* passages contaminates its virtuosic cachet, whereas adopting *più difficile* passages adds to its technical monstrosity. Ossia passages of extended length can even mount a convincing ontological challenge to a composition. Emil von Sauer's 1917 edition of Liszt's *Don Juan* Fantasy, for instance, relegates an extensive ossia written by Liszt to the appendix. In doing so, Sauer determines a clear favorite among two choices that, at least in Liszt's design, are to be treated as equal. Yet Sauer, who was affiliated with Liszt between 1884 and 1886, justifies his decision on account of modern performance tradition, in which Liszt's 119 measures of music are "seldom played in the concert hall these days."[46]

A year after Sauer's edition appeared, Ferruccio Busoni released his "instructive edition" of Liszt's *Don Juan* Fantasy. Busoni justified his copious and carefully notated deviations from Liszt's score as emanating from the same performance tradition that inspired Liszt to write down his fantasy in the first place.[47] In other words, the "editor" Busoni eagerly took on the ossia's inherent mandate to become co-composer. While his results might come off as monstrous aberrations of a sacrosanct urtext, they underscore how Liszt's ossia passages routinely defamiliarize the work to which they belong, adding an atraditional dose of surprise.

The ubiquity of the ossia in Liszt's oeuvre also serves as a powerful reminder that the performer—and not the composer—ultimately has the final say in how a piece of music is presented. Indeed, much has still been left unsaid, for *Schlaflos!* and *Vallée d'Obermann* are only tips of an enormous, mostly unexplored iceberg: Liszt's rendition of the waltz and act 2 duet from Gounod's *Faust* (S. 407 / LW A208), for instance, presents the pianist with 384 possible versions; the *Mephisto Polka* (S. 217 / LW A317) 16,384 renditions; and the fantastic arrangement of the *William Tell* Overture (S. 552 / LW A54) just over one billion (2^{30}) authorized permutations. In good virtuoso fashion, then, Liszt invites pianists to tailor his music according to personal taste, technical ability, and audience desire, thus ensuring innumerable challenges and rewards for generations to come.

Notes

1. For instance, consider the case of Busoni, as discussed in Erinn E. Knyt, "'How I Compose': Ferruccio Busoni's Views about Invention, Quotation, and the Compositional Process," *The Journal of Musicology* 27, no. 2 (2010): 224–64.
2. As Martin Edin notes about Henselt's additions of his own cadenzas to his editions of Chopin's piano music, "The fact that Henselt had his amplifications printed in a system that runs parallel with the original text is a sign that he considered it important to show, in a most pedagogical manner, which amendments he had made and how they relate to the original text.... Through printing his elaborations in an *ossia* system Henselt presents his cadenzas as alternative ways of performing the transitions rather than obligatory ones. The cadenzas are suggested to, but not imposed upon, the pianist" ("Cadenza Improvisation in Nineteenth-Century Solo Piano Music According to Czerny, Liszt, and Their Contemporaries," in *Beyond Notes: Improvisation in Western Music of the Eighteenth and Nineteenth Centuries*, ed. Rudolf Rasch [Turnhout: Brepols, 2011], 177–78).

3. Letter of December 2, 1868 to Sigmund Lebert, in *Franz Liszt's Briefe*, ed. La Mara (Leipzig: Breitkopf & Härtel, 1893–1903), 2:133: "In den Sonaten finden Sie einige Varianten, die mir ziemlich *zutreffend* scheinen. Mehrere Stellen ... habe ich im modernen Claviersatz umgeschrieben und schmeichle mir, dass Schubert damit nicht unzufrieden wäre" (original emphasis).

4. Although Kullak does not use the term "ossia," his approach has clearly been received as one. See, for instance, David Fallows's write-up of "Ossia" in *The New Grove Dictionary of Music and Musicians*, 2nd edn., ed. Stanley Sadie (London: Macmillan, 2001), 18:774, in which he documents its occurrence "in scholarly texts, readings from other sources or alternative interpretations of the same source." Incidentally, "ossia" is not given its own entry in the *Sachteil* of *Die Musik in Geschichte und Gegenwart*, 2nd edn., gen. ed. Ludwig Finscher (Kassel: Bärenreiter, 1997).

5. While today the ontology of music is a highly contested concept—what is "real" in the music, especially when "music" can be written, performed, and/or heard?—Kullak almost certainly did not think in such terms. Indeed, he believed that a single, fixed reading of Beethoven's concerto could be reconstituted using a process in which extant sources were collected, processed, and prioritized, with one ultimately emerging as being closest to the composer and therefore ranking as the most important. In this sense, his editorial method is not much different than that still used by today's editors—and expected by today's performers. See James Grier, *The Critical Editing of Music: History, Method, and Practice* (Cambridge: Cambridge University Press, 1996), esp. 1–37 and 96–143. At least among some of today's editors, however, "ossia" has been used to designate a variant of particularly high quality, such as in the *New Bach Edition*'s score of J. S. Bach's toccatas: "In some instances the early sources already contain divergent readings, while in others the later sources present self-sufficient and musically logical departures. Such cases have been incorporated in our text on *ossia* staves or in footnotes. This has enabled us to avoid combining textual forms occurring separately in the sources; it has also prevented us from consigning to the Critical Report alternative readings which, though less well substantiated, may well have originated with Bach himself. *Ossia* staves indicate well documented variants from the early sources, while footnotes refer to less well documented variants in later copyists' MSS." See Bach, *Toccaten*, ed. Peter Wollny (Kassel: Bärenreiter, 1999), vi. Robin Langley's edition of John Field's nocturnes is similarly peppered with alternative passages in ossia-like presentation, due to the fact that Field—like Liszt—was a habitual reviser of his music. Thus, Langley explains that "modern performers should feel at liberty, as Field would have done by improvisation, to choose differently between the given texts in each individual performance" (John Field, *Nocturnes and Related Pieces*, ed. Robin Langley [London: Stainer and Bell, 1997], xxiv).

6. For compositions by Liszt that exist in multiple versions, it is rare to find him porting ossia passages from the earlier version to the later version without alteration. One particularly interesting situation comes in his *Réminiscences de Lucrezia Borgia* (S. 400 / LW A71b), where ossia passages from the first version of 1840 become the main reading of the second version of 1848.
7. Based on information kindly provided to the author by Patrick Rucker, only Pascal Rogé featured this ossia in his 1969 recording of Liszt's piano works (Decca Eloquence 480 3150).
8. While Jeffrey Kallberg has argued that Chopin's tendency to compose variants into authorized editions released simultaneously are in fact "essential to the aesthetic mode of existence of Chopin's music, as understood both by Chopin and by his audiences in the 1830s and 1840s," Liszt's presentation of simultaneous readings of a passage in a single source has no parallel in the compositional practices of his contemporaries, Chopin included (Jeffrey Kallberg, "The Chopin 'Problem': Simultaneous Variants and Alternate Versions," in *Chopin at the Boundaries: Sex, History, and Musical Genre* [Cambridge, MA: Harvard University Press, 1996], 215–28, at 215).
9. Ossia passages also appear in Liszt's four-hand and two-piano music, selected orchestral works (such as the Doppler-Liszt orchestral arrangements of six of his Hungarian Rhapsodies), and lieder. A small number of ossia passages in this last genre have occasionally been the subject of scholarship, including Edwin Hughes, "Liszt as Lieder Composer," *The Musical Quarterly* 3, no. 4 (1917): 390–409, and Philip Friedheim, "First Version, Second Version, Alternative Version: Some Remarks on the Music of Liszt," *The Music Review* 44, nos. 3–4 (1983): 194–202.
10. J. A. Fuller-Maitland, "Ossia, Oppure, Ovvero," in *A Dictionary of Music and Musicians*, ed. George Grove (London: Macmillan and Co., 1880), 2:615. My emphasis. Fuller-Maitland's entry was carried over without change in the second edition of Grove's *Dictionary* of 1900.
11. Taste, like improvisation or the respectability of the ossia, is contingent. See Richard Taruskin, "Liszt and Bad Taste," *Studia Musicologica* 54, no. 1 (2013): 87–104.
12. See Jeff R. Warren, *Music and Ethical Responsibility* (Cambridge: Cambridge University Press, 2014), esp. 165–73, in which the author provokes readers to consider other people's music as either inheritance or gift.
13. Liszt provides three short ossia passages that only minutely differ from the main readings in the first version of his arrangement of *La romanesca*, for which Rena Charnin Mueller and Maria Eckhardt give the publication date as 1832–33 in "Liszt, Franz: Works," in *The New Grove Dictionary of Music and Musicians*, 2nd edn., ed. Stanley Sadie (London: Macmillan, 2001), 14:787. However, the edition of this work recently published as supplement volume

10 to the *New Liszt Edition* gives the date of publication as 1840. See Franz Liszt, *Consolations, Grand solo de concert (Earlier Versions) and Other Works*, ed. Adrienne Kaczmarczyk and Ágnes Sas (Budapest: Editio Musica, 2014), xxxi–xxxii.

These artistic awakenings include witnessing Paganini play in April 1832, meeting Marie d'Agoult in early 1833, and hearing the revised version of Berlioz's *Symphonie fantastique* in May 1833. As a foil to the public Berlioz and Paganini works, at this time Liszt also composed the *Apparitions* (1834) and single-movement *Harmonies poétiques* (1833–34), whose preface begins with the gnostic phrase: "These verses [i.e., this music] are addressed only to a select few" (Ces vers ne s'adressent qu'à un petit nombre). Tellingly, none of these private works bear ossia passages, despite their heavy technical and interpretative demands.

14. An excellent, annotated translation of Schumann's famous 1835 review of Berlioz's *Symphonie fantastique* can be found in Ian Bent, ed., *Music Analysis in the Nineteenth Century: Volume 2, Hermeneutic Approaches* (Cambridge: Cambridge University Press, 1994), 161–94. Schumann's evaluation of Liszt's arrangement appears on pp. 189–90.

15. Jacques Derrida, *Of Grammatology*, trans. Gayatri Chakravorty Spivak (Baltimore: John Hopkins University Press, 1997), 200.

16. Unfortunately, the edition of this work for the *NLE* (series 2, vol. 1) replaces the phrase "exécuté par l'auteur" with the misleading and inadequate expression "facilité."

17. In Derridean terms, the "Clochette" Fantasy offers an outsized accretion of the typical way in which Paganini's art was transferred to the piano by Liszt's contemporaries. See Jonathan Kregor, "Forging 'Paganinis of the Piano' in the 1830s," *Studia Musicologica* 54, no. 2 (2013): 115–34.

18. Letter of May 2, 1832 to Pierre Wolff, in *Franz Liszts Briefe*, 1:7. "Oui, un artiste, tel que tu demandes, tel qu'il en faut aujourd'hui!"

19. The ossia as presented in measures 24–40 of Liszt's arrangement features groups of four thirty-second notes in the left hand and lower voice of the right hand, while Schumann's original features groups of triplet sixteenth notes.

20. Franz Liszt, "Revue critique: Compositions pour piano, de M. Robert Schuman [sic]," *Revue et gazette musicale de Paris* 4, no. 46 (November 12, 1837): 488–90. See Nancy B. Reich, *Clara Schumann: The Artist and the Woman* (Ithaca, NY: Cornell University Press, rev. ed. 2001), 194–202, for a pithy overview of Clara Schumann's turbulent professional relationship with Liszt. Alexander Stefaniak considers her programming and performance strategies from the 1830s and early 1840s in "Clara Schumann's Interiorities and the Cutting Edge of Popular Pianism," *Journal of the American Musicological Society* 70, no. 3 (2017): 697–765, esp. 707–52.

21. Jim Samson, *Virtuosity and the Musical Work: The "Transcendental Studies" of Liszt* (Cambridge: Cambridge University Press, 2003), 86.
22. See Franz Liszt, *6 études d'après Paganini pour piano*, ed. Alfred Cortot (Paris: Éditions Salabert, 2003 [orig. 1949]), 3n2.
23. Letter of September 30, 1838 in *Franz Liszts Briefe* 1:22–23. "Vous ferez bien aussi, je crois, de réimprimer à la suite cette même *Étude facilitée*, que je vous ai envoyée également. Ce second arrangement est de M. Schumann, jeune compositeur d'un très-haut mérite. Il est plus à la portée de tout le monde, et aussi plus exact que ma *paraphrase*" (original emphasis). Notably, Liszt instructs Pacini to print Schumann's version "right after" (*à la suite*) Liszt's own, which did not happen.
24. [Robert Schumann,] "Etuden für das Pianoforte. F. Liszt. Bravourstudien nach Paganini's Capricen f. d. Pfte bearbeitet," *Neue Zeitschrift für Musik* 16, no. 34 (April 26, 1842): 134. "Wenn die Schumann'sche Bearbeitung mehr die poetische Seite der Composition zur Anschauung bringen wollte, so hebt Liszt, aber ohne jene verkannt zu haben, mehr die virtuosische hervor."
25. Facility is relative, and the *ossia più facile* that Liszt supplies for *Abschied* in measures 109–68 still puts the work out of reach to all but the most advanced pianists.
26. *NLE* 1:2, 21.
27. Incidentally, and unlike *Vallée d'Obermann*'s ossia passage, today every professional pianist plays this particular ossia, including Kissin, Bolet, and Argerich.
28. Therefore, this material as presented in the excellent supplemental volume 6 of the *NLE*, edited by Adrienne Kaczmarczyk, has not been used for the present study.
29. See Michael Saffle, "Early Italian Editions of Liszt's Works," *Revista de Musicología* 16, no. 3 (1993): 1781–94.
30. It should be acknowledged that the *NLE* occasionally does not distinguish well between true ossia passages and later, independent revisions to a passage (i.e., differences among chronologically different versions of a work), thus resulting in unusual editorial methods, such as that described by editor Imre Mező for Liszt's solo-piano arrangement of Beethoven's Septet in E-flat Major, op. 20 (S. 465 / LW A69): "The editions listed contain the same transcription in several versions. For the 1886 edition Liszt simplified the music in that he included the *ossia più facile* of the earlier editions in the main text throughout and omitted the earlier main text everywhere which was more difficult to play. By omitting the octave doublings he simplified measures 166–69 of the first movement as well. The present edition contains the final, 1886 version including the portions of the earlier editions omitted or changed by Liszt above or under the main text, eventually in footnotes and indicating in each case which source they have been taken from. As a result, on performing the main text, the final

version of the transcription can be heard and by inserting [the] quasi ossia [of] any parallel section we may reach back to the earlier versions" (*NLE* 2:22, xii). In other words, Mező employs ossia staves to fashion a source-critical composite score similar to that discussed above in note 5.

31. *NLE* 1:1, viii. For the most part, *NLE* editors have followed this editorial principle, but there are exceptions: a footnote for Hungarian Rhapsody no. 14 includes a modification "suitable for pianos with a smaller range" (1:1n64), while a note in the first edition of the Schubert/Liszt *Ständchen* over the chromatic run at measure 106 ("à l'Octava per i Cembali à 7 octavi" [i.e., extend this run up another octave on a seven-octave piano]) is implemented by *NLE* editors Andreas Krause and Imre Sulyok without comment in the critical report (153).

32. *NLE* 1:1, viii.

33. No complete English translation of this important resource exists, but see Kenneth Hamilton, "Performing Liszt's Piano Music," in *The Cambridge Companion to Liszt*, ed. Kenneth Hamilton (Cambridge: Cambridge University Press, 2005), 171–91, esp. 177–91.

34. Preface by Imre Sulyok and Imre Mező, dated May 1987, in *NLE* 2:4, x.

35. A cadenza for Henrik Gobbi is also included in the *NLE* volume for *Un sospiro*, measure 52, from a supplemental source.

36. Employing this famous passage in performance may be desirable if the pianist also programs the equally famous *Consolations*, whose fourth piece concludes (mm. 27–31) with the exact same progression as *Un sospiro*'s main reading.

37. For instance, Liszt instructed a student playing *Gaudeamus igitur* (S. 509 / LW A246) at a master class to "take the *ossia* each time in bars 123–30. He [Liszt] had the triplets in the left-hand *ossia* in bars 257–64 especially well projected and played this passage very *staccato* and lively, almost impudently." At other master classes, Liszt recommended performing the ossia passages in measures 292–97 of the Second Ballade in B Minor and measures 150–72 of the second movement of the Beethoven-Liszt Seventh Symphony. See August Göllerich, *The Piano Master Classes of Franz Liszt, 1884–1886*, ed. Wilhelm Jerger, trans., ed., and enlarged by Richard Louis Zimdars (Bloomington: Indiana University Press, 1996), 39, 45, 83, and *passim*.

38. Peter Szendy, *Listen: A History of Our Ears* (New York: Fordham University Press, 2008), 58.

39. Kenneth Hamilton, *After the Golden Age: Romantic Pianism and Modern Performance* (Oxford and New York: Oxford University Press, 2007), 257: "And of course, when the authority of the performer reaches that of a hierophant, it vies with that of the composer. A much larger degree of interpretative, even re-creative, freedom must be expected and allowed."

40. See Bryce Morrison, review of Perl's *Liszt Selected Piano Works Volume 3* (Classics 74321 71768-2), http://www.gramophone.co.uk/review/liszt-selected-piano-works-volume-3, accessed March 1, 2017. *Vision* also features ossia passages for the left hand at measures 38–39, 48, and 50.
41. For instance, Cyprien Katsaris plays the provided ossia passages in the repeated sections of Liszt's arrangement of Beethoven's Sixth Symphony (and also adds some of his own material to the "Storm" movement) in Beethoven/Liszt, *Symphonies Nos. 1–9* (Teldec 60865).
42. Liszt, *Transcendental Études* (Myrios Classics MYR019).
43. *NLE* 1:15, 124. The passages concerned replace measures 328–38 and 446–51.
44. Franz Liszt, *Musikalische Werke* (Leipzig: Breitkopf & Härtel, 1927), series 2, vol. 9 (*Verschiedene Werke für Pianoforte zu 2 Händen*).
45. On the one hand, situating *Schlaflos!* amid other introspective, unsettled pieces of Liszt's contradictory late years, Dolores Pesce posits that its open-ended conclusion "indicate[s] that Liszt found no easy, pat answer to his existential questioning. Not surprisingly, he chose not to publish such works which would have revealed his vulnerability to his public." See Pesce, *Liszt's Final Decade* (Rochester, NY: University of Rochester Press, 2014), 220. On the other hand, Alan Walker (*Franz Liszt, Volume 3: The Final Years, 1861–1886* [Ithaca, NY: Cornell University Press, 1996], 442) suggests that Liszt composed the final ossia passage of *Schlaflos!* for the general public, since he "knew that some of his contemporaries might find his first conclusion unacceptable."
46. Franz Liszt, *Klavierwerke*, vol. 8 (*Opern-Phantasien für Klavier zu zwei Händen*), ed. Emil von Sauer (Leipzig: Peters, 1917), 26: "im Konzertsaal heute kaum noch verwendet."
47. Busoni's preface, dated June 1917 and attached to his *Grosse Kritische Instruktions-Ausgabe* of Liszt's Fantasy, is translated as "Mozart's *Don Giovanni* and Liszt's *Don Juan* Fantasy" in *The Essence of Music and Other Papers*, trans. Rosamond Ley (New York: Dover, 1965), 89–95.

Chapter Five

Brahms "versus" Liszt

The Internalization of Virtuosity

David Keep

For all of virtuosity's striking qualities, it resists definition. In part, this is due to the multiplicity of its interacting dimensions. In the context of nineteenth-century piano music, Jim Samson has described virtuosity's "relational field" through its connections between at least four constituent parts: text, instruments, performer, and audience.[1] Here virtuosity's "object-status" and "event-status" are always in tension: the performer's engagement with the text draws them "right into the heart of the work," while the instrumental idiom is projected to the audience. In Samson's view, execution of idiomatic figures supports the moment of virtuosity and compels the audience's attention, highlighting the performer's abilities above all. Although the difficulties of execution are often genuine in such situations, at times the emphasis on fostering their clear perception can magnify the actual demands made on the performer to appear greater than they might be. However one may define "difficulty" in a performance context, its presence plays a foundational role in the understanding of virtuosity. Sigismond Thalberg's "three-hand" technique is an example of how perceived difficulty can be maximized from the listener's perspective, when a passage's demands are perhaps not as great as they seem. Such passagework, in its display, projects engagement with difficulty to the audience as audibly as possible. Thus, the relational field of virtuosity described by Samson centers on the performer's external projection of difficulty and its effective transcendence to the listener. Yet what would happen if this relationship were rearranged while still preserving virtuosity's emphasis on overcoming difficulty? For example, what if difficulty's projection were downplayed, while less immediately appreciable challenges (such as dense contrapuntal textures, unidiomatic passagework, or terse presentation of thematic material) for the performer were intensified by the demands of the musical text, purposefully without making audience perception a critical component? In this reconfiguration, the instrument serves as a channel through which both the performer and listener are drawn toward the musical text, centering attention perhaps less on the performative gesture and more upon the work in the abstract. In terms of the second relational field discussed above, the composer's text in this configuration maximizes experienced difficulty for the performer while shielding the listener from awareness of this aspect of music making. Instead, the listener's attention is drawn foremost to the text's attributes rather than to the displays of the performative act. If the work is particularly complex, the listening experience can become primarily centered upon the challenges of processing a composition's internal workings.

These two contrasting configurations of the relational field further the tension between distinct nineteenth-century listening habits. The first prioritizes the "event-status" that emphasizes the individual as the main participant within the "cult of virtuosity," and the second engages the "object-status" of the musical composition, stemming from the rise of the work concept in western European music.[2] Both types of listening presuppose above-average abilities in music making, since they often rely upon pronounced knowledge of or engagements with difficulty in some capacity. Taken together, their juxtaposition underscores the tension between bourgeois Romantic taste for event-status and elite-artistic Romantic taste for object-status, and may be said to have sown the seeds for the chasm between traditional and modern taste endemic to the twentieth century. Despite their differences, both habits were at play in the rise of virtuosic nineteenth-century piano music and can contextualize the diverse compositional approaches to virtuosity shaped by contrasting aesthetic aims.

But, one may ask, does the reconfiguration of Samson's relational field still recognize virtuosity? In other words, is virtuosity manifest only when the transcendence of difficulty is readily perceived by the listener? Or is virtuosity a function of the successful engagement of difficulty through the performer's experience, regardless of the listener's perception? Perhaps any answer will depend on one's aesthetic position, but it may be fair to claim in general that music of any true virtuosity must engage the performer with exceptional difficulty, real or perceived, and that the performer must transcend this difficulty through the act of compelling execution. Without such execution, virtuosity is merely an idea. In the composer's score, it remains only a prescription; in the ears of the audience, it is likely a recollection of a past event. Though the sum of the relational field must be accounted for to understand the multidimensional aspects of virtuosity as a historical phenomenon, its crux is the moment of effective execution.

The two relational fields also juxtapose the nature of demands made by a work; for we will always want to ask whether these are primarily "physical/technical" or "musical," descriptors commonly used by musicians to categorize difficulty. In many ways, this characterization only scratches the surface of the demands a performer faces. There are many other difficulties that must be overcome to rise to the occasion of virtuosity. From a twenty-first-century solo piano recitalist's perspective, these include the challenges of memorizing repertoire (often an hour of music or more); keeping works spontaneous and fresh while remaining faithful to a composed text that has already been played thousands of times; investing one's emotions, psychological state, and spirit into a performance; as well as committing the communication of one's own ideas to an audience through playing music (most often) written by someone other than oneself. These are only some of the many demands placed upon a performer in realizing a virtuosic execution. Thus, isolating virtuosity's demands as either physical/technical or musical can be only a limited part of the whole picture. Moreover, the separation of these somewhat arbitrary categories overlooks the fact that musical solutions can often make physical difficulties manageable. Specific demands aside, difficulty of some variety must be in place for virtuosity to occur so that the performer has challenges to transcend through compelling execution. Virtuosity and difficulty may not be equivalent, but in varying aesthetic contexts their relationship takes diverse forms.

In the interest of exploring virtuosity's conceptual boundaries through its relationship to difficulty, this essay will follow the thread of execution through passages from three musical compositions. From the performer's perspective, each work prominently engages with difficulty, though not all of these works are understood to be "virtuosic." Their composer, Johannes Brahms, is not often considered to be one of the great composer-virtuosos, like Paganini or Liszt. Nevertheless, despite his characterization as a staunch conservative composer of serious German art music, as well as the "anti-pope" who was thought to oppose Wagner, Liszt, and the New Germans, virtuosity was in fact a lifelong concern for Brahms. Coming to musical maturity in the mid-nineteenth century meant that Brahms had to develop his reputation as a composer of serious music while also responding to the demand for virtuosity. The following section will examine the contexts for virtuosity in Brahms's career, particularly as they relate to the example of Liszt, whom Brahms knew well, both personally and professionally, demonstrating how both versions of the relational field—or rather, the continuum between them—can be implemented to understand a specifically Brahmsian conception and practice of virtuosity. For the remainder of this essay, Samson's relational field will be referred to conveniently as "externalization" and the second relational field will be referred to as "internalization." Examples of both occur in Brahms's music, but the pieces discussed here, the Paganini Variations, op. 35, the Rhapsody in B Minor, op. 79, no. 1, and the Intermezzo in F Minor, op. 118, no. 4, map a progression across the continuum: the Paganini Variations are certainly an example of Brahms's engagement with externalized virtuosity, whereas the rhapsody features a mixture of internalization with some passages of marked externalization, while the intermezzo essentially internalizes its virtuosic difficulties. Of course, the meaning of difficulty proves variable in these contexts and is flexible based on the performer and their unique abilities. Nonetheless, accounts of each piece and the challenges they present will be described based on my own performance experiences as a pianist.

The intention here is, obviously, not to argue that Brahms's output as a whole fits the Lisztian virtuoso mold. Indeed, it is evident that difficulty has varying aesthetic purposes in the music of these two composers. The interest in this essay instead lies in examining how far one might be able to extend the conception of what virtuosity entails. The intermezzo, on the one hand, clearly fails to qualify as a "virtuosic" work, yet no pianist has ever argued that Brahms's late intermezzi are "easy" pieces, since they pose considerable challenges in many ways. On the other hand, while the Paganini Variations could hardly be more conspicuously examples of externalized, indeed Lisztian, virtuosity—specifically and frankly so, insofar as we understand Brahms's intentions—they also exhibit a significant degree of internalized virtuosity, Brahms wanting to be, as it were, a better sort of Liszt.[3] For Liszt's part, he said of the Paganini Variations: "I am happy to have been of service to Brahms in his variations through mine; it gives me great pleasure."[4] Even for composers as different as Brahms and Liszt, virtuosity in some capacity was a shared priority. Through thinking about Brahms's response to virtuosity across the continuum proposed above, we may be able to refine our sense of virtuosity's range of application, at least in an aesthetic and conceptual sense.

Contexts for Brahmsian Virtuosity

Brahms was forced to deal with virtuosity as a cultural phenomenon both as a performer and as a composer. For these reasons, we must consider virtuosity's influence on Brahms's music as a whole, even if his aesthetic outlook did not consistently prioritize the display of technical skill in a traditionally virtuosic sense. Framing this discussion with the language of externalization and internalization will contextualize the approaches to virtuosity in his music.

Brahms's earliest attempts at forging a musical career were centered on developing his skills as a virtuoso pianist. Though Brahms never heard Liszt perform in his prime (i.e., during the years of his European tours, 1839–47), he entered an arena dominated by Liszt's example, with its concomitant emphasis on the Romantic virtuoso as hero.[5] Born in 1833, Brahms's official 1848 recital debut was given in his early teens (though he appeared as a soloist on shared recital programs by 1847), just as Liszt was retiring from the active performing phase of his career.[6] In Brahms's early performances, he played works that were popular in Hamburg's music scene, primarily salon music, though these appeared alongside pieces by Beethoven and some of his own compositions.[7] Significantly, he demonstrated a "continuing preference" for Thalberg's music in programming his recitals, performing works such as the *Grande fantaisie et variations sur "Don Juan,"* op. 14, and the *Andante final de Lucie de Lammermoor varié*, op. 44. While Brahms's involvement with Thalberg's music perhaps did not last long beyond these early years, it is significant that he was exposed to such music in a formative stage of his career. Coming from a poor family, Brahms nevertheless received a decent overall musical education but later in life lamented how much he had to make up for its shortcomings.[8] Perhaps in hindsight the older Brahms saw the concern with pianistic virtuosity as a path that could have been bypassed if he had received a more rigorous compositional training. Launching his career as a pianist in the "heyday" of an "ultra-virtuoso idiom," Brahms's concern with virtuosity came about in the environment of these cultural pressures.[9]

Roger Moseley has recounted how Brahms's experiences as a pianist were formative in this regard, describing the ways in which Brahms's identities as performer and composer overlapped and diverged.[10] While still primarily a touring pianist, Brahms's concerto debut in 1859 of his Piano Concerto no. 1 in D Minor, op. 15, was met with harsh reviews. In this instance, his playing was criticized, but the reviews were generally negative toward the composition itself as well.[11] With expanded career options following the success of the German Requiem, op. 45, after 1868 Brahms found financial security in composing, taking the pressure off his virtuoso performing ambitions. From this point on, his playing probably began to deteriorate. If Brahms truly believed that virtuosity was nothing but showy, distracting excess, this would have realistically been the end of his pianistic career. Instead, with the debut of his Piano Concerto no. 2 in B-flat Major, op. 83, one of his most externally virtuosic and internally difficult compositions for piano, Brahms took the stage no fewer than twenty-one times to perform it as soloist in the season of 1881–82. Accounts of the performances often comment on the rough quality of Brahms's pianism but emphasize the success of the work itself.[12] Liszt remarked that this concerto was "one of the very best" even if "[Brahms] plays it a little sloppily himself. Bülow plays it beautifully."[13] At least in considering the unveilings of his two piano concerti—which occurred at very different stages in his career—Brahms's interest in his own externalized pianistic virtuosity appears to have diminished; the increasing importance of the work concept supported a growing internalization, drawing the listener and performer toward the work and away from the performer's display. In both cases, Brahms felt compelled to be the soloist as well as the composer, highlighting the importance attached to taking on significant difficulty as a virtuoso, apparently even without always transcending such challenges, while also writing serious music.

This narrative highlights the pressures put upon composers who sought cultural prestige in the nineteenth century: the growing canon of masterpieces from the Viennese classics provided constant competition, and current composer-virtuosos raised the bar for expectations regarding performance. Consequentially, composers like Brahms, as well as his mentor, Robert Schumann, sought ways to engage with virtuosity by composing works of great difficulty that they themselves might not be able to perform, unlike a Paganini or a Liszt. This speaks to the value composers ascribed to virtuosity in their music, even those who saw themselves as continuing the tradition of German art music. Alexander Stefaniak has observed that "for Schumann and many of his musical and literary colleagues, discussions about virtuosity often revolved around an anxiety intimately connected to their professional identities."[14] For Brahms, this aspect of his musical identity perhaps motivated his continual attempts at improving his pianistic abilities through his *51 Übungen* and other technical studies on musical material by Chopin, Schubert, and Bach, as well as the Variations on a Theme by Paganini, op. 35. Moseley has described how these efforts by Brahms "dissect" and "demystify" virtuosity, as he sought to study the magic of virtuosity to refashion it into something that could be achieved through hard work, continuing Czerny's example.[15] Accounts of Brahms's playing also describe how he seemed to relish challenges at the keyboard.[16] But through his considerable efforts, Brahms's pianism could not project virtuosity with the ease and efficacy that Liszt's abilities could.

While Brahms might have failed to warm to Liszt's music, he had nothing but effusive admiration for Liszt's playing: "If you never heard Liszt, you really have nothing to say.... His piano-playing was something unique, incomparable, inimitable."[17] Brahms mentioned to Klaus Groth about himself and other pianists in relation to Liszt: "Of course, we are also capable of playing the piano, but none of us possesses more than a few fingers of his two hands."[18] He could not resist the draw of magnetic virtuosity from a player as unprecedented as Liszt, and one can sense that his respect was mixed with a certain degree of envy. As was the case for many pianists in the nineteenth century, Liszt's playing set an example for Brahms that shaped the desired standard for his own performing. Furthermore, it may be the case that Liszt's decision to pursue composition full-time had just as much of an effect on Brahms as his virtuosic performing. Even though Brahms was a talented pianist, it appears that he put the most stock in presenting himself to the musical world as a serious composer, first and foremost. In a way, Brahms's career as a virtuoso pianist was a means to this end. Once he had attained a certain stature as a composer, performing did not have the same appeal or urgency that it had previously. But by this point, the attraction of virtuosity had already been rooted deeply in his musical sensibility and can be seen to have affected numerous aspects of his career as a composer.

For all that Liszt and the mania of midcentury virtuosity influenced Brahms, the hesitation to embrace it wholeheartedly was widespread among musicians who saw themselves as proponents of serious German music. John Daverio has observed that Schumann's attitudes toward virtuosity's problems and possibilities were closely mirrored by Brahms.[19] Stefaniak has argued that Schumann demonstrated in his musical compositions and journalistic criticism simultaneously supportive and hesitant attitudes toward virtuosity.[20] To locate in Schumann's and Brahms's approaches a fundamental opposition between the lofty goals of serious German art music and the worldly aspirations toward virtuosity seems to be a misapprehension. Though virtuosity was often perceived as having a morally dubious aura, its appeal could clearly not be ignored.[21] For example, Eduard Hanslick's review of Brahms's First Piano Concerto remarked on its use of "serious virtuosity," demonstrating an attempt to balance pervasive ambivalence toward and admiration for virtuosity.[22] One might speculate that virtuosity's internalization in Brahms's music was a strategic normalization of a controversial musical trend. Fitting within serious compositions the thrills and challenges of immense difficulties gives purpose and function to virtuosity within the context of "the work," thereby avoiding negative associations of unrestrained moral decadence.

For all that the rise of virtuosity instituted a new cultural environment characterized by pressures and expectations that Brahms's predecessors—those to whom he sought to link himself by continuing the tradition of serious music—did not face, the later composer's sense of virtuosity was strongly shaped by such composers, particularly through the influence of Beethoven and Chopin. Some of Brahms's most strikingly external virtuosic statements such as the Piano Sonata in C Major, op. 1, and the concluding fugue of the Variations on a Theme of Handel, op. 24, demand that the pianist transcend the instrument in a manner similar to Beethoven's "Hammerklavier" Sonata, with its exceptional difficulty in both the first movement and its massive fugal close. In addition, though Chopin's music is not documented among the recital repertoire of Brahms's early piano performances, it is difficult to imagine that the young composer had not encountered Chopin's music. Brahms's Scherzo in E-flat Minor, op. 4, reflects many aspects of Chopin's four scherzi. Rather than coming off as a light-hearted joke, Brahms's piece is a tour de force of demonic energy with considerable dramatic sweep. Here, as in Chopin, virtuosity is instrumentalized for distinct expressive purposes. In much of Beethoven's and Chopin's music at their best, virtuosity arises as a composed feature reserved for local, rhetorical dramatic purposes in a manner quite different from mid-nineteenth-century event-centric virtuosity. Most often, the use of virtuosity in Beethoven and Chopin could be effectively considered as a component within an internalizing relational field that prioritizes the work concept over the projection of the performer's skills. But, of course, no performer of these composers' works would argue that this amounts to a decrease in the emphasis on technical skill, which is more than required to compellingly play such repertoire, and it must certainly be admitted that externalized virtuosity is featured in various types of works from both earlier composers as well.

Brahms's approach frequently follows this trend in his works and perhaps intensifies the tendency toward internalization. However, there are numerous piano works by Brahms that strike a public, extroverted virtuosic tone. For example, the Piano Sonata no. 2 in F-sharp Minor, op. 2, is quite Lisztian with its passagework and cyclic form.[23] More so than most of the piano works, the Paganini Variations and the concerti raise virtuosity to the level of public spectacle. External virtuosity is not limited to the works for piano; it is projected in other works such as the Violin Concerto in D Major, op. 77, the Double Concerto for Violin and Cello in A Minor, op. 102, and the Piano Quartet no. 1 in G Minor, op. 25. However, the majority of Brahms's works tend to avoid external display, deemphasizing the performer's role in this regard while magnifying features of the work.

Brahms's compositional language itself shares a number of traits in common with ways the virtuosic impulse became manifest in nineteenth-century piano music. For example, a notable feature of Brahms's compositional language is the synthesis of many disparate idioms and stylistic elements for virtuosic effect.[24] One of the stylistic topics regularly invoked in Brahms's works featuring a distinctive realization of virtuosity is the use of an idealized Hungarian Gypsy idiom. Brahms evidently had a strong fondness for importing Hungarian Gypsy elements into his music, which, as Daverio observes, "resulted in a powerful influence upon his productivity."[25] Inspiring both soulful, sentimental melancholy in a melodic capacity as well as passages of "lighter, popular, wild" music, the Gypsy influence on Brahms resulted in recreations of style that are often quite externally virtuosic.[26] Daverio's analysis of the Double Concerto has shown that Brahms's notion of bravura writing for strings was decisively shaped by the Gypsy persona, not to mention the striking example of the opus 25 Piano Quartet *alla zingarese* finale.[27] The freedom and panache of Brahms's conception of Gypsy music is often fundamentally virtuosic through its expressive purposes. At the same time, Brahms's imagined style of the Hungarian Gypsy has striking elements in common with Liszt's folk renditions for piano, particularly the highly virtuosic Hungarian Rhapsodies. For this reason, it is perhaps not a coincidence that many instances of the *style hongrois* in Brahms's music are virtuosic in tone.[28]

Another significant re-creative aspect of Brahms's composed virtuosity is the importation of string figuration via Paganini. Daverio has noted that both Schumann and Brahms were enchanted by Paganini's music throughout their lives.[29] Both were certainly fascinated with the ways Liszt found immediate use of Paganini's string figuration in his own legerdemain at the keyboard. Some of the most striking examples of Liszt's virtuosic figuration came as a result of the importation of Paganini's string writing, which strongly influenced Brahms, especially Liszt's celebrated *Paganini Études* (1838/1851).[30] Notably, many of Brahms's chief attempts at composing overtly virtuosic works deal with importation of string figuration into the realm of the keyboard. The left-hand study of the Bach Chaconne, the Paganini Variations, and the G-minor Bach studies demonstrate a sustained interest in violin figuration and the ways it might influence pianistic virtuosity, as well as exploring what might be still possible under the imposition of severe limitations, as in the Chaconne.

Re-creativity is a fundamental technique for Brahms's approach to the piano's sonic capabilities, using the instrument to re-create orchestral sounds. In this way, employing the piano as a means for conjuring other instrumentations in a virtuosic fashion is decidedly Lisztian (Liszt's monumental transcriptions of the Beethoven Symphonies being a prime example). Schumann's comment about Brahms's early sonatas being "veiled symphonies" speaks to the orchestral character of his first published compositions for piano.[31] John Rink has even suggested that the weaknesses of writing in the early piano works stem from Brahms's ideas being held back by pianistic means while attempting to compose ideas of symphonic scope.[32] In particular, Rink cites the opus 15 Concerto as the first time that Brahms breaks out of a pianistic conception, allowing musical ideas to manifest themselves in the appropriate instrumental scale. Malcolm MacDonald has remarked that "Brahms's works have been open to charges of inconcinnity, or at least ambiguity," in regard to genre, as a result of his treatment of various instruments and the scale of ideas employed in works composed for them, especially between the chamber works, orchestral works, and concerti.[33] Much like Lisztian transcriptions, this pianistic approach constitutes a fundamental trait of virtuosic piano writing in Brahms's works.

A further consequence of stylistic re-creativity, especially in nineteenth-century piano writing, pushes the piano to do things it normally does not do in idiomatic writing. Clearly taking their cue from Beethoven, both Brahms and Liszt sought to write pieces for the piano that could reinvent what the instrument was itself increasingly capable of. The expressive goals of the two composers are often quite different, but both envisioned the piano as a canvas that was seemingly inexhaustible in its capabilities. As a result, Brahms and Liszt treated the piano as an instrument with a progressively versatile expressive voice. However, one difference that might be drawn between the two in this regard is that Brahms was often more strict about the fixed nature of the composition while somewhat flexible about its realization (the geneses of op. 15 and the Piano Quintet in F Minor, op. 34, for example, demonstrate this clearly), whereas Liszt was more flexible about fluidity of the work concept (with his multiple versions of the *Transcendental Études*, his frequent ossia passages, and improvisatory treatment of paraphrases and transcriptions), while perhaps more strict about its realization, often composing primarily for the piano as his virtuosic instrument of choice.[34]

Finally, Brahms's attitude toward composing for his nineteenth-century audience (and perhaps future audiences) resonates with an internalized role of virtuosity. By intensifying the emphasis on musical complexity in his works, Brahms placed considerable weight upon the listener's ability to absorb dense music. Eduard Hanslick wrote that in opus 118 and opus 119 for piano "there is much ore buried in these pieces, and this ore will be long conserved," hinting that the works could not be fully absorbed and appreciated through casual listening.[35] The ways in which Brahms's music stretched the listeners' capabilities centered on how "the relationship of detail to form, sequential logic to structure as recalled after an initial hearing—comprehending the irreversibility—became a challenge."[36] The aesthetic dimension of these demands made the issue a serious one for Brahms. As Leon Botstein writes, "All this made demands on the listener's skill, given that mere 'playing around' (*Spielerei*) was not at stake but deep inner communication through ordered musical sounds."[37] The conclusion that Botstein draws is that "the density of temporal consciousness and the demands made on the powers of discrimination and remembrance by Brahms's music were severe, even by contemporary standards."[38] Thus, in Brahms's music, the listener's responsibility and the performer's role become quite similar. The magnetic pull within an internal relational field draws both significantly toward the musical text. This reconfiguration still requires an intense engagement with difficulty in the performer's role, while also demanding much from the listener. Contrasting strongly with the role of listener as a passive spectator that observes external display, in this new context the listener is drawn toward internalized virtuosity itself to comprehend the complexity of the work.

Taking these contextual factors from Brahms's capacities as a pianist and composer into consideration, it is apparent that virtuosity was very much on Brahms's mind throughout his career. However, its manifestation is quite different from the midcentury ultra-virtuosity of Liszt and others. The differences stem mainly from aesthetic positions on externalization or internalization, and on the value of difficulty. Although Brahms's music occasionally enters the realm of public virtuosity, it spans the continuum and centers most frequently upon internalization. Even in performances of very private and deceptively modest works such as the late intermezzi, Brahms attached a positive value to difficulty in playing his works. In a letter to Clara Schumann, he savored the challenges of playing the Intermezzo in E Minor, op. 116, no. 5, a work that eschews external display in favor of compositional artifice.[39] In regard to difficulty, performers of Brahms's music rarely separate his works into categories such as the "virtuosic, difficult" works that engage externalization from the "simpler, less technically demanding" works that internalize their demands. Indeed, an intense engagement with difficulty is found almost in all of Brahms's works, prompting Moseley's conception of virtuosity, which characterizes the phenomenon in terms of reconfiguration:

> Brahms did not eliminate virtuosity from the discourse of his thematic arguments; rather, he reconfigured it, treating it as a minimum requirement for the performer while simultaneously transferring its attributes to the compositional realm. For those playing Brahms's music, fidelity to the text and virtuosity became one and the same, in that the latter was required merely to realize the former.[40]

An understanding of virtuosity in this context is quite different from the one that we may perceive in the tradition of Paganini and Liszt. But the examples of these composer-virtuosos had a significant impact on the development of a Brahmsian virtuosity, for the cultural value of seriousness, difficulty, and the loftiness of music in this historical moment made it impossible to ignore the magnetism of virtuosity as a desired artistic phenomenon. Thus, the following accounts of passages from piano works by Brahms demonstrate this reconfiguration of virtuosity, as the emphasis upon engagement with difficulty is internalized in various degrees to draw the relational field as a whole toward the work, away from the performative act.

The Roles of Virtuosity in Brahms's Piano Works

To highlight the shifting relational field and its changing physical and musical demands in three works by Brahms, each example investigates a similar type of pianistic virtuosity. In its own way, each example draws focus to multiple musical locations at once, challenging one's ability to effectively coordinate different skills simultaneously. In the order presented, the three pieces progress from external to internal types of virtuosity.

The first example, Brahms's Paganini Variations, contains a few passages indebted to the three-hand technique, a virtuosic display popularized by Thalberg in works such as his *Moses* Fantasy, op. 33, which was taken up widely as a stock virtuosic gesture in nineteenth-century piano music (for his part, Liszt endeavors to out-Thalberg Thalberg in his *Réminiscences de Norma*, S. 394 / LW A77, and his Third Concert Étude, *Un sospiro*, S. 144/3 / LW A118/3).[41] The three-hand technique serves as a characteristic instance of an externalized relational field of virtuosity. Crafted to showcase filigree and passagework embellishing a thematic idea, the technique vividly creates the impression of exceptional difficulty via textural saturation. In reality, the execution of this technique is not nearly as difficult as it sounds, optimizing the capacity for the listener to perceive the soloist's technical prowess.

Often the melodic idea being embellished in this scenario will not be an exceptionally complex one. For the technique to be effective, the complexity materializes instead from the added voices and figuration, not necessarily from the thematic idea itself being rich in detail. The layering of relatively simple musical ideas upon one another through textural accumulation leads to a virtuosic effect. The three-hand technique showcases the pianist's ability to juggle three different musical registers of the piano with only two hands. While the three-hand technique's execution requires skillful physical coordination, it presents musical difficulties as well. For a passage to sound as though it features three hands playing at once, the melodic idea must be voiced as the top priority of projection, with bass support coming at a close second, and the third priority being inner harmonic voices constituted as sweeping arpeggio and scalar passagework, shaped in ebbs and swells. If the passage is played with equal voicing in all parts, the density in sound and volume will occlude the perception of three individual textural strands. Liszt's Schubert song transcriptions are excellent examples of musical renditions that require the utmost sensitivity to shaping and voicing (particularly in instances of the three-hand technique) to capture the effect of Schubert's lieder, even though great skill is required to compellingly execute the transcriptions. In a physically focused gesture such as the three-hand technique, the effect of transcendence must be achieved through musical means.

Although perhaps not a staple gesture in Brahms's music, the split coordination characteristic of the three-hand technique shapes exceptionally difficult passages found in works like the Paganini Variations. In their extreme demands upon the performer's coordination as well as their unusually open-ended formal organization, these variations challenge and emulate the example of Liszt's virtuosic piano works, especially number 6 from the *Grandes études de Paganini* (S. 141 / LW A173, 1851), based on the same theme. Paganini's elemental and transparently structured theme from the A-Minor Caprice offers ideal musical material for withstanding numerous additions of textural layers while recognizably retaining its original form. In many ways, the virtuosity demanded by Brahms's take on the work is externalized, but the level of difficulty imposed upon the performer is relentless, transcending the magnified perception of difficulty experienced in a typical display of the three-hand technique.

Example 5.1. Brahms, Variations on a Theme of Paganini, op. 35, book 1, var. 14, mm. 1–4

Published with the subtitle *Studien für Pianoforte*, Brahms's Paganini Variations are divided into two books. The concluding variation, number 14 of book 1 from opus 35 demands virtuosic divisions of coordination at its outset (ex. 5.1).

The scalar thirty-second-note line in the middle range of the piano is passed between the two hands, requiring the pianist to shape continuously as a single voice. The punctuating octave gestures in the high and low registers provide a slower rhythmic component that stabilizes the passage, although the leaps add another level of difficulty. At any interpretation of the notated allegro tempo, this passage is immensely challenging to perform; instead of the typical three-hand technique's projected difficulty, with its comparatively less difficult demands in execution, all aspects of the passage are difficult in this instance. The relatively simple harmonic structure of the caprice theme is maintained (save for a new tonicization of C-sharp minor), and the virtuosic interest throughout the variation is generated from the addition of layers of figuration.

Variation 7 of book 2 also draws upon a three-hand texture and is exceptional in its rhythmic complexity (ex. 5.2). The right hand is initially in $\frac{2}{4}$ meter while the left hand is in $\frac{3}{8}$. Although cross-rhythms occur in many of Brahms's works, the demands in this variation's opening four measures call for four eighths in the right hand against nine triplet sixteenths in the left hand. This texture is complicated further by large leaps in the left hand, as an A bass pedal tone forces regular leaps over an octave in span throughout the passage. Continuing at the *poco più vivace* tempo from variation 6, these leaps are difficult enough to perform with the left hand alone. Adding the thematic material from the caprice in the right hand makes the passage fiendishly challenging. The variation continues to maximize difficulty in each continuing passage, as measures 5–8 of the variation break the right hand's octaves into sixteenths, embellishing the initial four against nine to create

Example 5.2. Brahms, Variations on a Theme of Paganini, op. 35, book 2, var. 7, mm. 1–24

eight against nine.[42] The intensification continues as the $\frac{2}{4}$ and $\frac{3}{8}$ switch between left and right hands in measures 9–16 and switch back again in measures 17–24. Once more, an effective execution of this passage's virtuosic demands requires a musical solution for a technical problem. The tempo is fast enough that one cannot feel every note of the eight against nine; realistically, the three against four must be the structural cross-rhythm while faster diminutions fall within larger gestures.[43]

Brahms's response to Liszt in the Paganini Variations occasionally implements displays of virtuosity that project difficulty to the listener in an overwhelmingly obvious fashion, but the principal manner in which his work challenges Liszt is through its unparalleled difficulty confronting the performer, which is not always made apparent to the listener through overt display.[44] Although still bent on engaging with public virtuosity, this reflects a shift in the relational field: attention is not solely focused on projecting difficulty to the listener; that difficulty is also maximized upon the performer rather than minimized. This is not to say that Liszt's works do not make their own imperceptible demands upon the pianist, but Brahms's Paganini Variations uniquely focus their virtuosity within the performer, with less attention to the ways that the listener might appreciate it. For example, the duration of the cross-rhythm passage is so brief that its effect is almost transitional, barely occupying the temporal spotlight that traditional three-hand effects often shine upon the performer's virtuosity.

The organization of opus 35 reflects other ways that Brahms sought to enter the arena of external virtuosity by emulating a Lisztian compositional perspective. Most of Brahms's independent variation sets for piano derive stylistic and structural features from the theme in ways that affect large-scale organization. For example, the Variations on a Theme by Schumann, op. 9, frequently quotes Robert's and Clara's works and showcases the young Brahms's own double personalities à la Schumann; the Variations on a Theme by Handel, op. 24, implements varieties of neobaroque textures and summarize the work's conclusion with a grand fugue; and the Variations on a Hungarian Song, op. 21, no. 2, retains the irregular meter of the theme for the majority of its duration, exploring various tropes of the *style hongrois* throughout. The Paganini Variations take Liszt's virtuosic standard as a starting point for complex figuration but in their organization also project uncharacteristically flexible attitudes for Brahms about the work concept. The division of the variations into two equal-length parts effectively creates two similar narratives that both end with climactic final variations. The result of playing the two books together is like playing the same piece twice. The beginning of the second book even repeats the unadorned main theme. While this may just underscore the pedagogical nature of the work as a set of studies, opus 35 has often attracted pianists to perform both books as a complete whole. Performers have sought to remedy opus 35's redundancy in various ways, by cutting one of the climactic final variations and reordering the inner variations (Arturo Benedetti Michelangeli) or by choosing simply to play one book by itself (Emil Gilels).[45] One might even claim that Brahms's exploration of open-form virtuosity fails to cohere as a creative response to Paganini's theme; instead, it is centered on giving the performer numerous options to showcase virtuosity. The flexibility leaves one wondering whether the structural integrity of the variations would be in any way affected by the composition of a third or even a fourth book of variations. In addition, the Paganini Variations are one of Brahms's only works to share material with the *51 Übungen*, suggesting even further a uniquely relaxed attitude from an otherwise discreet composer who habitually destroyed evidence of pre-compositional activity.[46]

Another feature of the Paganini Variations that speaks to its un-Brahmsian approach to virtuosity is its Lisztian use of ossia passages. Brahms employs optional ossias most often as simpler versions for difficult passages, for instance, in the alternate version of the left hand at the conclusion of book 2, variation 14, which breaks octaves to avoid leaps (ex. 5.3a).[47] Book 2, variation 8 marks one of the only examples in Brahms's works to provide an ossia that is not simpler than the original (ex. 5.3b). Instead, it presents harmonically altered material and figuration in sixths instead of the predominant thirds in the original version and offers another rendering of the entire variation. By giving the performer these options, which are not based on providing a simpler path, Brahms loosens the sense that there is a definitive version of this variation. This allows the performer to choose between two quite different musical manifestations of this particular variation (or possibly options for varied repeats), reflecting multiple compositional pathways in a style that occurs much more frequently in Liszt's works.[48] Put in even more extreme terms, based on whichever of the two books of the Paganini Variations is considered to be the "original," the other might even be thought of as an ossia composition itself.

Example 5.3a. Brahms, Variations on a Theme of Paganini, op. 35, book 2, var. 14, mm. 89–101

Example 5.3b. Brahms, Variations on a Theme of Paganini, op. 35, book 2, var. 8, mm. 1–12

Example 5.4. Brahms, Rhapsody in B Minor, op. 79, no. 1, mm. 1–5 b. 1

The B-Minor Rhapsody, op. 79, no. 1, constitutes a more characteristically Brahmsian engagement with virtuosity. Its internalization of difficulty is present from the outset (ex. 5.4). This is a passage that demonstrates the severe demands Brahms's music frequently makes upon listeners. Physically, the opening of the rhapsody is not challenging for the pianist in a virtuosic sense. Musically, the listener and performer are presented immediately with three separate contrapuntal strands that move by different intervals. Conceived as an aural "three-hand technique," this passage contains three separate events that, in the notated agitato tempo, constitute an uncompromising premise for the listener's engagement with the work's materials. Describing the rhapsody's opening as an example of "tiered polyphony," Brent Auerbach observes that in this compositional style "the increased contrapuntal activity" results in "pieces that are deeply complex, ones a listener could not hope to fully appreciate in one or even several hearings."[49] He suggests that this type of difficulty is reserved for piano or chamber works, perhaps for the sake of repeated performances for the listener to fully grasp the works and their complexity. Significantly, Auerbach's description of virtuosity warns against conceptualizing the rhapsody as a piece centered on display: "Brahms consistently cautions pianists not to obscure the dense material with excess speed and not to spoil the heightened emotional states of these special works by transforming them into flashy, virtuosic showpieces." This is not to say that the rhapsody is without instances of external virtuosity.

Brahms draws the work's tension from the symmetrical cyclic patterns at its outset, juxtaposing them to the asymmetrical harmonies of the traditional tonal system. The resulting clash erupts in powerful climaxes. Auerbach observes that the cyclic patterns of the opening have significant consequences on the harmonic organization of the Rhapsody's first sixty-seven measures, as they compose out a larger cycle of their own and trace a hexatonic path through various key areas.[50] Frank Samarotto has written that "the cyclic drive through equal intervals is an obsession of this conflict-ridden piece."[51] Samarotto reads the cyclic progression as a generator of conflict against the

Example 5.5. Brahms, Rhapsody in B Minor, op. 79, no. 1, mm. 49–66

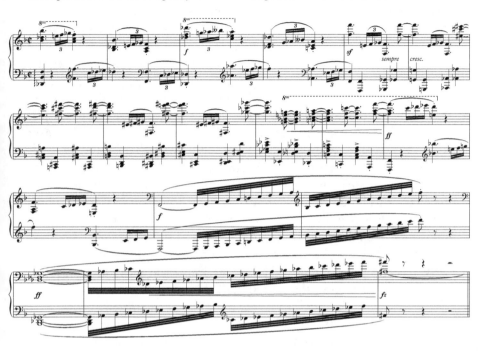

backdrop of authentic tonality from a Schenkerian perspective. The internal friction intensifies to such an extent that a dramatic scalar passage in measures 62–66 erupts in a moment of external display (ex. 5.5). Describing the moment as an "earthquake, a tectonic shift in the foundations of tonal space," Samarotto reads what seems initially to be a deceptive cadence in B-flat minor "in reality to be F♯ forcibly supplanting F-natural through sheer force of will."[52] Whereas Auerbach interprets this passage as a continuation of the hexatonic path, Samarotto regards it as a rupture against nature or, in other words, a harmonic event at odds with the tonal system within which Brahms's works were composed. However one interprets the structure of the passage, it is overwhelmingly evident that Brahms chose the most pronounced clash between the conflicting elements of the rhapsody's opening section—the force of the cycles versus the governing tonal backdrop—as the moment to unleash a virtuosic scalar flourish.

The bare ascending scales of this passage are strikingly austere, recalling the conclusion of Chopin's G-Minor Ballade, op. 23. Both instances prioritize virtuosic internalization by imbuing their respective local contexts with dramatic seriousness. Other passages in the rhapsody's A section make considerable physical demands upon the pianist. For example, measures 40–63 build an orchestral soundscape—in the manner of Brahms's re-creativity of larger instrumentations—requiring the pianist to leap regularly from one register to another, manage dense textural sonorities, and effectively voice and shape melodic and harmonic content in the process. Auerbach describes measures 53–62 of this passage as "thunderous, virtuosic music," which "forces pianists to claw their way up the keyboard one two- or four-note fragment at a time."[53] The closing of the A section intensifies the physical demands upon the pianist, as measures 81–89 stretch the hands with wide arpeggiated chords and registral leaps, heightening the emotional intensity of the passage (ex. 5.6). This brings to mind another virtuosic moment in Chopin, noted by Charles Rosen, as a point at which physical strain and emotional expression work in tandem: the climax of the "Winter Wind" Étude in A Minor, op. 25, no. 11 (mm. 81–84).[54] Furthermore, the rhapsody's notated meter is disturbed by the intensity of the physical gestures in the concluding measures leading up to the A section's final cadence, as the power of the rhapsody's "tectonic shifts" affect various musical parameters. Overall, the rhapsody's features described here draw attention within a relational field toward the work. The climactic passages of display emphatically underline the conflicts of musical process begun early on in the work, while the more subdued, unassuming moments of the rhapsody are dense with musical detail that challenge even the most attentive listener. If the rhapsody can be considered a virtuosic work, it must be framed within a relational field that prioritizes the listener's and performer's attention toward the work,

Example 5.6. Brahms, Rhapsody in B Minor, op. 79, no. 1, mm. 81–93

constituting a substantially internalized virtuosity with occasional tendencies toward externalization.

Moving even further from music of external display, Brahms's late piano miniatures (like those of the late Liszt) engage difficulty in ways that almost eschew physical strain. For all that we might not think of these works as virtuosic by the standards of the time, they were initially criticized for some of the same reasons that showpieces were looked down upon as lesser art forms. A preoccupation with technique was often cited as a problem in Brahms's late style.[55] Christian Martin Schmidt and Margaret Notley have drawn attention to the aspects of Brahms's late style that drew criticism for their single-minded preoccupation with certain compositional techniques. Building upon Schmidt's discussion of these types of works, Notley observes that some of the late piano miniatures such as the E-Minor Intermezzo, op. 116, no. 5, and the F-Minor Intermezzo, op. 118, no. 4, were "concerned with compositional speculation and virtuosity, the 'prominence of artifice' Schmidt notes, to an extent that supports calling them mannerist."[56] The negative response to these works as being contrived, aloof, and overly concerned with the demonstration of compositional skill strikes a similar tone to the negative responses that characterized virtuosic showpieces as being unnatural, unfeeling, and manipulative. An extreme stylistic opposite of what could be called externally "virtuosic," Brahms's "mannerist" concern with compositional artifice in his late works continues an aesthetic concern to engage with difficulty through an entirely internalized set of virtuosic demands.

In particular, Notley describes Brahms's F-Minor Intermezzo, op. 118, no. 4, as an example in which the composer "took musical artifice to an extreme," citing its relentless focus on canonic imitation.[57] These internalizing tendencies in the F-Minor Intermezzo draw the relational field increasingly toward the musical text, moving as far as possible from an external conception of virtuosity. Steven Rings observes that the intermezzo's opening phrase begins with a focus on strict inversion that becomes progressively more flexible toward its end, passing attention instead to a focus on strict canonic activity (ex. 5.7).[58] Retroactively, Rings notes that the canon has been sounding since the beginning of the piece, aurally submerged in slower rhythmic values beneath the flowing triplets that highlight the inversion between the hands. Citing the "piece's agitated *Stimmung*," Rings argues that the release of this pressure is an important cause for the easing of tension leading to the phrase's cadence at measure 11. The language Rings uses strongly suggests an inner impetus driving the music, one that strives to keep its knotty complexities from reaching the surface in an overt fashion.

Example 5.7. Brahms, Intermezzo in F Minor, op. 118, no. 4, mm. 1–14

The tension of the work is founded upon the play of canonic audibility and inaudibility highlighted above by Rings, and this motivation continues in the work's arresting B section (ex. 5.8). The gradual relaxation of tension continues here, as extraneous noncanonic material falls away, leaving only the bare canon in a moment of extraordinary calm. In fact, the passage is so bare and continues for such a proportionally lengthy segment of the composition that commentators such as Edward Cone have found it to be problematic.[59] Cone seeks to examine the reasons for the discomfort he experiences in Brahms's works in which "structural or expressive intent seemed unclear" or in which he heard "some of Brahms's most celebrated lyrical utterances as developing in an almost uncontrolled manner." But he finds the opposite problem in the intermezzo's B section: an "excessive rigidity of pattern" that lasts for "forty almost tunelessly bare measures." His solution for understanding the B section is found through comparing it to the figuration of piano accompaniments in Brahms's lieder, since they similarly provide pared-down harmonic patterns, adding melodic flourishes only at the ends of phrases or stanzas. Drawing a comparison to Schumann's famously notated but unsounded "inner voice" in the Humoreske, op. 20, Cone suggests that the intermezzo's B section implies a melodic voice that is meant to be thought and not played, "to be heard with the inner ear." He goes on to propose that "the entire piece is not intended to be performed—exposed to an audience—but only to be played privately, for oneself."[60] If one is convinced by Cone's reading, the intermezzo's internal difficulties are maximized in the work's most unassuming passage, while the pianistic requirements of the passage are minimized to extreme simplicity. In effect, the B section requires the

Example 5.8. Brahms, Intermezzo in F Minor, op. 118, no. 4, mm. 51–91

engagement of three essential voices: two sounding canonic voices and one implied inner voice. Internalizing a virtuosic division of coordination, the B section's cyclical traversal of key areas by major thirds (A-flat major in mm. 52–67, E major in mm. 68–75, and C major in mm. 76–83) projects symmetry against the intermezzo's asymmetrical authentic tonal framework (as in the rhapsody), perhaps signifying further internal tension in a moment otherwise marked by serenity on the surface.

While physical difficulties and displays of technical skill are not a focus of the intermezzo, its emphasis on internal relationships and possible demands on the performer's and listener's imaginations create uniquely difficult challenges of their own. Along the continuum of virtuosity's relational field, if the intermezzo is still within range, it would have to be quite far from externalization.

Internalized Virtuosity in Brahms and After

Having considered virtuosity in the context of three works of Brahms, with an eye to comparisons with Liszt, let us revisit the research question of this essay: Is virtuosity possible only when difficulty is outwardly projected, or can it also materialize when demands are maximized upon the performer without display? While one may regard the question as primarily an aesthetic one, the continuum spanning externalization and internalization highlights the significance of difficulty as a constituent element of virtuosity. Using these examples to test virtuosity's conceptual boundaries, at what point does virtuosity cease to exist? Must we use a different vocabulary to describe Brahms's engagement with transcendental difficulty? If such difficulty does not contribute to virtuosity, is it then missing something? Is virtuosity's existence contingent upon the aesthetic appeal of display, so as to exclude music like that of most of Brahms? Through documenting the contextual aspects of Brahms's musical career that demonstrate his engagement with the discourse of virtuosity and after reflecting on the challenges of performing his music, I concur with Moseley that in Brahms's music, "fidelity to the text and virtuosity became one and the same" and additionally that the reconfiguration of virtuosity's relational field presents listeners with virtuosic challenges of their own.[61]

Through the engagement with difficulty, virtuosity's magnetism thrives. The dichotomizing of its demands through externalization or internalization is merely a construction, and a crude one at that, given the complexity and richness of musical experience. However, such a framework can at least provide a vocabulary for exploring virtuosity's limits and investigating it within diverging aesthetic contexts. Many accounts of Brahms's music have claimed, in one way or another, that it eschews virtuosity, even to the extent of being "anti-virtuosic." While understandable, given the deeply private, personal aspects of his later works, that label fails to account for the pervasive engagement with difficulty in Brahms's composing, including in the most unassuming and apparently simple works. Given virtuosity's dependence on difficulty, it is worth reevaluating the diverse roles difficulty can play in making a musical utterance virtuosic.

This is not to claim a revisionist stance on Brahms's historical context. As Notley has argued, many of Brahms's ideas were entrenched within a Viennese liberal worldview, and his attitudes toward virtuosity must be considered within that lens.[62] However, especially with Brahms, it is all too easy to avoid investigating aspects of his music that seem to fall outside of his associated categories. Daniel Beller-McKenna has written about the tendency, stemming from the association of Brahms with "absolute music," to view his works outside of time and origin, born of an impulse "to distance Brahms's music from the context of Germany and the second half of the nineteenth century."[63] He traces this as an "outgrowth of the Brahms-Wagner dichotomy," which in many ways, incorporates a "Brahms-Liszt" antithesis that shapes our attitudes toward virtuosity in Brahms's music. While Brahms and Liszt were in many ways quite different in their compositional outlook, seeing their relationship in terms of mutually exclusive poles obscures attributes their works clearly share.

In conclusion, it is intriguing to consider the repercussions of Brahms's incorporation of virtuosity into his compositions upon later music. As J. Peter Burkholder has boldly argued, "Brahms is the single most important influence on twentieth-century classical music—not in the way it sounds, but in how we think about it, how composers think about it, how music behaves, why it is written, and how composers measure their success."[64] Positing that Brahms became the starting point of musical modernism through artistic purpose rather than style, Burkholder also writes of the significant impact this had upon the intensifying demands of the listening experience. A further element of Brahms's output that shaped later music was his ability to seamlessly incorporate highly varied styles from numerous eras into his musical language, even incorporating the externalized virtuosity of Liszt. But Brahms's use of virtuosity for specific compositional purposes, as seen especially in the rhapsody and the intermezzo, speaks to a type of virtuosity that becomes an essential part of the work itself.

With this in mind, it is striking to consider one of the most famous compositional engagements with virtuosity in the twentieth century: Luciano Berio's *Sequenzas*, written in the span of 1958 to 2002. Janet Halfyard's description of this epic output resonates with the Brahmsian process of internalization and fits nicely in Burkholder's overarching narrative of Brahms's influence on musical modernism:

> By acknowledging the virtuosity demanded by the Sequenzas, Berio reinstates it as an acceptable and respectable concept in serious music, but he consciously separates his idea of virtuosity from the historical image of the empty-headed performer who is "apt to regard the written work as a mere vehicle for his own art." Berio's new virtuoso is an altogether different creature, a performer with the same technical abilities but without the suggested ego of their historical counterpart, who will therefore primarily seek to serve the needs of the composition rather than merely to thrill the audience with brilliant but, by implication, superficial displays of technique. Virtuosity now becomes an integral aspect of the composition itself, part of how it creates meaning rather than separate from it.[65]

From the uplifting morally to "acceptable and respectable" standards within "serious music," to the idea of serving the "needs of the composition" rather than purposes of display, and last but certainly not least, reinforcing the notion that virtuosity can be reconfigured to constitute part of the composition itself, the influence of Brahmsian virtuosity upon the "music of the future" becomes palpable.

Notes

1. Jim Samson, *Virtuosity and the Musical Work: The "Transcendental Studies" of Liszt* (Cambridge: Cambridge University Press, 2007), 2.
2. Samson summarizes his introduction's motivation as "progressively mediating this opposition, which arguably boils down to a developing opposition between the musical performance and the musical work" (ibid., 7).
3. In a letter to Hans Rosbaud, Arnold Schoenberg confided that "there is nothing I long for more intensely (if for anything) than to be taken for a better sort of Tchaikovsky—for heaven's sake: a bit better, but really that's all. Or if anything more, then that people should know my tunes and whistle them" (*Arnold Schoenberg Letters*, ed. Erwin Stein, trans. Eithne Wilkins and Ernst Kaiser [London: Faber and Faber, 1964], 212).
4. August Göllerich, *The Piano Master Classes of Franz Liszt, 1884–1886*, ed. Wilhelm Jerger, trans., ed., and enlarged by Richard Louis Zimdars (Bloomington: Indiana University Press, 1996), 10.
5. As described by Samson, the Romantic virtuoso "stood for freedom, for Faustian man, for the individual in search of self-realization—free, isolated, striving, desiring. Heroically overcoming his instrument, he was a powerful symbol of transcendence. The type was represented most clearly by two men: Paganini and Liszt" (*Virtuosity and the Musical Work*, 75).
6. Florence May, *The Life of Brahms*, 2nd edn. (London, 1948), 1:85–87, cited in *A Brahms Reader*, ed. Michael Musgrave (New Haven, CT: Yale University Press, 2000), 19.
7. Kurt Hofmann, "Brahms the Hamburg Musician 1833–1862," in *The Cambridge Companion to Brahms*, ed. Michael Musgrave (Cambridge: Cambridge University Press, 1999), 17–19.
8. Richard Heuberger, *Erinnerungen und Johannes Brahms*, ed. K. Hofmann (Tutzing, 1976), 95, recollected Brahms's thoughts on his musical education: "neither Schumann nor Wagner nor I learnt.... Schumann took one path, Wagner the other, I yet a third. Yet none of us actually learnt properly. None of us passed through a systematic school. In truth it was afterwards that we learnt" (quoted in, and translated by, Michael Musgrave, *A Brahms Reader*, 62).

9. John Daverio, *Crossing Paths: Schubert, Schumann, and Brahms* (New York: Oxford University Press, 2002), 200.
10. Roger Moseley, "Between Work and Play: Brahms as Performer of His Own Music," in *Brahms and His World, Revised Edition*, ed. Walter Frisch and Kevin C. Karnes (Princeton, NJ: Princeton University Press, 2009), 137–66.
11. Eduard Bernsdorf, *Signale für die musikalische Welt* (9 February 1859), 71–72: "Herr Brahms has deliberately made the pianoforte part of his concerto as uninteresting as possible.... Herr Brahms's technique as a pianist does not attain the standard that we have a right to expect of today's concert pianists" (Moseley, "Between Work and Play," 139).
12. An example from an anonymous critic, "Stuttgart," *Allgemeine Musikalische Zeitung* 16/51 (1881): 810–11: "We must remember that [Brahms] is primarily a composer.... Details lack finish, and his playing often seems somewhat colorless, but on the whole he grips the audience through his objective and stylish rendering" (Moseley, "Between Work and Play," 143).
13. Göllerich, *The Piano Master Classes of Franz Liszt, 1884–1886*, 11.
14. Alexander Stefaniak, *Schumann's Virtuosity: Criticism, Composition, and Performance in Nineteenth-Century Germany* (Bloomington: Indiana University Press, 2016), 12.
15. Moseley, "Between Work and Play," 142. The learned vs. inherently possessed aspects of virtuosity are thoughtfully considered by James Deaville, "A Star Is Born? Czerny, Liszt, and the Pedagogy of Virtuosity," in *Beyond the Art of Finger Dexterity*, ed. David Gramit, (Rochester, NY: University of Rochester Press, 2008), 52–66. Brahms's exercises and études clearly emulate Czerny's emphasis on the learned aspects of virtuosity.
16. George Henschel, *Personal Recollections of Johannes Brahms* (Boston: R. G. Badger, 1907), 18, describes how Brahms played the octave trills of the First Concerto: "He would lift his hands up high and let them come down on the keys with a force like that of a lion's paw. It was grand!"
17. Max Kalbeck, *Johannes Brahms*, rev. ed. (Berlin, 1912–21; repr. Tutzing, 1976) 1:90, quoted and translated in Moseley, "Between Work and Play," 139.
18. Quoted in Peter Clive, *Brahms and His World: A Biographical Dictionary* (Lanham, MD: Scarecrow Press: 2006), 299.
19. Daverio, *Crossing Paths*, 201.
20. Stefaniak, *Schumann's Virtuosity*.
21. Dana Gooley, "The Battle against Instrumental Virtuosity in the Early Nineteenth Century," in *Franz Liszt and His World*, ed. Christopher H. Gibbs and Dana Gooley (Princeton, NJ: Princeton University Press, 2006), 75–111, traces the antipathy expressed toward virtuosity during its rise.
22. Eduard Hanslick, "In dem erste Satze des Brahmsschen Concertes grollen die Gewitter der Neunten Symphonie" (*Concerte, Componisten, und Virtuosen der*

letzten fünfzehn Jahre: 1870–1885 [Berlin: Allgemeine Verein für Deutsche Literatur, 1886], 109–11, cited in Alexander Stefaniak, "'Poetic Virtuosity': Robert Schumann as a Critic and Composer of Virtuoso Instrumental Music" [PhD diss., University of Rochester, 2012], 24).

23. F. E. Kirby, *Music for Piano: A Short History* (Pompton Plains, NJ: Amadeus Press, 1995), 234. Indeed, all three of Brahms's early piano sonatas demonstrate elements of Lisztian cyclicism and thematic transformation, an influence on Brahms's later practice of developing variation. See Walter Frisch, *Brahms and the Principle of Developing Variation* (Berkeley: University of California Press, 1990).

24. Peter H. Smith, "Brahms and Subject/Answer Rhetoric," *Music Analysis* 20, no. 2 (2001): 231–32, describes Brahms's very fusion of past stylistic elements as "virtuosic": "The idea that a procedure culled from the Baroque tradition can interact with a sonata-form practice based on the Viennese tradition, in the service of characteristically nineteenth-century formal relationships, brings us back to our point of departure. With the perspective of hindsight and our own present interest in the past, we are in a better position to appreciate the virtuosity and inventiveness of Brahms's engagement with tradition."

25. Joseph Joachim called it Brahms's "friendly predilection for Hungarian vintages," in *Briefwechsel, Johannes Brahms im Briefwechsel mit Joseph Joachim*, ed. Andreas Moser (Berlin: Deutsche Brahms Gesellschaft, 1908 and 1912), 290, quoted in Daverio, *Crossing Paths*, 212.

26. Daverio draws attention to the significant number of vigorous, celebratory examples of Brahms's Hungarian style, while also addressing its ability to inspire great pathos as well (ibid., 215).

27. Ibid., 191–242.

28. Brahms's transcultural interest in Gypsy idioms is usefully considered alongside Shay Loya, *Liszt's Transcultural Modernism and the Hungarian-Gypsy Tradition* (Rochester, NY: University of Rochester Press, 2011). Loya's argument concerning the gradual internalization and submersion of the *verbunkos* style within Liszt's later works parallels the present study's consideration of Brahms's gradual internalization of virtuosity.

29. Daverio, *Crossing Paths*, 210–11.

30. Ibid., 201.

31. Robert Schumann, *On Music and Musicians*, ed. Konrad Wolff, trans. Paul Rosenfeld (New York: Pantheon Books, 1946), 253: "Sitting at the piano he began to disclose wonderful regions to us. We were drawn into even more enchanting spheres. Besides, he is a player of genius who can make of the piano an orchestra of lamenting and loudly jubilant voices. There were sonatas, veiled symphonies rather [*mehr verscheierte Sinfonien*]." The first sentence leads one to wonder: Is Schumann talking about Brahms's playing or his compositions?

32. John Rink, "Opposition and Integration in the Piano Music," in *The Cambridge Companion to Brahms*, ed. Michael Musgrave (Cambridge: Cambridge University Press, 1999), 81.
33. Malcolm MacDonald, "'Veiled Symphonies?' The Concertos," in *The Cambridge Companion to Brahms*, 156.
34. See Samson, *Virtuosity and the Musical Work: The "Transcendental Studies" of Liszt*. On Liszt's re-creativity as virtuoso, Susan Bernstein, in *Virtuosity of the Nineteenth Century: Performing Music and Language in Heine, Liszt, and Baudelaire* (Stanford, CA: Stanford University Press, 1998), 112, writes, "Liszt presents a spectacle of alteration. His consistent inconsistency forms the very consistency of the virtuoso—an inconsistency determined by the oscillation between egotistic protrusion and transmissive self-effacement," while Charles Rosen, in *The Romantic Generation* (Cambridge, MA: Harvard University Press, 1995), 502–3, writes, "At what point Liszt ceases to paraphrase and starts to compose is a question that often makes very little sense . . . composition and paraphrase were not identical for him, but they were so closely interwoven that separation is impossible."
35. Eduard Hanslick, *Fünf Jahre Musik [1891–1895]* (Berlin: Allgemeiner Verein für deutschen Literatur, 1896), 259, quoted in Steven Rings, "The Learned Self: Artifice in Brahms's Late Intermezzi," in *Expressive Intersections in Brahms: Essays in Analysis and Meaning*, ed. Heather Platt and Peter H. Smith (Bloomington: Indiana University Press, 2012), 30.
36. Leon Botstein, "Time and Memory: Concert Life, Science, and Music in Brahms's Vienna," in *Brahms and His World, Revised Edition*, ed. Walter Frisch and Kevin C. Karnes (Princeton, NJ: Princeton University Press, 2009), 19.
37. Ibid., 19.
38. Ibid., 22.
39. Letter of early October 1892, Litzmann, *Clara Schumann und Johannes Brahms*, 2:479, trans. Styra Avins and Josef Eisinger, in *Johannes Brahms: Life and Letters*, ed. Styra Avins (New York: Oxford University Press, 1997), 698 (Moseley, "Between Work and Play," 143).
40. Ibid., 142.
41. Kenneth Hamilton, "The Virtuoso Tradition," in *The Cambridge Companion to the Piano*, ed. David Rowland (Cambridge: Cambridge University Press, 1998), 58.
42. Brahms's *51 Übungen* provide a helpful series of steps to achieve gradual comfort with the execution of rhythmic combinations, beginning with three against four in 1a and 1b, four against five in 1c and 1d, and six against seven in 1e and 1f. Additionally, Brahms features six against seven in virtuosic scalar flourishes in measures 266–67 and 361–63 in the fourth movement of the Second Piano Concerto, op. 83.

43. Julian Hook, "How to Perform Impossible Rhythms," *Music Theory Online* 17, no. 4 (2011), addresses rhythmic difficulties in performing Brahms's piano music as well as works by other composers from the nineteenth century.
44. Julian Littlewood, *The Variations of Johannes Brahms* (London: Plumbago Books, 2004), 104, observes, "Nonetheless, these variations are entitled 'Studies' and contain some of the most dazzling pianism in Brahms's solo compositions, yet without the extrovert virtuosity found in his piano concertos. For instance, variations I/5, I/6 and II/7 are taxing examinations of typically Brahmsian metrical conflict and dislocation, yet many concertgoers would be unlikely fully to appreciate the pianistic challenges these rhythms pose as compared with, say, a spectacular but deceptively straightforward Lisztian cascade of double octaves."
45. Johannes Brahms, *4 Ballades op. 10, Variations on a Theme by Paganini op. 35*, Arturo Benedetti Michelangeli, Aura Music, recorded 1973, released 1999; Johannes Brahms, *Variations on a Theme by Paganini, op. 35, Book 1*, Emil Gilels, Melodiya, recorded in 1983.
46. The performer of the Paganini Variations is prepared for no. 11 from book 2 is by exercise 29. Exercises 5 and 6 prepare for book 2, no. 9.
47. The Variations on an Original Theme, op. 21, no. 1, also employ *più facile ossia* passages. Furthermore, Brahms composed an entire *più facile* version of the opus 39 Waltzes.
48. [Ed.] See Jonathan Kregor's chapter on Liszt's ossias in this volume.
49. Brent Auerbach, "Tiered Polyphony and Its Determinative Role in the Piano Music of Johannes Brahms," *Journal of Music Theory* 52, no. 2 (2008): 318.
50. Ibid., 295.
51. Frank Samarotto, "Against Nature: Interval Cycles and Prolongational Conflict in Brahms's Rhapsody, op. 79, no. 1," in *A Composition as a Problem III: (Proceedings of the 3rd International Conference on Music Theory)*, ed. M. Humal (Tallinn: Scripta Musicalia), 100.
52. Ibid., 101.
53. Auerbach, 303.
54. Rosen, *The Romantic Generation*, 382. His description is striking in regard to the audience's appreciation of the passage's difficulty: "The very positions into which the hands are forced here are like gestures of exasperated despair. It would seem as if the physical awkwardness is itself an expression of emotional tension. The public does not, I think, generally realize the amount of pain actually attendant upon virtuoso pianism."
55. [Ed.] See Shay Loya's chapter in this volume.
56. Margaret Notley, *Lateness and Brahms: Music and Culture in the Twilight of Viennese Liberalism* (New York: Oxford University Press, 2007), 59. Notley refers here to Christian Martin Schmidt, *Brahms und seine Zeit* (Laaber: Laaber Verlag, 1998), 89, cited and translated in Notley, 40–41. Some reviews critical

of Brahms's late works that support Notley's claims described some pieces as "perpetual playing with techniques," in "W. Fr.," *Neues Wiener Tagblatt*, 15 February 1889, and also cite melodic ideas as continually disrupted by "the sands of rhythmic-harmonic artifice," in "k. st.," *Illustrirtes Wiener Extrablatt*, 14 February 1889.

57. Notley, *Lateness and Brahms*, 59.
58. Steven Rings, "The Learned Self: Artifice in Brahms's Late Intermezzi," in *Expressive Intersections in Brahms: Essays in Analysis and Meaning*, ed. Heather Platt and Peter H. Smith (Bloomington: Indiana University Press, 2012), 43–45.
59. Edward Cone, "Brahms: Songs with Words and Songs without Words," *Integral* 1 (1987): 31–33.
60. Ibid., 36. For more on the aesthetic and structural aspects of inner voices in Brahms's works, see Diego Cubero, "Inwardness and Inner Melodies in Brahms's Piano Works," *Music Theory Online* 23, no. 1 (2017).
61. Moseley, "Between Work and Play," 142.
62. Notley, *Lateness and Brahms*, 15–35.
63. Daniel Beller-McKenna, *Brahms and the German Spirit* (Cambridge, MA: Harvard University Press, 2004), 4–5.
64. J. Peter Burkholder, "Brahms and Twentieth-Century Classical Music," *19th-Century Music* 8, no. 1 (1984): 75.
65. Janet K. Halfyard, "Provoking Acts: The Theatre of Berio's *Sequenzas*," in *Berio's Sequenzas: Essays on Performance, Composition and Analysis*, ed. Janet K. Halfyard (Farnham: Ashgate Publishing, 2007), 115. Halfyard's internal reference is to Warren D. Allen, "Art and Virtuosity," *Bulletin of the American Musicological Society*, 11–13 (1948): 78.

Part Two

Lisztian Virtuosity: Theoretical Approaches

Chapter Six

The Practice of Pianism

Virtuosity and Oral History

Jim Samson

When you revisit your own books long after their publication their weaknesses stare back at you, clear as daylight. The principal casualty of my book on Liszt is performance, and specifically performance history.[1] The problem is partly that the historical dimension of the ideal types I proposed in that book was not adequately explored, but it is also that, despite the title, I focused on prescriptions for virtuosity rather than on virtuosity itself. My intention in this chapter is to offer a corrective to this by reflecting on virtuosity as a dimension of performance rather than of composition.

The Phrasicon

When Nicholas Cook announced that "we are all (ethno)musicologists now," he invited us to reflect on labels and on borders.[2] In the end, his provocation served only to confirm that although practitioners may resist the tendency of labels to control and conserve, the labels somehow endure and with them a bundle of associated, and deeply embedded, research curricula. Subdisciplinary borders are not that easily erased, but the borderlands have become more interesting. There has been a convergence of interests and methods, and this has allowed for unusual cross-flows and challenging adjacencies. This chapter takes as its starting point one such borderland exchange. At the very time it was commissioned I was working on traditional epic singing in the meta-regions surrounding the Black Sea, a topic about as far removed from pianism as one might imagine.[3] Could there be anything from my work on epics that might have a bearing on traditions of pianism? At the very least there might be a handful of suggestive prompts.

Epic traditions draw upon an oral repository that remains for the most part inaccessible to us. Of course some of that repository has been captured on record, but its fluid, variable character is prone to be compromised by the recording medium, which also imposed specific constraints. And anyway we did not always have recording. How much do we really know about epic singing in a prerecording age? Now all of this could apply in more or less every particular to traditions of pianism. And we could take the analogy a stage further. Epic singing, unlike many other genres of traditional music making, possesses an extensive written trace as well as an oral repository. And, self-evidently, so does the practice of pianism. Indeed it is by way of that written trace that both these cultural practices have been most characteristically studied, and for this very reason the ontology of their products has been overdetermined—overspecified—by notated forms.[4]

One prompt from the study of epics concerns a body of writing on the textualization of oral epics, which not only deconstructs the dichotomy between orality and literacy but also explores the implications of cohabiting oral and literary forms. I think of Lauri Honko's application of so-called intersemiotic translation to epic traditions.[5] This concept, introduced by Roman Jakobson, promotes translation across media and systems.[6] It is not necessary to explore in detail how Honko draws upon it. The main point is that it encourages a fluid and compound understanding of manifest form, countering or supplementing a purely text-based analysis. The ontology of epics is neither one thing nor the other, we might say, but both. And if we speak of a text, it should be a hypertext.

Crossing over to pianism, this invokes the moment when a pianist-composer steps from the piano to the desk and picks up a pen. It is the interface between a world of sound, where an embodied musical thinking is extended by the technologies of the keyboard, and a world of notated forms, where it is extended by the quite different tools of pen and paper. That interface bears examination. Some scholars (Saul Novack, for instance) and some composers (Alexander Goehr, for instance) have argued for a qualitative distinction between thinking in sounds and thinking in concepts, maybe a bit similar to the distinction psychologists make between procedural and declarative knowledge.[7] Novack referred to a "mind-ear axis." Then again, it could be that the former is really just a speeded-up version of the latter (I have not encountered any discussion of a "mind-ear axis" among music psychologists, even those—Nicolas Donin, for instance—engaged directly in studying the creative process). In any case, the symbiosis involved in that moment of transfer is of some interest. So-called 4E cognition could well have some traction on it, and I have already gone halfway with my reference to an "embodied" musical thinking "extended" by different tools and technologies; later I will get to the other two Es: "enacted" and "embedded."[8] But there are other angles, and I will address one of them now, by way of a further prompt from the study of epic.

I refer here to Parry's and Lord's notion of anterior speech, a formula-based, generative corpus of material that has some capacity not just to mediate oral and literary forms but to program that compound understanding of form advocated by Lauri Honko.[9] And this is reinforced by ethnographic studies of the learning process of epic singers, especially in Turkic traditions, emphasizing the importance of aural schemata to each stage of the apprenticeship.[10] So what can we carry across from this? Thanks to scholars such as Robert Gjerdingen, we have come to appreciate the hidden world of orally transmitted schemata—the phrasicon—that not only helped to determine learning processes but also shaped musical narratives in art music of different kinds in the eighteenth century.[11] Now Gjerdingen's phrasicon functions in almost every way like Parry's and Lord's "anterior speech," and it continued to do so right through to at least the late nineteenth century.[12] It is one of those borderland convergences I spoke of earlier.

It would be a Herculean task to document the gradual shift of emphasis between a declining tradition of aural teaching models (the partimenti and solfeggi of the Italian conservatories) and an ascendant tradition of notated exercises in north European cultural capitals. These latter are of two classes. There were the contrapuntal-compositional exercises associated with theory treatises by Johann Kirnberger and Johann Albrechsberger in particular,[13] and there were the practical keyboard exercises (études or *leçons*) associated with the rise of modern conservatories.[14] In respect of this shift of emphasis the early nineteenth century represented an era of transformation in music pedagogy, and with complex political and cultural histories lurking in the background (the work of Cynthia Gessele on the Paris Conservatoire remains informative here).[15] But in any case the lexical bundles in notated exercises of both kinds continued to function as a kind of anterior speech in the Parry and Lord sense. Although he appears not to have published on the subject, Ludwig Holtmeier beautifully makes the case at the piano, as he demonstrates how a wealth of late-classical repertory, including Beethoven and Schubert, reworked and elaborated standard formulae drawn from the compositional treatises.[16]

Now when I wrote *Virtuosity and the Musical Work* I was aware of a phrasicon, though I did not actually use the word. My phrasicon—my anterior speech, if you like—consisted of what I then called "ideal types": genre markers, musical-rhetorical figures, and idiomatic figures. I do not renounce any of that, but if I were writing the book today I would have more to say about a phrasicon, thanks to the work of Gjerdingen and Holtmeier and of others such as Giorgio Sanguinetti.[17] I would want, in other words, to locate it within a wider context. And actually that might point me yet again to the folklorists, for example, to what Richard Baumann has called the "generic patterning" of epics, a semi-latent mode of construction, or assemblage, that in turn may presuppose, and may even have promoted, a mode of generic listening.[18] Might there be parallels with generic hearing in pianism? We all know there are limits to what can be recovered from earlier practices. Even so, there may be things we can say, even about listening. Everyone recognizes that the rhythmic pattern in Chopin's sonata movement spells out a controlling "funeral march" genre, but in an age of structural hearing, or under the long shadow cast by that age, we could miss—because of its metrical placement—the role of that identical pattern as a passing generic fragment in the A-minor prelude, especially in light of the prevailing *Affekt*. In an age of generic hearing, we might have been more inclined to pick it up.

I am already confronting the history in my title. In fact, virtually every author I have cited, whether folklorist or theorist, addresses history first and foremost, specifically how we might do historical justice to oral traditions: to performance. The Parry and Lord answer was to commute between a notated historical trace and a contemporary oral practice, basically between Homer and the Yugoslav epics. Their system—and that is not really too strong a word to describe their analysis of epic—was all about restoring the balance between oral and notated forms. We might seek to do something similar with pianism by commuting between score and improvisation. And if we do so, we will certainly expose yet again the Parry and Lord paradox, which is that improvisation can both stretch and also freeze the conventions of composition. It is as true of pianism as it is of epic poetry. The commute would invoke yet again the historical phrasicon, all those aural models and notated exercises that were in part occulted during what Reinhard Strohm called, with heavy irony since he does not believe in it, "the age of the work-concept."[19] The phrasicon is all about a shared pool of schemata, assimilated partly by osmosis but based on the habit formation that comes with formulaic learning processes in both composition and performance. It allows a heavy dose of historical hermeneutics to complement, and in some cases to counter, the findings of formal analysis.

The Emancipated Performer

To return to *Virtuosity and the Musical Work*, I reiterate that this book was really about musical materials and not about "enactment," to cite a third category of 4E cognition. Of course, I sketched in some background on performance traditions, including Italian operatic and violin schools and later schools of pianism. But all this was at a level of some generality. Had I sought greater specificity, I might have singled out performers and performing styles, as Kenneth Hamilton did in parts of his book *After the Golden Age: Romantic Pianism and Modern Performance*.[20] But that path is not exactly straightforward. Indeed, it is pitted with conceptual potholes. Just about any framework you adopt—teacher-pupil genealogies, national schools, generations—risks foundering on the difficulty of reconciling the special and the typical, a problem, incidentally, that should haunt our attempts at compositional history equally. In fact, it should probably haunt the ethnomusicologists too; witness the collector who invariably seeks out the best singers. And all this before we come up against what Oliver Strunck called the "impenetrable barrier of oral traditions," a barrier that has relevance to pianism too.[21]

The biggest of the potholes is the paradigm of interpretation within which discussions of musical performance were trapped for such a very long time.[22] So powerful was (is) this paradigm that it embraced even those performers who appeared most blatantly to resist it. I was reminded of it when reading Claudio Arrau, a performer who reflected long and hard on his own and others' playing. At one point Arrau contrasts the pianism of Schnabel with that of Edwin Fischer. Schnabel is regarded as the "supreme intellectual authority," the "servant of music"; Fischer is "volcanic, eruptive," often "*selbstherrlich*," "not above putting in things that are not in the score."[23] The space between these two approaches is of course real, and it has its own history. It was opened up in the nineteenth century, following an earlier understanding of performance as the final stage (in rhetorical terms, the execution) of a much less differentiated process of making music.[24] Liszt himself, in his essay on Clara Schumann, made a valiant attempt to reach across the space and hold together the two diverging positions. For all that performers should show the most profound respect for the masterpieces of the great composers, "virtuosity is not a submissive handmaid to the composition."[25]

By the early twentieth century the space was maximally wide. It is no surprise that Arrau was on the side of fidelity to the text, but he was quite unable to resist the attractions of the other position. Of one performance by Busoni he conceded that "it was so marvellously done, and so creatively, that you had to accept it," though you could never regard it as "a final interpretation."[26] He said something similar about Rachmaninoff as pianist.[27] The space is indeed real, but the key point is that it is not a space between composer and performer. What is at stake is the attitude to the score, not to the composer's "idea." On one shore—Stravinsky is standing there—that idea was embodied in a notated text. On the other shore—Busoni is there—it could only be imperfectly realized in the text, but it might be made accessible through the text in the hands of an inspired performer. In effect, this reorders a Platonic degenerative sequence, such that the performance, although subsequent to the text, might come closer to the ideal form of the work. Actually, Busoni's reworking of Schoenberg's opus 11, number 2 takes this a stage further, by recording on the page his attempt to find the idea lurking behind what he perceives to be Schoenberg's imperfect notation; this particular reworking is not remotely covered by the aesthetics of transcription. In any case, the point is that what unites Stravinsky and Busoni is a default position that recognizes the authority of the composer's idea.

Yet elsewhere Arrau introduces a quite different thought. He acknowledges that some composers may actually need a little help, identifying certain pieces that he says "have to be made" and thus highlighting not just the collaborative but the redemptive role of the performer.[28] He was citing Liszt in particular here. *Mazeppa* and *Harmonies du Soir* (from the *Transcendental Études*) are pieces that, according to him, "have to be made." Compare Alfred Brendel's observation that Liszt "faithfully and fatally mirrors the character of the interpreter."[29] Not everyone will like how Arrau "makes" the transcendentals in that late recording. But at least there can be little doubt about the overall strategy, which is to allow backgrounds to become foregrounds by promoting figuration and the left-hand layer and thus distancing what some might take to be melodic blatancy or overrehearsed harmonic shifts. It is a redemptive strategy, but for me at least there is a cost: a laboured *Feux-follets* whose rallentandos make the theme present and significant rather than elusive and insubstantial, a distinctly, almost perversely, understated *Eroica*, and more besides. It is all in keeping with the organicist readings of the later recordings, in contrast to the modernist readings of the early ones, which were no doubt apt reflections of the cultural ecology of Berlin in the 1920s and early 1930s.

Let us stay with this one performer for a bit as we zoom in further on enactment. The two phases of Arrau's recording history—pre- and post-Philips—are a mantra of criticism, and they are most easily compared through repeat recordings of the same pieces: Ravel's *Jeux d'eau*, the Chopin Ballades, and most telling of all Schumann's *Carnaval*, where Arrau's ideas on psychoanalysis offer an irresistible explanatory framework. André Tubeuf goes so far as to suggest that "Schumann was an existential test for [Arrau], an obviously double identity, to which he must restore its lost unity."[30] He was referring, of course, to the later recording. The timings alone speak volumes (the early recording is "ruthlessly driven," in the words of one Berlin critic), and that is true of the other doubles I mentioned, with the later recording invariably the more expansive (the one exception is Chopin's Ballade no. 2, op. 38, but this is because Arrau completely rethought the opening theme). In other ways too, the early and late readings seem to inhabit radically different expressive worlds, and Arrau himself came to view the hard-edged, brittle quality of the early recordings with some distaste. Then there emerged what we might call a "last style": performances of Bach and recordings of Chopin, Debussy, and late Schubert, including the C-Minor Sonata (D. 958), about which Arrau had something to say. He referred to passages of the finale that he used to play "in an almost graceful way. Now I feel very strongly that the whole movement is very tragic, very close to the idea of death."[31]

Arrau was describing there what he considered a property of the work, one that he took some time to recognize. But that property really existed only in his own mind. When he recorded the Schubert he was generating, not recovering, musical meanings. In other words, whatever Arrau may have said about interpretation, his recording history makes concrete something that few of us would quarrel with these days, which is that not just certain pieces but *all* pieces have to be made. And that goes for technical, as well as expressive, properties, if indeed we can separate the two. Charles Rosen used to tell students that he could not really say where a voice actually begins in one of those passages of freely idiomatic counterpoint in Chopin; the performer has to make a decision about that. Now of course I am not speaking of laissez-faire. Performers constantly negotiate between the self and the forms, but the forms have less to do with the composer's idea, even if that were available, than with pedigreed performance praxes that over time have become a sedimented layer of the work's identity. It is true that the emancipated performer is widely recognized by scholars of so-called performance studies these days;

they speak of scripts rather than texts (Nicholas Cook), of "performance in" rather than "performance of" a work (Christa Brüstle).[32] But it is striking, all the same, that the flagship studies exploring expression in performance still tend to be work bound rather than topic generated, which actually would make more sense.[33] We pay lip service to the emancipated performer, but does our analysis really register this? Does our history? If we truly accepted that the composer does not hold a monopoly over signification, we would surely allow performers a much stronger claim on our reading of history than they currently enjoy. And if we did that, a number of other things, including gender balance and the geographies of centers and peripheries, would shift around a bit within our narratives.

The Practice

If I were to rewrite the Liszt book today, I would certainly elevate the practice of performance, and I emphasize the term "practice." In several publications I have advocated "the practice" as a primary category of cultural history.[34] Again, it is an approach that has been alive and well in ethnomusicology for many years, and I will allow one last prompt from that direction. In her discussion of oral traditions of epic, Margaret Beissinger remarks that epics take their identity from the relational context in which they are embedded (and here I cite the fourth element in 4E cognition), describing them as "texts embedded in an interdependent web of context, performative event, performer, and audience," and she goes on to illustrate how the shifting relations between enabling occasions, marked poet-musicians, and performance arenas invest these texts with particular power.[35] To make that specific, we might invoke the epic traditions of the Don Cossacks. If we view those traditions as a historically changing practice, we will note an emergent ethos of professionalism that in its turn produced a culture of virtuosity. I refer here not just to the singular compound of heterophony and polyphony but also to the wordless bravura descant characteristic of this tradition, comparable to the wordless *krimanchuli* of Gurian polyphony in Georgia. In both the Don Cossack and the Gurian cases, virtuosity is the point, and in the case of the *krimanchuli* I would be happy to recycle the language I used in the Liszt book: an occlusion of reference, a surrender to mechanism, and the stigma of the gratuitous (you just need to ask an East Georgian song master what he thinks of the Gurian tradition).

Now in theorizing practices it is all but obligatory to invoke Pierre Bourdieu, who argues that all practices, including cultural practices, are a priori political: they are, in other words, power-impregnated.[36] This is because the social spaces, or "fields," to use Bourdieu's terminology, that are generated by practices establish institutions, rules, schemes of domination, legitimate opinions, and so on and so forth. And insofar as these fields possess an autonomous status, practitioners serve to legitimate the forms and beliefs of the field as though they are self-evident; they become a kind of "second nature." Bourdieu is not in need of endorsement from me, but I do find this a persuasive way of conceptualizing a practice, apart from one thing. His schema, at least as I read him, leaves limited space for an ethos, which I take to be of cardinal importance.

This is where Alasdair MacIntyre's understanding of a practice comes in, not as a replacement for Bourdieu but as a qualifier.[37] It is an understanding grounded in neo-Aristotelian ethics. For Aristotle, without virtues you cannot flourish, or in modern terms, you cannot achieve a sense of personal authenticity. Now MacIntyre reworks the Aristotelian position on virtues by arguing that they are embedded in historically grounded social practices, but he still stresses the moral goods inherent in these practices, and he sees them as internal goods; in other words, right actions are not instrumental or utilitarian but are determined by the ethos of the practice. Thus for MacIntyre the interests of a practice potentially diverge from those of the institutions that house it and may indeed have been originally generated by it. As institutions tend toward reification, they tend to lose touch with the ethos of the practice.

So how might this bear on the history of pianism? How is pianism embedded? Let us look at two historical moments. Consider first the pre-recital practice of the early nineteenth century. Bourdieu might want to show that this practice generated and was dependent upon interconnected and increasingly specialized agencies—piano manufacturer, publisher, promoter, critic, teacher, performer, composer—all addressing the needs of a new kind of consumer, and he might want to explore the power relations that arose from their interaction, bearing in mind that several of these agencies were conflated to a single agent. MacIntyre, on the contrary, might want to remind us that this practice, like any other, demanded of its participants the exercise of virtues as well as skills, and virtues are recognized as such in relation to an underlying ethos. If we were to generalize that ethos from the critical record, we might describe it as the need to maintain a balance between the mercantile and the aesthetic values of a developing instrument. In relation to this, virtuosity tips the scales toward the former value.

Now leap forward a century and note how the practice of pianism has changed. Bourdieu might note that the institution hosting this later practice is now the recital, and he would note further that the real focus of the recital is not now a multiply exemplifying event (it may point to a genre, a venue, an instrument, or a technique), but rather an aesthetic object (the musical work) and a concept (an interpretation). MacIntyre meanwhile might argue that the ascendancy of interpretation also changed the underlying ethos of the practice, which one might now define as the need to maintain a balance between a liberal realization of the self and a contractual acknowledgment of collective norms and inherited knowledge—which is more or less the same as the "self and the forms" mentioned earlier. Here virtuosity takes on a rather different meaning, one that prioritizes the subject over the ideal subject. It captures me in the moment, like a selfie ("I was there, then"), as distinct from enshrining the self ("I did that, so remember me"). By the way, both Bourdieu and MacIntyre might note that the practice began to change yet again when the recital yielded in its turn to the recording, when we move, in a word, into a post-recital age.

This understanding of a practice, as promoted by Bourdieu and qualified by MacIntyre, provides a flexible framework within which the constellation of elements involved in performance events might be ordered and reordered at different times and in different places. It would enable us to locate the changing faces of virtuosity historically, and without the crude binarism that often accompanies it. I mean here the widely peddled idea that virtuosity is best viewed in a binary relation to idealist values (either via the embodied subject or via one or other model of economic determinism). As indicated by the recent monograph by Žarko Cvejić, *The Virtuoso as Subject: The Reception of Instrumental Virtuosity, c.1815–c.1850*, this may indeed go some way to explaining why virtuosity was critically panned at a specific historical moment in the mid-nineteenth century, though the critical record is less cut and dried than Cvejić suggests.[38] But it has more limited purchase on the resurgence of virtuosity in the early twentieth century, of which editing praxes as well as recordings speak eloquently. There is work along these lines on Chopin editions at the turn of the century, including editions by Liszt pupils.[39] And it is all the more instructive because the Chopin source tradition is less permissive than the Liszt: no less complex but less permissive. Liszt, as everyone knows, put his personal stamp on all kinds of remembered fragments and alternative versions of his music. I doubt that the idea of a linear source chain can carry much meaning in this context, to say nothing of the multiple ossias discussed elsewhere in this volume.[40] And to the extent that it does, should it include, for example, piano rolls by pupils, an important part of what we might call a living Liszt tradition? The questions are endless. In any case, Zofia Chechlińska's study of these fin-de-siècle Chopin editions isolates a layer of virtuosity and holds it up for inspection, teaching us a great deal in the process about performance practice. As for the radical reformulation of virtuosity associated with some of the New Music of the post–World War II years (the Berio *Sequenzas*, inter alia), even the softest form of binarism will not help us much with this. It tells another story.

Prescribing Virtuosity

These meditations on performance history all locate their subject matter within the broader field of human communication. The intention has been to nuance a discourse of today, one that stresses agencies, localities, and events. However, I am not inclined to abandon totally a discourse of yesterday, one that locates its subject rather within the field of an evolving human consciousness, given expression in significant, and innovatory, cultural works. My final thought, then, will be a brief nod toward yesterday, referencing the two composers who together created the most enduring repertory to have been molded, at least in part, by the impulse to virtuosity. It will be a reflection on music by Chopin and Liszt, with the intention of cutting through to certain essentials. Without doubt it will incur the usual penalties for reductionism of this kind.

Let us consider four composers of the early Romantic generation: Chopin, Liszt, Mendelssohn, and Berlioz. I want to suggest two separate pairings. First I propose a fault line that has Chopin and Mendelssohn on one side and Liszt and Berlioz on the other, and my further proposal is that this has its origins in musical education. For Chopin and Mendelssohn, both technical training and more general thinking about music were deeply and firmly rooted in eighteenth-century texts and ideas: actually the same texts and the same ideas, by and large, though there are differences, and they are very telling.[41] Now it is obvious that on one level these two composers drew very different conclusions from a similar pedagogical background; just think of how they each processed their principal mentor, Johann Sebastian Bach. But on another level it was precisely this similar background that set them both apart from Liszt and Berlioz, the former of whom had only a year of rigorous, sustained, week-in-week-out training with Salieri, while the other approached his studies with several teachers (including Reicha) with circumspection if not skepticism.[42]

Now I think that lurking behind this is a distinction between genealogical and generational thinking.[43] Chopin and Mendelssohn were sons of their fathers, metaphorically speaking, and they remained committed to a classical, even a rule-bound, understanding of the musical work. Liszt and Berlioz, in contrast, were members of a cohort and held a contrary, idealist view of the work. The *Symphonie fantastique* might perhaps represent a symbolic inauguration of that particular cohort. There had never been anything quite like it.[44]

My other pairing is more obvious, but I think less defining. Here we would group together Chopin and Liszt as pianist-composers who continued to work within, even as they transcended, the framework of a postclassical, bravura pianism that took shape in the 1820s.[45] Mendelssohn pointedly rejected that world, and Berlioz praised the Almighty that he had never been part of it. (And by the way Berlioz's precise comments on this give an interesting negative spin to the idea of a phrasicon: "When I think of the appalling quantity of platitudes for which the piano is daily responsible—flagrant platitudes which in most cases would never be written if their authors had only pen and paper to rely on and could not resort to their magic box—I can only offer up my gratitude to chance which taught me perforce to compose freely and in silence and thus saved me from the tyranny of keyboard habits, so dangerous to thought, and from the lure of conventional sonorities, to which all composers are to a greater or lesser extent prone.")[46] Now Chopin and Liszt certainly found very different ways of transforming the elements of postclassical, popular pianism in their mature music, but I suggest that we can understand those differences best if we remember that the two composers were located on different sides of my initial fault line. This is what lay behind the descriptors of virtuosity I used in my book, respectively, "neobaroque" and "Romantic," though I would not use the second term today.

A more forensic examination would show that the particular, and very different, rearrangements of elements from postclassical pianism made by Chopin and Liszt inaugurated innovatory style models that had a very long reach. The source elements in popular pianism were to a degree formulaic: a melodic basis in opera and popular genres of the time, squared off against, or combined with, a restricted repertory of idiomatic figurations. Now these formulae were themselves reifications of more nuanced classical devices, and their transformation in Chopin, and to a lesser degree Liszt, was in part about reinstating that classical *ars subtilior* (in one text on Chopin I referred to a synthesis of classical and postclassical elements).[47] In part, though, it was about adding new layers of complexity.

In Chopin, the complexity is more often than not a property of structure, which I know opens up a number of questions about structure, and it resulted in a model of pianism that looked to Debussy even as it remembered Bach. Yet postclassical starting points remain explicit both in the profile of the musical materials and in the manner of their juxtaposition. What really happens in Chopin is that both the melodic layer and the figuration become dense with information, and on the whole they do so separately (needless to say, I speak of an orientation, not a uniform practice). In Liszt, the complexity was more often about richness of surface, which of course reopens the questions about structure and even about the possibility of structure. In practice this amounted to a quite different model of pianism, with a different arrangement of postclassical elements and a different (and weaker) classical ancestry. It is a model in which melody and figuration are not so much squared off against one another as superimposed or entangled in mutual dependency. And again it is a model with a future, albeit Ravel rather than Debussy. Given these differences, it might be thought ironic that Liszt is the one accused of being episodic. Actually, I think it may be the right call. What we really need to ask is why it should be an accusation. Why is it not all right to be episodic?

I am only too well aware that this glance toward yesterday positively begs for elaboration, but it is not really possible to take it further in the present chapter. I include it mainly because I want to affirm the explanatory value of stylistic analysis and stylistic history, whose findings continue to illuminate musical works. But let us not forget, within certain limits, and on particular occasions, a performer can turn any of those findings on its head.

Notes

1. Jim Samson, *Virtuosity and the Musical Work: The "Transcendental Studies" of Liszt* (Cambridge: Cambridge University Press, 2003).
2. Nicholas Cook, "We are All (Ethno)musicologists Now," in *The New (Ethno)musicologies*, ed. Henry Stobart (Lanham, MD: Scarecrow Press, 2008), 48–70.
3. This research embraced Russian *byliny*, Ukrainian *dumy*, the epics of the Don Cossacks, and the music associated with the Nart sagas of the Caucasus. Parallel and overlapping traditions of epics are found among the Turkic peoples of Central Asia and eastern Anatolia, as well as among Tatar and Balkar-Karachaev communities.

4. Among the other subjects illuminated by such borderland exchanges is the study of medieval chant, where again oralists have freshened the field after a long-lived history of manuscript-based scholarship. The subtitle of Peter Jeffery's seminal text is significant: *Re-envisaging Past Musical Cultures: Ethnomusicology in the Study of Gregorian Chant* (Chicago: University of Chicago Press, 1992). So too is the title of Timothy McGee's monograph: *The Sound of Medieval Song: Ornamentation and Vocal Style according to the Treatises* (Oxford: Clarendon Press, 1998). Special interest attaches to Georgian liturgical chant in this respect, since most of the tradition has been transmitted orally. See John A. Graham, "The Transcription and Transmission of Georgian Liturgical Chant," PhD Dissertation (Princeton University, 2015).
5. Lauri Honko, "Text as Process and Practice: The Textualization of Oral Epics," *Textualization of Oral Epics*, ed. Lauri Honko (Berlin and New York: Mouton de Gruyter, 2000), 3–54.
6. Roman Jakobson, "On Linguistic Aspects of Translation," in *On Translation*, ed. A. Reuben Brower (Cambridge, MA: Harvard University Press, 1959), 232–39.
7. Saul Novack, "Aspects of the Creative Process in Music," *Current Musicology* 36 (1983): 137–50; Alexander Goehr, *Finding the Key: Selected Writings of Alexander Goehr* (London and Boston: Faber and Faber, 1998), 82.
8. Sometimes subsumed within "enactivism," this is a way of understanding cognition by relating it both transitively and intransitively to its environment. Relevant publications are Humberto R. Maturana and F. J. Varela, *The Tree of Knowledge: The Biological Roots of Human Understanding* (Boston: Shambhala Publications, 1992 [1987]), and Francisco J. Varela, E. Thompson, and E. Rosch, *The Embodied Mind: Cognitive Science and Human Experience* (Cambridge: MIT Press, 2017 [1991]).
9. Milman Parry, *The Making of Homeric Verse: The Collected Papers of Milman Parry*. 2nd edn., ed. A. Parry (Oxford: Oxford University Press, 1987 [1971]). See also Albert Lord, *The Singer of Tales*, 2nd edn., ed. S. Mitchell and G. Nagy (Cambridge, MA: Harvard University Press, 2000 [1960]).
10. Yıldıray Erdener, *The Song Contests of Turkish Minstrels: Improvised Poetry Sung to Traditional Music* (New York: Garland Publishing, 1995). See also Natalie Kononenko Moyle, *The Turkish Minstrel Tale Tradition* (New York: Garland Publishing, 1990).
11. Robert O. Gjerdingen, *Music in the Gallant Style* (Oxford: Oxford University Press, 2007).
12. Robert O. Gjerdingen, "Gebrauchs-*Formulas*," *Music Theory Spectrum* 33, no. 2 (2011): 191–99.
13. Johann Philipp Kirnberger, *Die Kunst des Reinen Satzes*, 2 vols. (Berlin: Decker und Hartung, 1771–79), and Johann Georg Albrechstberger, *Anweisung zur Composition* (Leipzig: J. Brietkopf, 1790). For a detailed look at the lineage

of these treatises (and of the popular Seyfried version of Albrechstberger), see Ian Bent, "Steps to Parnassus: Contrapuntal Theory in 1725 Precursors and Successors," in *The Cambridge History of Western Music Theory*, ed. Thomas Christensen (Cambridge: Cambridge University Press, 2002), 554–602.
14. Such exercises were initially developed for non-keyboard instruments, notably at the Paris Conservatoire. The pioneering work for keyboard was Johann Baptist Cramer's *Étude pour le pianoforte, contenant 42 exercises* of 1804, later subsumed by his *84 études*. See Peter Ganz, "The Development of the Etude," PhD Dissertation (Northwestern University, 1960).
15. Cynthia M. Gessele, "The Institutionalization of Music Theory in France: 1764–1802," PhD Dissertation (Princeton University, 1989).
16. I witnessed this at the third International Orpheus Academy for Music Theory held at the Orpheus Institute in Ghent in 2008.
17. Giorgio Sanguinetti, *The Art of Partimento: History, Theory, and Practice* (Oxford: Oxford University Press, 2012).
18. Richard Baumann, "Verbal Art as Performance," *American Anthropologist* 77 (1975): 290–311.
19. Reinhard Strohm, "Looking Back at Ourselves: The Problem with the Musical Work-Concept," in *The Musical Work: Reality or Invention?*, ed. Michael Talbot (Liverpool: Liverpool University Press, 2000), 128–52.
20. Kenneth Hamilton, *After the Golden Age: Romantic Pianism and Modern Performance* (Oxford: Oxford University Press, 2008).
21. Oliver Strunck, *Essays on Music in the Byzantine World* (New York: Norton, 1977), this passage on 60–61.
22. Dennis Libby articulates this as follows: "The performer was made to feel that his highest calling . . . was to subject himself to the composer's will as the means by which his masterpieces were communicated to the world" (quoted by Albert Cohen in *The Cambridge History of Western Music Theory*, ed. Thomas Christensen [Cambridge: Cambridge University Press, 2002], 549).
23. Joseph Horowitz, *Conversations with Arrau* (London: Collins, 1982), 113.
24. Greg Dikmans, "The Performer as Orator: Rhetoric and Historically Informed Performance," PhD Dissertation (University of Melbourne, 2000).
25. Originally published as the first of six portraits in *Neue Zeitschrift für Musik* (1854–56), Liszt's essay on Clara Schumann was later reprinted in *Franz Liszt: Gesammelte Schriften*, ed. Lina Ramann (Leipzig: Brietkopf & Härtel, 1881–99, vol. 4, 1882), 193.
26. Horowitz, *Conversations*, 87.
27. Ibid., 93.
28. Ibid., 134.
29. Alfred Brendel, *Musical Thoughts and Afterthoughts* (Princeton, NJ: Princeton University Press, 1976), 78.

30. In his sleeve note for the Icon box set, "Claudio Arrau, Virtuoso Philosopher of the Piano," re-issued on EMI Classics (2011).
31. Horowitz, *Conversations*, 126.
32. Nicholas Cook, "Between Process and Product: Music and/as Performance," *Music Theory Online* 7, no. 2 (2001); Brüstle has addressed this in several publications; see, for example, "'Performance studies'—Impulse für die Musikwissenschaft," in *Musik mit Methode: Neue kulturwissenschaftliche Perspektiven*, ed. Corinna Herr and M. Woitas (Köln, Weimar, and Wien: Böhlau, 2006), 253–68.
33. Nicholas Cook, "Squaring the Circle: Phrase Arching in Recordings of Chopin's Mazurkas," *Musica Humana* 1 (2009): 5–28.
34. Jim Samson, "The Practice of Early-Nineteenth-Century Pianism," in *The Musical Work: Reality or Invention?* ed. M. Talbot (Liverpool: Liverpool University Press, 2000), 110–27.
35. Margaret H. Beissinger, "Why Does Epic Survive? A Comparison of Balkan Oral Traditions," in *Balkan Epic: Song, History, Modernity*, ed. Philip V. Bohlman and N. Perković (Lanham, MD: The Scarecrow Press, 2012), 53–80.
36. Pierre Bourdieu, *Esquisse d'une théorie de la pratique, précédé de "Trois études d'ethnologie kabyle"* (Paris: Librairies Droz, 1972).
37. Alasdair MacIntyre, *After Virtue: A Study in Moral Theory*, 3rd edn. (Notre Dame, IN: University of Notre Dame Press, 2007 [1981]).
38. Žarko Cvejić, *The Virtuoso as Subject: The Reception of Instrumental Virtuosity, c.1815–c.1850* (Newcastle upon Tyne: Cambridge Scholars Publishing, 2016).
39. Zofia Chechlińska, "Ze studiów nad źródłami do scherzo F. Chopina," *Annales Chopin* 5 (1960): 82–194.
40. [Ed.] See Jonathan Kregor's contribution to the present volume.
41. Larry R. Todd, *Mendelssohn's Musical Education: A Study of his Exercises in Composition* (Cambridge: Cambridge University Press, 1983); Jim Samson, "Chopin and the Traditions of Pedagogy," in *New Paths: Aspects of Music Theory and Aesthetics in the Age of Romanticism*, ed. Darla Crispin (Leuven: Leuven University Press, 2009), 115–27.
42. Liszt's brief period of private study with Antoine Reicha took place in 1826 (see Rémy Stricker, "Franz Liszt et Antoine Reicha," *Studia Musicologica* 42, no. 1–2 [2001]: 9–24), the same year that the (older) Berlioz began his course with Reicha at the Paris Conservatoire (see David Charlton, "Learning the Past," in *Berlioz; Past, Present, Future*, ed. Peter Bloom (Rochester, NY: University of Rochester Press, 2003). The explanatory value of the Reicha connection for both composers raises issues too big and too complex to explore here. They relate to Reicha's singularity as a theorist, and especially to the competing priorities of counterpoint, harmony, and melody in the shaping of musical phrases. See Keith Chapin, "Antoine Reicha and the Three Identities of the Learned Musician," in *Antoine Reicha, compositeur et théoricien*, ed. Louise Bernard de

Raymond, J-P. Bartoli, and H. Schneider (Hildesheim: George Olms, 2013), 109–18. There are suggestive remarks, though in need of qualification, in Charles Rosen, "Battle over Berlioz," a review of Julian Rushton, *The Musical Language of Berlioz*, in *The New York Review of Books*, April 26, 1984.

43. I have found this double axis of genealogy and generation a useful heuristic in several corners of music history, and I have sometimes found it helpful to link it to Alain Badiou's understanding of the "event," since an event—something from the edge of the void, so to speak—can change genealogical thinking to generational thinking. See Alain Badiou, *Being and Event*, trans. Oliver Feltham (London: Bloomsbury, 2013). Original: *L'être et l'événement* (Paris: Seuil, 1988).

44. Erlend Hovland has an interesting take on the singularity of harmonic processes in the *Symphonie fantastique*; see his "Berlioz Fantasizing at the Guitar: Some Remarks on the Compositional Practice in the *Symphonie fantastique*," *Music & Practice* 3 (2017).

45. [Ed.] On the emergence of brilliant-style and bravura pianism, see Robert Doran's contribution to this volume.

46. Hector Berlioz, *The Memoirs of Berlioz*, trans. David Cairns (London, Toronto, Sydney, and New York: Granada Publishing, 1970 [1969]), 47.

47. Jim Samson, *Chopin [The Master Musicians]* (Oxford: Oxford University Press, 1996), 165.

Chapter Seven

Liszt's Symbiosis

The Question of Virtuosity and the Concerto Arrangement of Schubert's *Wanderer* Fantasy

Jonathan Dunsby

In Liszt reception, the role of Schubert's piano writing as a model of pianistic virtuosity is little discussed, certainly not in comparison with discussion of the influential virtuosity of Carl Czerny and, above all, the violin virtuoso Niccolò Paganini.[1] There is no intention here to try to refocus the rather dubious received view of this aspect of Schubert's own creativity, with its tendency to regard his solo piano writing as somehow only tangentially, almost accidentally virtuosic. Yet as Liszt was well aware, some Schubert requires from the virtuoso pianist as high a degree of technical accomplishment as almost any contemporaneous repertoire. While Liszt would not find in Schubert such a tour de force as, say, the finale of Beethoven's Piano Sonata, op. 106 ("Hammerklavier")—and, after all, probably no music from the second and third decades of the nineteenth century can be compared with that monumental call on dexterity and endurance—nevertheless there are far from isolated examples in Schubert of virtuosity required at a level of which Liszt had sought, in his developing early years, to make himself uniquely capable, to make himself—as everyone knows he intended—the "Paganini of the piano." Examples of Schubert's virtuosic extremes known to Liszt could include the finales of the Piano Sonata in C Minor (D. 958) and the compositionally earlier Piano Sonata in A Minor (D. 748), both published just over a decade after Schubert's untimely death in 1828; and they would certainly include the Fantasie in C Major, op. 15 (D. 760), the most technically demanding of Schubert's works, of which the composer reportedly exclaimed "the devil may play it!" after getting stuck in the last movement during a private performance.[2]

The work came to be known as the *Wanderer* Fantasy, very possibly a title that Liszt himself put into circulation.[3] Liszt's involvement with the *Wanderer* included making an edition of the solo version in later life, when he was commissioned by the Stuttgart publishing firm of Cotta in 1868 to provide items by Weber and Schubert, including the *Wanderer*, for a series of "Instructive Editions."[4] It was "through Liszt's performances of Schubert's great Fantasie . . . that the work was first brought to public attention. . . . During his halcyon years as a touring virtuoso, in the 1830s and 1840s, the work turns up frequently in his recital programs."[5] Then a few years later, as we shall see, he turned the *Wanderer* into a majestic piano concerto (*Franz Schuberts Grosse Fantasie*, S. 366 / LW H13, 1851), the main topic of this chapter—though first we shall gain some orientation, in Liszt's creative responses to Schubert, through another key facet of his legacy, the lied arrangements.[6]

Liszt's Schubert Lied Arrangements

Only relatively recently has it become recognized that Liszt's Schubert lied arrangements were not meant essentially to disseminate professionally treasured music to uninitiated soirée and recital audiences but as a vehicle for Liszt's own keyboard virtuosity. They were intended for those who probably already knew Schubert's lieder or who at least had a good idea of what the originals must have been like. In Liszt's fifty-six compositions based on Schubert's lieder—compositions for which the modern term in Western artistic circles would more likely be "interpretations" rather than arrangements—virtuosity was at the top of his creative agenda. His vision was to apply this virtuosity to the most highly poetic, received compositional cannon of modernity, to works of art by Schubert that represented what we might call "peak expression" in terms of Romantic sensibility, taken to the heights of human feeling that, in the decades following Schubert's death, musical Europe was universally recognizing in his compositions. Liszt was effectively consolidating a new genre here, offering not merely new solo works that are songlike but for piano, not merely "songs without words" of the kind widely popularized by Mendelssohn, but actual song converted into instrumental pieces embodying state-of-the-art virtuosity.[7] Even when the original poetic texts might be included in the printed score, to guide the executant as to the "affect" required in performance, and even though Schubert's melodies "sing" through the kaleidoscopic musical textures, nevertheless the voice has been definitively transformed. We might even care to speculate, aesthetically, that Liszt produced in the strongest cases something more evocative of the lied's true artistic nature, of its *vocality*,[8] than could be present in the original Schubert lieder, in their compositionally constrained medium, and with their potentially distracting poetic texts; perhaps the Schubert who, according to Theodor Adorno, knew as no other the superficiality of verbal language—"the uselessness of words in this deep place where poems offer nothing but the materials, and words are incapable of breathing life into them. The wanderer follows nothing but empty words into the deep, rather than their bright illuminated intention"—would have been uniquely placed, had he been granted his three score years and ten, to appreciate Liszt's instrumental purifications and heroic elaborations of some of his lieder music.[9]

With that in mind, Philip Friedheim's dull characterization of that repertoire as technical display does contain a kind of impoverished truth:

> Liszt seems not so much to have desired to stimulate an interest in Schubert as to demonstrate his own ability to perform anything at the piano. It would seem that when this music was published, it was designed not to bring Schubert's music to a greater public but rather to impress Liszt's admirers with his extraordinary keyboard technique. These works, like certain early seventeenth-century operas, were published primarily as souvenirs of the occasion.[10]

Demonstrations of virtuosity they certainly were, but surely their printed versions were much more than souvenirs; for there is abundant evidence in the scores themselves, to those familiar with his style, that Liszt poured into them, for the most part, his every ounce of creative skill and imagination. The *Winterreise* set was entitled, significantly, "melodic études." Its seriousness of compositional purpose, enshrined in the epithet "melodic," implying as it does something far deeper than sonic and gymnastic creativity, is not to be underestimated, as Jonathan Kregor argues strongly.[11] Just as Liszt's hugely admired contemporary Schumann had expounded the idea of song as a higher form of poetry, so Liszt, in this immediately successful, and widely imitated lieder-inspired repertoire culled from Schubert, was promoting the étude as—so to speak—a higher form of song.[12] And, much as the issue of virtuosity may not arise in many of the Schubert lieder themselves, as a repertoire they certainly could be potential sites of virtuosity, or occasionally sites of actual virtuosity, as in the barely performable piano part of "Der Erlkönig," which will reappear here shortly.

Bearing in mind those introductory remarks, perhaps the reader can be reoriented from the previously customary position, prominent in about the first century of Liszt reception and still often to be encountered, which was to see his engagement with Schubert as somehow naively disrespectful rather than symbiotic. Witness Olga Samaroff, a formidable pianist of the early twentieth century, who was the first woman to give a debut recital in Carnegie Hall, in 1905, and whose advocacy of Schubert's piano music was truly far sighted; yet she could not resist the rhetoric that deifies the work of one "brain" and deplores any intrusion into the genius of Schubert's hallowed works: "The kind of instrumental effectiveness in writing I have in mind *must be born of the same brain that creates the music*. Liszt's well-meant arrangement of the *Wanderer* Fantasie for piano and orchestra, his embellishment of the simple Schubert waltzes in his 'Soirees de Vienne,' and his florid arrangements of several songs are not welcome to the real Schubert-lover, even though they unquestionably sprang from his own love of the music."[13] It is an assumption of this chapter that there are nowadays, nearly a century later, Schubert lovers and indeed Liszt lovers of an altogether different stripe.

The Virtuosity of the *Wanderer*

Liszt's *Wanderer* Concerto, a "symphonic arrangement for piano and orchestra," was completed in 1857, thirty-five years after Schubert's original composition in 1822, during Liszt's boyhood. We do not know anything about the circumstances in which Liszt first encountered Schubert's masterpiece, but Liszt's piano teacher Czerny was certainly well aware of the *Wanderer*.[14] Those circumstances involve the further inflection as to genre that in this period Liszt was developing his creative thinking about the concerto, with which he was concerned directly in conceiving his own two piano concertos (published in 1856 and 1861, respectively, but composed over a long period). Generally, he was giving sustained thought to mastering extended forms of composition, if with a caution fueled by the contemporaneous professional and public lack of appreciation of, in particular, his ultra-modernistic Piano

Sonata, S. 178 (1853), the "B-Minor Sonata," which would take decades to become an acknowledged, enduring masterpiece, posthumously.[15] Thomas Kabisch offered a compelling study of Liszt's compositional intentions in the *Wanderer* arrangement (one of the ancillary purposes of this chapter being to disseminate knowledge in English of Kabisch's insightful monograph, published only in German), intentions further clarified by Detlef Altenburg and Kregor.[16] Kregor is surely right to have refocused critical attention in general on Liszt's transcriptions as "great acts of creativity" and also "great works of originality," opening the way for intense study in this case of what Liszt, as the consummate master of pianism, made for us of Schubert's own, perhaps little-acknowledged virtuosity.[17]

Such discussions are inevitably inflected by the gap between score and realization in the case of what was originally a piano solo. Kabisch writes of the "unconstrained, indeterminate [*chaotisch*] sound" of Schubert's—and it could be anyone's—piano writing.[18] A great deal of the voicing that produces motivic emphasis and shaping, and inner melodies, is merely latent in a piano score, only ever realized in actual performance. Did the *Wanderer* sound like a virtuoso work when Schubert played it (or gave up playing it halfway through, according to the anecdote cite above)?[19] We simply do not know. That gap between score and realization can be closed in certain ways by means of pedagogically oriented editions: Artur Schnabel's edition of the Beethoven piano sonatas and Alfred Cortot's editions of most of Chopin's piano works are well-known examples of versions of the score entailing multiple interpretive inflections, inscribing on the printed page the detail of supposedly ideal performances.[20] There is a Cortot study score (*édition de travail*) of the *Wanderer*, which includes no fewer than eighty-eight footnotes offering advice on interpretation and technique, far in excess of the relatively sparse advice implicit in Liszt's 1868 edition mentioned above.[21] (Alan Walker credits Liszt with being a scholarly pioneer in scrupulously identifying in his edition, typographically, every suggestion for interpretation that was not actually by Schubert himself.)[22]

Alfred Brendel judged that Schubert's piano works, such as the *Wanderer*, "often surpassed the possibilities of his instruments," Brendel offering, that is, a kind of modernist, compositional aesthetic of a work written for the future.[23] It might therefore seem strange that in that future the *Wanderer* came to be seen as an extreme example of virtuosity not only for its time but for any era. Equally strange is any inquiry into its contemporaneity, from the point of view of pianistic demands, given that technically it seems to require nothing more than is to be found in repositories such as Czerny's *School of the Virtuoso*, op. 365. Perhaps the reason for that double puzzle—if the premise is that in respect of virtuosity it was both ahead of its time yet also nothing special in its time—is that in this case virtuosity is harnessed not to relatively trivial Western art music, of the kind that was a commonplace in the thousands of *Kleinmeister*-generated études, variations, character pieces, and similar that were the daily fare of early nineteenth-century consumers, but to a composition of such expressive intensity and structural drama that it clearly ranked alongside the masterpieces of the Viennese triumvirate, which had rapidly become sanctified, during Liszt's youth, as a standard of aesthetic excellence. In recent scholarship, nearly two centuries after the *Wanderer* was composed, it still garners awe from a technical point of view alone. Hye-Won Jennifer Cho, for example, enthuses that "what truly stands out in the *Wanderer* Fantasy—and what distinguishes it from so much of Schubert's prior piano writing—is its virtuosity. None of the previous seven piano sonatas or any other of his piano works show off the virtuosic possibilities of the piano—or present such numerous and varied technical difficulties."[24]

Liszt's Compositional Reasoning

The main musical-analytical focus of this chapter, however, is on the kinds of modification of Schubert's piano writing made by Liszt and the reasons. Although some of Liszt's emendations—also evident in his earlier two-piano arrangement and his later pedagogical edition of the original *Fantasie*—can be considered technically more advanced than in Schubert's original version, mostly Liszt's stance is to clarify, to update for the more recent piano, and to remove some of the features that he seems to have considered to be egregiously taxing for the pianist. In the *Wanderer* Concerto Liszt inscribed a wealth of compositional response to Schubert's pianism, from which we might conclude that his intention was not so much "transcription" or "arrangement" but *symbiosis*, a re-energization of Schubert's modernist virtuosity.

Probably the first place in Liszt's arrangement to which any pianist would turn is the passage of octave figures, involving both hands, in the first movement (exx. 7.1a and 7.1b). This passage can be said to be emblematic of Schubert's comprehensive understanding of virtuosity, since there are various ways in which it could have been written to make it slightly less challenging technically, without truly destroying its climactic impact. On the lighter and probably shallower action of whatever piano Schubert had in mind, his writing here is undoubtedly a little easier to execute than on a modern concert grand piano of any make.[25] If we want more extensive evidence from Schubert about octave scalar passages, perhaps the best and the best known, one of extreme or even excess virtuosity, appears in the closing measures of the Piano Sonata in A Minor (D. 784), which is regarded as virtually unplayable on a modern piano such as an American Steinway, at least, if it is to be at the same speed as the *allegro vivace* of the rest of the movement (ex. 7.2).[26] Even one of the twenty-first century's most accomplished pianists, Mitsuko Uchida, renowned for the musical integrity and technical virtuosity of her Schubert piano sonata interpretations, recorded the last ten measures of this sonata movement at slightly, but distinctly, slower than the average tempo of the D. 784 finale as a whole.[27]

One thing for sure is that the original *Wanderer* octave passage would have presented no real pianistic difficulty to Liszt himself. We need only look at the opening of his arrangement of Schuber's lied "Der Erlkönig" (S. 558/4 / LW A42/4, 1837–38) to see how, in addition to the notorious, wrist-sapping repeated octaves in the right hand, Liszt has doubled the original left-hand part to employ, in this new version that has become a "Study in Octaves" (fig. 7.1b), precisely the kind of octave scalar figure that Schubert had used, for purely artistic reasons—that is, not in any sense as an "étude"—in the *Wanderer*, at a commensurate speed (fig. 7.1a).[28] David Montgomery cites this passage from the *Wanderer*, which has been considered by many commentators in recent decades of both Schubert and Liszt scholarship, in his discussion of tempo choice, making at least three points relevant to our

Example 7.1a. Schubert, *Wanderer* Fantasy in C Major, D. 760, with annotation to show the rhythmic motive, mm. 160–66

Example 7.1b. Liszt, *Franz Schuberts Grosse Fantasie*, S. 366, from m. 161 of Example 1a

Example 7.2. Schubert, Piano Sonata in A Minor, D.784, finale, mm. 258–69

discussion: "The opening of the last movement shows no value smaller than an eighth note, and from a purely technical point of view the entire movement can be played faster than the first movement (a fact which many pianists seek to use to advantage, as often as not to divert the listener's attention from the problems which he or she has had with the octaves at the end of the first movement)."[29] First, note how Montgomery takes it for granted that our well-known passage is a moment of extreme technical challenge in the *Wanderer*, and he is not discussing the practice of amateur pianists but factors that professionals have to bear in mind. Second, there is a subtext to his considerations here, in that he regards the "finale" of the *Wanderer* as more easily playable than the first movement, at least in respect to the first movement ending.[30] The finale is positively rippling with sixteenth-note passagework after the initial quasi-fugal exposition, but it does all lie rather naturally under the hand and is perhaps no more advanced technically than is to be found in the moderately difficult sonatas of Beethoven, and thus Montgomery's subtext about an easier, thus less virtuosic finale is hardly counterintuitive. It strongly invites the question, though, whether Liszt felt any easing of the technical difficulty of the finale in the piano part of his symphonic arrangement, compared with Schubert's *Wanderer*, to be necessary, which would therefore seem unlikely—a question to which we shall return on various counts. Third, there is the implication that performances of Schubert's *Wanderer* are typically defective in their overall structural grasp. That is surely the implication of Montgomery's surmise that "many" pianists are seeking to divert listeners' attention from an overly slow first movement, or a first movement that left the impression of having slowed down, by closing the whole work in a rapid tempo. This may seem a minor point about pianists who typically cannot quite aspire to the virtually limitless technical options of the ideal piano virtuoso, such as Liszt himself is believed to have been. Yet it would nevertheless be a telling one, assuming it to be plausible, bearing in mind that Schubert's *Wanderer* is typically exhibited as the model of one Romantic ideal, the grand, organic structure, by virtue not only of its thematic transformation but also of its creative nature as a giant compositional canvas, an expressive marathon, which was to resonate through any number of major nineteenth-century works, from Liszt's Piano Sonata in B Minor (completed 1853) to—in the medium of chamber music—Schoenberg's *Verklärte Nacht* for string sextet (1899). However that may be, the idea that a local point of nearly unachievable virtuosity can determine a strategic approach to the interpretation, at least regarding tempo, of the entire composition provides an intriguing example of a concrete link between technique and structure.

What we see in example 7.1b, Liszt's version of this short passage, momentous from the point of view of Schubert's inherent virtuosity, is how Liszt is, as it were, not particularly interested in what he probably regarded as the superficial issues of Schubert's original. The sixteenths are played, with consummate, effective ease, by woodwind and strings. Meanwhile, the piano picks out the essence of the passage, and what Liszt was hearing here is undoubtedly the sforzatos that Schubert has so carefully marked, hoping to ensure that in his measures 161–65 the principal rhythmic motive of the entire work will not be lost (see bracket *x* on ex. 7.1a). There is a natural tendency for the four-note octave runs here to be sensed by the pianist as upbeats to their goal, and Schubert's original sforzatos were quasi-analytical markings, indicating that those apparent goal tones (mm. 161/3 and 162/3) must also function not only as goals but also as the initial tones of the *Wanderer* motive. Without occluding the ambivalence, this is exactly what Liszt has ensured in performance by piano and orchestra: even in a scrappy performance—such as one may hope never to experience—Schubert's musical intention would be clear to hear, as contrived by Liszt's otherwise faithful arrangement of these focal measures. Whether Liszt has therefore misrepresented the "affect" of this passage remains a moot point. Kabisch seeks to exonerate Liszt's arrangement of the passage by noting how "the configuration in (motivically independent) layers prevents the climax from arriving too effortlessly, diminishing the energized sound of the original."[31] Others might say that Liszt has to some extent sanitized Schubert's virtuosity, replacing superhuman achievement in performance with, perhaps, merely human

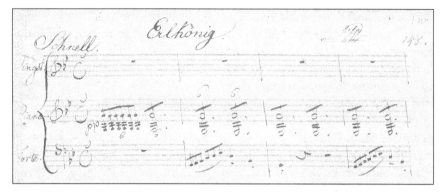

Figure 7.1a. Schubert, "Der Erlkönig," holograph manuscript, 1815

Figure 7.1b. Liszt, "Der Erlkönig" arrangement, S. 558/4, mm. 1–5

triumph or some such simpler affect, to the detriment of Schubert's original and higher purpose. Yet it is conceivable—as a middle, critical way—that Liszt's architectural mind was at work here, for he knew that the piano would be highlighted, in his arrangement, in the fugal opening of the "finale" (as will be explained here in due course), in a way that would have rendered Schubert's original pianistic climax at the close of the first movement premature, thus in need, symbiotically, of a fix that would do nothing to harm Schubert's bigger picture.

Kabisch's critical stance is in general highly favorable to Liszt's changes to the *Wanderer*, and it would seem unproductive to point to "solutions" Liszt found in his arrangement that could arguably be regarded as unnecessary distortions of the artistic meaning of Schubert's original. It is well known that Liszt was fully conscious of the need to justify the potential artistic distortion in transcriptions or arrangements of other composers' masterpieces. As he so memorably pointed out in the preface to his Beethoven's Fifth, Sixth, and Seventh Symphony transcriptions:

> The poorest lithography, the most incorrect translation, still gives a vague idea of the genius of a Michelangelo and of a Shakespeare. Even in the most incomplete reduction one will sometimes find half-faded traces of the master's inspiration. . . . I shall be satisfied if I carry out the task of the intelligent engraver, the conscientious translator, who precisely grasps the spirit of the work and thereby contributes to the circulation of the masters and the sense of the beautiful.[32]

That artistic credo is, typically for Liszt, conceived as relating to the deepest levels of artistic value, as is obvious from his reference to Michelangelo and Shakespeare, whom we hardly regard as examples of mere virtuoso display in their artistic products. Nevertheless, virtuosity as a quarry for dissemination can surely be part of the deeper message of a masterpiece, and this is surely a vital quality of the *Wanderer* that seems to have impelled Liszt to reimagine it in the concert hall with large (for its day) orchestra, in an epic dialogue implied by the very idea of concerto.[33]

Actually, it is evident in Liszt's score for his symphonic arrangement of Schubert that painstaking creative thought has been given to how to configure the available forces, which means in effect how to tame a virtuoso solo composition into a dramatic scenario led by the piano but with meaningful integration of everything on stage in the performance. For instance, entirely predictably perhaps, Liszt begins with an orchestral tutti. Of course he was familiar with precedents for piano solo openings or initial incursions, such as in Mozart's Piano Concerto no. 9 in E-flat Major (K. 271) and more immediately relevantly to Liszt's creative arsenal the Fourth (op. 58) and Fifth (op. 73) Piano Concertos of Beethoven. Yet Schubert had already set up the opening of the *Wanderer* in purely musical terms as a kind of simulacrum of tutti and solo, comparing his *fortissimo* opening with the almost immediate thematic reprise in measures 18 and following, *pianissimo*, and with slight, soloistic variation. Looking at the ensuing plan of the work, Kabisch usefully provides a conspectus on the overall handling of instrumental forces by Liszt. Although this may strike some readers as an exercise in rather dull, descriptive musicology, nevertheless the account of Liszt's instrumental architecture has a somewhat alluring flavor in that it recovers exactly the kind of "compositional"—or perhaps one should call it re-compositional—thought process that must have been in Liszt's conscious awareness. The elaborate structuring of complex music does not arise in some kind of intuitive compositional haze but has to be planned. Centuries' worth of brilliant Western composers, along with their sketches and drafts, even including the Mozart who was Romantically portrayed as some sort of intuitive naïf from whom music simply poured forth, have testified to that careful pre-compositional work. Kabisch writes:

> In each movement of the Fantasy, Liszt favors a particular kind of sonority and thus emphasizes the contrast between elements of the cycle within the double-function form. The first movement begins with a tutti sound, includes some characteristic passages where the orchestral instruments are used soloistically, and develops the separation of the orchestra into relatively independent groupings of strings and woodwind. He does the same in the second movement, which is notable for the frequent appearance of orchestral solos, joining the piano in presenting melodic material (bar 227ff.) or accompanied by the piano (bar 223). The scherzo . . . continues the idea of contrast between strings, woodwind, and piano solo, gathering in a tutti only towards the end of the movement. And lastly, the finale leads from initial separation of the orchestral groups to tutti (bar 639ff.), bar 667ff.), thus reversing, so to speak, the narrative of the first movement. . . . The structural features of the original play a decisive role in the partly new realization, where extra features are to be regarded as enhancements or reductions of Schubert's piano writing.[34]

For our purposes, however, a more probing question is whether Liszt has implicitly approved, through his symphonic arrangement, of Schubert's virtuosity or consistently sought to improve, update, or enhance that virtuosity, as he was perfectly entitled, and uniquely gifted, to do. That perspective casts some new light on all those passages, of which there are many, where Liszt has not only retained the grace and subtlety of Schubert's piano writing, but also retained Schubert's own virtuoso piano style. Example 7.3a offers such a case, in that this original passage at a climactic point of Schubert's second, slow "movement" is retained intact by Liszt, as example 7.3b shows. There are any number of ways, subtle or decisive, in which Liszt could have recast measures 223 and following of the Schubert, but he leaves undisturbed its organic outgrowth from Schubert's progressive rhythmic diminutions leading to this: nor does he vary Schubert's carefully controlled use of register; and the unobtrusive melodic commentary, using the "Der Wanderer" theme, introduced in horns and solo trumpet provides compositional continuity that could not have been available to Schubert writing for piano solo—one may speculate that this is exactly the kind of enhancement Schubert himself would have made if transcribing for larger forces, though of course we can never know.[35]

Example 7.3a. Schubert, *Wanderer* Fantasie in C Major, D. 760, m. 231

Example 7.3b. Liszt, *Franz Schuberts Grosse Fantasie*, S. 366, m. 224

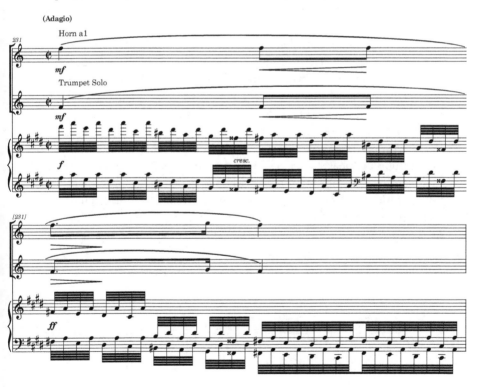

Where Liszt does not retain intact the virtuoso kind of writing in Schubert of which he must surely have regarded Schubert as being the best judge, we can expect to be able to identify some strong creative reasoning. Examples 7.4a and b offer a telling example. Liszt's version distills his creative response to Schubert's essentially simple buildup to the third movement climax that will introduce the fugue. A concerto, in a large auditorium, requires a certain textural clarity where the piano is not occluded unnecessarily by the orchestra, and that Liszt achieves by two, elegant new takes on Schubert's music, replacing triplet eighths with duple eighths and reversing the vertical direction of the piano right-hand figuration so that in the two-measure hypermeasures the piano emerges texturally high up on the hypermetrical offbeats.[36] In addition—but there is no assumption here about in what order Liszt may have thought of these inflections—on the downbeat of measure 564 and then repeatedly in the ensuing measures of this section, Liszt's strings play the principal melodic motive of the scherzo, which maps in to the duple-eighth piano figuration (perhaps the introduction of the scherzo motive was what gave him the idea of how to replace Schubert's figuration rhythmically—but in reality how to treat these measures probably occurred to Liszt all at once, given that human inspiration does not dwell on cause and effect). The "creative reasoning" here was not in the detail but in Liszt's idea that this strategic passage of the *Wanderer* had to be, in a concerto version, reconceived: Schubert's buildup to the end of the scherzo, in a dramatic helter-skelter ride to the catharsis of the finale fugue, is necessarily translated into a dialogue between orchestra and piano.

The idea of transparent creative reasoning probably also applies to that most important phase of Liszt's reconception of Schubert, the work's ending. Example 7.5a shows Schubert's original (from measure 711), the kind of passagework that has done little to obviate the reputation of this movement, as mentioned above, from exhibiting the "finale problem," in this case by dissolving into what might be regarded as essentially vapid arpeggios. What

Example 7.4a. Schubert, *Wanderer* Fantasy in C Major, D. 760, m. 564

Example 7.4b. Liszt, *Franz Schuberts Grosse Fantasie*, S. 366, m. 562

we see in example 7.5b is Liszt's interpretation of Schubert's conception from two different points of view. First, he recognized the potentially oppressive prominence of sixteenth-note passagework earlier in the finale by eliminating it here, which is also to recognize the likely different acoustic situation of a concerto performance, where sonic glitter is so easily dissipated into the wastes of public architecture; there is also a sense of modernization in the substitution of bravura piano writing for what he probably regarded as an outdated *stile brillante*.[37] Second—and this was perhaps more decisive in Liszt's idea of eliminating the passagework—he has decided to round off his symphonic arrangement with a military topic, which is undoubtedly the effect of the dotted rhythms shown in the horns and trumpets, fifth and sixth staves down in example 7.5b. This military topic caps the whole orchestral story of the finale in Liszt's reading, present from the orchestra's initial entry after the piano solo fugal opening, as shown in example 7.5c, where horns and trumpets alternate with strings to produce a continuous dotted note, military-topic trope on Schubert's original. Liszt probably drew on a passage in the middle of Schubert's original finale (ex. 7.5d, measures 667, 671, and 675ff.), developing an idea from the insistent principle motive of the scherzo (ex. 7.5e), which, we should note for good measure, was itself clearly drawn from the "Der Wanderer" lied motive indicated in example 7.5f.

Creative reasoning can also apply, of course, to features that Liszt does retain intact. This is nowhere more evident than at the opening of the finale, where Liszt made the architecturally significant decision to allow the piano to play, entirely solo, the complete fugal exposition. Calling this section a

Example 7.5a. Schubert, *Wanderer* Fantasy in C Major, D. 760, mm. 709–14

Example 7.5b. Liszt, *Franz Schuberts Grosse Fantasie*, S. 366, mm. 709–13

Example 7.5c. Liszt, *Franz Schuberts Grosse Fantasie*, S. 366, mm. 629–32

Example 7.5d. Schubert, *Wanderer* Fantasy in C Major, D. 760, mm. 667–78

Example 7.5e. Schubert, *Wanderer* Fantasy in C Major, D. 760, mm. 245–52

Example 7.5f. Schubert, *Wanderer* Fantasy in C Major, D. 760, mm. 189–90

fugal "exposition" is justified by the action of the four "voices" presenting the subject in an orthodox way, in tonic (measure 598), dominant (measure 606), tonic (measure 615), then tonic again (measure 631), in what has the effect of tenor/alto/soprano/bass order texturally. There is also a countersubject that is as identifiable as in any late baroque fugues that Schubert might have studied, and the return of the subject in measure 659 in the bass, after episodic development from measure 631, further confirms the generic reference.[38] It is only the fact that the "fugue" then fuses with developmental and cadential elaboration that prevents the genre from being fully realized. After all, had he wanted, Schubert could easily have realized those generic, formal expectations with one resounding recurrence of the fugue subject near the end of the piece. That recurrence almost anywhere in the last 53 measures of the 122-measure movement would have turned it into a regular example of fugal form as such, and this tells us how penetrating was his creative vision in this hybrid, which might well represent a scenario of the old giving way to the new, if Schubert had some kind of historical subtext in mind.[39] For all we know this procedure might even have been Schubert's response to the fugal finale of Beethoven's mighty "Hammerklavier" Sonata, op. 106, completed in 1818 and published the following year, three years before the *Wanderer*, and if so, as an alternative take on how the fugue could be assimilated into Romantic sensibility, as a fragment rather than some kind of neoclassical apotheosis. However that may be, Liszt preserved the "exposition" not only literally but, as it were, super-literally, in that during its brief but structurally prominent course—and after a momentous buildup in the closing forty-six measures of the scherzo—the piano does something that was not available to Schubert: it silences the orchestra. Within the original *Wanderer* as a whole, the fugue has something of the place of a cadenza, of course, an effect that would probably not have been lost on Liszt and may have been part of the creative reasoning that led him to make it so prominent as a piano solo. It was, in all likelihood, especially important to Liszt to therefore emphasize, sonically, Schubert's original organic vision in relating, by means of strong thematic reminiscence, the fugue "subject" to the work's opening (compare exx. 7.6a and 7.6b), and the long-term link Liszt thus established between orchestral tutti opening and piano's fugal "victory" that opens the finale could hardly be more decisively represented in terms of the forces Liszt chose to employ in his arrangement.

There is a double aspect to this material from the point of view of expressive intention, difficult though it is to be forensic about aspects of music that one can but envisage, as opposed to scrupulously analyze. To the extent that

Example 7.6a. Schubert, *Wanderer* Fantasy in C Major, D. 760, mm. 1–3

Example 7.6b. Schubert, *Wanderer* Fantasy in C Major, D. 760, mm. 598–99

the fugue may represent a kind of cadenza, a solo feature of the concerto genre, this passage will tend to give the impression of a brilliantly improvised rather than predetermined section. Even if Liszt's audiences may have known Schubert's original perfectly well, or if in any case they assumed the fugue to have been hard-wired into the composition of Schubert's original, nevertheless in the context of Liszt's arrangement it is transformed into that mercurial, spontaneous, risk-laden creative moment of an improvised, fugal cadenza by the very genre, the concerto, that Liszt brought to the music. As a second aspect, the fugue is also, in Schubert's original, a brilliant section of piano writing that gives the impression of virtuosity, of, one might say, inscribing virtuosity as a topic rather than offering it as a fact, given that these measures are, in reality, not particularly hard to perform but *sound as if* they are.[40]

There are other layers of historical reference too. First, and obviously, Liszt was subscribing to the classical concerto tradition of beginning a finale with a memorable solo passage, imitative or not, and this is a generic stamp that in one way or another hovered over the entire nineteenth-century piano concerto repertoire, explicitly or otherwise. Second, and perhaps more specifically here, is the generic character of the concerto as a kind of contest, about which Dana Gooley writes at some length with regard to Liszt's concerto practice in general. Gooley notes that there was always something subtle in Liszt about the relationship between virtuoso and orchestra, with a marked preference for the kind of creativity where the battle is already won: "Liszt, like his virtuoso contemporaries, played compositions in which the orchestra has a decidedly subsidiary role . . . with moments of conflict appearing only rarely. A sense of struggle came from other elements of the performance: the acoustic relationship of solo and tutti, and the visual dynamism of his performing style."[41] It seems that in the finale's fugue Schubert has done Liszt's concerto work for him, in that a certain territory has already been demarcated compositionally as a kind of "victory" for the fugue. Schubert reception history has often described as a weakness his repeated struggle to find an effective compositional solution for casting a finale as part of a large overall symphonic structure. Of course, this kind of challenge was certainly not unique to Schubert, which Michael Talbot's research on the "finale problem" makes abundantly clear.[42] It might be said that in this case Liszt has deftly turned a "weakness" into a creative victory.[43] The creative vision of a Schubert *Wanderer* recast as a Liszt concerto is a powerful way of resolving its "finale problem," for at a stroke, in Liszt's conception, the fugue gains a comprehensible and generically appropriate role.

The Transcendental Schubert

That feature of Liszt's arrangement is so effective that we must wonder, in closing, whether he has discerned and realized something that was in Schubert's mind all along. Was the *Wanderer* conceived as a kind of concerto by its composer in the first place? It was certainly a completely new genre providing a general structural model that was taken up by any number of Romantic and modern composers, not least Liszt himself. But was it specifically also a "virtuoso concerto for piano solo"? Did Liszt's arrangement realize a latent quality just as Schubert might have done, at least in respect to the instrumental configuration of the finale and perhaps in fact overall in various important respects, some of them indicated above? If that is reasonable critical speculation, it brings an altogether deeper meaning to the idea of a symbiotic relationship between the Schubert of the *Wanderer* and the Liszt of its symphonic arrangement, a relationship in which the "same brain"—to repeat Samaroff's misguided ideal mentioned above—is not necessarily the only route to creative success.

The present writer's early experience of Schubert was as a composer of the early Romantic virtuoso movement, and the experience of showpieces such as the F-Minor *Moment Musical*, op. 94, no. 5 (D. 780), or particularly technically challenging movements such as the scherzo of the Piano Sonata in D Major (D. 850), and the finale of the Piano Sonata in C Minor (D. 958), did everything to confirm this picture of a contemporary of Beethoven, who was developing state-of-the-art textures, techniques, and effects in the period, when advanced pianism had begun to completely escape the possibility of amateur performance—when Chopin, Schumann, and Liszt were approaching their teenage years and, along with numerous contemporary compositional *Kleinmeister* who were nevertheless master pianists, were about to rewrite the script when it came to what was possible at the keyboard. It was only later, after reading books on the history of music and eventually scholarly articles and dissertations, that I began to sink into the general habit of thinking of Schubert's piano writing as being one of the least important topics in the evaluation of his music. It was in the history of Schubert reception that this story developed in the later nineteenth century and has been perpetuated to some extent ever since. Yet for Liszt himself, there was no meaningful Schubert reception history. It was Liszt above all who put Schubert on the canonical map as a largely unknown and misunderstood composer—hence the many contemporaneous accounts of how, as one critic put it, "Schubert can become comprehensible only through Liszt's playing."[44] And it would seem obvious that Liszt regarded Schubert as a composer of music that was not only memorable, intense, charming, soul-searching and so on—indeed chthonic, to use Adorno's word—but also on message with Liszt's own mission to create pianism of a virtuosity the likes of which had never been heard before: "transcendental" virtuosity, virtuosity that sets its own standards for the creative imagination, virtuosity that, as Schumann would have said, amounts to a "higher form" of pianism. While the evidence for Liszt's creative intentions in his involvement with the *Wanderer* seems to be exhausted factually, its challenge to our historiographical imagination remains, or so it has been argued here. This writer, at least, believes that Liszt's Schubert was Schubert the virtuoso, in the sense of the composer of virtuoso music. Liszt's Schubert was the Schubert who not only failed to disseminate his own piano writing to any lionizing public but, from all we know, never wished to do so. This was very likely because, with his mind of a genius, Schubert well knew that others could do that better, Liszt being, very shortly after Schubert's untimely death, the consummate other who did precisely that for him.

Notes

1. [Ed.] See chapter 1 of this volume for a discussion of the influence of Czerny's compositions on Liszt.
2. Quoted in Heinrich Kreissle von Hellborn, *Franz Schubert, A Musical Biography*, trans. Edward Wilberforce (London: W. H. Allen, 1866), 60. For more about D. 748, see below.
3. In the rest of this chapter, Schubert's D. 760 will be referred to for convenience simply as the *Wanderer*. There is only one passing reference, beyond this note, to the song, cited throughout the musicological literature on both Liszt and Schubert, on which its thematic material was based, "Der Wanderer," op. 4, no. 1 (D. 489).
4. See below for further comment on editions.
5. Alan Walker, *Reflections on Liszt* (Ithaca, NY: Cornell University Press, 2005), 188.
6. Liszt also made an arrangement of the *Wanderer* for two pianos (S. 653 / LW C5), on which he began work at some time after 1851 and which was published in 1862.
7. For an even-handed and informative survey and critical appreciation of Liszt's versions of Schubert lieder, see Charles Madsen, "The SchubertLiszt Transcriptions: Text, Interpretation, and Lieder Transformation," PhD Dissertation (University of Oregon, 2003).
8. For various references to "vocality" in the context of contemporary musicological concepts, see Benjamin Binder, Jonathan Dunsby, Wayne Heisler, Jennifer Ronyak (convenor), Kira Thurman, and Laura Tunbridge, "Studying the Lied: Hermeneutical Traditions and the Challenge of Performance," *Journal of the American Musicological Society* 67, no. 2 (2014): 543–82.
9. Theodor Adorno, "Schubert (1928)," *19th-Century Music* 29, no. 1 (2005): 12. In this quotation the "wanderer" to whom Adorno refers is, ambiguously, the listener in general, "He who crosses the threshold between the years of Beethoven's death and Schubert's" (ibid., 7), as announced in the first line of Adorno's essay "Schubert" and referred to, specifically, some eight times; but also, in the immediate context, the wanderer who is the subject of *Winterreise*, Song no. 4, from the poetry of which Adorno is about to quote here; and also by reasonable inference the wanderer of the *Fantasie* that Adorno has just been discussing. Part of Adorno's subtle literary creativity in this essay is also the undoubted, repeated reference to himself, as author and celebrant of the Schubert centenary, "wandering" through Schubert's world. The ambiguity is both confirmed and clarified in the first-person plural of the famous, admittedly opaque closing lines: "We cry without knowing why, because we are not yet what this music promises for us. We cry, knowing in untold happiness, that this music is as it is in the promise of what one day we ourselves will be. This is music we cannot decipher, but it holds

up to our blurred, overbrimming eyes the secret of reconciliation at long last" (ibid., 14).
10. Philip Friedheim, "The Piano Transcriptions of Franz Liszt," *Studies in Romanticism* 1, no. 2 (1962): 87.
11. Jonathan Kregor, *Liszt as Transcriber* (Cambridge: Cambridge University Press, 2010), 76–78.
12. As discussed extensively in Beate Perrey, *Schumann's Dichterliebe and Early Romantic Poetics: Fragmentation of Desire* (Cambridge: Cambridge University Press, 2002).
13. Olga Samaroff, "The Piano Music of Schubert," *The Musical Quarterly* 4, no. 4 (1928): 600, emphasis added. It is no coincidence that Olga Samaroff was writing in 1928, for this was the centenary year of Schubert's death, which also inspired the aforementioned essay published that year by Theodor Adorno, its translation being referred to several times in this chapter (Adorno, "Schubert [1928]"). Samaroff's condemnation is typical of contemporaneous hubris that flew in the face of compositional history, if by implication it would also condemn, for instance, Bach's many recompositions of Vivaldi concertos.
14. See Jay Rosenblatt, "The Concerto as Crucible: Franz Liszt's Early Works for Piano and Orchestra," PhD Dissertation (University of Chicago, 1995), for an account of the genesis of Liszt's arrangement.
15. The Piano Concerto no. 1 in E-flat Major (S. 124 / LW H4), first conceived in 1830 and famously premiered in 1855 with Berlioz conducting and Liszt as soloist, is often cited as Liszt's visionary test bed for extended composition. Bartók is often quoted in the literature for judging, in 1936, that this concerto was "the first perfect realization of cyclic sonata form, with common themes treated on variation principles. After Liszt's time this solution of formal problems came to acquire more and more importance" (*Béla Bartók Essays*, ed. Benjamin Suchoff [London: Faber and Faber, 1976], 503). Less often quoted is Bartók's earlier 1911 opinion that although the concerto's "formal innovation" is "perfect," nevertheless "in content it is not at all satisfying, because the greater part of it is empty fireworks" (ibid., 452). The halo of critical recognition regarding formal construction that surrounded Liszt's first concerto is also a symptom of the contemporaneous historiographical failure to recognize Schubert's claim to have first dramatized the potential of "cyclic sonata form ... on variation principles," despite Liszt's concrete attempt—the topic of this chapter—to draw public attention to the *Wanderer* Fantasy.
16. Thomas Kabisch, *Liszt und Schubert* (Munich/Salzburg: Emil Katzbichler, 1984); Detlef Altenburg, "Franz Liszt and the Legacy of the Classical Era," *19th-Century Music* 18, no. 1 (1994): 46–63.
17. Kregor, *Liszt as Transcriber*, 4.
18. Kabisch, *Liszt und Schubert*, 135, my translation.
19. This is not the place to elaborate on the question of what kind of pianist Schubert himself was. The writer's opinion is that there is much research still to

be done on that question, and that musicological opinion to date, quoted from one era to the next without hard evidence, is probably not to be taken seriously. Related statements such as that "Schubert was not a composer for the virtuoso" (Philip Radcliffe, *Schubert Piano Sonatas* [London: BBC Music Guides, 1967], 9) have fortunately come to be seen as cliché rather than informed opinion.

20. Schnabel and Cortot are mentioned here because their outstanding editorial work dates from the age of recording, and each was a definitive performer of the works they edited; and yet a performance offers a contingent, provisional kind of knowledge, compared with which pedagogical editions are so much richer and more reliable.

21. Alfred Cortot, Study Score, Schubert's *Wanderer* Fantasy (Paris: Salabert, 1954).

22. Walker, *Reflections on Liszt*, 185. See also Vera Wolkowicz, "Liszt's Edition of Schubert's 'Wanderer' Fantasy: Arrangement or Instructive Edition?," unpublished research paper (University of Cambridge, 2013), https://www.academia.edu/5940447, accessed 2 December 2019, which is, to this writer's knowledge, the most recent, English-language study of Liszt's work on his *Wanderer* edition and a valuable repository of information and opinion. She seems to conclude, while also supporting Kregor's influential characterization of Liszt's transcriptions as having had multiple objectives, that the *Wanderer* edition is definitely more instructive than creative. Compared with the symphonic arrangement, that is clearly the case. This may seem an arcane type of debate, but Wolkowicz is aware of a body of opinion among modern musicologists criticizing Liszt for his incursions into Schubert's originals, and in that sense she is defending Liszt's scholarly as well as his artistic integrity.

23. Alfred Brendel, *Alfred Brendel on Music: Collected Essays* (Chicago: A Capella Books, 2001), 151n7.

24. Hye-Won Jennifer Cho, "Performance Practice Issues in Franz Schubert's Fantasy in C Major ('Wanderer Fantasy'), D. 760" (DMA Dissertation, UCLA, 2010), 44.

25. For general information on the piano in Schubert's day, see, for example, Malcolm Bilson, "Schubert's Piano Music and the Pianos of His Time," *Studia Musicologica Academiae Scientiarum Hungaricae* 22, no. 1/4 (1980): 270, which includes some discussion of this work.

26. I am grateful to Alexander Kobrin for sharing with me his authoritative views on the playability of classical and Romantic octave scales. It is difficult to find meaningful analogies to this case in the piano literature. For example, octave scalar passages in Mozart and Beethoven have long been presumed to be glissandi, which are not overly challenging technically on the shallower and lighter action of contemporaneous pianos; and not even the notorious octave passage closing Chopin's "Black Key" Study, op. 10, no. 5, is truly analogous, since passing over the black-key pentatonic "scale" in octaves is a glissando-like

technique (anyone who tries to perform Chopin's passage at speed transposed to white keys can ascertain how categorically distinct are the physiological limits of white-key as opposed to inherently less challenging black-key successions).
27. Mitsuko Uchida (CD, Philips 475 6282PB8).
28. This is a matter of opinion as to fine detail. The maximum likely speed of the "Der Erlkönig" arrangement is about 140 bpm, as also of the *Wanderer* first movement, though packing four notes into a beat rather than three, and thus more challenging; as with ex. 7.2 from D. 784, a local relaxation of the tempo at the *Wanderer* passage is, in the writer's experience of contemporary practice, typical and could be argued to be expressively appropriate, regardless of technical issues.
29. David Montgomery, *Franz Schubert's Music in Performance: Compositional Ideals, Notational Intent, Historical Realities, Pedagogical Foundations* (Hillsdale, NY: Pendragon Press, 2003), 236.
30. Bear in mind that the *Wanderer* is a single-movement work, although its multi-movement, symphonic disposition—first movement with many of the characteristics of a "sonata form," followed by slow movement, scherzo, and finale—is unmistakable.
31. Kabisch, *Liszt und Schubert*, 137, my translation.
32. Quoted in Kregor, *Liszt as Transcriber*, 131–32, which also includes Liszt's original French text (ibid., 250–51).
33. We shall see below that Dana Gooley characterizes Liszt's own concerto practice as the composition not of inherent struggles so much as celebrations of solo virtuosity with orchestral support.
34. Kabisch, *Liszt und Schubert*, 134, my translation.
35. This passage is discussed in Jonathan Dunsby, "Adorno's Image of Schubert's *Wanderer* Fantasy Multiplied by Ten" *19th-Century Music* 29, no. 1 (2005): 12, in response to Adorno's description of the slow movement as a place where rather than merely musically describing death, as another composer might do, Schubert takes us there musically to show us around: "Adorno has left us no hint of what this musical relationship between mm. 206–14 and 231–35 may be about, although it requires no great leap of the musical imagination to suppose that if the original measures are our way in to a deathscape, then the later reinscription of those measures is the outburst of a memory of it" (ibid., 44).
36. The parallel passage in the initial hearing of the scherzo, which is in the traditional "da capo" form of scherzo-trio-scherzo, begins at measure 305 and formally at its incipit, measure 303.
37. [Ed.] See Robert Doran's chapter in this volume for an exploration of the relation between bravura piano writing and the *stile brillante*.
38. Theorists might want to argue that this latter is a kind of "false entry," with some justification in the sense that in the centuries-long tradition of fugal theory "false" means non-schematic according to certain fugal norms. Since Schubert's *Wanderer* "fugue" dissipates into fantasy-conclusion in the service

of the overall constructional strategy of the composition, this "entry" is "false" not only fugally but as a kind of Schubertian formal pun. It appears, both unexpectedly and not, in the dialogue between fugue and dissipation. Liszt rendered it pounded out by the entire string section, *fortissimo* and *marcatissimo*, against the piano's virtuoso countersubject gymnastics: it is not difficult to see this place in the symphonic arrangement as an example of Liszt's exact translation of Schubert's original compositional strategy.

39. Hesitate though one must to indulge in hoping to read a composer's mind, it is also true that Schubert could not conceivably have undertaken the huge labor of composition of a work like the *Wanderer* without pondering the purpose and novelty of his own decision-making process.
40. [Ed.] On the idea of the perception of virtuosic difficulty, see in the present volume the editor's introduction and David Keep's chapter.
41. Dana Gooley, *The Virtuoso Liszt* (Cambridge: Cambridge University Press, 2004), 114.
42. Michael Talbot, *The Finale in Western Instrumental Music* (Oxford: Oxford University Press, 2001).
43. Unfortunately, Adorno never, at least in those of his writings that were published, explained what exactly he thought was wrong with the *Wanderer* finale, but there was certainly something, as the following, rather obscure and puzzling comment from 1928 makes clear: "That the finale of the B-Minor Symphony could not be written has something to do with the shortcomings of the finale of the *Wanderer* Fantasy; it is not the dilettante who cares passionately about how a piece is destined to end, but Schubert" (Adorno, "Schubert (1928)," 28).
44. Kabisch, *Liszt und Schubert*, 135, my translation.

Chapter Eight

From the Brilliant Style to the Bravura Style

Reconceptualizing Lisztian Virtuosity

Robert Doran

During his formative years as a child prodigy, well before his "transcendental" breakthroughs in the realm of virtuosity in the late 1830s and early 1840s, Franz Liszt made his mark on music through his amazing improvisations, but also through the performance of a select group of works for piano and orchestra that were considered to be the pinnacle of piano virtuosity in their day. Superseding Beethoven's mighty "Emperor" Concerto, op. 73, premiered only a decade prior but already "outmoded,"[1] these works—Hummel's Piano Concertos in A Minor, op. 85, and B Minor, op. 89, and Weber's *Konzertstück*, op. 79[2]—were the epitome of what is now called the "brilliant style," the postclassical (as Jim Samson terms it) approach to virtuosity that flourished in the 1820s.[3] In fact, the two Hummel concertos were published, and the Weber piece composed, during the same year, 1821.[4]

In 1822, Liszt was placed under the tutelage of Beethoven's student Carl Czerny, himself a prolific exponent of the brilliant style.[5] After ten months, Czerny allowed the eleven-year-old phenomenon to make his Viennese debut with Hummel's A-Minor Concerto, creating a sensation. A reviewer in the *Allgemeine Zeitung* enthused, "A young virtuoso has, as it were, fallen from the clouds, and compels us to the highest admiration. The performance of this boy, for his age, borders on the incredible, and one is tempted to doubt any physical impossibility when one hears the young giant, with unabated force, thunder out Hummel's composition, so difficult and fatiguing, especially in the last movement."[6] The reviewer makes two important points: (1) that Hummel's concerto is especially "difficult and fatiguing" (even for adults, presumably), thereby foregrounding the extreme virtuosity of the composition itself; and (2) that the young Liszt "thunders out" the Hummel concerto with "unabated force," an observation that most likely pertains to Liszt's specific performance, rather than to any objective quality suggested by the score.[7] Indeed, the latter point presents a rather odd description of brilliant-style virtuosity. Although, at this time, Liszt might be considered to be "a prisoner of the *style brillant*,"[8] to the extent that the brilliant style is associated with *lightness* (in both senses of being easy on the ears and of implying the lighter touch required in clearly articulated, rapid passagework) Liszt can already be said to be pushing the boundaries of this style, effectively prefiguring the thicker, heavier, "thundering" pianism of what we shall call the "bravura style" of the mature Liszt.

With regard to the first point, virtuosity is certainly an essential feature of brilliant-style pianism, revealing a shift in audience expectation and compositional goals, both of which were trending in the direction of a greater public display of the performer's skill. Concerto performances were the primary vehicle for this shift, insofar as they would become, beginning in the 1820s, the exclusive province of professional *virtuosos*, namely those capable of executing the latest and most advanced technical innovations with aplomb. Difficulty (actual or perceived) was thus a new feature of the art music of the period.[9] Beethoven ensured that his piano concertos could be played by the talented amateur (recall that Archduke Rudolf premiered the "Emperor" Concerto) as well as the conventionally skilled professional (indeed they are considerably less daunting than solo piano compositions such as the "Hammerklavier" Sonata, op. 106, and the "Diabelli" Variations, op. 120, or even the "Waldstein," op. 53, and "Appassionata," op. 57, Sonatas, for that matter). But Hummel sought in his A-Minor and B-Minor Concertos to showcase some of the most virtuosic and challenging piano writing, putting them out of reach of all but elite professionals (or child prodigies)—like the composer himself, the leading pianist of the day and a former prodigy who had studied (and lived) with Mozart. (This tradition extends into the first half of the twentieth century, in the piano concertos of composer-pianists Rachmaninoff and Prokofiev, considered to be among the most difficult of all piano compositions in the standard repertoire.) In these two Hummel concertos, virtuosity is seamlessly woven into the fabric of the work, as opposed to being confined to cadenzas, transitions, and final flourishes. These works also reveal a more extroverted or "popular" form of virtuosity, increasingly opposed to the private virtuosity of Beethoven's late piano works, which were for a long time considered inscrutable.[10]

In the 1830s brilliant-style virtuosity gradually gives way to the new bravura style of Thalberg and Liszt. In many respects this shift tracks closely with the evolution of the piano itself, from the lighter Viennese action associated with the brilliant style to the increasingly powerful sonority and more responsive action of the pianos of the 1830s and 1840s, in particular that of the Érard piano, of which Liszt became an early champion.[11] Thus, as I noted in my editor's introduction, bravura virtuosity was as much a function of developments in piano manufacturing as it was of developments in the way the piano was played and composed for. However, Liszt would take the virtuosic implications of these design innovations to technical and musical heights none of his contemporaries could have imagined. Indeed, of his cohort, only Liszt was able to elevate and transform the popular virtuoso pianism of 1830s and 1840s, and he did so, as I shall explore in this chapter, by means of a modernist aesthetic.

To be sure, Liszt's transcendence of the brilliant style by modernist means is not a new or even a controversial topic. Carl Dahlhaus already observed in his seminal *Nineteenth-Century Music* that "the convoluted modernity of the musical material [of the *Dante* Sonata] provoked 'excessive' harmonic effects, interspersed with unusual dissonances and violent changes of key. This kept Liszt's virtuosity from devolving into mere 'brilliance,' the pianistic equivalent of the derivative, classicist harmony and melody of the Thalbergs and Kalkbrenners."[12] This said, one of the principal contentions of this chapter is that we do not often perceive the complex relations Liszt developed between a new bravura pianism and the brilliant-style of execution and composition on which he was weaned. Indeed, in his contribution to this volume, Kenneth Hamilton reveals the deep influence of brilliant-style works such as Czerny's Sonata, op. 7 (c. 1820) and Weber's Piano Sonatas on Liszt's art.[13] But in this chapter I am less concerned with the question of influence than with what one might call a *musical dialectics*, that is, the negation, preservation, and elevation to a higher level of musical substance—a musical *Aufhebung*.

Bravura versus *Brillante*: A Revolution in Style

The musical or expressive term "bravura" derives from its use in describing spirited vocal music in the Italian style, specifically the *aria di bravura*. The entry for "bravura" in *Grove Music Online* reads as follows (oddly there is no entry for *brillante* or "brilliant style"):

> The element of brilliant display in vocal or instrumental music that tests the performer's skill. The term was particularly common in the 18th century with the *aria di bravura*, also known as the *aria d'agilità*. John Brown (*Letters on Italian Opera*, 2/1791) remarked that such arias were "composed chiefly—indeed, too often—merely to indulge the singer in display"; and Mozart said of the aria for Constanze, "Ach, ich liebte" in *Die Entführung aus dem Serail*, "I have tried to express her feelings, as far as an Italian bravura aria will allow it" (letter dated 26 September 1781).[14]

Several things jump out from these definitions: (1) the idea of a test of skill, that is, difficulty, or at least the appearance of difficulty, is paramount; (2) the idea of empty display—the superficial or superfluous aspect that is later associated with virtuosity, including the idea that bravura might be musically limiting, as Mozart implies; and (3) the use of the word "brilliant" as a roughly interchangeable with "bravura," instead of a term of contrast, as will become the case beginning in the 1830s.[15]

In the Lisztian context it is the literal meaning of "bravura" as courage or swagger that will become important, eventually displacing its synonymous association with "brilliant." Although Jim Samson, in his *Virtuosity and the Musical Work*, often uses the terms "bravura" and "brilliant" interchangeably,[16] he nevertheless notes that in Liszt "the word *bravura*, ubiquitous in the titles of the brilliant style, can be seen in a new, gendered light, with a suggestion of machismo, of the exploits of medieval chivalry or folk heroism."[17] And "the total command of technique also involved a sense of sacrifice; it was hard won, and that (ethical) quality was of its essence, suggestive of heroic resolution, a difficulty magnificently and bravely overcome (*di bravura*)."[18] A contemporary commentator from the 1830s in fact noted Liszt's "over-heroic treatment of the instrument," which did not take "into account the weakness of the piano frame."[19] As Dana Gooley explores in his *The Virtuoso Liszt*, it is indeed the heroic, or Napoleonic-heroic, aspect that will come to define Lisztian bravura.[20]

Like the term "bravura," *brillante* originated as an indicator of musical expression. Defined as "the use of rapid passages for virtuoso display or intense feeling,"[21] in piano music this typically meant single-note (and double-note—thirds—in Hummel especially) passagework in the upper registers of the keyboard. *Brillante* then emerges as a category of musical style (*stile brillante*) to describe the type of virtuosity that flourished in the period 1810–30, a kind of interregnum between classicism and Romanticism, particularly in the works for piano and orchestra of composer-pianists such as Weber, Hummel, Czerny, Moscheles, Kalkbrenner, the early Chopin, and the early Mendelssohn (who, though only one year older than Chopin, composed brilliant-style works for piano and orchestra well into the 1830s: Piano Concerto no. 1, op. 25, in 1831; *Capriccio Brillant*, op. 22, in 1832; and *Rondo Brillant*, op. 29, in 1834).[22] Even the casual listener will be struck by the remarkable similarities between Chopin's two piano concertos (1829–30) and those of Hummel referenced above—particularly the fact that both feature, as Leonard Ratner puts it, a "contrast between the brilliant-vigorous and the gentle-cantabile."[23] Although many of the works of this period were highly regarded by contemporaries—Hummel's F-sharp Minor Piano Sonata, op. 81, and Weber's four piano sonatas chief among them—such important pieces are rarely performed or recorded today. This leaves a relatively large lacuna in the musical consciousness of the contemporary listener, who suffers from a skewed sense of the Romantic piano aesthetic—as if Chopin and Liszt simply followed Beethoven and Schubert with nothing of consequence in between. There is thus a tendency to ascribe an originality to the early Chopin he does not truly deserve. Samson and Kornel Michałowski note in their entry on "Chopin" in the *Grove Music Online*:

> Excluding the two earliest, written in his eighth year, there are seven solo polonaises of this kind composed in Warsaw, and we may add the *Polonaise brillante* op. 3 for cello and piano. They are pieces of considerable accomplishment. But they are hardly "Chopinesque," and they give the lie to any notion that Chopin's unique sound world was somehow present from the start, that it appeared from nowhere, fully formed. The idiomatic figuration in these works was in fact closely modelled on an extensive repertory of post-Classical concert music, and it reached its zenith in the *Grande polonaise brillante* op. 22 [1830–31] for piano and orchestra, which must rate as one of the peaks of the "brilliant style."[24]

Liszt's pianistic art similarly emerged from the brilliant style, but his strategies for overcoming it were very different from Chopin's.

Let us consider a simple but paradigmatic example from Liszt's virtuoso period, his 1838 showstopper *Grand galop chromatique* (S. 219 / LW A43), which, as I mentioned in my editor's introduction, is one of a small number of works Liszt regularly programmed and was by far his most popular *original composition* of the late 1830s and 1840s.[25] It was also featured by other major pianists of the day, such as the Russian prodigy Anton Rubinstein, who played it as the final item in his first concerts in Paris. Rubinstein's biographer observes that "in performing such works as Thalberg's fantasies and Liszt's *Grand galop chromatique* (frequently included in Liszt's own programs), the young Rubinstein exhibited eloquent proof of his skill in the mechanical execution of music composed in the grand bravura style."[26] In other words, the young Rubinstein wanted to be counted as an exponent of the new virtuosity then represented by Thalberg and Liszt, just as Liszt had used Hummel in his early years to signal his mastery of the brilliant-style virtuosity then in vogue.[27]

Although now eclipsed by such warhorses as the First Mephisto Waltz and the Second Hungarian Rhapsody, the *Grand galop* should not be discounted as a mere historical curiosity; it is in many ways a pivotal work in Liszt's early oeuvre and performing career. Since it was his only well-known, fully original work of the virtuoso period, it played a crucial role in defining Liszt as a composer, for better or worse. (Such was its popularity that Liszt published four-handed [S. 616 / LW B2, 1838] and simplified [S. 219bis] versions of the piece.) Its relation to Chopin is instructive. On one level, the piece can be read as a kind of bravura parody of the sparsely linear, perpetual-mobile (brilliant-style) figuration of Chopin's A-Minor Étude, op. 10, no. 2, with which it shares the technical requirement of using 3–4–5 right-hand figuring for the ascending chromatic scale with chords that is at the heart of both works (exx. 8.1a and 8.1b). Liszt thus invites comparison of his bravura virtuosity—in this case, its slyly demonic, boisterous, unrestrained, and extroverted qualities, as well as its thick textures—with the tightly restrained, classical (or even baroque) virtuosity of Chopin's étude.[28] Even the opening (but recurrent) fanfare-like figure (ex. 8.1b) mischievously (but respectfully) recalls the opening of Chopin's *Grande valse brillante*, op. 18 (ex. 8.1c), in the same key of E-flat major. (Liszt begins unconventionally with the fanfare on C♭, a half step above the harmonically expected B♭, as in Chopin's waltz.) These similarities are simply too obvious not to be intentional.[29]

On another level, however, Liszt's showpiece can be read as performing a commentary on the brilliant style itself. The allusion to the salon virtuosity of Chopin's opus 18 Waltz is certainly an indication of this, but the inclusion of an interlude marked *brillante* (ex. 8.1d), repeated four times without alteration, makes it explicit.

Example 8.1a. Chopin, Étude op. 10, no. 2, mm. 1–2

Example 8.1b. Liszt, *Grand galop chromatique*, S. 219, mm. 1–12

Example 8.1c. Chopin, *Grande valse brillante*, op. 18, mm. 1–6

Example 8.1d. Liszt, *Grand galop chromatique*, S. 219, mm. 69–78

The four identical repetitions of the *brillante* interlude would seem to represent a nostalgic gesture toward the old-style—brilliant and salon—virtuosity with which Liszt achieved fame as a prodigy and then as a young adult in Paris. That Liszt's effort was intended not for the exclusive, *haut-bourgeois* / aristocratic salon but rather for the democratic masses of the concert hall serves to separate the new from the old Liszt, just as his recently composed *Grandes études* (1837) separated Liszt's new transcendental (and modernist) bravura from the largely vapid, Czerny-inspired brilliant figuration of the *Étude en douze exercices* (1826) on which they were based.[30] In both cases, a certain quaintness or innocence of the brilliant style is compared to the revolutionary accomplishments of Liszt's bravura aesthetic. The more cultivated audiences of the time would have no doubt perceived the *Grand galop* as a kind of hybrid: at once nostalgic and new, oriented toward the popular taste with its rollicking accompaniment and yet harmonically challenging with its implacable chromaticism.

Now, of course it was showpieces like the *Grand galop* that tended to give the term "bravura" a bad reputation, thereby pointing to the great fissure between mid-nineteenth-century concepts of "serious" music and the exigencies of the burgeoning concert scene. Consider, for example, the definition of "bravura" in the 1880 *Grove Dictionary*: "The notion of effect for effect's sake is perhaps involved in the term. Beethoven therefore can never be said to have written bravura pieces, though many of his pieces require the greatest skill and are extremely brilliant."[31] Clearly the perceived excesses of Liszt and other virtuosos of the 1830s and 1840s affected the meaning of the term "bravura," which by 1880 (but most probably earlier), and unlike "brilliant," implied a value contrast between Romantic virtuosity and the classical profundity epitomized by Beethoven (and later by Brahms). This can be seen as a general consequence of the way in which, as Samson puts it, virtuosity draws "the listener away from the qualities of the work toward the qualities of the performer" and in this manner "highlighted technique rather than substance, the moment rather than the whole. . . . It encourages us to wonder at the act, rather than to commune with the work and its referents by way of the act."[32] Thus effective performance qualities come to be seen as poor work qualities, even if one can argue that work-virtuosity becomes a new avenue for musical experimentation. With Liszt, we do not have to choose between the crowd pleasing or the avant-garde (and the *Grand gallop* can be regarded as both). Dahlhaus observes that "whatever the deficiencies of Paganini's own compositions, he evidently made Liszt aware of the potential of virtuosity for formally integrating 'experimental' musical material, and conversely the potential of a radically modern musical idiom for giving virtuosity a substance lacking in the fashionable style [i.e., the brilliant or salon style] in which he had grown up."[33] In other words, Liszt saw in virtuosity a revolutionary musical force, not simply a means of showcasing one's abilities; and it was this specifically *modernist* impulse that infused Lisztian virtuosity with its epoch-making significance.

According to the 1880 definition quoted above, there is no bravura in Beethoven. But his student Czerny certainly did not think so. In Czerny's 1839 tract *On the Proper Performance of All Beethoven's Works for Piano* (part of his *Pianoforte-Schule*, op. 500), we find that the term *Bravura* (the same word in German) abounds in his descriptions of Beethoven's works. Speaking of Beethoven's Piano Sonata, op. 7, Czerny writes that "the passages in semiquavers" are to be played "with great bravura and fluency."[34] Of opus 31, number 3, Czerny notes that "the Finale must be performed with the greatest vivacity, lightness, power, and bravura," and he refers to the "bravura passages" of the finale of the "Hammerklavier" Sonata, op. 106.[35] Czerny also uses the term "brilliant" as a quasi-technical, expressive indication. Thus Czerny avers that "although animated," the first movement of opus 22 is "yet not properly brilliant"; and of the first movement of the "Pathétique" Sonata (op. 13) he notes that "the following Allegro is extremely impetuous and excited, by which this composition acquires its brilliant character, in the symphony style."[36] However, the first movement of opus 110 is "by no means brilliant."[37] Whereas for Czerny "brilliant" and "bravura" are distinct categories of expression, they also can be complementary, as when he directs that the conclusion of the last movement of the "Pastoral" Sonata (op. 28) be played "very quick and brilliant, and with bravura," while the finale of the "Funeral March" Sonata, op. 26, should be "rendered interesting by an equality of touch, and by delicate shading of the ascending or descending movement, without departing from its character by a too sentimental performance, or by brilliant bravura playing."[38] Indeed, as mentioned above, many works in the brilliant style used the term "bravura" in their titles.

Czerny also saw brilliant and bravura as complementary in his own compositions, as evidenced in his contribution to the collaborative *Hexaméron* (organized by Liszt in 1837), indicating that his variation should be played *vivo e brillante*, while also writing *con bravura* over the first measure, thus implying that it should apply to the whole piece. However, by 1844, when Czerny published his *The Art of Finger Dexterity*, op. 740, it appears as if he had begun to see "bravura" as designating a specific technique of execution or an autonomous style in *contrast* to brilliant-style writing and execution, as illustrated in the last two exercises of the set, which he describes, respectively, as "Octaves-Bravura" (*Oktaven mit Bravour*, no. 49, ex. 8.2) and "Bravura in Touch and Tempo" (no. 50). These examples clearly reveal the influence of Thalberg and Liszt. Even if Czerny's music and studies are generally in the brilliant style, Czerny nevertheless recognizes the importance of the new bravura piano aesthetic. Liszt himself remarked that "later on, [Czerny] did not set himself up against some of the progress that had been made in technique, but contributed materially to it by his own teaching and works."[39]

Example 8.2. Carl Czerny, *The Art of Finger Dexterity*, op. 740, no. 49, mm. 1–8 (*Oktaven mit Bravour*)

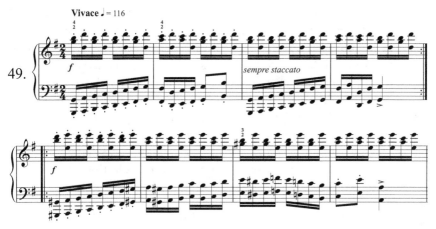

It is instructive to note how Liszt was sometimes moved to transform brilliant-style works into bravura ones, as he did with Weber's *Konzertstück*, of which Liszt published his own edition with alternate passages in 1880. And one could also mention in this context Liszt's 1851 concerto arrangement of Schubert's *Wanderer* Fantasy (discussed in Jonathan Dunsby's chapter in this volume). Presumably these represent Liszt's own (early) performance practices, and they appear to jibe with firsthand accounts of the young Liszt. Gooley notes that Liszt's version "not only enriched the sonority, but also rewrote the performer's bodily choreography. Whereas the body of Weber's virtuoso sweeps along the horizontal axis of the keyboard, Liszt's arms and wrists are constantly approaching the keyboard vertically. By transforming rapid fingerwork into vertical gestures, Liszt offered a spectacle of domination and violence that, in the special circumstances of the *Konzertstück*, displaced to an image of heroic military valor."[40] Indeed, although he speaks nominally in terms of "embellishments,"[41] what Gooley is describing is in effect a shift in style: a break with brilliant-style performance practices, which involves a physical dimension as well as musical one, namely a shift from the horizontal movements of the brilliant style (rapid finger work) to the vertical gestures (octaves, leaps, alternating hands) of bravura pianism, with all of its heroic connotations (bravery, daring).

I should add that the "violence" was not only gestural but also inhered in the very sonority of Lisztian bravura virtuosity, which not only enriched but departed significantly from the beautiful aesthetic exemplified by Chopin and Thalberg. While there are a few moments of violence in Chopin (such as the crashing chords in the coda of the B-Minor Scherzo, op. 20), in general, as Charles Rosen points out, "Chopin's aesthetic is that of the beautiful in terms of sonority and texture. This is why he is the most listenable to those who don't know or care for classical music."[42] Indeed, no one associated "terror" with Chopin's or Thalberg's virtuosity, as they did with Liszt. This would also explain why Thalberg was initially more popular than Liszt in the late 1830s. His beautiful aesthetic was simply easier to digest and to appreciate than was Liszt's violent and modernist bravura (as evidenced especially in his études of that period), which can be identified with the aesthetic concept of *sublimity*, a notion to which Rosen appears to point, as in this passage:

> The piano was taught to make new sounds. These sounds often did not conform to an idea of beauty, either Classical or Romantic, but they enlarged the meaning of music, made possible new modes of expression. On a much larger scale, Liszt did for the piano what Paganini had done only a few years previously for the violin. Listeners were impressed not only with the beauty of Paganini's tone quality but also with its occasional ugliness and brutality, with the way he literally attacked his instrument for such dramatic effect. Liszt made a new range of dramatic piano sound possible, and in so doing he thoroughly overhauled the technique of keyboard playing.[43]

Rosen thus reconfigures Dahlhaus's insight about Liszt and Paganini according to the cardinal eighteenth-century contrast between the sublime and the beautiful: bravura virtuosity in the sense of Paganini and Liszt is no longer assimilable to the sense of beauty or conventional taste (let us recall that taste involves beauty, not sublimity, in Kant's aesthetics); it contains a brutality and ugliness that can be understood only in terms of sublimity.[44]

According to Kant's theory, the sublime object is in fact a kind of *ugliness* (boundless formlessness or a threatening natural force); it does *violence* to our sensibility (in Kantian terms, it is contrapurposive for our judging faculty), and by this very violence it puts us in touch with our supersensible vocation (the rational-noumenal overcoming of a phenomenal presentation of sensibility). Kant writes, "That which . . . excites in us the feeling of the sublime, may to be sure appear in its form to be contrapurposive for our power of judgment, unsuitable for our faculty of presentation, and as it were doing violence to our imagination, but is nevertheless judged all the more sublime for that."[45] Hence the *paradoxical* feeling of being both overwhelmed and elevated, inferior and superior, humbled and exalted that is the hallmark of the sublime. I call this in my book on the sublime the "dual structure" of the experience of sublimity.[46] Gooley observes that "listening to Liszt was the aural equivalent of the experience of the sublime, often overwhelming or terrifying the listener."[47] While here Gooley evinces a more Burkean understanding of the sublime as terror, in a later chapter of his book Gooley would appear to integrate both the elevating/uplifting (divine) and overwhelming (demonic) aspects, remarking that "Liszt's bravura has the capacity to be coded holy as well as diabolical."[48] (Samson similarly notes that "for Schumann [Liszt] was a 'demon exercising his powers,' while intriguingly, for Clara [Liszt] invoked the other side of that noumenal coin; he was 'divine'; he could be compared to no other virtuoso. He is the only one of his Kind. He arouses fright and astonishment.")[49] In short, I think Gooley's *The Virtuoso Liszt*, like Charles Rosen's *The Romantic Generation*, can be seen as structured by the aesthetic opposition between the beautiful and the sublime, with Thalberg playing the same "beautiful" role for Gooley that Chopin does for Rosen and Liszt playing the "sublime" role for both.[50]

Broadly speaking, then, we can see the dichotomy between the brilliant and bravura styles as mapping onto the beautiful/sublime contrast, even if there are complications to this basic model (as with Paganini and Thalberg, who can be considered under the rubric of brilliant or bravura depending on one's focus).

The "Storm Rondo" and the New Bravura Aesthetic

Despite the highly innovative and seminal quality of his two sets of études, op. 10 and op. 25, Chopin's attitude toward piano virtuosity remained decidedly classical, even restrained. He effectively ignores most of the major changes in execution and the new bravura figuration that Liszt and others pioneered in the 1830s and 1840s: tremolando to imitate orchestral textures (especially in transcriptions but also original pieces such as *Vallee d'Obermann*, first version from 1837–38, S. 156/5 / LW A40a/4); rapid note repetition (*Tarantella*, first version from 1840, S. 159/4 / LW A53/4); glissandos (Tenth Hungarian Rhapsody, S. 244/10 / LW A132/10, 1847);[51] extended declamatory or virtuosic double-octave passagework (as in *Funerailles*, S. 173/7 / LW A158/7, 1849, and the Sixth Hungarian Rhapsody, S. 244/6 / LW A132/6, 1847— Chopin's "Octave Étude," op. 25, no. 10, being an exception in his oeuvre); long trills combined with melody notes in one hand (Beethoven had suggested this technique in the finale of the "Waldstein" Sonata, op. 53, but Liszt certainly took it to new heights, as in his *Fantaisie sur des motifs favoris de l'opéra "La sonnambula" de Bellini*, S. 393/1 / LW A56/1, 1841); rapid, broken octaves blurred by the pedal to create a "surging" effect (as in Liszt's *Transcendental Étude* no. 11, *Harmonies du soir*, 1837/1851); to say nothing of Thalberg's widely admired "three-hand" technique (imitated by Liszt in the *Réminiscences de Norma*, S. 394 / LW A77, 1841, and the Third Concert Étude, *Un sospiro*, S. 144/3 / LW 118/3, 1845–49) and Liszt's patented interlocking chromatic octaves (sometimes termed "blind" octaves, as employed in the middle section of the *Don Juan* Fantasy, S. 418 / LW A80, 1841).[52] Chopin certainly developed his own inimitable, piano-specific sound, but this sound was inevitably tempered by a musical asceticism that recoiled from the larger palette of virtuosic effects. Liszt, on the contrary, could see no reason to dismiss any technical innovation for which he could find a musical use. Liszt's conception of what musical uses the piano could be appropriately assigned, from the exotic textures of the Hungarian Rhapsodies to the orchestral sonorities of his Beethoven and Wagner transcriptions—his virtuosic eclecticism, one could call it—represented a fundamentally different approach to the piano. But this eclecticism also led to charges of "vulgar" piano writing, defined as that which extended too far beyond "classical" limits toward a "tasteless" bravura. ("Tasteless" tends to be a relative judgment; Chopin apparently considered Beethoven's "Hunt" Piano Sonata, op. 31, no. 3, to be "vulgar.")[53]

A case in point is the often-derided tremolando technique. In fact, most of the new techniques listed above can be considered as varieties of the tremolo (the rapid repetition or alternation of one or more notes), the trill being the most common form on the piano (Paganini's "Tremolo" Caprice, no. 6 is also nicknamed "The Trill"), even if it is not usually categorized as such. One of the chief virtues of this technique was to mitigate or even eliminate what was considered to be the main drawback of the piano vis-à-vis other instruments, the piano diminuendo, the immediate decay and inalterability of a tone after a key is stuck. The desire to "solve" the problem of the piano diminuendo was addressed by both manufacturing and performance-based innovations. In 1812, Sebastian Érard obtained a patent for a *forte-piano à son continu* (piano with a continuous sound), which featured "a sustaining mechanism that secures the hammer to the string via a toothed or rotating wheel."[54] A decade later, Érard developed his famous double-escapement action, enabling a "continuous sound" by a different means, namely rapid note-repetition. On the performance side, the increased use of the damper pedal, not regularly employed prior to 1800 (for reasons of taste more than of technology), allowed the piano to "sing" by creating the illusion of sustained tone.[55] But it was the tremolando technique that counteracted the piano diminuendo most effectively and spectacularly.

It is often assumed, erroneously, that this technique was originally developed in the context of transcription to imitate specific orchestral sonorities (strings in particular, which had a long tremolando tradition) and hence is not idiomatic or proper to the piano—which might therefore explain Chopin's aversion to it. Referring to Chopin, Alan Walker observes, "We search almost in vain for the tremolando, that stock-in-trade device used by so many of Chopin's contemporaries and generally cheapened by them. The tremolando is an orchestral effect that sounds ungainly on the piano keyboard because it does not naturally spring from it."[56] But the tremolando is no more foreign to the piano aesthetic than the use of the sustaining pedal, both of which started to draw intense interest circa 1800.

In fact, one of the earliest and most iconic uses of this technique was by Daniel Steibelt (1765–1823) in a work *with orchestra*: the third movement of his Piano Concerto no. 3 in E Major, op. 33 (1798), nicknamed "L'orage" (the storm), which was quite popular at the time.[57] Richard Wigmore observes:

> Steibelt's finale [to his Third Piano Concerto] caused a sensation, as he surely calculated it would. Headed "Rondo pastorale, in which is introduced an imitation of a storm," the movement exploits the current fashion for naive pictorial effects. Musette drones and the nasal sonority of strings playing close to the bridge enhance the rusticity of the opening tune, while the storm that erupts in the middle of the movement features swirls of diminished sevenths and liberal use of tremolo—something of a Steibelt speciality. Within a few years this "storm rondo" was being played in salons and concert halls across Europe.[58]

This piece effectively establishes the storm-tremolo topos that Liszt would make his own (e.g., the tremolo-heavy storm scene in *Vallée d'Obermann*), and it may have been this extramusical association, more than the ubiquity of this technique in transcription, that gave Chopin pause.

Beethoven was reportedly on one occasion outshone by Steibelt's extensive and innovative use of the piano tremolando. Commenting on a concert held in Vienna in 1800, which precipitated the supposed "duel" between Steibelt and Beethoven, the latter's future student Ferdinand Ries relates that "[Steibelt] played a quintet of his own composition, improvised, and produced a great effect with his *tremolandos*, which were something quite new then. Beethoven could not be persuaded to play again."[59] While the simple octave roll in the first movement of Beethoven's "Pathétique" Sonata in C Minor, op. 13 (1798), was most likely inspired by similar octave rolls in the openings of Clementi's Piano Sonata in C Major, op. 2, no. 2 (1779), and Mozart's Piano Sonata in C Minor (K. 457, 1784), Steibelt's influence might well be seen in the more atmospheric tremolandos that punctuate the "Marcia funebre" movement from the Sonata in A-flat Major, op. 26 (1800–1801), where they are coupled with the sustaining pedal. This is in fact the first pedal indication in Beethoven's piano sonatas, thus emphasizing the co-emergence of the two techniques as constituting new possibilities in piano sound. A contemporary of Steibelt noted in 1833 that

> [Steibelt] had in his manner of making tremolos something that was thrilling, and when he combined it with a broad, noble melody, brought out loudly by the right hand, or by the left hand crossing over, one could hardly believe that one single person was capable of producing such an effect. These tremolos, in which one never heard any action-noise, and which produced truly connected sounds, I have never heard executed well after him except by Mr. L[ouis] Adam.[60]

It was no doubt the "thrilling" aspect of the tremolo device that attracted Liszt in his overhaul of piano technique: the thickness of texture, the greater volume, and the pedal blurring, not to mention the added virtuoso control (especially of dynamics) that could be achieved, contrasted markedly with the limpidity and restraint that characterized the brilliant-style pianism of the 1820s.

Looking at the final "Allegro Moderato" section of the "Storm Rondo" (ex. 8.3), the figuration looks more specifically Lisztian than anything in Beethoven. Liszt will in fact use the exact same figuration (left-hand chord alternating with thumb at the distance of an octave in the bass), not only in his orchestral transcriptions (e.g., the overture to Rossini's *William Tell*, S. 552 / LW A54, 1838), but also in original compositions such as his *Grande Étude / Transcendental Étude* no. 6, *Vision* (1837/1851, a kind of funeral march),[61] creating a similar wall of sound. Of course, a more refined use of the tremolo, namely a rapid octave roll with damper pedal to imitate an organ sustain, could cohere with the brilliant style, as in the opening measures of Weber's A-flat Major Sonata, op. 39 (which Liszt admired and seemingly imitates in the opening of his Second Legend, *St. François de Paule marchant sur les flots*, S. 175/2 / LW A219/2, 1862–63).[62] But Steibelt's storm-tremolo announced a new piano aesthetic, one that took more than thirty years to find its champion.

Example 8.3. Daniel Steibelt, Piano Concerto no. 3 in E Major, Third Movement, "Storm Rondo," *Allegro moderato*, mm. 1–4

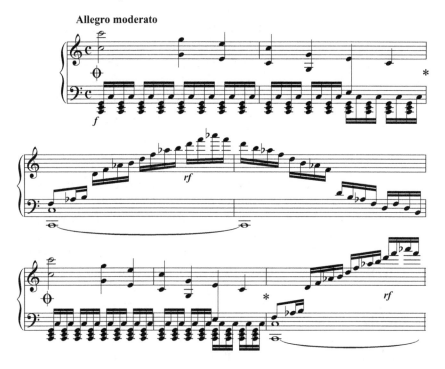

It is certainly no accident that tremolando technique is extensively explored in Liszt's études, in particular the first *Paganini Étude* (based on the "Tremolo" Caprice, cited above) and the final *Transcendental Étude* (*Chasseneige*). Liszt begins one set and ends the other with the tremolo, thereby underlining its special prominence in his approach to the piano. In terms of its mitigating effect on piano diminuendo, rapid arpeggios with sustaining pedal are perhaps the nearest equivalent, and Chopin certainly had no qualms about using arpeggios with abandon: opus 10 begins with and opus 25 ends with lavish arpeggio études. But it is their use in opus 25 no. 1, nicknamed the "Aeolian Harp," that most approximates the tremolo effect. In this étude Chopin creates a continuous chordal sound that swells and recedes according to the performer's will. Liszt's *Chasse-neige* bears more than a superficial resemblance to the "Aeolian Harp" Étude, not only in terms of continuity and control of sound but also in terms of the wide leaps in opposite directions with the fifth finger of each hand, accompanied by arpeggios (Chopin) / tremolos (Liszt) in both hands occupying the middle of the keyboard.[63] The idea that Chopin's arpeggio technique in this étude is somehow more virtuous, piano specific, or effective than Liszt's tremolando technique in *Chasse-neige*—both of which similarly seek to overcome piano tone decay—is a position I think few would defend today. Nevertheless, given the violence and sheer novelty of the tremolo effects in *Chasse-neige* (pointing toward the impressionism of Ravel), this étude is highly emblematic of Liszt's modernist, bravura-style virtuosity, intended in many respects to counter Chopin's more "classical" model.[64]

Transcendental Bravura and the Anti-brilliant Style

Indeed, it is in Liszt's two great sets of études, the six *Études d'exécution transcendante d'après Paganini* and the twelve *Grandes études*, composed and published in the late 1830s, that the contrast with brilliant-style virtuosity is most apparent and self-conscious. Given that both sets endeavor to erase as much as possible the brilliant style of their models—Paganini's *24 Caprices* (1820) and Liszt's own very early *Étude en douze exercices* (1826)—remaking them in the image of Liszt's experimental, bravura-style virtuosity, they were perhaps bound to suffer from excess. These études in fact aspire to be the *antithesis* of the brilliant style and thus can be considered *anti-brilliant-style* works; for they define themselves by a *conscious refusal* of brilliant-style tropes and figure-types, forging an alternate path to extreme virtuosity. In the *Grandes études* Liszt had a freer hand to "recompose," as Samson puts it, since it was a matter of reworking his own compositions. Most strikingly, Liszt eliminates virtually all of the scalar figuration—a mainstay of the brilliant style that abounds in the *Douze exercices*, the only exception being the very brief *Preludio* (no. 1), an explicit homage to Czerny, the dedicatee of the set (and even here the passagework gives way to un-brilliant-like, massive *fortissimo* chords halfway through). There are otherwise only two single-note, scalar passages in the entire *Transcendental Études*, and significantly both were added to the 1851 revision: in the introduction appended to no. 4, *Mazeppa*, and in the climactic moment of no. 12, *Chasse-neige*, both of which involve massive pedal blurring to achieve a surging effect—the exact opposite of the way scales are used in the brilliant style.[65]

Liszt cannot be similarly bold in eliminating all brilliant-style figuration from the Paganini set of 1838, given that it is, for the most part, a sort of "transcription," however loosely the originals are followed.[66] It thus resists recomposition in a way that the *Étude en douze exercices* does not. Liszt must employ other strategies, typically a thickening of the texture (double instead of single notes, added contrapuntal lines). But the constraint of transcription of works by another composer makes him even more prone to excess. For he is also in a relation of rivalry vis-à-vis the model: that is, Liszt does not merely wish to imitate, but also to *outdo* Paganini, while still following his example (that of uniqueness in virtuosity, as I observed in my editor's introduction).

To review the revisions of these two sets undertaken in the early 1850s is to perceive divergent strategies relating to Liszt's view of the relative successes and failures of the two efforts. No longer narrowly focused on demonstrating his distance from the brilliant- and salon-style virtuosity of his youth and early adulthood, Liszt can confidently trim the excesses and put musical thoughts ahead of other concerns. This "definitive," more work-oriented version of his two étude sets is slightly less modernist—and more Romantic-poetic, hence the added descriptive titles—and somewhat less technically challenging; but it is virtuosically more effective and projects an aesthetic that is still radically divergent from the virtuosity of the 1820s.[67] In the Paganini set, the "streamlining" is more extreme, reflecting Liszt's realization that his early effort to transform brilliant violin writing into bravura piano writing simply did not work, for the most part. He consequently makes them more properly transcription-like and less a virtuoso elaboration; the maximalist impulse has become a minimalist one.

The best illustration of this is certainly number 4, of which there are two versions in the 1838 collection. It is the only piece in the set to have multiple versions, thus highlighting Liszt's quandary. Version 2 (ex. 8.4) demonstrates most vividly how Liszt overshoots the mark in attempting to create difficulties for the pianist equivalent to those encountered by the violinist. With its double notes and full-handed chords, Liszt introduces an extremely thick and unwieldly texture that completely obscures the vivacious charm of the violin original. Liszt is obviously trying too hard to be "transcendental," and the étude ends up sounding more like an exercise than a composition.

In the 1851 revision (ex. 8.5), Liszt throws in the towel, as it were, reducing the score to a single staff, mirroring the violin score in letter and spirit. The *con bravura* in the climactic moment of version 2 (1838) is appropriately changed to simply *vigoroso* in the 1851 revision.

Example 8.4. Liszt, *Études d'exécution transcendante d'après Paganini* no. 4, version II, S. 140 (1838), mm. 56-61

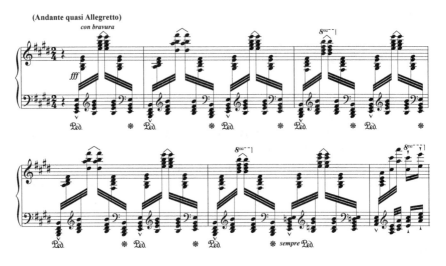

Example 8.5. Liszt, *Grandes études de Paganini* no. 4, S. 141 (1851), mm. 51–54

This is admittedly an extreme example in the set. In other respects Liszt may have gone too far in the minimalist direction. Number 5 is a case in point. Liszt removes many of the contrapuntal textures as well as the cleverly effective coda. Vladimir Horowitz, in fact, preferred the 1838 version, as evidenced by his stunning recording of it in 1930 (along with the 1851 version of no. 2). He also performed this version in his early concerts.[68] I think that a case can be made for the reintegration of some elements of the earlier into the later version of the Paganini studies, in those cases where Liszt went too far in paring things back.[69] Such an effort would not be worthwhile, however, with respect to the *Transcendental Études*, for the reasons cited above.

Finally, it is worth noting that the Breitkopf & Härtel edition of Liszt's complete études in three volumes, edited by Ferruccio Busoni and published in 1911,[70] actually *translates* the French title of the *Transcendental Études, Études d'exécution transcendante*, as *Bravour-Studien* in German and *Bravour-Studies* in English, thereby establishing a linguistic equivalence between "transcendental execution" (*exécution transcendante*) and "bravura."[71] Busoni's edition thus implies that Lisztian bravura does not simply refer to popular virtuosity, namely, showpieces like the operatic fantasies or the Hungarian Rhapsodies, as the more pejorative definition cited above assumes,[72] but also, and perhaps more properly, to works of stunning technical experimentation, high poetic sensibility, and audacious musical sonority—in a word, *modernist virtuosity*. Finally, the hyphenated title indicates the double meaning of "studies in bravura" and "bravura studies": that is, these études both initiate the (advanced) student into the technical challenges of the new transcendental virtuosity, and demonstrate its possibilities to a wider public.

Liszt's Dialectical Virtuosity

Let us now look at some contrastive uses of the expressive and titular indications *brillante* and *bravura*, to see how, increasingly, these denote divergent styles of composition and performance. While Chopin used *brillante* for the French titles of several of his earlier compositions—*Introduction and Polonaise brillante* in C Major, op. 3 (for cello and piano, 1829–30), *Variations brillantes* in B-flat Major on "Je vends des scapulaires" from Hérold's *Ludovic*, op. 12 (1833), *Grande valse brillante* in E-flat Major, op. 18 (1833), *Andante spianato et grande polonaise brillante* in E-flat Major, op. 22 (1830–34), *Trois grandes valses brillantes*, op. 34 (1831–38)—he never uses the term "bravoure" in any of his titles. Liszt, however, only rarely uses *brillant* in his French titles—in his first compositions as a teenager in the 1820s, *Variations brillantes sur un thème de Rossini* (S. 149 / LW A4, 1824), *Impromptu brillant sur des thèmes de Rossini et Spontini* (S. 150 / LW A5, 1824), a fantasy from the 1830s, *Réminiscences de "La juive" (Fantaisie brillante sur des motifs de l'opéra de Halévy)* (S 409a / LW A20,

1835), and a *Mazurka brillante* from 1850 (S. 221 / LW A168). Liszt's use of "bravura" in his composition titles is more extensive: one of his earliest pieces, by which he sought to define himself as an adult virtuoso, is the *Grande fantaisie de bravoure sur "La clochette" de Paganini* (S. 420 / LW A15, 1832–34); but there is also the youthful *Allegro di bravura* (S. 151 / LW A6, 1824–25) and *Rondo di bravura* (S. 152 / LW A 7, 1824–25); and in the 1830s we find the *Grande valse di bravura (Le bal de Berne)* (1836, revised in 1850–52 as *Valse de bravoure*, S. 214/1 / LW A32B), *Hexaméron: Morceaux de concert; Grandes variations de bravoure sur la marche des Puritains de Bellini* (S. 392 / LW A41, 1837–38, arranged for piano and orchestra around the same time and for two pianos in 1840 and again in 1870); and in 1846 there is the *Tarantelle di bravura d'après la tarantelle de "La muette" de Portici* (S. 386/1 / LW A125, revised under the same title in 1869). For comparison, Thalberg has two (French) titles with *brillant* and none with any form of *bravoure*.[73]

As Liszt's usage would seem to indicate, the French terms *bravoure* and *brillant* were seen as somewhat interchangeable in the 1820s. By the mid-1830s, however, with the brilliant style going out of fashion, the word largely disappears from the titles of the works of the pianist-composers, including Chopin, who may have also wished to assert his individuality vis-à-vis his earlier, more imitative period. *Bravoure* took on a new meaning in the post-brilliant piano aesthetic, as indicated in the subtitle of the *Hexaméron*, a work that features many brilliant-style variations of various contemporary pianist-composers, surrounded, as it were, by Lisztian bravura (Liszt provided the introduction, interludes, and finale to the work). This tension between bravery and brilliance is borne out in the modern dictionary (*Merriam-Webster*) definition of "bravura":

Bravura noun
Definition of *bravura* (Entry 1 of 2)
1 *music*: a musical passage requiring exceptional agility and technical skill in execution
2: a florid brilliant style
3: a show of daring or brilliance
Bravura adjective
Definition of bravura (Entry 2 of 2)
1: marked by a dazzling display of skill
2: ornate, showy[74]

With the Romantic-pianistic revolution in the 1830s, the "bold" and "daring" connotations of the term come to be emphasized, overshadowing and displacing the "brilliant" (florid) aspect. While brilliant-style virtuosity might have been somewhat "daring" for its time, it now pales when compared with the derring-do of the Lisztian virtuosity of the late 1830s, with its violent runs in double (or interlocking-chromatic) octaves, gargantuan tremolando effects, treacherous leaps, and the astonishing thickness and bewildering complexity of texture.

Even if, as noted above, Chopin never uses *bravoure* in the title of any of his compositions, he nevertheless employed *con bravura* as an indicator of expression, thereby evincing a contrastive understanding of brilliant and bravura. This is exactly one indication of *con bravura* in all the Chopin études. It occurs, somewhat surprisingly, in a "slow" étude, opus 10, number 3, sometimes called "Tristesse," at the beginning of the cadenza (m. 46).[75] The texture is thicker here than in most of the other études, with both hands performing rapid sixths in contrary motion, descending from the upper to the middle register of the keyboard—an impressive virtuoso display far removed from brilliant-style figuration. With *con bravura* Chopin thus indicates virtuosic "daring" rather than brilliance. (He was also no doubt concerned that the mostly tranquil character of the piece might otherwise lead the performer to render the cadenza in a languid or meditative manner.) *Con bravura* thus doubles as a technical requirement: it raises the level of difficulty, effectively making the passage the most formidable of the piece (keeping with Chopin's practice of having the middle section of the études be a bit more technically challenging than the surrounding sections, although similar figuration is used).

As with *con bravura*, there is only one indication of *brillante* in the études, found just two études later at the head of opus 10, number 5, the "Black Key" Étude, thus applying to the whole piece. This étude is almost stereotypically in the brilliant style: lightness abounds with its rapid, leggiero, and single-note passagework in the upper register of the keyboard; the piece requires a light touch and is also lighthearted. As with the "brilliant" interludes in Liszt's *Grand galop*, discussed above, the étude is perhaps best interpreted as a kind of homage to the high brilliant style of the previous decade. Simon Finlow writes:

> From the mannerisms of the "brilliant style," for example, there were a number of distinctive virtuoso resources. A typical device was one characterized by

rapid triplet semiquavers and *leggiero* touch. . . . In his well-known étude in this manner, op. 10 no. 5, Chopin presents the pianist with a brilliant right-hand figure whose outline and structure are uniquely circumscribed according to a specific topographical feature of the keyboard. . . . The scintillating effect of this harmony combined with the glittering bravura passagework which distributes it across the keyboard is without precedent in the piano music of Kalkbrenner or any other exponent of the "brilliant style."[76]

Note that Finlow feels compelled to use the term "bravura" to contrast Chopin's "brilliant style" with that of earlier composer-pianists.

Chopin's contrasting usages of *brillante* and *con bravura* would appear to establish at this relatively early date (1829–32) that bravura virtuosity was qualitatively different from the virtuosity of Hummel, Czerny, and Weber in the 1820s, as well as from the salon virtuosity of the Paris of the early 1830s (Herz, Pixis, Hiller, etc.), and, perhaps more importantly, that it could cohere with works of a serious nature.

As for Liszt, given that, as noted above, the main purpose of his two sets of études was to develop a virtuosity shorn of brilliant-style elements, we are not surprised that there is only one *Grande étude* (1837) that contains an indication of *brillante*: in number 2 Liszt writes *leggermente brillante* next to the ascending, right-hand, triplet figuration in measures 12–13 and *sempre forte e brillante* for its repetition later in the piece (seemingly a brief gesture toward Chopin's opus 10, number 2, in the same key of A minor, with its similar leggiero ascending-descending right-hand movement).[77] Save for the Czerny-inspired *Preludio* (no. 1), these are the only four measures in the entire set that can be considered "brilliant." Tellingly, however, Liszt removes the *brillante* indication from the 1851 revision, replacing it with *leggiero*, thereby expunging the only explicit reference to the brilliant style from the *Transcendental Études*.

Even though, as noted above, the two sets of études can themselves be broadly considered "bravura" in terms of conception, they also contain a few expressive indications of *con bravura*. We find *staccato con bravura* in the last iteration of the theme in *Grande étude* no. 4 (*Mazeppa* in later versions), an indication retained in the separately published 1840 version (S. 138 / LW A172/4); but it is changed into *allegro deciso* in the 1851 revision, thereby altering the character of the section.[78] (Presumably, Liszt thought that the listener, not to mention the performer, would tire of so much bravura in one piece.) Near the end of number 5 (*Feux follets*), there is an *energico con bravura* section, which serves to mark a moment of high tension in an otherwise quiet, ethereal piece. In the 1851 revision Liszt adds a comma, *energico, con bravura*, thereby creating two expressions from one. In number 10 of the

Grande études, fff con bravura is indicated for the return of the dotted-rhythm theme (in the home key of F minor), with *marcatisso il basso* written under it (for the bass clef); but both expressions are replaced in the 1851 version by *marcato*, no doubt to emphasize the more solemn character of this passage in the revision.

The one unaltered instance of *con bravura* in the 1851 version of the *Transcendental Études* is found in the double-octave passage of number 7, *Eroica* (ex. 8.6), perhaps the most treacherous double-octave passage in Liszt, in that it combines full chords with octaves at different intervals. It would appear that the use of the term is intended to steer the performer away from a

Example 8.6. Liszt, *Études d'exécution transcendante* no. 7, *Eroica*, S. 139, mm. 87–102

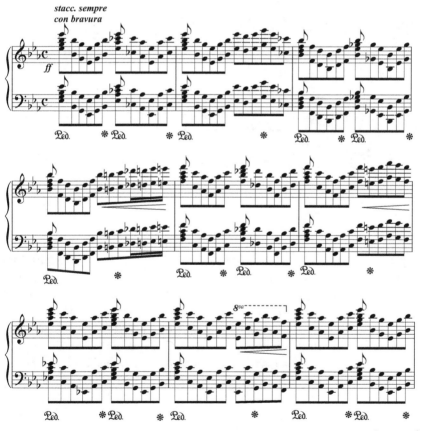

(continued)

Example 8.6.—*(concluded)*

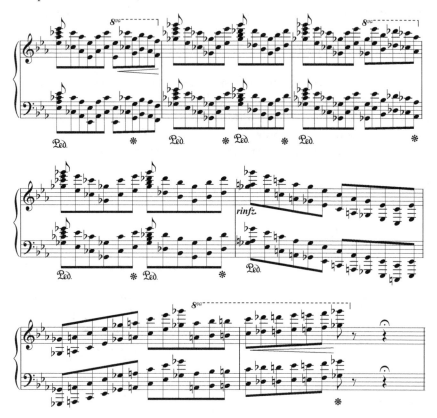

lackadaisical approach to the piece. In one of his master classes Liszt's reportedly commented on a student's performance of the octave passage thus: "not so merry and dancelike, but rather strike into it with strength; for once those fellows really ought to be boxed on the ears!"[79] As we saw with opus 10, number 3, the *con bravura* indication also changes the degree of difficulty of the passage, which a pianist might be tempted to take at a slower, grandioso tempo (though it in fact follows an *animato il tempo* indication twenty-two measures earlier). Liszt apparently recommended a rather brisk tempo for the entire piece, faster than might otherwise be suggested by the march-like main theme.[80]

What is most striking in Liszt's use of *con bravura* expressive indications is its recurrent juxtaposition to *brillante* in many important passages. Indeed, one is tempted to assume some kind of larger significance. Let us take the two piano concertos. In the section headed "Più mosso" (ex. 8.7) in the last major section ("Allegro marziale animato") of the Piano Concerto no. 1 in E-flat Major, Liszt indicates *non legato brillante* for a four-measure passage that features an arpeggio-like figuration (reproducing the "scherzo" theme from the third section of the work). This is followed by a seven- (or perhaps ten-) measure passage marked *con bravura*. There is no doubt that Liszt intends a real contrast in virtuosic tone here, which is not always brought out in performance.

We find a similar juxtaposition in the section titled "Un poco animato" from the Piano Concerto no. 2 in A Major. Here we have a fourteen-measure section marked *brillante*, containing some of the most technically challenging and impressive figuration of the concerto (based on a peculiar arm momentum that comes into play only at full speed, thus making it difficult to practice), followed by a three-and-a-half-measure *fortissimo* passage in double alternating octaves (with no expressive indication) (exx. 8.8a and 8.8b). Here the contrast is most evident, obviating the need for a *con bravura* marking

Example 8.7. Piano Concerto no. 1 in E-flat Major, S. 124, *Più mosso*, mm. 427–32

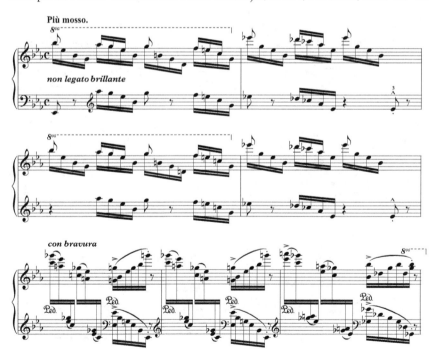

Example 8.8a. Piano Concerto no. 2 in A Major, S. 125, *Un poco animato*, mm. 442–45

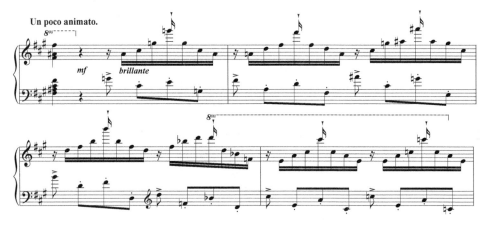

Example 8.8b. Piano Concerto no. 2 in A Major, S. 125, *Un poco animato*, mm. 454–59

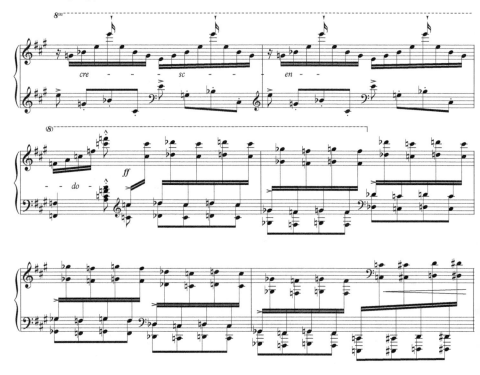

(rapid *fortissimo* octaves are inevitably bravura in Liszt). Although the octave passage looks at first glance like a transitional, cadenza-like flourish devoid of motivic content, it in fact cleverly echoes the main theme of the concerto—thereby emphasizing the economy of Lisztian virtuosity, which, far from seeking "effect for effect's sake," in fact contributes to the development of the musical figures.[81]

Another similar example is found in the finale, marked *allegro animato*, of the same concerto. Again, an explicitly marked *brillante* passage (ex. 8.8c) precedes a *con bravura* passage (ex. 8.8d) that occurs just a few measures later, bridging to the final flourishes that bring the concerto to a thundering close.

We can make two points regarding these examples from the concertos: (1) the fleeting *brillante* passages might be interpreted as a nostalgic gesture in an otherwise bravura context (as in the *Grand galop*, discussed above); and (2) in a period after the brilliant style has fallen out of favor, composers perceived the need to make explicit the brilliant character of certain passages, which might otherwise be misinterpreted. It is thus significant that in the cited examples the *brillante* marking *precedes* that of *con bravura*, as if indicating a reversion to the rule or norm.

This pattern of juxtaposition is not limited to the concertos. In the *Don Juan* Fantasy, of 1841, an eight-measure section marked *brillante* (and *scherzando*) is followed by a two-measure *con bravura* passage (exx. 8.9a and 8.9b). Here again, it would appear that Liszt is not only contrasting, but is also some way uniting brilliant and bravura styles of execution and composition—a *dialectical* virtuosity.

This dialectical virtuosity is found not only in Liszt. Let us consider the example of Schumann's *Symphonic Études*, op. 13, which, like Liszt's *Transcendental Études* exists in two versions from the same two periods, a first version from 1837 and a revision from 1852. In the 1837 version, Étude 6 is marked *agitato* with the expressive subheading *con gran bravura*. This is followed immediately by Étude 7, marked *allegro molto*, with the expressive subheading *sempre brillante*. As in the Liszt examples cited above, this back-to-back juxtaposition of the brilliant and bravura manners is too blatant not to be intentional. (The finale is also marked *allegro brillante*, connoting a lighter, champagne-like character in contrast to the darker cast of the rest of the work.) Interestingly—or tellingly—in the 1852 revision, Schumann removes the expressive subheading *con gran bravura* from the corresponding "Variation" (as the études are called in the later version) but leaves intact the *sempre brillante*. Whether "bravura" had become too pejorative, passé, or

Example 8.8c. Piano Concerto no. 2 in A Major, S. 125, *Allegro animato*, mm. 518–20

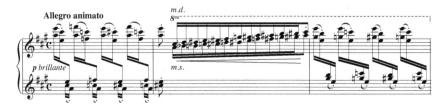

Example 8.8d. Piano Concerto no. 2 in A Major, S. 125, *Stretto (molto accelerando)*, mm. 542–45

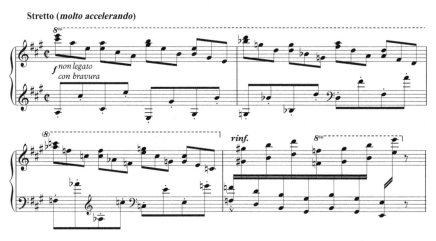

simply represented a brand of pianism from which Schumann sought to distance himself, its removal is certainly significant, particularly in view of what I have observed throughout this chapter.

In conclusion, I would like to emphasize that virtuosity, specifically bravura virtuosity such as I have defined it in this chapter, can be said to possess a dual function in Liszt's work: (1) that of increasing the musical and poetic intensity (and corresponding sense of excitement and wonder in the listener), which is similar to the role virtuosity plays in Chopin; and (2) that of a tool of modernism, that is, the aesthetic of avant-garde innovation and audacity

Example 8.9a. Liszt, *Réminiscences de Don Juan*, S. 418, Andantino, variation 2, *tempo giusto*, mm. 271–76

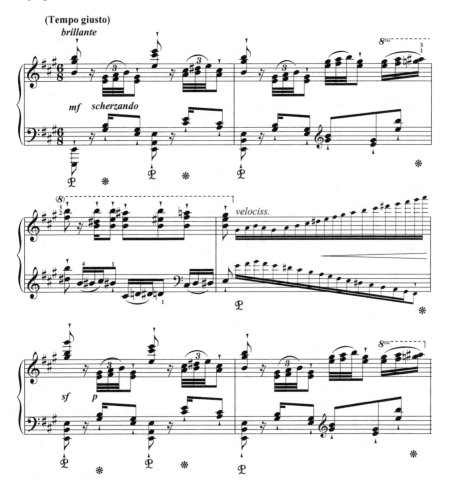

Example 8.9b. Liszt, *Réminiscences de Don Juan*, S. 418, Andantino, variation 2, *tempo giusto*, mm. 280–85

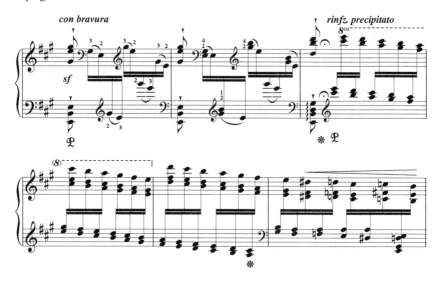

similarly at work in Berlioz and Wagner, which separates it from Chopin-style virtuosity.

This said, I would nevertheless challenge, as far too narrow and simplistic, the stereotypical dichotomy between a "classical" Chopin, who supposedly never lowered himself to the level of popular pianism, and a "vulgar" Liszt, whose bravura aesthetic catered to the popular taste, even if there is some truth in it, particularly in regard to their respective attitudes toward public performance. Certainly, Chopin's association with the extroverted, brilliant style in his youth, which continued into early adulthood, reveals an artist eager to find approval and acceptance through the public performance of his own works and the display of his pianistic skills—in particular, in his several compositions for piano and orchestra, all created and performed during Chopin's brief "virtuoso period," 1828–33. In addition, Chopin's dedication of the opus 10 Études to Liszt, and his opus 25 set to Liszt's romantic partner, Marie d'Agoult, indicates a sincere admiration for Liszt's capacities as a *musician*, and not merely as a performer, strictly defined. The following 1841 testimonial from François-Joseph Fétis, one of the era's most perceptive and influential critics, is instructive:

Those who, at the concert [Liszt] gave in Liège, heard him improvise, as I did, a marvelous caprice upon apparently incompatible themes suggested by members of the audience; those who saw him read at sight music laced with death-defying technical difficulties and hastily set down in all but unreadable hands, playing at speeds that surprised even the authors, with such effortlessness at to suggest the performance of mere bagatelles; those, finally, who know that all music of any value whatsoever is stored away in Liszt's mind in such a way as he is able instantaneously to perform whatever piece by whatever celebrated composer that one might care to name—those persons, I say, know that Liszt is the most complete musician of our time as well as the most accomplished virtuoso.[82]

Musician *and* virtuoso. Although it is often observed that Chopin thought little of Liszt as a composer (with the caveats that he could not have known the mature Liszt of the 1850s and that Chopin disparaged most of the compositions of his contemporaries in any case), this belies the fact that, as Fétis implies, for Liszt, perhaps more than for any other musician in the nineteenth century, performance was continuous with creation.[83]

There is thus little point in distinguishing improvisation, inspiration, execution, and elaboration in Liszt's art, even if later in his career he embraces the work concept.[84] While Liszt's new style of bravura virtuosity, like Chopin's early efforts, tended in some respects in his touring years toward the public taste (the opera fantasies, the virtuoso transcriptions, the *Grand galop*), it nevertheless represented a true *modernist* revolution in keyboard technique, sound, and ultimately composition, which at once negated and preserved—as in the Hegalian *Aufhebung*—many aspects of brilliant-style pianism. I thus broadly agree with Rosen when he observes that "critics often write as if Liszt's innovations in piano technique were merely ways of playing lots of notes in a short space of time, instead of inventions in sound."[85] And with Dahlhaus, who goes so far as to call Liszt a "musical *fauviste*," in describing the "amalgam of modernity and primitivity" in the *Dante* Sonata.[86] Indeed, Liszt's marriage of musical experimentation with technical daring and sheer virtuosic violence, particularly in the two sets of études, the *Don Juan* Fantasy, and later in major solo works such as *Funérailles*, the B-Minor Sonata, the *Dante* Sonata, and the First Mephisto Waltz, defined a virtuoso aesthetic that changed the course of nineteenth-century music, affecting even those, like Brahms, commonly thought to be "anti-Liszt."[87]

Notes

1. For his very first public performance, at the age of nine (October 1820), Liszt played not Beethoven but a more recent piano concerto by Beethoven's student and secretary Ferdinand Ries (the Concerto in E-flat Major, op. 90, 1816). As a point of comparison, when Czerny made his debut as a nine-year-old child prodigy 1800, it was with Mozart's Piano Concerto, no. 24, in C Minor (K. 491), composed in 1786. (Beethoven's first two piano concertos were not published until 1801.) Beethoven's Fourth Piano Concerto, op. 58, one of the most performed of all concertos today, suffered for decades from almost complete obscurity: there were seemingly no public performances of the work from its premiere, with Beethoven as soloist, in 1808 until it was resurrected by Felix Mendelssohn, who performed it (as soloist) in Leipzig in 1836.
2. Piano sonatas, like chamber music, were still considered intimate works whose virtuosity was correspondingly more introverted. The extroverted virtuosity at the time was reserved mostly for works with orchestra, as well as for public improvisations.
3. See Jim Samson, *Chopin [The Master Musicians]* (Oxford: Oxford University Press, 1996), esp. chapter 6: "'A New World for Myself'—Issues in Musical Style"; and Jim Samson, *The Music of Chopin* (Oxford: Clarendon Press, 1985), chapter 3, "*Stile brillante.*" See also Roman Ivanovitch, "The Brilliant Style," in *The Oxford Handbook of Topic Theory*, ed. Danuta Mirka (Oxford: Oxford University Press, 2014), 330–54.
4. Hummel's A-Minor Piano Concerto, op. 85, was composed in 1816 and his B-Minor Piano Concerto, op. 89, in 1819; Weber's *Konzertstück* in F minor, op. 79, was published in 1823.
5. Although today known almost exclusively for his numerous volumes of vapid but useful exercises for piano, Czerny composed a large number of works that were well regarded at the time. See Kenneth Hamilton's chapter in this volume.
6. Review of the December 1822 concert, quoted in Alan Walker, *Franz Liszt, Volume 1: The Virtuoso Years, 1810–1847* (New York: Alfred A. Knopf, 1983), 78.
7. Of course, Liszt may have played differently on different occasions, and he no doubt had off nights, like all performers (in addition, of course, he was just a boy and could not have been expected to have the consistency of a seasoned professional). Several months later, playing a different Hummel concerto, Liszt made a less satisfying (and less thundering) impression: "The eleven-year-old boy Liszt gave a concert on Sunday, April 13 in the small Redoutensaal at noon. He played the great piano concerto in B Minor by Hummel, Variations of Moscheles, and a Fantasy. One has to allow this talented boy sufficient due; he played with fluency and elegance, although he lacked physical strength, a lack that one noticed particularly in the performance of the concerto" (*Allgemeine*

musikalische zeitung, April 26, 1823, quoted in Allan Keiler, "Liszt Research and Walker's 'Liszt,'" *The Musical Quarterly* 70, no. 3 [1984], 387).
8. Carl Dahlhaus, *Nineteenth-Century Music*, trans. J. Bradford Robinson (Berkeley and Los Angeles: University of California Press, 1989), 135.
9. See my editor's introduction for a more extensive discussion of difficulty as it relates to virtuosity.
10. This distinction between private and public performance would eventually collapse, however, in Liszt's invention of the solo piano "recital," even if Liszt's programs would be considered eccentric by today's standards and more often than not were governed by popular taste. (Prior to Liszt's innovation, concerts were invariably variety shows, such as benefit concerts, featuring a wide array of musical forces.) Let us recall that in an age in which opera fantasies, *variations brillantes*, and improvisations based on themes submitted by the audience were de rigueur for the virtuoso, Liszt gave the first documented public performance of Beethoven's "Hammerklavier" Sonata, in the Salle Érard in 1836, which prompted Berlioz to proclaim Liszt the "pianist of the future": "A new Oedipus, Liszt, has solved it [the riddle of the Sphinx, the "Hammerklavier" Sonata], solved it in such a way that had the composer returned from the grave, a paroxysm of joy and pride would have swept over him. Not a note was left out, not one added ... no inflection was effaced, no change of tempo permitted. Liszt, in thus making comprehensible a work not yet comprehended, has proved that he is the pianist of the future" (quoted in Walker, *Franz Liszt, Volume 1*, 236, original source: *Gazette Musicale*, June 12, 1836).
11. See Olivia Sham's chapter in this volume.
12. Dahlhaus, *Nineteenth-Century Music*, 136.
13. An interesting discussion of the brilliant style in John Field's piano concertos is to be found in Julian Horton, "John Field and the Alternative History of Concerto First-Movement Form," *Music & Letters* 92, no. 1 (2011), 43–83.
14. *Grove Music Online*, "Bravura," entry by Owen Jander.
15. Kornel Michałowski and Jim Samson use the term in this way to describe the early Chopin's engagement with the brilliant style: "Chopin's early 'brilliant' polonaises, which have little in common with the later 'heroic' works composed in Paris (the only ones the composer himself chose to publish), indicate that in a very short time he managed to assimilate many of the standard materials of bravura pianism. Essentially they are essays in virtuoso figuration and exuberant right-hand ornamentation, complete with hand crossings, wide leaps, trills and double trills, arpeggio-based passage-work, and other stock-in-trade devices of the pianist-composer" (*Grove Music Online*, "Chopin").
16. For example: "[Postclassical concert music] was music designed to be popular, and happy to accept this commodity status. Its basic ingredients were a bravura right-hand figuration that took its impetus from the light-actioned Viennese and German pianos of the late eighteenth century" (Jim

Samson, *Virtuosity and the Musical Work: The "Transcendental Studies" of Liszt* [Cambridge: Cambridge University Press, 2003], 19).
17. Ibid., 82.
18. Ibid., 77.
19. Quoted in Kenneth Hamilton's chapter in this volume. Original source: Dezsô Legány, *Unbekannte Presse und Briefe aus Wien 1822–1886* (Vienna: Boehlau, 1984), 38–40.
20. See Dana Gooley, *The Virtuoso Liszt* (Cambridge: Cambridge University Press, 2004), esp. chapter 2, entitled "Warhorses: Liszt, Weber's *Konzertstück*, and the Cult of Napoleon," where he writes, "Liszt's bravura performances, whether solo or with orchestra, presented his audiences with a drama of violent struggle and domination that repeatedly displaced to an image of heroic battle valor, even when the music lacked military *topoi*. . . . The battle trope thus offered a second 'alibi' for his aggressive, dominating bravura style" (115).
21. Leonard G. Ratner, *Classic Music: Expression, Form, and Style* (New York: Schirmer, 1980), 19. Quoted in Ivanovitch, "The Brilliant Style," 331.
22. Stephen Hough has recorded all these works on one CD: *The Romantic Piano Concerto*, Vol. 17 (Hyperion, 1997). The piano concertos of Camille Saint-Saëns might be said to constitute a late brilliant-style pianism.
23. Ratner, *Classic Music*, 219. Quoted in Ivanovitch, "The Brilliant Style," 330.
24. Samson and Michałowski, "Chopin," *Oxford Music Online*.
25. Liszt performed the *Grand galop* more than any other piece during his German tours. See Michael Saffle, *Liszt in Germany, 1840–1845: A Study in Sources, Documents, and the History of Reception* (Stuyvesant, NY: Pendragon Press, 1994), table 2, 187.
26. Philip S. Taylor, *Anton Rubinstein: A Life in Music* (Bloomington and Indianapolis: Indiana University Press, 2007), 13.
27. During one of his master classes, Liszt "related that he had been frightened when he heard Rubinstein play the C-Minor Etude (probably op. 25, no. 12) of Chopin. He thought that the instrument would break into pieces. But he said: 'it suited him well'" (August Göllerich, *The Piano Master Classes of Franz Liszt, 1884–1886*, ed. Wilhelm Jerger, trans., ed., and enlarged by Richard Louis Zimdars [Bloomington: Indiana University Press, 1996], 27). No doubt many said the same in reference to Liszt himself in his early years.
28. There is more than a superficial resemblance between Chopin's opus 10, number 2, and Bach's Prelude in D Major (BWV 850) from the first book of the *Well-Tempered Clavier*.
29. Indeed, as Nicolas Dufetel notes in his chapter in this volume, a reference to Chopin's opus 18 is found in one of Liszt's sketchbooks.
30. Alfred Brendel writes, "Liszt was the first to depart from the salon. To the displeasure of some contemporaries, he democratized the concert by occasionally performing for an audience of thousands in large theaters like Milan's La

Scala. This required a different projection of music" (Brendel, *Music, Sense and Nonsense: Collected Essays and Lectures* [London: The Robson Press: 2015], 233–34).
31. *A Dictionary of Music and Musicians (A.D. 1450–1889)*, ed. George Grove (London: MacMillan, 1879, vol. 1, 272). The entry continues, "Bravura: (Italian: courage, bravery). A style of both music and execution involving the display of unusual brilliancy and technical power; music written to task the ability and test the courage of the artist" (271–72).
32. Samson, *Virtuosity and the Musical Work*, 74, 84.
33. Dahlhaus, *Nineteenth-Century Music*, 135.
34. Carl Czerny, *On the Proper Performance of All Beethoven's Works for Piano*, ed. Paul Badura-Skoda (Vienna: Universal Edition, 1970), 28.
35. Ibid., 46, 55.
36. Ibid., 35, 33.
37. Ibid., 56.
38. Ibid., 38.
39. Quoted in Kenneth Hamilton's contribution to this volume. Original source: Letter of March 17, 1856, in *The Letters of Franz Liszt*, Volume 1, ed. La Mara, trans. Constance Bache (New York: Scribner's, 1894), 266. For more on Czerny, see the excellent anthology *Beyond* The Art of Finger Dexterity: *Reassessing Carl Czerny*, ed. David Gramit (Rochester, NY: University Rochester Press, 2008).
40. Gooley, *The Virtuoso Liszt*, 99.
41. "[The *Konzertstück*'s] predominantly right-hand passagework, outlining scales and arpeggios with single-tone figurations, belongs to the Viennese 'brilliant' style of the early nineteenth century. Liszt made this piece his own by introducing a wide range of embellishments" (ibid., 99).
42. Charles Rosen, *The Romantic Generation* (Cambridge, MA: Harvard University Press, 1995).
43. Ibid., 492.
44. In his *Anthropology from a Pragmatic Point of View*, Kant stipulates that "the sublime is therefore not an object for taste, but rather an object for the feeling of emotion [*das Gefühl der Rührung*]" (Immanuel Kant, *Anthropology, History, Education*, ed. Gunter Zoller and Robert B. Louden [Cambridge: Cambridge University Press, 2007], 347).
45. Immanuel Kant, *Critique of the Power of Judgment*, trans. Paul Guyer and Eric Matthews (Cambridge: Cambridge University Press, 2001), 129. I comment on this passage in my book on the sublime as follows: "The sublime . . . involves a special kind of encounter with ugliness (and a special kind of dissatisfaction), which, though contrapurposive for our faculty of presentation, for the accord between the imagination and the understanding (the beautiful), is nevertheless purposive for the mind as a whole" (Robert Doran, *The Theory*

of the Sublime from Longinus to Kant [Cambridge: Cambridge University Press, 2015], 212).
46. See ibid., 8–12.
47. Gooley, *The Virtuoso Liszt*, 47.
48. Ibid., 248.
49. Samson, *Virtuosity and the Musical Work*, 81.
50. I should note the continuing relevance of the idea of the sublime in understanding virtuosity in music studies. See especially chapter 4, "Virtuosity and the Rhetoric of the Sublime," of Alexander Stefaniak's *Schumann's Virtuosity: Criticism, Composition, and Performance in Nineteenth-Century Germany* (Bloomington: Indiana University Press, 2016), 124–54.
51. Octave glissandos had been occasionally used by Beethoven, most notably in the coda to the finale of the "Waldstein" Sonata, op. 53, and in the first movement of the First Piano Concerto, op. 15. Both works are in C major, thus enabling such glissandos.
52. Interestingly, Liszt does not employ blind or interlocking octaves in either of his two piano concertos, though he does use them to great effect in *Totentanz*. There is certainly an association in Liszt between the diabolical, the key of D minor, and the use of interlocking octaves, as this short list shows: *Totentanz*, the *Dante* Sonata, the *Don Juan* Fantasy, *Mazeppa* (*Transcendental Étude* no. 4).
53. Alan Walker recounts: "[Chopin's] admission that he regarded the E-flat major Sonata, op. 31, no. 3 as 'very vulgar' until he heard Hallé play it in Paris in the 1830s, speaks volumes" (Walker, *Fryderyk Chopin: A Life and Times* [New York: Farrar, Straus and Giroux, 2018], 16). One assumes that Chopin's distaste was directed at the last movement of this sonata. See also Richard Taruskin, "Liszt and Bad Taste," *Studia Musicologica* 54, no. 1 (2013): 87–103.
54. Ingrid J. Sykes, "*Le corps sonore*: Music and the Auditory Body in France 1780–1830," in *Music and the Nerves, 1700–1900*, ed. James Kennaway (London: Palgrave, 2014), 85.
55. The fortepianists of the period would have been perplexed at Anton Rubinstein's later pronouncement that "the soul of the piano is the pedal," since the use of the damper pedal on the fortepiano of that time was more of a special effect.
56. Walker, *Chopin*, 267. The only real tremolandos in Chopin are those that occur at the end of the exposition and recapitulation in the first movement of his two piano concertos, where they serve essentially as a kind of trill (mimicking the Mozartean trill that invariably occurs at the same moment in his piano concertos). This use can thus be regarded as "classical." In fact, Brahms does the same in his Second Piano Concerto, op. 83, even if the tremolo/trill is more Lisztian/modernist in sound (it basically imitates the trill at the interval of a ninth found in the last section of Liszt's *Don Juan* Fantasy).
57. The rondo was published in a separate edition for piano solo in 1818 by Duboisat in New York.

58. CD notes to Howard Shelley's recording of Steibelt's Piano Concertos nos. 3, 5, and 7 on Hyperion Records (2016), https://www.hyperion-records.co.uk/dc.asp?dc=D_CDA68104&utm_source=youtube&utm_medium=youtube_taster, accessed September 15, 2019.
59. Quoted in Andrea Botticelli, "'Creating Tone': The Relationship Between Beethoven's Piano Sonority and Evolving Instrument Designs, 1800–1810," PhD Dissertation (University of Toronto, 2014), 61. Original source: Ferdinand Ries, *Beethoven Remembered: The Biographical Notes of Franz Wegeler and Ferdinana Ries*, trans. Frederick Noonan (Arlington: Great Ocean Publishers, 1987), 70–71.
60. Quoted in ibid., 63.
61. Busoni claimed that it depicted Napoleon's funeral.
62. See Kenneth Hamilton's chapter in this volume for an analysis of these measures in Weber's sonata.
63. Although, as mentioned above, the Lisztian tremolo is most often found in his transcriptions and storm scenes (e.g., *Vallée d'Obermann*), the tremolo is also featured in climactic moments in his B-Minor (final presentation of the "grandioso" theme) and *Dante* Sonatas (final section).
64. According to Samson, Liszt's dedications to Czerny and Chopin of volumes 1 and 2, respectively, of the 1837 Ricordi edition of the *Grandes études* "served to mark out his separation from Chopin's neo-baroque virtuosity no less than Czerny's post-Classical virtuosity" (*Virtuosity and the Musical Work*, 109).
65. One might also cite the rather unwieldly (on a modern piano) scale-like motif of the 1837 version of number 8, *Wilde Jagd*, which is replaced by an alternation between the hands, creating a chopping effect. See Olivia Sham's chapter in this volume for a discussion of this.
66. The first is after the Sixth Caprice (with the introduction and coda of the Fifth). The famous *La campanella* no. 3, counts as an original work, since it is merely based on themes by Paganini, not on a particular Caprice.
67. Indeed, as Samson has explored, "[Liszt] himself made it clear that he regarded the results [of his revision] as not as alternative versions, but as improvements and replacements" (*Virtuosity and the Musical Work*, 135). This is not only due to Liszt's changing attitude toward virtuosity but also to the evolving piano, which had reached a new plateau in terms of manufacturing and design around 1850.
68. These can be found on YouTube. In his memoires, Arthur Rubinstein remarked of having attended Horowitz's recital at the Théâtre des Champs-Élysées in Paris (June 3, 1932): "I do not remember the entire program, but I shall never forget the two Paganini-Liszt études, the E flat and E major ones [nos. 2 and 5]. There was much more than sheer brilliance and technique; there was an easy elegance—the magic something which defies description" (Rubinstein, *My Many Years* [New York: Alfred A. Knopf, 1980], 255).

69. For example, I heard Peter Klimo (second prize at the 2014 International Franz Liszt Piano Competition in Utrecht) play the entire Paganini set in a recital at the Eastman School of Music in 2018, and he used a few passages from the 1838 version of no. 2 to great effect, e.g., the rapid, double-note scales in thirds in the 1838 version (measures 6 and 8, and their repetition in the recapitulation), instead of the single-note scales of the revision.
70. These are currently available in a Dover reprint edition. In this edition, "bravura-studies" is replaced by a more literal translation: "Etudes for Transcendental Technique."
71. For Alan Walker, however, the era of "transcendental" virtuosity, as codified in the title of book 4 of the first volume of his Liszt trilogy: "The Years of Transcendental Execution, 1839–1847," begins a year or two *after* the composition of the two étude sets.
72. "The notion of effect for effect's sake is perhaps involved in the term."
73. These are: *Grandes Valses brillantes*, op. 47, and *Souvenirs d'Amérique, Valses brillantes*, a new version of *Valse mélodique*, op. 62.
74. https://www.merriam-webster.com/dictionary/bravura, accessed September 16, 2019. The online *Oxford Living Dictionary* similarly has "great technical skill and brilliance shown in a performance or activity. The display of great daring" (https://en.oxforddictionaries.com/definition/bravura, accessed September 16, 2019).
75. Chopin's metronome marking for this étude (100 bpm), usually disregarded, indicates quite a brisk pace.
76. Simon Finlow, "The Twenty-Seven Etudes and Their Antecedents," in *The Cambridge Companion to Chopin*, ed. Jim Samson (Cambridge: Cambridge University Press, 1992), 57.
77. There is only one indication of *brillante* in the *Douze exercices*: in no. 8 in C Minor.
78. Lisztian transcendental-style staccato could either be *con bravura* or *brillante*. In number 5 of the 1838 Paganini set, for example, there is an indication of *sempre staccato e brillante*.
79. Göllerich, *The Piano Master Classes of Franz Liszt*, 66.
80. "[Liszt] let the tempo be taken very allegro, much faster than I would have imagined" (ibid., 22).
81. See my editor's introduction to this volume for an expansion of this point.
82. François-Joseph Fétis, "Études d'exécution transcendante pour le piano, par F. Liszt" (*Revue et Gazette musicale de Paris*, May 9, 1841), introduced and translated by Peter Bloom in the chapter "Fétis's Review of the Transcendental Etudes," in *Franz Liszt and His World*, ed. Christopher H. Gibbs and Dana Gooley (Princeton, NJ: Princeton University Press, 2006), 427–39, here 435.
83. What Samson says of Chopin in this regard applies even more so to Liszt: "For the early nineteenth-century composer-pianist the borderline between

improvisation and composition was in any case a good deal less clear than it is today. A composition would as often as not begin life as an improvisation, and there are accounts of Chopin's agonized attempts to formulate on paper an idea already perfectly realized at the piano" (Samson, *The Music of Chopin*, 48). Liszt's "agony" plays out in the multiple versions of many, if not most of his works.

84. See Kenneth Hamilton's chapter in this volume for an exploration of this very point.
85. Rosen, *The Romantic Generation*, 508. But Rosen does not focus specifically on the meaning of bravura in Liszt, which I think is key to understanding the revolution in keyboard virtuosity Rosen endeavors to analyze.
86. Dahlhaus, *Nineteenth-Century Music*, 135–36.
87. See especially Rosen's analysis of the work, by which he sets out to rehabilitate the early Liszt: "The *Réminiscences [de Don Juan]*, written in 1841 as Liszt was setting out on the most spectacular triumphs of his career as a virtuoso, the tours of Germany and Russia, has won, as Busoni observed in the preface to his edition, 'an almost symbolic significance as the highest point of pianism.' In it, Liszt displayed almost every facet of his invention as a composer for the piano. That the tunes are by Mozart is largely irrelevant; the work is one of Liszt's most personal achievements" (*The Romantic Generation*, 539).

Part Three

Virtuosity and Anti-virtuosity in "Late Liszt"

Chapter Nine

Harmony, Gesture, and Virtuosity in Liszt's Revisions

Shaping the Affective Journeys of the Cypress Pieces from *Années de pèlerinage* 3

Dolores Pesce

My 1990 article "Liszt's *Années de pèlerinage*, Book 3: A 'Hungarian' Cycle?" argues that Liszt conceived the *Années de pèlerinage: Troisième année* as a true cycle, with musical and conceptual links to his homeland Hungary.[1] *Années* 3 carries us through Liszt's reflections on death via its four threnodies and the consolation he found in Christianity via its three religious pieces. *Années* 3's multiple references to Hungary's second national anthem "Szózat" suggest that Liszt infused his metaphysical reflections with thoughts of his homeland. *Années* 3 is further unified through tonal and motivic features.

This essay offers an in-depth interpretation of two of the cycle's threnodies, *Aux cyprès de la Villa d'Este 1* and *2* (S. 162/2 and 3 / LW A283/2 and 3, 1877).[2] Liszt's multiple surviving versions of the two works allow me to examine my interpretations against firsthand evidence. My analysis uncovers intersecting concerns on Liszt's part as he revises: how to "work out" each piece's seminal harmonic concept, how to enhance plaintive gestures, and how to bring virtuosic textures into play. With respect to the last, Liszt engages virtuosity in a multifaceted way. As a composer-performer, Liszt desires to "command" his instrument and have those who perform his music do likewise: as virtuosos, they expose the keyboard's sonic potential revealed through diverse textures, whether in lyrical or dramatic passages. Significantly, Liszt's revisions of the two threnodies often increase their sonic exploration of the keyboard not simply for its performative value but also as a vehicle for expression within each piece's overall affective trajectory.

In sum, this chapter proposes to show that the final version of each Cypress piece can be understood in terms of an affective journey. While each threnody evokes a tone of lament, of plaintiveness in its opening motive, neither is limited to a single affect. As Liszt develops a harmonic plan linked in some way to these germinal motives, he also traces an affective trajectory that complicates the lament theme. In *Aux cyprès 1*, on the one hand, the unstable opening motive yields to a stable lyrical melody. In the quietude of what follows, Liszt offers a glimpse of solace achieved through religious faith, though still tinged with the pain of grief. *Aux cyprès 2*, on the other hand, offers a musical unfolding in which the plaintive force of the opening motive is dissipated through its interaction with musical material that is uplifting in character, though not necessarily religious. The opening motive appears at the end in an identifiable, albeit altered form, signifying hope and a step forward in the emotional journey of grief.

Liszt and Musical Expression

Liszt used a number of musical formations which musicologists now call "musical topics"—characteristic gestures with particular associations established in the early eighteenth century.[3] By Liszt's time, many of the conventional topics of the classical style had gone out of use, but dances remained, along with some general categories such as pastoral and martial. Some topics are merely picturesque, while others may carry with them a particular expressive content, for example, a lament motive elicits a sense of grieving; a pastoral topic, calm; and a heroic topic, grandeur. Music topics could also be kinds of utterance, such as *bel canto*, based upon an operatic model; and rhetorical, "speaking," or recitative-like, which Liszt borrowed from Beethoven's instrumental music.[4] Topics may appear as fully worked-out pieces, that is, *types*, or as figures and progressions within a piece, that is, *styles*.[5] As will be argued below, the Cypress pieces present topics as styles within a given work.

We tend to focus on Liszt as a promoter of program music, of works that explicitly acknowledge an extramusical connection through an attached title or "program" of some sort. Yet even in his 1855 essay on Berlioz's *Harold in Italy*, a forum for his espousal of program music, Liszt recognized instrumental music's inherent power to express ideas on its own, to "poeticize." At no time during his long compositional career did Liszt discard this early nineteenth-century metaphysical concept of musical poetics, which positioned music in first place within an artistic hierarchy, above even poetry itself.[6] Consistent with this belief in music's power to express ideas on its own, Liszt drew upon musical markers such as major and minor, register, texture, articulation, rhythmic activity, dynamics, and chord quality that had expressive connotations within European art music as a whole.[7] Through a combination of conventional musical topics and more general expressive musical devices, many tied to a tonal syntax, Liszt created his works, with or without a programmatic title.

Throughout this essay, I shall employ the term "affect" when referring to *what* Liszt's music expresses. Defining the term concretely is difficult, particularly given that within modern psychology, different taxonomies position "affective" as part of the "cognitive" domain, or "cognitive" as part of the "affective" domain. Taking into account the underlying assumption of both views, one can regard affect as the "subjective and conscious aspect of feelings and emotions."[8] Accordingly, when Liszt conveys an affect within a piece, he expresses his understanding of the experience of a particular emotion. Affect becomes the "idea" of the work.

Short pieces may encompass a single affect, but a longer piece more typically presents some affective contrast, as, for example, in the B section of an ABA form. In a classical symphony, each of the four movements presents a distinctive affect, within a broad framework of expected tempo and key relationships, but not necessarily of prescribed affects. With Beethoven's Fifth Symphony, on the contrary, audiences came to experience a specific affective trajectory, of struggle to triumph, which became a particularly cogent expressive archetype for subsequent composers. Robert Hatten refers to an archetype such as "struggle-to-triumph" as an "expressive genre" that could cut across formal genres, thereby allowing its appearance in settings outside the four-movement symphony. For Hatten, an "expressive genre" is the broad topical field that organizes the expressive states of a work.[9] In the following discussion, I use "expressive genre," "affective trajectory, or journey," and "expressive archetype" interchangeably.

As stated earlier, Liszt subtitled the Cypress pieces in *Années* 3 "threnodies," thereby guiding the listener to expect each work to communicate an affect of lament and grieving. The opening melodic material of each piece meets that expectation by supplying a suitable "lament" musical topic. But Liszt presents other musical topics and more general expressive musical devices that create an affective trajectory in each work. Though not as clear cut as the struggle-to-triumph expressive genre of Beethoven's Fifth, *Cyprès 1* suggests a movement from lament to religious consolation, while *Cyprès 2* conveys a weakening of the topos of lament and a sense of hope. In both cases, Liszt reveals to his listeners a subtle understanding of the emotional experience of grieving.

A final issue in Liszt's approach to expressive content concerns the role of virtuosity. As Márta Grabócz has noted, Liszt developed a "new virtuosity technique" in the 1830s in response to two stimuli: the possibilities offered by the mechanical action of the English Broadwood piano, which he was the first well-known performer to use; and the influence of Paganini, precipitating a transfer of violin virtuoso techniques to the piano.[10] Without a doubt, Liszt's music requires a virtuosic performer who can reveal for a listener the varied palette of the keyboard, whether in delicate, lyrical passages or in dramatic evocations. While "virtuosic" tends to be used more frequently in connection with the latter, it is interpreted here to encompass sonic keyboard explorations more generally. Significantly, within his revisions of the two Cypress pieces, Liszt manipulates textures to serve his affective message. Specifically, as I endeavor to show, he employs "virtuosic" textures hand in hand with musical topics and more general expressive devices to shape his ideas about grieving.

Aux cyprès 1

Table 9.1 summarizes the melodic and harmonic features of two versions of *Aux cyprès 1*: on the left, the final version, consisting of 214 measures, on the right, the first surviving version, 181 measures. On occasion, I also refer to a printer's copy, not included in the table.[11] Gray shading indicates differences between the first and final versions. The main area of discrepancy occurs in measures 87–130, that is, before the second appearance of the piece's lyrical melody at measure 131. What issues did Liszt confront at this point?

By way of answer, we turn to the three main motivic/thematic elements. Motive 1a unfolds D–E♭–C♯–D, whose chromatic neighbor-tone motion

Table 9.1. *Aux cyprès de la Villa d'Este (Thrénodie 1)*, S. 163/2, melodic and harmonic structure of first and final versions

	FINAL VERSION				FIRST SURVIVING VERSION			
mm.	No. of mm.	Melodic material	Key	Expressive marking	No. of mm.	Melodic material	Key	Expressive marking
1–24	24	motive 1a, neighbor motion D E♭ C♯ D	implied G key, over F♯ bass	*Andante* bass sempre legato	24	motive 1a,	implied G key, over F♯ bass	*Quasi Andante*
25–32	8	trans. motive, descending B♭ F♯ E♭ D	B♭⁺ triad over F♯ bass		8	trans. motive, descending B♭ A F E♭ D	B♭⁺ triad over F♯ bass, then B♭ triad	
33–46	14	motive 1b D E♭ C♯ A	g, then modulates	*molto accentuato*	14	motive 1b	g, then modulates	*Un poco più Lento molto accentato*
47–58	12	**lyrical melody**	G♭	*appassionato*	12	**lyrical melody**	G♭	*appassionato*
59–62	4	trans. motive, B♭ A G, F♯ F E	C♯°⁷		4	trans. motive	C♯°⁷	

(continued)

Table 9.1.—*(concluded)*

	FINAL VERSION				FIRST SURVIVING VERSION			
mm.	No. of mm.	Melodic material	Key	Expressive marking	No. of mm.	Melodic material	Key	Expressive marking
63–78	16	motive 1b	F♯ pedal, with chords D, f♯, F, a♯ = aug. triad	*tranquillo, sotto voce*	16	motive 1b	F♯ pedal, with chords D, f♯, F♯, a♯ = aug. triad	*un poco agitato*
79–86	8	motive 1a	chromatic ascent	*poco a poco accelerando*	8	motive 1a	chromatic ascent	*poco a poco accelerando*
87–98	12	motive 1a	C♯ bass, **implied f♯ key**	*Più agitato*, r.h. *sempre legato*, bass *marcato*, alternating with *tremolando*	8	diatonic melody, 3rd doubling	**E major**	
99–106	8		chromatic ascent over C♯ bass					
107–30	24	motive 1a	C♯°7 over bass C♯; bass moves to C B	*un poco accel.*, bass *tremolando*; *un poco rall.*	8	motive 1a	4♯ sig. (E triad to A♯°7)	*Più mosso*

131–42	12	**lyrical melody**	bass B, key of G	Tempo 1 *appassionato*	12	**lyrical melody**	bass B, key of G	*Più mosso molto appassionato*
143–67	25	transitional motives	momentary emphasis on E tonality		17	transitional motives	momentary emphasis on E tonality	
168–75	8	**lyrical melody (cont.)**	G		11	chordal skeleton	G	
176–90	15		chromatic descent	*senza agitazione, e molto legato, then un poco più marcato (ma poco)*	15		chromatic descent	*dolce senza agitazione*
191–214	24	D D♯ E, E E♭ D, abstracted from motive 1a	G, muddied by 3rd-related chords, then prolonged IV to I, then IV–VII°7–V7/I–I		24	D D♯ E, E E♭ D, abstracted from motive 1a	G, muddied by 3rd-related chords, then prolonged IV to I, then IV–V–I	
Total	**214**				**181**			

Example 9.1. *Aux cyprès de la Villa d'Este (Thrénodie 1)*, S. 163/2, final version, motive 1a, mm. 1–10

Example 9.2. *Aux cyprès de la Villa d'Este (Thrénodie 1)*, S. 163/2, final version, motive 1b, mm. 33–40

around D presents a musical topic of lament appropriate to Liszt's designation "threnody" (ex. 9.1). Motive 1b represents a rhythmicized version, in which the neighbor-note movement is no longer completed but leaps upward (ex. 9.2). The lyrical melody's main gesture ascends stepwise from a neighbor-tone figure, then falls back by a leap of a fourth (ex. 9.3). This gesture of unfulfilled yearning occurs twice more, each at a lower pitch level, followed by a concluding, largely chromatic descent of four measures, also signaling an emotional uncertainty.

As shown in these three examples, Liszt sets up F♯ to G as the piece's primary harmonic inflection by starting with an F♯ pedal in the bass; F♯ moves to G at the start of motive 1b; the lyrical melody follows in G♭. Table 9.1 indicates that G♭ is next enharmonically respelled as F♯ in measure 63, again sounding as a pedal, after which motive 1a is incorporated into a chromatic ascent at measure 79. Liszt's harmonic challenge was how to get from that chromatic passage to the return of the lyrical melody in G major.

Example 9.4 contains version 1, starting at the equivalent of measure 79, through the opening phrase of the lyrical melody at its return in measure 131. After eight measures in which the outer voices largely trace ascending

Example 9.3. *Aux cyprès de la Villa d'Este (Thrénodie 1)*, S. 163/2, final version, lyrical melody, mm. 47–62

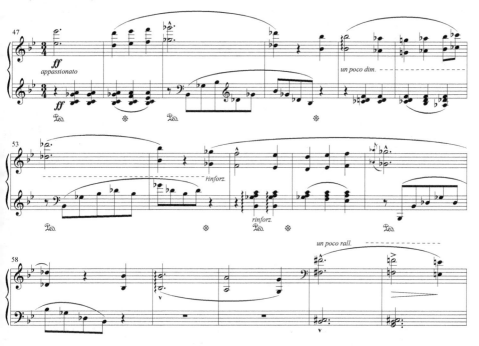

chromatic lines, Liszt makes a startling turn to E major at measure 87 and presents eight strictly diatonic measures, beginning with a repeated-note, fanfare-like figure, whose rhythm carries over into an ascending line, followed by a smoothly descending gesture in parallel thirds. Liszt follows this diatonic segment with a phrase of six measures, which presents motive 1a at the outset, and moves from an E triad to an A♯ half-diminished seventh chord.[12] Liszt crosses out the six-measure phrase (shown by *X*s) and extends it to eight at the *più mosso*, intensifying the presence of motive 1a in a now consistently syncopated texture. Nonetheless, he retains roughly the same chordal framework beginning on an E triad and ending on an A-sharp seventh chord, now fully diminished. In this rewrite, the chord voicing leads smoothly into the return of the lyrical melody in G: the lowest-sounding A♯ moves to B, while the highest-sounding E remains on that tone.

As table 9.1 shows, in his revisions Liszt eliminates at measure 87 the E-major, diatonic statement entirely. Presumably, he questioned the abrupt

Example 9.4. *Aux cyprès de la Villa d'Este (Thrénodie 1)*, S. 163/2, first version equivalent of mm. 79–131

turn to an unambiguous diatonic E major in a piece that otherwise offers more subtle tonal manipulations. In his revision, after the chromatically rising lines from measures 79–86, Liszt expands the sixteen-measure, restricted registral utterance of the earliest version into a significant section of forty-four measures (mm. 87–130). While motive 1 remains the primary building block, Liszt now gradually increases its sense of anxiety and agitation, created through a combination of virtuosic textures, unstable harmony, and expanding dynamics (described below).[13] This extended middle section also allows Liszt to address the unbalanced sectional lengths in his earliest version (see table 9.1). The middle section of version 1 consists of only forty measures, versus the sixty-two measures of its opening and seventy-nine of its final section. Liszt's final version aligns that middle section with the outer section proportions: at sixty-eight measures, it falls closer to the preceding sixty-two and following eighty-four measures.

A detailed look at the expanded middle section brings into focus Liszt's textural and harmonic manipulations leading to the return of the lyrical melody at measure 131. As shown in example 9.5, at measure 87, a C♯ bass pedal situates the entire section in an implied F-sharp minor. In the first passage (mm. 87–98), the right hand unfolds arpeggiated chords over three octaves in rapid eighth notes, while the left hand alternates motive 1a (marked *marcato*) and tremolandos, also spanning three octaves. Over the C♯ bass pedal, the right hand traces an upper line of A–A♯–B (see circled notes). The second passage (mm. 99–106) retains the C-sharp bass pedal, while the right hand continues its chromatic ascent upward: B♯–C♯–D–E♭–E. In this passage, the registral exploration broadens even further, with the left hand spanning three octaves, the right hand, four. Example 9.6 reveals that, in the printer's copy, Liszt crossed out a first try at measure 99, which did not involve the virtuosic hand-crossing of the final version.[14] Continuing with example 9.5, in the final passage (mm. 107–30), the only one with an equivalent in the first version, the left hand presents a constant tremolando in the lowest octave of the keyboard, while the right hand travels three octaves upward, then downward, with motive 1a exposed on the ascent. (Liszt provides a left-hand ossia of sweeping, virtuosic arpeggios that cover three octaves.) While the earlier version of this passage notates a move to a diminished seventh chord on A♯, Liszt now respells that sonority as a C♯ diminished seventh (see arrows framing the passage), in accordance with the C♯ bass pedal, after which C♯ then slides through C to B, preparing the return of the lyrical melody's opening sonority at measure 131.[15] Thus this middle section highlights the tension-ridden motive 1 in an explosive

Example 9.5. *Aux cyprès de la Villa d'Este (Thrénodie 1)*, S. 163/2, final version, mm. 87–130

(continued)

Example 9.5.—*(concluded)*

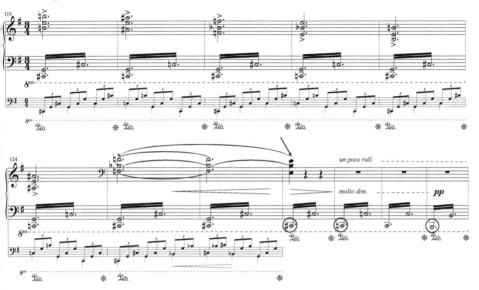

Example 9.6. *Aux cyprès de la Villa d'Este (Thrénodie 1)*, S. 163/2, printer's copy, mm. 99–100

uncertainty. But in his revisions, Liszt brings a relatively fuller sense of resolution to the lyrical theme during its second appearance at measures 168–75 (see table 9.1). As shown in example 9.7, the earliest version of those measures contains merely a chordal skeleton at that point, with neighbor-tone movement around the tone D. The revision in the printer's copy reveals how Liszt fleshes out the lyrical melody's presence, though he continues to fuss with how to get from its ending G sonority (first arrow) to the repeat of that sonority at measure 175 (second arrow). In the final revision, he eliminates

Example 9.7. *Aux cyprès de la Villa d'Este (Thrénodie 1)*, S. 163/2, earlier equivalents of mm. 168–75

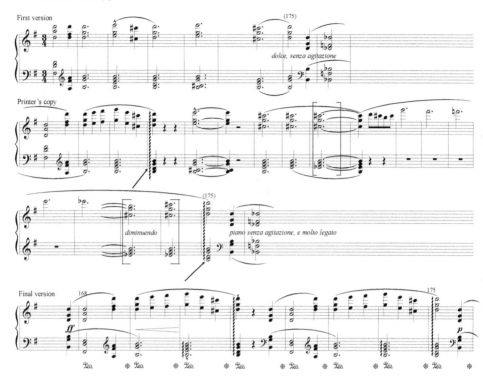

texture characterized by rapid rhythmic movement, registral expansion, and an increase in dynamics from *f* to *fff*. The sonorous virtuosity of this section undoubtedly heightens an affect of volatility inherent to the motive and its unstable harmonic context.

Nevertheless, the section's buildup is not unidirectional. At measures 116–27, the right hand makes a deliberate descent featuring dissonant *rinforzando* chords, followed by three measures in which the left hand plays the tones C to B alone, *molto diminuendo* to *pp*. The ascendancy of motive 1a, with its seemingly overriding anxiety, has been, in effect, curtailed. In turn, although the lyrical melody appears at measure 131 in the harmonically important key of G, its appearance does not signal complete resolution, for a number of reasons. Its supporting tonic sonority at measure 133 is in first inversion and not prepared by a structural dominant, and the melody unfolds essentially as it did at the outset (compare mm. 47–62 and 131–47), thereby still conveying a sense of emotional the diminished seventh chords and descending chromatic line that occur between the arrows of the printer's copy and instead simply repeats the phrase. The harmonic palette is now essentially diatonic throughout, and the tonic chord in measure 169 is solidly preceded by a dominant, albeit not in root position. The melody itself changes shape so that after a stepwise ascent, it rounds back to its initial pitch, creating a sense of closure lacking when it fell a fourth. Finally, Liszt enriches the single-register utterances of the earlier versions by positioning the melody's initial upbeat and downbeat in a lower register, thus grounding it and contributing to its climactic utterance at a *fortissimo* dynamic level (versus *forte* at m. 131). This enhanced keyboard exploration contributes a virtuosic dimension to this passage, which, in combination with the now diatonic palette, as well as melodic and harmonic closure, transforms the yearning character of the lyrical melody into one of assurance.

Table 9.1 reveals that the remainder of the piece shows little change between the first and final versions. After the climactic statement of the lyrical theme at measures 168–75, Liszt retains a fifteen-measure transition that reintroduces a chromatic line, now descending, played *piano, senza agitazione, e molto legato*, then a second time *un poco più marcato (ma poco)*. These very explicit performance designations suggest an affective interpretation: chromaticism signals unease, as it has from the outset; but now, on its return after the confident lyrical theme at measure 168, the unease is muted, with some attempt at resurgence in the second phrase, to be played "just a little bit more *marcato*."

In the generally subdued final twenty-four measures beginning at measure 191 (see ex. 9.8), Liszt combines a number of expressive devices to suggest a further affective change in the aftermath of the confident statement of the lyrical theme. He introduces third-related sonorities in succession, specifically G major, B major, G-sharp minor, E minor, and C major, at a *piano* dynamic level, creating a calm, awe-filled atmosphere.[16] A sense of imminent transcendence is conveyed by the right-hand reaching upward: it sounds each sonority, then repeats it an octave higher against the grounded bass line, creating an upper-voice movement of D–D♯–E (see circled notes). While this gesture abstractly links back to the tension-ridden opening motive 1a, the pitches now inch upward instead of circling back to D. A further sense of release from the confined motion occurs when E leaps to the G at measure 201. G, as the highest tone of this final passage, is supported by a IV chord that initiates a recurring plagal progression, albeit with a shifting metrical placement of the tonic in various voicings. Liszt likely intends this distinctive progression, the "Amen" cadence of hymnody, set in a high register, to

Example 9.8. *Aux cyprès de la Villa d'Este (Thrénodie 1)*, S. 163/2, final version, mm. 191–214

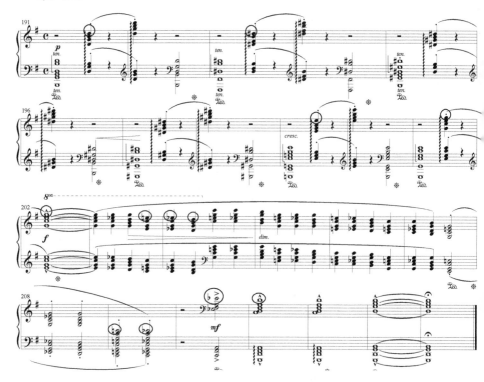

function as a musical topic for religious solace, enhancing the affect of awe created by the preceding third-related chords. Nonetheless, the E–E♭–D linear motion embedded in this final passage (see circled notes) reverses the uplifting D–D♯–E gesture and tinges the subdominant with a passing minor flavor. After this subtle manipulation, the final G-major tonic in root position, preceded by V⁷/I unmistakably represents a secure resting point.[17]

In summary, while beginning with tension encapsulated in its plaintive musical topic, motive 1a, *Aux cyprès 1* reaches a point of relative stability in the second appearance of its lyrical theme, in G major, a seemingly inevitable goal: Liszt leads the listener from the implied G of the opening, through an extended emphasis on G♭ reinterpreted as F♯, back to G. Yet even within the stable G area of the lyrical theme, Liszt insinuates that moving past one's grief is not straightforward. In revising the transition between the lyrical melody's two appearances at measures 131 and 168 (see ex. 9.9), he adds

Example 9.9. *Aux cyprès de la Villa d'Este (Thrénodie 1)*, S. 163/2, final version, mm. 142–67

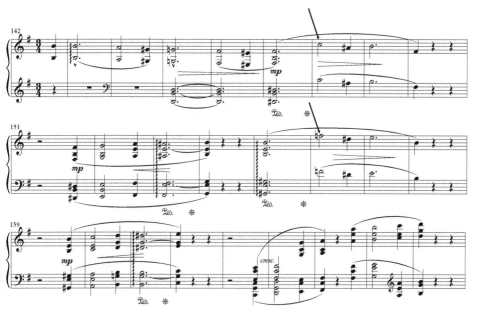

two exposed plaintive gestures played in octaves at measures 148–50 and 156–58. Related to both the chromatic neighbor figure of motive 1a and the falling fourth of the lyrical melody, these expressive gestures momentarily weaken the positive affect associated with the ensuing multiple scalar ascents that build to the assured statement of the lyrical theme at measure 168. Furthermore, in the final section of the piece, the extended plagal progression is tinged with the pathos of a slide through E♭ as E moves to D. Though Liszt designs the piece so that the plaintive motive 1a yields to the assured lyrical melody in G, he subtly reminds us, even during a concluding evocation of religious solace, of the affect that motivates the work. Grief lingers in the background.

Aux cyprès 2

Aux cyprès 2 survives in two early versions and a printer's copy.[18] I here focus on the earliest version, held at the Library of Congress (see table 9.2).[19]

Table 9.2. *Aux cyprès de la Villa d'Este (Thrénodie 2)*, S. 163/2, melodic and harmonic structure of first and final versions

	FINAL VERSION				LC VERSION		
mm.	No. of mm.	Melodic material	Key	Expressive marking	No. of mm.	Melodic material	Key
1–30	30	motive 1	e	*accentuato molto, pesante*	37	motive 1	e
31–46	16	motive 2	D♭ to e, c to B♭	none	12	motive 2	D♭ to e, c to B♭
47–60	14	motive 2	B♭ to b♭	*grandioso*	13	motive 2	B♭ to b♭
61–67	7	motive 1 (Tempo 1)	b♭	none	11	motive 1	b♭
68–75	8	arpeggios	F♯	*dolce legatissimo*	4	arpeggios	F♯
76–95	20	**lyrical melody**	F♯ to C♯	*sempre dolce e legato*	4	**lyrical melody**	F♯
96–105	10	motive 1	f♯	*espr. dolente*	8	motive 1	f♯
106–113	8	arpeggios	A	*sempre legatissimo*	4	arpeggios	A
114–135	22	**lyrical melody**	A to E	*sempre dolce e legato*	4	**lyrical melody**	A

136–145	10	motive 1	a	*espr. dolente*	8	motive 1	a
146–153	8	arpeggios	C	none			
154–161	8	**lyrical melody**	C7–A7–C♯°7 prog.	*appassionato*			
162–177	16	motive 2	**D♭ to B♭°7, c to C♯°7**	*marcato* (with *dolente* moments)	12	motive 2 over tremolo	e to c
178–191	14	motive 2	**B♭ to b♭**	*grandioso*	15	motive 2	**E (4♯ sign.)**
192–207	16	motive 1 (Tempo 1)	E°7 to A♭+	none	20	motive 1	E (4♯ sign.)
208–225	18	motive 1 with arpeggios	4♯ sign.	*legato*	8	arpeggios	no sign., G♯–F♯ prog.
226–240	15	arpeggios alone	E	none			
241–244	4	motive 1	E	*Più lento*			
Total	**244**				**160**		

Like *Aux cyprès 1*, *Aux cyprès 2* is based upon several motives and a lyrical melody. Motive 1 sounds a music topic of plaintiveness as it leaps down a fifth, then snakes chromatically upward a minor third (ex. 9.10). Motive 2 likewise contracts inward, evoking a sense of struggling against constraint through its numerous changes in pitch direction: it unfolds three leaps of a fifth or fourth upward in alternation with a descent of a third or second, then a stepwise motion up and back, with a final neighbor motion, all over a somewhat ponderous accompaniment (ex. 9.11). The lyrical melody at measure 76 consists of largely descending segments, which collectively move upward in register. Played *dolce e legato*, it conveys a calm mood, though its slowly realized ascent suggests an affect of yearning (see ex. 9.12).

As table 9.2 indicates, the structural unfolding of these primary materials in *Aux cyprès 2* is very different from what happens in *Aux cyprès 1*. In the second Cypress piece, the lyrical melody occurs in the middle section, as part of a tripartite complex consisting of motive 1, arpeggios, and the lyrical melody. This complex occurs three times. The arpeggios and lyrical melody work as a largely diatonic unit that supplants the chromatic, plaintive utterance of motive 1. (See ex. 9.12 for the first appearance of the complex at mm. 61–95.) Note that the arpeggios consist of two diatonic chords a third apart, F-sharp major and D-sharp minor, played *dolce legatissimo*, with no appreciable tension or sense of forward motion. As the arpeggios alternately ascend and descend, they create a calm, dreamlike mood. The lyrical melody at measure 76 contains a brief internal *crescendo* during its final phrase (mm. 85–92), when it ascends more quickly, with chromatic flavoring, then fades out in a quiet harmonic close on a perfect authentic cadence in measures 91–92. That cadence, sounded with the release of a final appoggiatura (D♯ to C♯), suggests a momentary fulfillment of the yearning that characterizes this melody.[20]

Does Liszt create a climactic moment, and, if so, where? (See table 9.2.) The third appearance of the lyrical melody at measure 154 seems somewhat promising with its *appassionato* performance indication (as opposed to *dolce* in its first two appearances). Yet, its short eight measures consisting of unresolved dominant seventh chords (in a third relation to one another) prevent us from hearing this utterance as a climax. The *grandioso* return of motive 2 in B-flat at measure 178 is also a potential climax, which becomes particularly apparent in a comparison to its first appearance at measure 47. In both cases, it is set up by a statement of motive 2 in D-flat major, at measures 31 and 162, respectively. As shown in example 9.11, if motive 2 at measure 31 evokes a sense of striving, of attempted release from constraint, then perhaps its immediately following diatonic, *grandioso* statement at measure 47 implies

Example 9.10. *Aux cyprès de la Villa d'Este (Thrénodie 2)*, S. 163/3, final version, motive 1, mm. 1–14

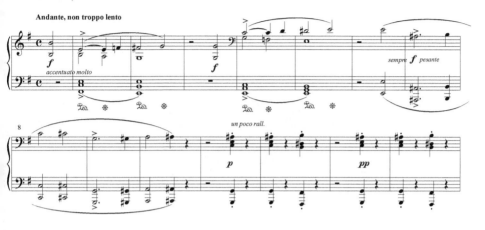

Example 9.11. *Aux cyprès de la Villa d'Este (Thrénodie 2)*, S. 163/3, final version, motive 2, mm. 30–53

Example 9.12. *Aux cyprès de la Villa d'Este (Thrénodie 2)*, S. 163/3, final version, first appearance of tripartite complex, mm. 61–95, with lyrical melody at m. 76

(continued)

Example 9.12.—*(concluded)*

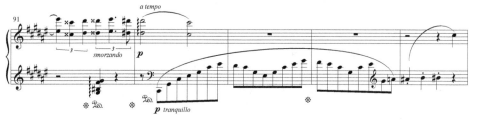

some release through its assertive nature. Yet we do not hear it as a point of arrival because it is not preceded by a dominant harmony, but instead by a *pianissimo* B♭ sonority. Liszt merely juxtaposes the two manifestations of motive 2 through this shared harmony. Significantly, when motive 2 returns at measure 162 (ex. 9.13), it carries with it textural and expressive changes. It now appears in the left hand, played *marcato*, accompanied by right-hand *pianissimo* tremolandos, which add overt tension to the earlier statement. Furthermore, Liszt marks the repeat of the neighbor-tone figure an octave higher *dolente* (see arrows), explicitly asking the performer to emphasize this plaintive component of motive 2. Thus, the earlier motive 2 preparation for the *grandioso* statement gives way, at measure 162, to a somewhat more complex emotional palette, where the sense of striving has been intensified and infiltrated by sorrow. This passage's chromatic tones, dissonance, and rich texture of tremolandos and *marcato* articulations provide an extremely stark contrast with the diatonic, *grandioso* statement of motive 2 at measure 178, causing its initial bare octaves to sound particularly empty.[21] Most importantly, by reintroducing the *grandioso* statement in B-flat major, Liszt reawakens the essential tonal crux established at the work's outset, between the tonic E and B-flat, a tension-ridden tritone relationship that seeks resolution. This tonal factor contributes to the inability of the *grandioso* motive 2 at measure 178 to provide a satisfying climax.

After having offered a less-than-convincing climax at measure 178, Liszt creates a final section, starting at measure 192, that largely features motive 1. As shown in example 9.14, motive 1 (Tempo 1) unfolds in equivalent fashion to measures 1–14 (see ex. 9.10): now in the left hand, the motive again arrests our attention, played *fortissimo* three times, followed by subdued chordal interjections. This restatement of motive 1 constitutes the last forceful moment in the piece. Significantly, at measure 208 Liszt brings motive 1 into the dreamy, arpeggiated texture introduced in the middle of the piece.

Example 9.13. *Aux cyprès de la Villa d'Este (Thrénodie 2)*, S. 163/3, final version, mm. 162–84, with *grandioso* motive 2 in B-flat

Under a four-sharp signature, the motive is uttered *espressivo* and *piano*, multiple times, on gradually ascending pitches (see circled left-hand inner-voice notes beginning in m. 209): G♯, A, B, settling in measure 225 on C♯, then D♯, after which it falls stepwise back to B, as dominant preparation for the Es that appear in both outer voices at measure 226. At the same time, the arpeggios trace their own counterpoint on B♯–C♯–D–D♯ (see circled right-hand notes), over bass notes G♯ and F♯, thereby also preparing the Es at measure 226. Motive 1's appearance *within* the arpeggio texture suggests that it has been absorbed into a new emotional space—calm, dreamlike in character. As the arpeggios and motive 1 slowly ascend, a sense of uplift is suggested, even as motive 1 retains its internal chromaticism. At measure 226, the arpeggios continue alone, now within an entirely diatonic palette that avoids dominant preparation, yet indicates E major through that triad's gradually increasing

Example 9.14. *Aux cyprès de la Villa d'Este (Thrénodie 2)*, S. 163/3, final version, mm. 192–244

(continued)

presence within the gentle flow of sonorities. In the last phrase that begins in measure 237, Liszt sounds a chromatic inflection C♯–B–C♮–B (see circled notes), as a reminder of the piece's initial tension. Nonetheless, the last utterance of motive 1, unaccompanied, takes its final pitch to G♯, thereby transforming the minor flavor of the opening motive into major.

I interpret this final section as signifying that the force of the plaintive motive has been dissipated. The motive neither finds a triumphant voicing, nor is it obliterated. Rather, its absorption *within* the dreamlike texture erases any sense of plodding or heaviness. It appears at the end identifiable, yet transformed. Now tinged with a major inflection, the plaintive motive signifies a step forward in the emotional journey of grief, one that has been touched by hope. This message is subtle, but effective, in comparison to the blatant attempt at climactic resolution by *grandioso* motive 2.

Example 9.14.—*(concluded)*

The availability of an early sketch of *Aux cyprès 2* invites an examination of my interpretation against the sorts of changes Liszt carried out. Table 9.2 reveals that, from the outset, Liszt intends a large-scale move from E minor to E major, but he dramatically changes where E major will appear. While in the earlier version, the *grandioso* motive 2 returns in E (equivalent to m. 178 in the final version), E emerges clearly only at the very end of the final version. This and associated revisions contribute to structural and tonal symmetry and to Liszt's affective message.

Example 9.15 reproduces what occurs in the early version immediately *before* the *grandioso* statement of motive 2 in E major: motive 1 (eight measures) and motive 2 (twelve measures), equivalent to measures 136 and 162 respectively. As shown in table 9.2, while Liszt retains the motive 1 passage at

Example 9.15. *Aux cyprès de la Villa d'Este (Thrénodie 2)*, S. 163/3, first version equivalent of mm. 136–83, with *grandioso* motive 2 in E major

measure 136 in his final version, he adds to it the arpeggios and lyrical melody that followed in the two previous complexes. He thereby creates structural symmetry on several levels: within the middle section by completing the third complex, and within the piece as a whole by significantly lengthening the middle section from 43 to 101 measures.[22] Framed by an opening of 60 measures and a final section of 82 measures, the middle section now commands attention because of its length as well as its distinctive progression of materials: *dolente* (motive 1), calm and dreamlike (arpeggios), and yearning (lyrical melody).

As shown in table 9.2, at the early version equivalent of measure 162, Liszt had already decided to present the opening motives in a mirror image, whereby the sequence of motive 1 to the motive 2 complex is reversed to the motive 2 complex, then motive 1. In revising this passage, he presents the motive 2 complex with essentially the same tonal plan heard at the outset (compare mm. 31–60 with mm. 162–91) and thereby delays the appearance of E major. As remarked earlier, by reintroducing the *grandioso* statement of motive 2 in B-flat major, Liszt reawakens the tonal crux between E and B-flat established at the outset of the work. Accordingly, the *grandioso* statement cannot be heard as climactic, and the listener continues to await resolution of the tritone relationship.

This harmonic ploy supports the affective message in a way that the first version does not. Although the first version manuscript is incomplete, its final surviving page suggests where Liszt was heading next (ex. 9.16). After the E-major statement of the *grandioso* motive 2, Liszt brings back motive 1 under a four-sharp signature, so that it sounds at the same pitch level as the piece's opening but now tinged as E major rather than E minor. The arpeggios follow, but Liszt had not yet decided to position motive 1 within that dream-like texture.[23] Of course, by already presenting motive 1 in E major, the following arpeggiated texture seems like an afterthought, without affective consequence, perhaps even contrived. Liszt apparently sensed this weakness. In his final version, beginning at measure 208, he brings the textural, tonal, and affective issues into mutually supportive play: a tonally unstable motive 1 moves *into* the arpeggiated texture, which dissolves its tension, in preparation for a final passage beginning at measure 226 that asserts E major. It seems appropriate that only the arpeggios are heard in this penultimate passage, given their demonstrable transforming power. They are largely responsible for the overall sense of uplift and calm that prevails from measure 208 to the end. In Liszt's hands, the arpeggio passage thus serves not only as virtuosic keyboard exploration, but also as an agent of change within an affective journey.

Another revision reveals Liszt working out the larger-scale tonal plan on a more minute level. Example 9.17 shows the opening measures of the work in the first and final versions. In the first version, the downbeat pitches of each statement of motive 1 fall on E, C, B, and G, while in the final version, they fall on E, C, A♯, and G, a linear form of the vertical sonority that follows, an augmented sixth sonority on IV, leading to the dominant B chord. The alteration in measure 7 (see final version) most immediately allows E and A♯ to be heard in juxtaposition, thus foregrounding the crucial tonal axes on E and B-flat. At the same time, this revision accentuates the upper-voice motion A♯ to B, an essential gesture in the piece's eventual move to E major. Once the *grandioso* motive 2 returns at measure 178 in B-flat major (recalling the

Example 9.16. *Aux cyprès de la Villa d'Este (Thrénodie 2)*, S. 163/3, first version equivalent of mm. 192–207

Example 9.17. *Aux cyprès de la Villa d'Este (Thrénodie 2)*, S. 163/3, comparison of opening mm., first and final versions

enharmonic A-sharp), the passage at measure 208 traces an ascending upper line that eventually leads to the tone B in measure 225. A♯ (B♭) thereby definitively resolves to B, in preparation for the entrance of E in the outer voices of the final passage that begins at measure 226.[24]

Thus, Liszt carries out a number of revisions to enhance the structural symmetry of *Aux cyprès 2* but also, as importantly, to ally his tonal plan with his affective message: the eventual resolution of the E and B-flat tritone relationship brings with it a sense of calm and uplift, essentially dissipating the tension inherent in the plaintive opening motive. When that motive sounds alone at the end, it suggests that grieving is not over, yet its final inflection to G♯ imparts to it a major flavor and a sense of moving forward with hope.

Finally, we address Liszt's revisions with respect to expressive gestures and virtuosic textures and their role in communicating his affective message. Example 9.18 shows the first appearance of motive 2 in the earliest surviving version, as well as in the final version. The arrows mark a C–B "sigh-like" gesture, which Liszt revises to include chromatic neighbor motion, C–B–A♯–B, producing a more plaintive tone, a gesture he then repeats an octave higher.[25] A second gestural revision occurs in the tripartite complex in the middle of the piece, which each time begins with motive 1. Example 9.19 shows the first of these motive 1 appearances, in its original and final versions. In revising the passage, Liszt simplifies the gesture to its bare minimum, drawing attention to its plaintive essence.[26] Thus, both gestural revisions intensify the plaintive aspect of grieving.

With respect to virtuosic passages and their expressive content, we have already noted the affective role of the arpeggios in Liszt's final version, from measure 208 to the end. In addition, a comparison of the first to final version reveals that he encased the lyrical melody in a more virtuosic texture to enhance its message. While the first version equivalent of measure 76 consists of a brief four-measure skeleton (ex. 9.20), the final version expands four measures into twenty, revealing the sonic richness of the keyboard at the midpoint of the work (see ex. 9.12, mm. 76–95). Together the hands sweep over four and a half octaves, five if one includes the preparatory arpeggios. Enveloped in this expansive landscape, the lyrical melody reaches upward, yearningly, then quietly dies away at the moment of its perfect authentic cadence. Liszt's pianistic texture, complementing the expansiveness and fluidity of the lyrical melody itself, provides a midsection foil to the measured, inwardly contracting motives 1 and 2 and their relatively more limited registral utterances. In this instance, we comprehend

Example 9.18. *Aux cyprès de la Villa d'Este (Thrénodie 2)*, S. 163/3, comparison of first appearance of motive 2, first and final versions

Example 9.19. *Aux cyprès de la Villa d'Este (Thrénodie 2)*, S. 163/3, comparison of first appearance of motive 1 in tripartite complex, first and final versions

Example 9.20. *Aux cyprès de la Villa d'Este (Thrénodie 2)*, S. 163/3, first version, first appearance of lyrical melody

"virtuosic" in the expanded sense described earlier: a sonically rich passage, albeit in a lyrical instead of a dramatic context (the arpeggiated textures are also of this sort). Although the lyrical melody does not serve a climactic role, it nevertheless contributes, through its virtuosic texture, to the affective contrast Liszt intends in the piece as a whole: plaintive and constrained versus hopeful and unimpeded.

Liszt created within his two Cypress pieces subtly different evocations of the human experience of lament, of grief. In *Aux cyprès 1*, the affective trajectory is essentially one of grief progressing to solace grounded in religious faith. Specifically, its plaintive motive yields to a stable, lyrical melody which exudes a sense of assurance; within the ensuing evocation of transcendence and religious consolation, only a tinge of disquiet remains. In *Aux cyprès 2*, on the contrary, the plaintive motive remains throughout, signaling that grief has not been overcome; instead, as the motive interacts with other musical material that is uplifting in spirit, though not specifically of a religious character, its intense affect of grief is attenuated. In its final iteration, the still identifiable motive communicates a sense of hope. The affective trajectory of the piece thereby evokes a sense of how an individual can take a step forward in handling grief, even though it retains its hold on the psyche.

In drafting and revising both pieces, Liszt relies upon musical topics, more general expressive devices, and virtuosic textures to realize fully these related, yet distinct affective journeys. In both pieces, unfolding his affective message goes hand in hand with working out a tonal crux established at the work's outset: in *Aux cyprès 1*, G to G-flat to G, in *Aux cyprès 2*, E to B-flat to E. While both tonal plans evoke tension that can be associated with the stress of grieving, the extremely unstable tritone relationship between E and B-flat is a particularly cogent expressive device in Liszt's evocation of grief.

In addition to offering insights into Liszt's modus operandi in the Cypress pieces, this essay contributes to a more refined interpretation of the expressive meaning of the cycle as a whole. While Liszt primarily treats death and lament in the four threnodies (*Aux cyprès 1* and *2*, *Sunt lacrymae rerum*, and *Marche funèbre*) and Christian consolation in the framing *Angelus* and *Sursum corda* and middle *Jeux d'eau*, the demarcation is not clear cut. By insinuating religious solace and a sense of hope respectively within the two Cypress threnodies, the cycle mimics what happens in real life—disparate emotional states are not always experienced at discrete points in time, but may intermingle. Thus, while the *Années 3* cycle paints the broad strokes of a journey to spiritual consolation, it also captures the emotional flux that occurs along the way.

Notes

1. Pesce, "Liszt's *Années de pèlerinage*, Book 3: A 'Hungarian' Cycle?" *19th-Century Music* 13, no. 3 (1990): 207–29.
2. *Années de pèlerinage: Troisième année* is published in the *New Liszt Edition* (hereafter *NLE*), series I, volume 8 (Budapest: Editio Musica Budapest, 1975). Examples from the published version (also referred to as "final version") are reproduced in this essay with permission from the publisher.
3. See Leonard Ratner, *Classic Music: Expression, Form and Style* (New York: Schirmer, 1980), 9–30. See also the more recent *The Oxford Handbook of Topic Theory*, ed. Danuta Mirka (Oxford: Oxford University Press, 2014).
4. Márta Grabócz, *Morphologie des oeuvres pour piano de Liszt. Influence du programme sur l'évolution des formes instrumentales* (Budapest: MTA Zenetudományi Intézet, 1986), 32, 54–56.
5. Ratner, *Classic Music*, 9.
6. Vera Micznik offers a revealing analysis of Liszt's statements within the Berlioz essay in "The Absolute Limitations of Programme Music: The Case of Liszt's 'Die Ideale,'" *Music & Letters* 80, no. 2 (1999): 210–12.
7. In *Musical Meaning in Beethoven: Markedness, Correlation, and Interpretation* (Bloomington: Indiana University Press, 1994), 2, Robert Hatten defines the term "markedness" as "a semiotic valuation of oppositional features that . . . accounts for relative specification of meanings, the coherence of meanings in a style, and the emergence of meaning within an expanding style competency." On p. 34, he abbreviates the definition to "valuation given to difference." For the purposes of this essay, my use of "marker" acknowledges Hatten's theory without adopting its terminology in full.

8. This definition appears in Denise Gill, *Melancholic Modalities: Affect, Islam, and Turkish Classical Musicians* (New York: Oxford University Press, 2017), 17. Gill offers this definition after discussing the various scholarly debates about how to differentiate affect from feeling or emotion (14–17).
9. Hatten, *Musical Meaning in Beethoven*, 67–90.
10. Grabócz, *Morphologie des oeuvres pour piano de Liszt*, 32–33.
11. B. Schott, Mainz, owned the early version and printer's copy. See note 18 below for more information on the printer's copy.
12. In the manuscript, Liszt added the sixth measure in the margin by extending his staff lines. The bass note remains on G♯, while the G♮ that appears in the right-hand of the previous measure is absent; thus one assumes that Liszt intended an unequivocal half-diminished seventh chord on A♯.
13. At measure 63, where Liszt had indicated *un poco agitato* in the first version, he substitutes *sotto voce* in the printer's copy, to which he adds *tranquillo* in the final version—presumably an attempt to slow down an inevitable buildup.
14. The first version is less pianistic and therefore more difficult to play.
15. Notwithstanding the framing notation of a C♯ diminished seventh, Liszt's interest in the E and A♯ relationship persists because the right hand emphasizes those tones as it ascends and descends in this passage, and Liszt actually notates the A♯ diminished seventh in measures 109, 111, 113, 115.
16. Richard Taruskin discusses cycles of third-related sonorities within Schubert's works in *Music in the Nineteenth Century*, *The Oxford History of Western Music*, vol. 3 (Oxford: Oxford University Press, 2010), chapter 2. Referring to a cycle of major thirds in the codetta of the first movement of the "great" C-major symphony, Taruskin writes, "Schubert is likely to entice us—and entrance us—with islands of mysterious repose amid the hurly-burly"; and about the opening passage of the Sanctus in the Mass in E-flat Major, he writes, "the Mass Sanctus, we may recall, is a representation of the song of the angelic hosts surrounding God's throne. Schubert's use of the cycle of thirds here was surely an attempt to render the scene in as sublime or 'unearthly' a manner as possible" (101). Taruskin thus characterizes these third-related progressions in Schubert's music as creating a particular affect—mysterious, even sublime. His interpretation of such progressions' affective content lends support to my perception of Liszt's succession of third-related sonorities as evoking a calm, awe-filled atmosphere.
17. The final version can be analyzed as two phrases of eleven and thirteen measures each. The early version also contains twenty-four total measures, but distributed into two phrases of thirteen and eleven measures respectively. One difference between the versions involve the D–D♯–E motion (mm. 191–201): in the first version, Liszt wrote out a phrase with D–D♯–E, then rewrote it to vacillate between D–D♯ several times before reaching E. The other difference resides in the final chord progression equivalent to mm. 201–14: though a bit

unclear, the E♭–D motion of the upper voice does not seem to fully incorporate the VII^{o7}–V^{7}/I progression of the final, though Liszt inserts a symbol to indicate that he will add something before the final sonority; that addition is not evident on the surviving pages.
18. One early version is held at the Library of Congress, ML31.H43a, no. 72, the second at the Musée Royal de Mariemont, Belgium, inv. 1115e. The printer's copy, once owned by B. Schott, Mainz, became part of the Julliard Manuscript Collection through a purchase in 2004.
19. A facsimile of the second early version is published in Mária Kovács, "Liszt's Manuscripts in Morlanwelz-Mariemont," *Studia musicological Academiae Schientiarum Hungaricae* 30, nos. 1–4 (1888), 321–32. This source is fragmentary, consisting of three noncontinuous pages. With respect to the final version, page 1 consists of the equivalent to mm. 1–36; page 2 consists of the equivalent to mm. 112–37; and page 3 consists of the equivalent to mm. 222–44.
20. Descending appoggiaturas figure throughout the melody; see e.g. mm. 78 and 82. In each case, the release of dissonance occurs over a chord *not* in root position, which mitigates a sense of true resolution. Only the appoggiatura at m. 92 sounds like a point of closure, however fleeting.
21. It is still not prepared by a structural dominant, but instead by a diminished seventh chord on a scale degree other than VII.
22. The lengthening in part results from additional modulations within each complex.
23. The arpeggios start with the same two chords found in the final version: G-sharp to F-sharp. The page ends after the F-sharp sonority and no additional pages have been located to date.
24. At the same time, the bass movement G–F♯–E from the work's opening is transformed into G♯–F♯–E within mm. 208–26.
25. As mentioned above, in the symmetrical return of motive 2 at m. 162 (see ex. 9.13), Liszt added to those two measures in the higher register the expressive designation *dolente*, a performed affect that accentuates the plaintive tone. Liszt wrote *dolente* in his own hand in the printer's copy at the equivalent of mm. 168 and 176 in the final version.
26. However, in the next two appearances of motive 1, at mm. 96 and 136, Liszt revises the texture to intensify the chromatic content and lend a sense of lethargy through circular eighth-note motion. This chromatic malaise contrasts with the dreamy, diatonic arpeggios that follow.

Chapter Ten

Anti-Virtuosity and Musical Experimentalism

Liszt, Marie Jaëll, Debussy, and Others

Ralph P. Locke

"We are still in the thralls of Liszt's pianism," writes musicologist J. Mackenzie Pierce in a recent issue of *Current Musicology*.[1] But what about piano works that do *not* seek, with high-virtuosic displays, to subjugate the listener and to hold her or him in thrall?

The topic is potentially large and multifaceted. For reasons of space, I restrict myself in the present chapter to introducing a newish and rarely used term, "anti-virtuosity," discuss its possible applications, and then focus on three short pieces, one each by three renowned pianist-composers: Liszt, Debussy, and Marie Jaëll. Jaëll was a major recitalist and pedagogue in her day and published her works with leading publishers (notably Heugel). Her music has recently been rediscovered, performed again by major artists, and recorded. (More on her in a separate section below.)

The three pieces discussed here exemplify the sort of anti-virtuosity that I have in mind: each is enterprising in its musical substance—even experimentally inclined—yet entirely avoids such virtuosic techniques as long passages of rapid finger work or impressive double-octaves. The three pieces bear a family resemblance to one another that I find suggestive of parallel concerns or compatible aesthetic values. Not least, each of the pieces allows us to wonder whether *non*-virtuosic piano writing may allow or even encourage a special kind of communication, or even communion, between player and composer.

I am not claiming any relation of influence among these three pieces. But I do not want to exclude that possibility. More basically, I do not mean to deny the possibility of a general influence from one composer to another. As we shall see, Jaëll knew Liszt and his music well (including some experimental late pieces, such as the near-baffling Third Mephisto Waltz [S. 216 / LW A325, 1883], which he dedicated to her); she showed him several of her major works for comment—or played them for him—when they were still in manuscript; and Liszt hailed the unconventional elements in her compositional style. Similarly, Liszt's works may find belated echo in more pieces by Debussy than has been generally noted.[2] (Debussy had heard Liszt play and had played for him, as we shall see.) Jaëll's pieces, as well, may have been models for Debussy. At the least, he admired and praised her writings on piano instruction and performance.[3]

These matters of influence and derivation surely deserve further study. The present chapter is more modest in its aim. It approaches from an unaccustomed angle the question of what complex piano textures, and relatively simple ones, can and cannot do, as seen in three unusually fascinating short pieces, all (perhaps not by chance) bearing titles having to do with the natural world: more specifically, with various kinds of inclement weather.

Types of Anti-virtuosity

Let me start with my term of choice, which is a recent and somewhat unusual one: "anti-virtuosity."[4] The obvious sense of the term is "negative attitudes toward virtuosity." As Olivia Sham has pointed out in her 2014 doctoral dissertation on virtuosity and Liszt, some musicians, critics, and concertgoers today continue to disparage elaborate pianistic writing by Liszt and others.[5] Not least, one still hears complaints that Liszt's desire to excite or overwhelm the listener produces results that are "tasteless," though the complainers rarely take care to indicate which precise features reveal the purported lack of taste (or, put differently, the presence of bad taste).[6]

An instance of what Sham refers to—what we might call default or garden-variety anti-virtuosity—appears in a recent issue of the *New York Times*. The prominent Soviet-born pianist Kirill Gerstein (now an American citizen), in an interview, derides the changes that Alexander Siloti made in the

Tchaikovsky First Piano Concerto during the early years after the work received its first performance. Gerstein offers a damning judgement: Siloti's supposed improvements reveal that the renowned pianist and pedagogue had a "tendency toward the superficially brilliant, and some traits of 19th-century pianism that are less noble."[7]

(A brief aside: loaded and moralistic language such as Gerstein uses in that remark worries me. Who is to say when brilliance is "superficial," hence to be derided, and when it somehow succeeds in being "noble" and thus deserves to be admired? Gerstein is certainly no stranger to Lisztian virtuosity, having recorded a highly regarded CD of the *Transcendental Études* in 2016.)

As I was saying, the basic, almost intuitive meaning of "anti-virtuosity" is an opposition to the excesses—however one defines those—of certain virtuoso performers and of what they play. But the term might also refer, potentially, to a critique not of virtuosic playing itself (nor, I might add, a critique of virtuosic singing) but rather of the musical world's *obsession* with displays of virtuosity. Schumann, as Alexander Stefaniak has explored, was a devoted exponent of anti-virtuosity in this sense, railing against the superficiality of the piano culture of his day but finding, in his own works, numerous ways to apply virtuosic techniques to what he considered deeper and more "poetic" purposes.[8]

Liszt himself observed, in several early published essays and polemics, that a performer's amazing dexterity can distract listeners from the profound musical truths that the art of music is, at its best, capable of conveying. He argued, furthermore, that these special abilities can risk turning the performer into what he termed an *amusoir*.

Liszt may well have invented that word. His early writings, as Jean Chantavoine noted a century ago, contain a number of neologisms and unusual usages.[9] *Amusoir*, at least when used as Liszt does here, suggests an amusement machine or entertainment device. A similar word, *amusoire* (with a final *e* and feminine in gender), had long been a normal word in French for "plaything": that is, an object, creature, or person with which or whom a person plays (or even toys) for his or her own amusement. But Liszt likely had something more precise in mind here.[10] By preferring the male-gendered term *amusoir*—by analogy to, say, *encensoir*: an incense-burner, which creates a sweet smell for people around it to enjoy—he meant to imply, I think, that a virtuosic musician such as him was too often considered a super-proficient mechanical device that creates amusement (for other people). Put another way, the masculine word *amusoir* is more active in the giving of amusement than the feminine word *amusoire*.

But being active does not grant an *amusoir* much true agency. (Similarly, an *encensoir* is not self-impelled to sweeten the air. Some human agent must insert the incense and set it alight.) The *amusoir* can only amuse on cue: the user hires the, let us say, *amusoir-pianiste*—the user is thus, figuratively, inserting a coin—and only then does the piano-playing *amusoir* give forth a wondrous, blazing, volcanic eruption of musical notes and gestures, creating an effect that impresses the listener and evokes images and feelings.

In objecting to the status (his own, at times) of being treated as an *amusoir*, Liszt was declaring himself to be "anti" virtuosity in a narrow but important sense: namely, he was seeking to unmask and oppose the ways in which virtuosic technique was often turned into a remunerative public event or a saleable product. (Virtuosity was, as we would say today, reified and monetized.)[11] One such marketable product was the printed score of a demanding piano piece, which the music lover could purchase, play (however capably or clumsily), and show to guests as tangible proof of his or her connection to high culture.[12] Another was a caricature drawing or statuette in which a famous pianist was shown as having fingers that were prodigiously long or grotesquely numerous.[13] Liszt's decision to scale back the extreme technical demands in some of his solo-piano pieces—for example, when he published the final revision of the *Transcendental Études* in 1852—is evidence of his own growing distance from what he, by that point, clearly felt were the virtuosic excesses of his earlier years.[14] Further evidence can be found in certain of the alternative (ossia) versions of passages that Liszt increasingly provided in his piano works, as Jonathan Kregor discusses in his contribution the present volume.

Easy Pieces, yet Problematic

I would like to focus in the remainder of this chapter on a third possible meaning for the term "anti-virtuosity." Some of Liszt's works pointedly refrain from elaboration, instead making the most of little. In particular, I am thinking here of certain pieces, or passages in larger pieces, that meet the following four criteria:

1. They resist the virtuoso's habitual impulse to impress his or her listeners with waterfalls of notes and attention-getting sweeps of the arms.[15] Instead, the musical materials are well within the technical abilities of an intermediate-level amateur.

2. Such pieces express or evoke moods or emotions that are very different from—and often darker or more doubt-filled than—the energetic agitation, forward drive, and surging passion so typical of Liszt's more virtuosic piano works.[16]
3. They achieve their unusual expressive ends by means of unusual, even experimental musical choices (e.g., highly dissonant harmonies, unclear tonal direction, phrases that break off . . .).
4. In the pieces that I have in mind, a short phrase may be repeated several times, or many times, and the repetition is relieved by slight shifts in pitch content, harmony, or figuration from one statement to the next. Sometimes a drifting scrap of forlorn melody enters, only to stop precipitously.

The first of these four criteria could be met by a number of "easier" pieces that Liszt wrote at different points in his career (e.g., *Le mal du pays*, from *Années de pèlerinage*, bk. 1, published 1855, S. 160/8 / LW A159/8; and *Il penseroso*, from *Années de pèlerinage*, bk. 2, published 1858, S. 161/2 / LW A55/2). It is when one adds criteria 2, 3, and 4 that the existence of pieces with a distinct anti-virtuosic aim, as I am suggesting, comes into view. The pieces—or passages in pieces—that fit all four criteria were mainly written in the last decade of Liszt's life. (The end of this chapter discusses some earlier instances in Liszt's own work and some works of other composers that may have inspired Liszt to write in this way.)

Liszt's blend of ascetic denial and experimentalism—including, of central relevance to this book, the absence of pianistic display—is familiar to many music students from the oft-anthologized *Nuages gris* of 1881 (S. 199 / LW A305; ex. 10.1). The title means, literally, *Grey Clouds*, though Liszt's alternate title for the piece (in German), *Trübe Wolken*, might be translated *Dark Clouds* or, more freely, *Heavy Cloud Cover*. The music of *Nuages gris* is as unsettled as a day when the sky is overcast and one fears that rain may soon fall or thunder be heard. The unsettled quality derives largely from the harmonic language, which flirts at times with a tonal center (G minor) but repeatedly undermines it with functionally ambiguous augmented chords. Liszt's fascination with augmented chords possibly derived from the scales used by the *csárdás* bands that so impressed him in his early and middle years. As Shay Loya and others have demonstrated, the style and practices of the *csárdás* bands influenced Liszt's compositions in ways that are overt (e.g., in the Hungarian Rhapsodies) but also in what we might call subterranean ways that avoid cultural evocation at the surface level.[17] As for the thunder

Example 10.1. Franz Liszt, *Nuages gris / Trübe Wolken*, S. 199 (1881, first published 1927)

G-minor tonic undermined by #$\hat{4}$, and by weak placement of $\hat{1}$ (on beat 4).

I^6 harmony (weak).

Five-step chromatic descent in top voice (→m. 20) harmonized with augmented triads against sometimes-dissonant B♭ and A pedals.

Semitone blur.   Augmented triad.

(continued)

Example 10.1.—*(continued)*

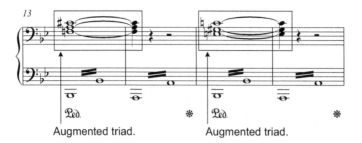
Augmented triad. Augmented triad.

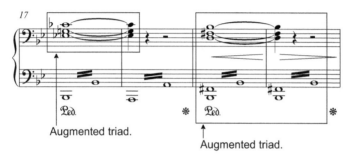
Augmented triad. Augmented triad.

Melodic fragments begin.

(continued)

Example 10.1.—*(concluded)*

that I mentioned as being a threatening possibility on a day when the sky is overcast, maybe some distant rumbling *is* heard in this piece: in the recurring left-hand octave tremolos, which the sustaining pedal, specified in the score, turns into a dissonant semitonal blur (mainly B-flats and A-naturals).

Perhaps we might choose to think of the music of *Nuages gris* as indicative not of external weather conditions and our reaction to them but, rather, of human moods and emotions generally. In that case, we might decide that the adjective from the German title—*trüb*—captures the piece's feeling-tone well: *trüb* means something like "gloomy," as for example when a person is discouraged or deflated by life's sorrows.[18] Alan Walker, in volume 3 of his magisterial biography of Liszt, draws attention to the depressed or despairing aspect of Liszt's psychological and spiritual state during the final decade of his life, and Dolores Pesce has recently demonstrated in detail the ways in which religion and a philosophy of principled resignation helped Liszt deal with these challenges.[19]

Much of the fascination, over many decades, with *Nuages gris* and other such pieces by Liszt (or passages in pieces by him)—for example, *En rêve / Notturno*, 1885 (S. 207 / LW A336) or the second half of *Schlaflos! Frage und Antwort*, 1883 (S. 203 / LW A322)—has focused specifically on two traits: their experimental approach to harmony or—a point rightly stressed by Walker—their way of trailing off at the end.[20] (The trailing off of melodic phrases *within* a piece, which I just noted in *Nuages gris*, is a related phenomenon. One encounters a number of these in, for example, the introduction to, and later moments in, *Die Zelle in Nonnenwerth,* version 4, published 1883, S. 274ii / LW N6.) Both of these traits contribute to the unsettling effect—the greyness, the *trüb*ness—of a piece such as *Nuages gris*.

One feature of *Nuages gris* has perhaps been considered too obvious to require much comment: the stripped-down quality of its piano writing, which results in the fact that anyone with a basic piano technique—an oboist, say, or a singer, a composer, a piano-playing philosopher, a "mere" music-loving amateur, or, I readily confess, a somewhat piano-challenged musicologist—can explore the piece on his or her own and have the sensation of communing directly with Liszt.

There is something democratic—in the sense of "open to all"—about a sparely written piece like this. The young Liszt might have said that it was, for that reason, "humanitarian."[21] The technical demands are as modest as those that amateur pianists could (and today can) encounter in thousands of far more predictable pieces, whether jolly or soothing, written and published during Liszt's lifetime. But, unlike in those pieces, the musical content in these late works by Liszt is quite unpredictable or even disturbing.[22] In the case of *Nuages gris*, not only is the harmony, with its emphasis on ♯4̂ and augmented triads, highly unstable and unresolved—we might call it "floating" or, like clouds, "drifting"—but the texture is also highly ambiguous. Are we to hear a meaningful melody in the top notes of the descending triads in measures 9–20? But those notes turn out to be nothing more than a chromatic scale descending slowly, two measures per melodic half step: less a melody than the materials out of which a normal melody might be built. Only in measures 25–32 do we encounter completely shaped melodic structures, and even these soon break off—as if even they were only phantoms of melodies that one remembers having heard in better years (or on sunnier days). The piece returns to slowish chromatic-scale ambiguity, now stated in bare octaves, and this time rising, with each half-step lasting less time than before (mm. 33–44) but often creating semitone clashes with some note in the left hand. (For example: the C over C♯ in m. 38, which, through a kind of voice exchange, becomes the equally inscrutable C♯ over C in m. 39.) Indeed, the passage spells out the entire twelve chromatic steps, from F♯ up to the next F♯, stopping balefully before the anticipated resolution on a high G (if we take the key of the piece to be G minor, hinted at in the opening measures). Liszt then ties things off with two highly ambiguous chords placed in the piano's ethereal upper register, the second of which indeed provides a high-G octave but in the context of what is, not surprisingly, an augmented triad (mm. 46–48) now over an utterly puzzling low A.

The radiating influence of Liszt's musically experimental and sometimes anti-virtuosic pieces is a matter that surely could use further study. Béla Bartók—once he discovered works such as the *Années de pèlerinage*, the *Harmonies poétiques et religieuses* (i.e., the ten-piece set, S. 172a / LW A61, 1847), the *Faust* Symphony, and *Totentanz*—began to advocate for Liszt as a bold explorer of musical terrain.[23] Arnold Schoenberg likewise praised Liszt's harmonic boldness.[24] But neither addressed Liszt's withdrawal from virtuosic keyboard technique in pieces such as *Nuages gris*. That Liszt was here foregoing his usual compositional persona and finding a new way to address the musical world, including performers of modest skill, was apparently not a topic that much interested composers or indeed other commentators, many of whom, being caught up in the polemics of modernism, tended to see accessibility (easy playability) as inevitably linked to highly predictable, popular, and conservative musical language.

Debussy, Walking in Liszt's Footsteps?

Still, some composers did begin to produce anti-virtuosic pieces analogous to Liszt's (whether directly influenced by them or not, as I said at the outset). One such case, I would propose, is Debussy's *Des pas sur la neige* (*Footsteps* [or *Footprints*] *in the Snow*; ex. 10.2), published in 1910 as the sixth piece in the Preludes for solo piano, book 1.

Debussy's snowscape inhabits a closely similar feeling-world to the cloudscape that is *Nuages gris / Trübe Wolken*. It even uses the same device of a repeated kernel that is gradually enriched by small doses of new material, including scraps of melody that enter above a recurrent left-hand figure or kernel. As for that kernel itself, it begins with a rising major second that is submitted to a several-seconds-long blur equivalent to what one might achieve (and what Liszt achieved in *Nuages gris*) with the sustaining pedal, though here it is accomplished by the fingers alone. When the major second expands to a minor third, the air clears, so to speak, only to become misty again when the measure-long kernel (and its dissonant interval of a major second) immediately returns.

Debussy is admittedly more tune-oriented in this piece than Liszt was in *Nuages gris* (written around twenty-eight years earlier). Already in measures 2–4 he begins to allow melodic fragments that are "expressive and sorrowful"—as the score indicates (*expressif et douloureux*)—to float above the rhythmically inchoate repeated figure from the opening. Those three measures are now expanded in range (cf. mm. 2–4 and 5–7: the rising scale, at first outlining an augmented fourth, now outlines a fifth, and so on), and the texture and tessitura increase as an additional voice is added below the initial rhythm (a descending line in "planing" parallel triads, so in a sense three additional voices), in contrary motion to the rising right-hand melody. Debussy builds tension further in measures 16–19 by contrasting a descending melody on top with an ascending melody in the bottom and—as always—the initial rhythmic figure (which is of course a two-voice unit in itself) in the middle. He tempts us into thinking we have now reached some kind of traditionally expressive, self-enclosed melody in measures 21–23 (*en animant surtout dans l'expression: p expressif et tendre*). But this segment ends by fragmenting into two-note groupings (mm. 23–25). Thus, time after time, the invitations to melodic thinking are withdrawn by the composer until, in the final measures, we are left in as much a state of mystery as we are at the end of Liszt's *Nuages gris*.

Example 10.2. Claude Debussy, Preludes, bk. 1, no. 6 (1910), bearing the after-title (at the bottom of the music) "... *des pas sur la neige*" (Footsteps—or Footprints—in the Snow).

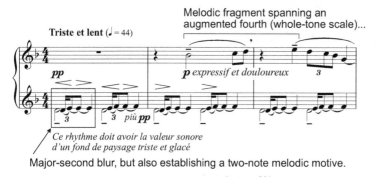

(continued)

Example 10.2.—*(continued)*

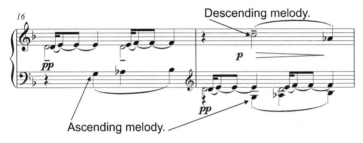

(continued)

Example 10.2.—*(continued)*

(continued)

Example 10.2.—*(concluded)*

(...Des pas sur la neige)

And, to return to my main point here, *Des pas sur la neige*, as a whole, sits at nearly the same place as *Nuages gris* on the spectrum of digital difficulty, namely, not difficult at all. *Des pas sur la neige* is one of Debussy's most democratic pieces, in the sense that it is "available to all." Not surprisingly, it is one of the pieces that Japanese musician Isao Tomita selected for his widely circulated RCA Victor LP entitled *Snowflakes Are Dancing*, which consists entirely of Debussy works arranged for synthesizer.[25] Yet *Des pas sur la neige* is also as evanescent as *Nuages gris*, scarcely forward-driving, rarely clear cut or "logical."

We know that Debussy spent parts of three days in the presence of Liszt (perhaps conversing with him, perhaps not), when the latter visited the Villa Medici in January 1886, during Debussy's stay there as a winner of the Prix de Rome. On January 8, 1886, Debussy and Paul Vidal played a two-piano arrangement of the *Faust* Symphony for Liszt. The next day, they played Chabrier's *Trois valses romantiques* for him.[26] And on the 13th, Liszt himself played three pieces for the assembled Rome Prize winners (among them Debussy and Vidal) who lived in the villa. These included *Au bord d'une source* (first published in 1840—S. 156/3 / LW A40a/2b—and republished, revised, in *Années de pèlerinage*, bk. 1, 1855—S. 160/4 / LW A159/4) and Liszt's transcription of Schubert's song "Ave Maria" (S. 558/12 / LW A42/12, 1837–38, published 1838). Nearly thirty years later, in 1915, Debussy would recall vividly "that art of making the pedal do a sort of *breathing*, which I noticed in Liszt['s playing], when I, because I was then in Rome [where Liszt spent much time in his last years], had the chance to hear him."[27] Nevertheless, there is, I believe, no evidence that Debussy knew, or even knew of, the most intensely exploratory late works of Liszt, and certainly not the unpublished ones, such as *Nuages gris*.[28] But perhaps he set his hand on a copy of some other late Liszt pieces, many of which are startling or disturbing in their own ways: for example, various compositions in Liszt's *Années de pèlerinage*, book 3 (S. 163 / LW A283, published 1883), the twelve technically modest movements that make up *Weihnachtsbaum* (S. 185a / LW A267, published 1882), or the remarkably stripped-down Two Church Hymns for Organ or Harmonium, consisting of *Salve Regina*—a setting of a Gregorian antiphon—and *Ave maris stella* (S. 669/2 / LW E27/2b, published 1877).

Marie Jaëll, a Disciple and an Original

The evidence is more abundant for a fairly direct influence of Liszt's meditative and anti-virtuosic late style in pieces by one of the most prominent members of Liszt's own circle: Marie Jaëll. In the next section, we will look at one of her pieces that is anti-virtuosic in the sense that this chapter is primarily discussing. But first we need to get a sense of the pianist and composer herself, since she is much less well known now than she was in her own day.

Marie Jaëll (1846–1925) was born Marie Trautmann, daughter of the mayor of Steinselz (today Steinseltz), which was, at the time, a largely German-speaking town in Alsace, near Weissenburg (today Wissembourg). The young pianist trained in Stuttgart (under Ignaz Moscheles) and Paris (under Henri Herz), married the noted Trieste-born, Viennese-based pianist Alfred Jaëll (who was fourteen years her elder), and performed widely throughout Europe as a prominent solo recitalist and, with her husband, in two-piano and four-hand repertoire, until Alfred's death in 1882 at the age of forty-nine.[29]

Jaëll, who lived most of her adult life in Paris, studied composition and orchestration with Camille Saint-Saëns over many years; she also studied with César Franck for a time. Jaëll performed, to great acclaim (often with the composer conducting), nearly of all of Saint-Saëns's piano-and-orchestra works. She also gave multi-concert overviews of the solo-piano repertoire of Beethoven (including all the sonatas, the first time anybody had played them all in Paris), Chopin, Schumann, and Liszt. Her lengthy booklet of program notes to her six-recital series in 1891 devoted to the major original solo works of Liszt (a booklet she revised somewhat for a second iteration in 1892) amounts to an aesthetic credo: she praises Liszt's devotion to music as a high, almost spiritual calling (as in most of the pieces in the three books of *Années de pèlerinage*) and is quick to chastise him when he slips back into mere showmanship. The *Grande valse di bravura* (S. 209 / LW A32a, 1836)—even in what she calls its "much-improved" second version (S. 214/1 / LW A32b, published in 1852, as the first of the three *Caprices-Valses*)— "still bears the imprint of being a 'piece of virtuosity,' a fact that deprives it of any serious interest."[30] Ouch!

Jaëll became a fixture of Liszt's circle, serving as a kind of personal secretary during her extended stays in Weimar in 1883, 1884, and 1885.[31] Among other things, Liszt asked her to correct the proofs of an edition of the *Faust* Symphony and repeatedly referred to the tonally experimental Third Mephisto Waltz (S. 216 / LW A325, 1883) as "your" piece. More precisely, she reports in her (rarely cited) program notes to her set of six recitals of Liszt's piano works (Paris, 1891) that Liszt wrote that piece for her, reworked it heavily after hearing her play it from manuscript, and then had her write the ending that appears in the published edition.[32] Somewhat later, he declared (in a letter) that her four-hand arrangement of the piece was a "jewel," and he helped her to get it published.[33]

Jaëll composed actively during much of her life, from the early 1870s to around 1915. She died in 1925 at age seventy-eight, having published many solo pieces, chamber works, and songs. She also—between 1896 and 1912— came out with no fewer than seven books on piano pedagogy.[34] These were based in part on physiological theories that were circulating at the time. In 1915, Debussy recommended one of her books to a friend for its guidance on piano pedaling.[35] On the European Continent some of her pedagogical principles are still followed by piano teachers who consider themselves part of Jaëll's lineage.[36]

Many of Jaëll's compositions are large in scale and technically demanding. These include a piano sonata (dedicated to Liszt), two piano concertos, a cello concerto (which is stronger, I think, than the two concertos for her own instrument), and an important song cycle based on her own poetic texts: *La légende des ours* (The Legend of the Bears). The song cycle also exists in a German version (*Bärenlieder*), the words penned, again, by the composer. Jaëll provided the long-standard French singing translation for editions of Brahms's *Ein deutsches Requiem* that can still be found in many libraries.[37] Most of all, Jaëll was considered both a virtuoso *and* a composer of originality and substance by at least three prominent composer-pianists of her day: Saint-Saëns, Liszt, and Brahms. We shall take each in turn.

Saint-Saëns was, over many years, Jaëll's friend, her main composition teacher, and her enthusiastic supporter. Nevertheless, as Florence Launay and Jann Pasler (and others) have pointed out, the increasingly unconventional, even daring musical language in Jaëll's compositions eventually led her mentor to express some disapproval. Jaëll did not suffer this rebuff in silence. On August 2, 1893, she offered to send Saint-Saëns, in manuscript, her recently composed piano-solo pieces *Ce qu'on entend dans l'Enfer / le Purgatoire / le Paradis* (What One Hears in Hell / Purgatory / Paradise), inspired by the three parts of Dante's *Divine Comedy*: "Il m'est venue une telle profusion et de si drôles d'idées dans une œuvre que je suis sur le point de terminer que je ne puis pas ne pas vous l'envoyer." (Such a profusion of such odd ideas have come to me, in a work that I am about to complete, that I cannot *not* send it to you.)[38] A follow-up letter five days later suggests that Saint-Saëns—despite his growing qualms—had agreed to receive and evaluate the new works. Jaëll, perhaps in response to something in his letter (which apparently does not survive), now brusquely rejected the very possibility that she had herself proposed:

> Quel intérêt voulez-vous que j'aie à vous envoyer mes manuscrits? Ils contiennent des idées *très neuves*, si Liszt était de ce monde elles lui auraient fait un plaisir énorme, il aurait été heureux de me dire: *Marchez en avant!* Je croyais que vous lui ressembliez!
>
> (But what point do you think there would be in my sending you my manuscripts? They contain *very new* ideas. If Liszt were still in this world, these ideas would have given him enormous pleasure. He would have been happy to say to me: "Forge ahead!" And I thought that you were like him!)[39]

Jaëll is not exaggerating. Liszt, by this point seven years dead, had, twenty-two years earlier, called her a "valiant, ambitious, and subtle composer"—high praise from someone who was quick to denounce anything mediocre or overly conventional. Liszt's remarks, in a letter to Marie's husband and piano-partner Alfred, are worth citing in full:

Cher Jaëll:

Comment m'excuser? Que votre amicale indulgence me vienne en aide, et m'obtienne aussi le pardon de votre compagnon d'armes et de célébrité, Madame Jaëll.

J'ai lu avec une attention passionnée ses "Méditations, Impromptus, Petits Morceaux, et la grande Sonate". Ces œuvres ont un cachet étrange; elles surabondent en nouveautés et hardiesses que je n'ose critiquer, mais que j'apprécierai mieux encore quand j'aurai le plaisir de les entendre jouer par leur vaillant, ambitieux et subtil compositeur.

(Dear [Alfred] Jaëll:

How can I be forgiven for this delay in responding? I hope your friendly indulgence will come to my aid and will also obtain this forgiveness from your companion-at-arms and companion-in-renown, Madame Jaëll.

I have read with intense interest her "Meditations, Impromptus, Smaller Pieces, and the Grand Sonata [dedicated to Liszt]." These works have a strange aura. They abound in new and bold ideas that I wouldn't have the audacity to criticize, and that I shall appreciate yet more when I have the pleasure of hearing them played by their valiant, ambitious, and subtle composer.)[40]

It is notable that Liszt did not feel the need to adjust the gender of his language to suit Marie's sex. She was a *compositeur* like himself, not a *compositrice*, a term he might have thought demeaning. And she was her husband's *compagnon*, not his *compagnonne*, which, likewise, could have suggested that she was a muse or helpmate, not a creative figure in her own right. (The word *compagnonne* did exist at the time: it was used by Victor Hugo, in his 1838 play *Ruy Blas*, to mean a woman who was ugly and mannish-looking, with facial hair and a stump-shaped nose.)[41]

In 1876 Liszt played (with Saint-Saëns) Marie Jaëll's remarkable waltz-set for piano four-hands: *Douze valses et finale*.[42] He also addressed, over the years, numerous letters to her with one of two salutations: "Chère admirable" (Dear admirable one) or "Chère Ossiana" (creating a nickname for her based on her symphonic poem *Ossiane*, about a mythical female poet and seer).[43]

Jaëll was the most significant woman composer in Liszt's entourage, indeed perhaps the only significant one. (I stress the word "significant." Sophie Menter composed a bit, and so surely did a few other women who were students or colleagues of Liszt.) Liszt allowed Jaëll to spend long hours reading and composing in his residence in the Weimar Altenburg.[44] He also commented extensively and encouragingly on some of her compositions before she sent them off for publication (notably the aforementioned large set of four-hand waltzes).[45]

Brahms, too, admired the fact that Jaëll performed her own compositions, instead of playing the same few Liszt pieces again and again, as was the "insipid" (his word: *fad*) practice of other "female piano players" (*Klavierspielerinnen*). Brahms described Jaëll as an "intelligent and witty person," and he said to some friends—with his habitual irony—that her pieces succeeded in being "as bad as Liszt's."[46] I suspect he meant this as a left-handed insult: in other words, as a compliment.

In short, though most of us know little or nothing about Marie Jaëll (and that included me, until recently), there is some reason to think that her pieces are far more interesting than the run of the mill. And so it proves to be, when one lives a bit with a piece like Jaëll's *On rêve au mauvais temps*. Either listening to it or playing it (as many enterprising amateurs today could easily do), one begins to sense how serious Jaëll was as a composer and how deeply grounded in some of the most accomplished techniques of musical composition of her day. One also sees why commentators today who have looked into her solo pieces of the 1890s see them as anticipating certain tendencies in late twentieth-century musical minimalism (a point to which I shall return).

A Jaëll Piece in the Spirit of Late Liszt

Jaëll's *On rêve au mauvais temps* is one of her many shortish pieces for piano solo that require only a very limited technique. Furthermore, like Liszt's *Nuages gris* and Debussy's *Des pas sur la neige*, it is irresolute rather than goal-directed. *On rêve au mauvais temps* (Dreaming of Bad Weather) is the last in her twelve-piece set entitled *Les beaux jours* (literally "Beautiful Days," but here implying days when the weather is fair). Jaëll composed a parallel twelve-piece set entitled *Les jours pluvieux* (Rainy Days). The two sets were published in 1894 by the distinguished firm of Heugel.[47] *On rêve au mauvais temps* seems to have been intended as a link to the *Pluvieux* set, because it is placed last in the fair-weather set. In parallel fashion, the rainy-day set refers to the fair-weather set by ending with a piece entitled *On rêve au beau temps* (Dreaming of Nice Weather). The two sets can thus become a single closed circle, at least in the mind of the player.[48]

It is surely not by chance that all three composers chose a weather-related title for their piece under discussion here, given that each piece seems to evoke a process or environment separate from the realm of goal-directed human action. *On rêve au mauvais temps* is also the kind of thing that Jaëll probably had in mind when, writing to a friend, she described her compositions as having a "scientifique" character; the word suggests, I suspect, that Jaëll viewed them as using a novel yet systematic approach and as thus being, to a degree, experimental.[49] She probably would also have described the two weather sets the way she described her three "Dante" sets to Saint-Saëns on August 2, 1893 (the same year she completed the "weather" pieces), namely as being full of "odd/funny ideas" (*de si drôles d'idées*). Or, to quote her next sentence in that letter: "On ne voit pas tous les jours de la musique comme cela." (One does not see music like this very often.)[50]

On rêve au mauvais temps (ex. 10.3) begins with a left-hand part constructed of a repeated simple scalar fragment using only the pitches 1, 2, and 3 (in G-sharp minor), alternating with a dominant pedal, the latter placed in what we might think of as the "tenor" voice. We immediately sense some oddity because degree 2 (A♯) is placed on the strong first and third beats of each measure. The right hand, in the "alto" voice, begins with a recurring and equally conjunct figure, consisting only of two pitches a half-step apart (i.e., degrees 1 and 7). Measure 5 introduces slow melodic phrases, which sound somewhat regretful or unemphatic, especially because the short notes are written as grace notes rather than as notes with a specified length. (Jaëll indicates that these *petites notes* should not be played *trop vite*. In other words, they are true melody notes: in measures 5–8 they help create a smooth melody line: 5 8 5 6 5 4.)[51] This opening melody ends with a clear descent from the dominant to the tonic (D♯ to G♯), but any sense of resolution is undermined by the fact that the entire melody has been accompanied by variants of that opening left-hand oscillation that, thanks in part to the persistent downbeat A♯ appoggiatura, somewhat blur the tonal sense. Indeed, the melody's resolving tonic note that I just mentioned (G♯ in m. 13) creates a notable clash with the simultaneous A♯ below it.[52]

Furthermore, the sustaining pedal is indicated as being depressed at the beginning of the piece. Even if one does not take this literally as an instruction to hold the pedal down throughout, any amount of pedaling will naturally create a blur from the various oscillating patterns in the left hand and in the right-hand alto part. The result thus somewhat resembles the blur created by the pedaled tremolos in Liszt's *Nuages gris* (composed around eleven years earlier).

Example 10.3. Marie Jaëll, *Les beaux jours*, no. 12: *On rêve au mauvais temps* (Dreaming of Bad Weather; 1894)

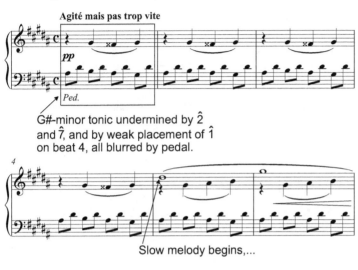

(continued)

Example 10.3.—*(continued)*

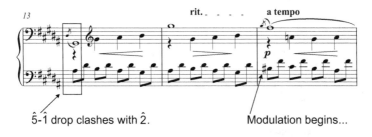

$\hat{5}$-$\hat{1}$ drop clashes with $\hat{2}$.   Modulation begins...

A♮°

(continued)

Example 10.3.—*(concluded)*

Return ≈ mm. 5–12.

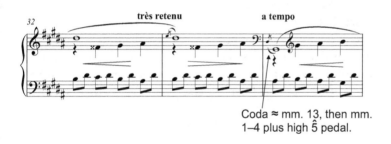

Coda ≈ mm. 13, then mm. 1–4 plus high $\hat{5}$ pedal.

Measures 15–26 modulate away, hesitantly, arriving at a tonal dead end (m. 23: a diminished-seventh chord on A) and then, after trying again, reach a new dead end (m. 26: an analogous chord on B♭). At this point, Jaëll seems to accept defeat in her wandering: she attempts to restore order by bringing back the two opening phrases of the piece (slightly reworked), but she gives them to us now in reverse order: first the original tune (mm. 5–13), then the piece's opening measures (mm. 1–4), allowing the piece to die away in the same mood of mild distress with which it began. The slight reworking in the final four measures (mm. 35–37) proves significant: the dominant pedal is stated not just, as originally, in the tenor voice (in short repeated notes) but now also in the soprano (in long notes). The change enables the piece to melt away, unemphatically, with a symbol of emptiness, desolation: an open fifth (G♯–D♯) in each hand.

The resemblances to compositional procedures in late Liszt are not coincidental.[53] Jaëll was, as a select member of Liszt's inner circle, more familiar with his late work than almost any other musician alive. And, in her own program notes for her series of six recitals of the major piano works by Liszt (Paris, 1892), she pointedly mentions how often his late pieces end with phrases that "expire as if the breath of God were leaving them."[54] Indeed, the recital by Jaëll that Brahms attended in 1888 (two years after Liszt's death) opened with her playing an unpublished piece—likely a late one—by Liszt, no doubt meant as a tribute to the one musician who had, more than any other, encouraged her to persevere in her own bold compositional experiments.[55]

Impossible (yet Very Playable) Objects

I would like to conclude with three somewhat loose sets of reflections on the pieces we have examined—Liszt's *Grey Clouds*, Debussy's *Footsteps in the Snow*, and Jaëll's *Dreaming of Bad Weather*—and pieces like them (whether those pieces allude to atmospheric conditions or not!).

First, where do such often strange-sounding pieces belong in the stories we tell about developments in musical style and pianistic writing? There is no single dominant arc or trend in music history any more than there is in history generally; rather, there are various simultaneous, overlapping, competing, and interacting tendencies or trends. One important trend is the triumphant rise of virtuosic exhibitionism and the adaptation of virtuosic techniques to important aesthetic purposes: for example, by Liszt in the B-Minor Sonata and by Ravel in *Gaspard de la nuit*. (And onward to such composers as György Ligeti.)[56] But perhaps another important trend, less often discussed, is the *withdrawal* from the display of high technique into a realm of seemingly private musical contemplation, where the smallest deviations register with the force of shifting tectonic plates.

Several commentators have drawn parallels between late Liszt and late twentieth-century minimalism.[57] Sébastien Troester, similarly, has noted similarities between certain pieces by Jaëll and the often modest yet conceptually challenging works composed by Erik Satie around the same time. Troester notes that Satie's famously atonal *Vexations* comes from around 1893. This was the very year Jaëll was completing and publishing her three "Dante" sets and her two "weather" sets.[58] And even Troester does not mention what strikes me as a conceptually daring piece, proto-minimalist in a sense, by Jaëll from the "fair weather" set: number 4, *Incendie de broussailes* (Brushfire) consists entirely of the notes of the tonic chord, made bearable (and even captivating) through keyboard passagework that, using the title as a guide, portrays fire moving slowly and then spreading quickly and scarily through dry weeds or bushes.[59] However much or little credence one wishes to give to these parallels between musical phenomena from eras separated by a hundred years or so (that is, Jaëll and Satie, on the one hand, and Reich and Glass, on the other), the very fact that the parallels have been posited reminds us that there may be other ways of "slicing" music history—other patterns we may wish to notice and explore—than the ones we are accustomed to reading and writing about.

Second, the seemingly contradictory (or at least counterintuitive) combination of technical simplicity, on the one hand, and harmonic and formal ambiguity and discontinuous or mysterious moment-to-moment succession of phrases and melodic materials, on the other, has largely escaped discussion as a historical trend or recurring phenomenon. Indeed, the process of composing in a mood of what we might call "desolate spareness" did not start with Liszt. I think of the harmonically disorienting Prelude, op. 28, no. 2, by Chopin (published in 1839), generally said to be in A minor. (It seems to open in E minor but does clearly end in A minor.) The Second Prelude does not fit the fourth of the criteria that I laid out at the beginning of the chapter, but it certainly fits the first, second, and third: technical ease, grimness of mood, and bold stylistic choices (here, harsh dissonances). The novelist André Gide specifically said that the Second Prelude was something to play on one's own, that is, in the privacy of one's home, not in concert.[60]

Lawrence Kramer, elaborating on Gide's thought, describes the piece as an "impossible object."[61] But my point, in part, is that, despite its harmonic ambiguities, Chopin's A-Minor Prelude is actually a very *possible* object . . . from the viewpoint of a player of limited skill. Pieces like this have a special potential in the musical life of humanity: they seem to evoke complex feelings and even some philosophical depth, similar to Liszt's aforementioned *Il penseroso* (e.g., doubt about the validity of "normal" optimism, reason, and so on), all while being perfectly playable by millions of amateur pianists around the world.

Another "precursor" in this respect is Schubert.[62] Liszt may have been encouraged by the powerful use of limited resources in certain Schubert songs that he knew well (not least from having transcribed so many of them for piano solo). I am thinking, for example, of "Die liebe Farbe," from *Die schöne Müllerin* (1823), with its tolling repeated note on the dominant and its brief, hopeful glimpse of the major mode (in each of its three strophes) and sudden return back to minor-mode despair; "Der Leiermann," which is the final song from *Winterreise* (1827); or "Der Doppelgänger" (1828), first published in the posthumous collection *Schwanengesang* (1829). Each of these handily meets criteria 1, 2, and 3: easy to play and sing for oneself (if not easy to perform meaningfully for a listening audience), most serious in mood, and employing musical materials that were unusual (at the time) or else—as with the repeated dominant and the minor-major contrast in "Die liebe Farbe"—familiar but used in a highly distinctive and expressively pointed manner.[63]

Likewise, various aspects of Liszt's strange and spare late piano solo works are anticipated in a few remarkable pieces from much earlier in Liszt's own compositional career. He occasionally turned out more or less "easy pieces" when it suited his expressive purposes, as in several movements from *Années de pèlerinage*, book 1 (published in 1858), such as the aforementioned *Le mal du pays*; or the Elegy no. 1 for piano, harp, and harmonium (S. 130a / LW D13a, published 1875; S. 130b / LW D13b is an arrangement of this for cello and piano); or some sacred pieces for organ or harmonium such as the aforementioned Two Hymns.[64] And, as Jonathan Kregor has demonstrated in *Liszt as Transcriber*, the late-period experiments with harmony and phrase structure strikingly recall passages in a few works that Liszt had composed as long ago as 1834, when he was twenty-three years old: the first *Apparition* (S. 155/1 / LW A19/1) and the equally astounding, and more extended, *Harmonies poétiques et religieuses* (S. 154 / LW A18—the piece that would later, in revised form, be renamed *Pensée des morts* as part of the collection entitled *Harmonies poétiques et religieuses*.[65] Indeed my criterion 4 for anti-virtuosic pieces—immediate repetition (literal or varied) of a single phrase—can be seen as an outgrowth of the numerous fantasy- and recitative-like passages that can be found in numerous of Liszt's works written at different points in his life.[66]

At times, and throughout his career, Liszt lingered, almost obsessively, in this disturbed yet quietly pensive realm, caring little whether his contemporaries would join him there. In such pieces, he was writing for what he once called, quoting Lamartine, "a certain few" (un petit nombre), namely people who are "meditative souls" (âmes méditatives).[67] Marie Jaëll explored that realm as well. Indeed, she reprinted Liszt's preface to the 1834 *Album d'un voyageur* in the program notes to her series of all-Liszt recitals in Paris (1891–92), drawing special attention to the phrase "a certain few."[68]

I said that the pieces I have been discussing are democratic, in that they require no advanced technique. But, of course, they are not crowd-pleasers and were never intended to be. They *can* be played by the multitude, but multitudes are not very likely to *want* to play—or listen to—such evasive or seemingly desultory musical statements. In that sense, they are (do I contradict myself?) anti-democratic, or at least anti-crowd. Indeed, Liszt's aforementioned preface to the *Album d'un voyageur* confides that, in that publication, he was (I highlight the crucial phrase) "addressing myself to a certain few *rather than the crowd*."[69]

Third, did other composers besides Jaëll do some exploring of this rarefied kind, encouraged by Liszt's more experimental compositions?[70] After all, we know that certain important members of Liszt's circle were intrigued by his unpublished late solo pieces (for example, the *Bagatelle sans tonalité*, S. 216a / LW A338, 1885) and that Arthur Friedheim, Hugo Mansfeldt, and others tried to bring one or another of them to performance (or even did so) over his objections.[71] Similarly, might some members of the circle have been intrigued—or inspired—by Jaëll's experimental pieces? The pieces were easily available for purchase: most of the ones for piano (such as the two "weather" or *Jours* sets, the three "Dante" sets, and pieces with mysterious titles such as *Prisme: Problèmes en musique* and *Sphinx*) were published quite promptly, by major firms, such as Gérard and Heugel, during Jaëll's lifetime. Further, we know that she played some of her pieces—though we often do not know which—at numerous gatherings of Liszt and his followers.[72]

In conclusion, I suspect that Liszt—that magnetic, ever-inventive genius—left marks on music history and on the concert repertoire that remain to be discovered. And also on the intensely private, *non-concert* repertoire, including pieces that are non- or even anti-virtuosic.[73] Because one of those marks—notable yet rarely mentioned—was his willingness to question the purpose and function, in human existence, of the very virtuosity of which he was the greatest living incarnation.[74]

Notes

I wish to thank Amy Bauer, Jonathan Bellman, Zbigniew Granat, Denis Herlin, Shay Loya, James Parakilas, and Jürgen Thym for comments or suggestions. Marie-Laure Ingelaere and other library staff at the University of Strasbourg kindly helped me obtain scans of the revelatory program booklets that Jaëll published for her six-concert series, in Paris, of Liszt's major original solo-piano works (1891, repeated 1892).

1. J. Mackenzie Pierce, review of James Q. Davies, *Romantic Anatomies of Performance* (Berkeley: University of California Press, 2014), *Current Musicology* 98 (2014): 151–55.
2. The single most-noted parallel is between the "water" imitations in Liszt's *Les jeux d'eaux à la Villa d'Este* from *Années de pèlerinage*, bk. 3 (S. 163/4 / LW A283/4, 1877, pub. 1883), and Debussy's *L'isle joyeuse* (1904).
3. See n. 35.
4. The word does not exist in the *Oxford English Dictionary*, with or without hyphen. It was used in an idiosyncratic way by Marc Couroux in regard to a 1973 piece for solo piano by Iannis Xenakis: "*Evryali* and the Exploding of the Interface: From Virtuosity to Anti-virtuosity and Beyond," *Contemporary Music Review* 21, no. 2–3 (2002), 53–67. On Schumann's "anti-virtuosic" stance, see n. 8 below.
5. Olivia Sham, "Performing the Unperformable: Notions of Virtuosity in Liszt's Solo Piano Music," PhD dissertation (London: Royal Academy of Music, 2014), 13. Sham cites Stephen Hough's remarks about the lieder transcriptions: they are "a touch tasteless" and amount to "a terrible lapse in judgement" (Stephen Hough, "Liszt: The Man Who Could Be a Touch Tasteless at Times," *The Telegraph*, July 25, 2011; Sham accessed this blog at http://blogs.telegraph.co.uk/culture/stephenhough/100055028/liszt-the-man-who-could-be-a-touchtasteless-at-times; it is no longer accessible).
6. See Richard Taruskin, "Liszt and Bad Taste," *Studia musicologica* 54, no. 1 (2013): 87–104.
7. David Allen, "A Concerto Minus Its Sequins," *New York Times*, February 1, 2017, C4. The headline in the online version is "Listen to Tchaikovsky, Stripped Down to His Intentions: Kirill Gerstein Will Play a Less Gaudy Version of Tchaikovsky's Piano Concerto No. 1." Gerstein refers to the Siloti

alterations as "sprinkles of MSG" on top of the concerto's "organic food." I would argue that one of the risks in using such metaphors (good nutrition vs. an empty flavor enhancer) is that the substantial elements of display that are present in Tchaikovsky's *own* version may be seen as, likewise, appealing but empty.

8. Alexander Stefaniak, *Schumann's Virtuosity: Criticism, Composition, and Performance in Nineteenth-Century Germany* (Bloomington: Indiana University Press, 2016), passim. Schumann's position relates to a more general aesthetic ideology that viewed German and Austrian musical traditions as emphasizing spiritual depth (profundity) and French and Italian traditions as emphasizing a more transient appeal to the senses (superficiality). See Holly Watkins, *Metaphors of Depth in German Musical Thought from E. T. A. Hoffmann to Arnold Schoenberg* (Cambridge: Cambridge University Press, 2011), esp. Chapter 4, "Robert Schumann and Poetic Depth."

9. See Jean Chantavoine's introduction to his edition of Liszt's early essays: Franz Liszt, *Pages romantiques* (Paris: F. Alcan, 1912).

10. See my "Liszt on the Artist in Society," in *Franz Liszt and His World*, ed. Christopher H. Gibbs and Dana Gooley (Princeton, NJ: Princeton University Press, 2006), 291–302 (here 300 n. 3). The *Trésor de la langue française informatisé* (*TLFi*) includes *amusoir* only as an alternative spelling of *amusoire* and makes no mention of Liszt's careful use of the non-*e* spelling. (See the entry for the two spellings at http://atilf.atilf.fr/tlf.htm; one enters the requested word in the box at upper-right labeled "Valider 1.") *TLFi* thereby misses the distinction that I propose above: between a child amusing him- or herself and a pianist providing amusement for others.

11. On the place of pianos and piano playing in European and American culture in the nineteenth century and beyond, see the wide-ranging chapters, by numerous contributors, in *Piano Roles: Three Hundred Years of Life with the Piano*, by James Parakilas, Douglas Bomberger, et al. (New Haven, CT: Yale University Press, 1999) and available as an e-book. Re-released in paperback in 2002 (with fewer illustrations) as *Piano Roles: A New History of the Piano*.

12. That music lovers bought highly demanding pieces as souvenirs of a recent performance they had attended by Liszt or another virtuoso is suggested by James Deaville, "Publishing Paraphrases and Creating Collectors: Friedrich Hofmeister, Franz Liszt, and the Technology of Popularity," in *Franz Liszt and His World*, 255–88.

13. For a study of one gifted artist's caricatural drawings and statuettes of piano virtuosos and other famous performing musicians, see H. Robert Cohen, "The Musical World of Dantan jeune: Subtle Distortions and Giants Reduced," in Peter Bloom, ed., *Music in Paris in the Eighteen-Thirties / La vie musicale à Paris dans les années Mil Huit Cent Trente* (Stuyvesant, NY: Pendragon Press, 1986), 135–208. The article includes numerous amusing illustrations.

14. Those changes resulted in part from developments in piano manufacture between the 1830s and the 1850s, such as the slight widening of each key on the keyboard (which eventually made certain stretches impossible).
15. This is true also of the piano parts in some of his later songs. See Jürgen Thym, "Crosscurrents in Song: Six Distinctive Voices," in *German Lieder in the Nineteenth Century*, ed. Rufus Hallmark (New York: Routledge, 2010, 2nd rev. ed.), 178–238, esp. 204, 206.
16. E.g., *Transcendental Étude* no. 4, *Mazeppa*; First Mephisto Waltz; Second Hungarian Rhapsody; and the two Piano Concertos.
17. See the extensive discussion of Liszt's fascination with the "Hungarian-Gypsy" bands (whose leaders and members were mostly Roma, but sometimes were ethnic Germans, Jews, or Slavs) in Shay Loya, *Liszt's Transcultural Modernism and the Hungarian-Gypsy Tradition* (Rochester NY: University of Rochester Press, 2011), and, more briefly, in my *Musical Exoticism: Images and Reflections* (Cambridge: Cambridge University Press, 2009), 135–49.
18. Indeed, the old *Gesamtausgabe*, taking its cue from the piece's German title rather than its French one, uses the English equivalent "Gloomy Clouds" (rather than "Grey Clouds").
19. Alan Walker, *Franz Liszt, Volume 3: The Final Years, 1861–1886* (New York: Alfred A. Knopf, 1996), 426–28, 431, 437–56; and Dolores Pesce, *Liszt's Final Decade* (Rochester, NY: University of Rochester Press, 2014). Pesce (171–208 of her book) gives *Nuages gris* in its entirety, discusses it, and lays out the publication history of the late works. Pesce also makes the strong point that *Nuages gris*, in particular, should not be taken as indicating that Liszt's mental state was primarily depressive in his later years. Many of the late pieces, she argues, encompass a message of religious consolation: they carry out a "paradigm of suffering and uncertainty yielding to hope and joy" (235).
20. See writings by Schoenberg, Alan Walker, the composer Mauricio Kagel, and others, quoted or summarized in James K. Wright, "Schoenberg's Liszt: 'Greater than an Artist: A Prophet!,'" in James Deaville and Michael Saffle, eds., *Liszt's Legacies* (Hillsdale, NY: Pendragon Press, 2014), 280–99.
21. On Liszt's 1835 call for a new "humanitarian" music that would meet the spiritual needs that the church was no longer addressing and would, simultaneously, serve political and social ends (e.g., a healthy nationalism or a concern for the rights of the poor), see my two articles "Liszt on the Artist in Society," in Gibbs and Gooley, *Franz Liszt and His World*, 291–302; and "Liszt's Saint-Simonian Adventure," *Nineteenth-Century Music* 4, no. 3 (1981): 209–27, and—correcting an error—5, no. 3 (1982): 281. One clear example of a "humanitarian" piece from his early years is *Lyon* (S. 156/1 / LW A40a/1, 1837–38), from the *Album d'un voyageur*, a piece that Liszt excluded when turning the *Album* into the *Années de pèlerinage*, bk. 1. For "democratic," in the text above, I might have been tempted to substitute "populist" had that word not recently—in the

political realm in both Europe and North America—acquired associations with authoritarianism (or even dictatorial and self-interested rule by a privileged few), intolerance of cultural and religious difference, and ignorance of history and science. In 2005, a politically more innocent era, Katharine Ellis was still able to use the word "populist" straightforwardly, characterizing Liszt's unusually strong concern—in his early years but also later as well—for the improvement of society and for the spread of musical education: "Liszt: The Romantic Artist," in *Cambridge Companion to Liszt*, ed. Kenneth Hamilton (Cambridge: Cambridge University Press, 2005), 1–13, here 12.

22. In this sense, *Nuages gris*, though playable by almost anybody who has mastered the basics of piano playing, which is to say millions of people around the world, remains intended for "un petit nombre" (see discussion below, in the paragraph containing n. 68).

23. See Béla Bartók, *Essays*, ed. Benjamin Suchoff (London: Faber & Faber, 1976), 409 (from an autobiographical article first published in 1921), 451–54 (from 1911), and 501–10 (from 1936). Bartók praised *Totentanz* for its "shattering"—or, perhaps better translated, "disturbing"—grimness and its avoidance of "empty fireworks" ("Liszt's Music and Today's Public," 452). A moment of great revelation, for many modernist composers, came with the first publication, in 1927, of such late pieces as *Nuages gris, Schlaflos! Frage und Antwort*, and *Unstern* in a volume of the Liszt *Gesamtausgabe* edited by José Vianna da Motta. See James Deaville, "Liszt and the Twentieth Century," in Hamilton, *Cambridge Companion to Liszt*, 28–56. On the more experimental features of many of the late works (including many posthumously published ones), see two chapters by James Baker, "Liszt's Late Piano Works: A Survey," and "Liszt's Late Piano Works: Larger Forms," in Hamilton, *Cambridge Companion to Liszt*, 86–119, and 120–51.

24. See n. 20 above.

25. See Matthew Brown, *Debussy Redux: The Impact of His Music on Popular Culture* (Bloomington: Indiana University Press, 2012), 66–74. The Tomita album is still available, as a CD rerelease on the Sony High Performance label.

26. Chabrier's work (completed in 1883) is for two pianos and is rich in "progressive" harmonic features, such as pentatonic writing and ninth chords. Years later, it continued to fascinate two composer-pianists, Ravel and Poulenc.

27. Details in François Lesure and Denis Herlin, eds., *Correspondance, 1872–1918* (Paris: Gallimard, 2005), 49n5, and in François Lesure, *Claude Debussy: Biographie critique* (Paris: Fayard, 2003), 83–84.

28. Denis Herlin informs me that, unfortunately, there is next to no evidence today of what scores Debussy may have owned (email, January 7, 2018).

29. Marie's married name was probably pronounced the German way in much of Europe during her lifetime (as Alfred's, I imagine, was, Trieste being part of the Austro-Hungarian Empire at the time), namely with an opening Y

sound. Nowadays it is more likely heard the French way (beginning with a Zh) because her fame remains strongest in the French piano-teaching world. The only published biographies of Marie Jaëll are inadequate in different ways. Hélène Kiener's is valuable primarily for its snippets from Jaëll's letters and diaries, and from writings about her by others: *Marie Jaëll, 1846–1925: Problèmes d'esthétique et de pédagogie musicales* (Paris: Flammarion, 1952). Catherine Guichard's biography of Jaëll is insufficiently researched, poorly organized, and unclearly translated: *Marie Jaëll: The Magic Touch, Piano Music by Mind Training*, trans. Cyrille de Souza (New York: Algora, 2004). Some of the sources excerpted by Kiener are found more completely in *Marie Jaëll: "Un cerveau de philosophe et des doigts d'artiste,"* ed. Laurent Hurpeau (Lyons: Symétrie, 2003).

Alfred's *Réminiscences de "Norma,"* op. 20 (a different work from Liszt's fantasy of the same name), has recently been made available on CD in a fine performance by Andrew Wright (*The Operatic Pianist*, vol. 2: Divine Art 25153). The performance is also at https://www.youtube.com/watch?v=5ujdRuq5G4I. A live recording by the same pianist includes the score for viewing: https://www.youtube.com/watch?v=pRXhqZp5RLU.

30. "Quoique Liszt l'ait sensiblement améliorée dans l'édition de 1852, elle n'a pas perdu l'empreinte du morceau de virtuosité qui lui ôte tout l'intérêt sérieux" (from Jaëll's 32-page program booklet for her 1891 six-recital series in Paris, p. 14). I used the rare copy of this booklet (bearing corrections in Jaëll's hand) that is now in the library of the University of Strasbourg (MRS JAELL, 18); henceforth: "Jaëll, Liszt program booklet." I also consulted the forty-page booklet that she used when she repeated, with some changes, the Liszt recitals in 1892 (MRS JAELL, 19). Cf. Laurent Hurpeau, "Liszt-Jaëll: Une correspondance méconnue," in Hurpeau, *Marie Jaëll*, 85–98 (97); and Marie-Laure Ingelaere, "Marie Jaëll: bibliographie sélective," in Hurpeau, *Marie Jaëll,*, 237–43 (242). The six concerts excluded Liszt's arrangements of his own non-piano works (e.g., for chorus or orchestra) and also omitted pieces based on materials that were not his own (e.g., the Hungarian Rhapsodies—many of which are based on tunes he had heard *csárdás* bands play—and the opera fantasies).

31. Many crucial facts about the life and career of Marie Jaëll can be gleaned from the various (topically organized) chapters in Hurpeau, *Marie Jaëll*, a multiauthor essay collection cited in n. 29. Several chapters in that book are particularly valuable for the numerous letters that they print, complete or in excerpt. The book also includes detailed lists of Jaëll's musical works (certain of which remain unpublished) and of her books and articles. The pianist Alexandre Sorel devotes a short but thoughtful chapter to Jaëll's compositional output ("L'œuvre de Marie Jaëll compositeur," 145–60). The quoted words in the subtitle of Hurpeau's book—"she's really something [*c'est un type*]: the head of a

philosopher combined with the fingers of an artist"—come from a remark of Liszt's, as relayed by Albert Soubies (Kiener, *Marie Jaëll*, 15–16).

32. Jaëll, Liszt program booklet, 28–29. Information accepted in the worklist in Hurpeau, *Maire Jaëll*, 236.

33. See letters from Liszt to Marie Jaëll (one undated, the other from 9 February 1884) in Hurpeau, "Liszt-Jaëll," 96.

34. Two others appeared posthumously (1927), and all nine of them were reprinted in 1998 by the Association Marie Jaëll (Paris). With Charles-Samson Féré she coauthored two articles on the psychological effects of hearing different intervals and rhythms. See Ingelaere, "Bibliographie sélective," 239–40. Féré was the head medical officer at the renowned Bicêtre hospital and former assistant to the pioneering neurologist Jean-Martin Charcot at the Salpétrière.

35. Debussy recommended Marie Jaëll's writings about piano pedaling in a letter to his publisher Jacques Durand, September 1, 1915 (Lesure and Herlin, *Correspondance, 1872–1918*, 1927). He specifically praised Jaëll's emphasis on letting the sound "breathe," a concern that is closely parallel to his comment on Liszt's playing, mentioned above.

36. See various France-based sites, notably http://www.mariejaell-alsace.net/.

37. This French translation appears in editions published by Rieter-Biedermann, C. F. Peters, and Eulenburg.

38. Jaëll to Saint-Saëns, 2 August 1893, in Laurent Hurpeau, "Correspondance Jaëll—Saint-Saëns: une Alsacienne et un maître à penser de la musique française," in Hurpeau, *Marie Jaëll*, 99–142 (here 121). Jaëll's relationship to Saint-Saëns is treated also (with brief quotations from letters) in Kiener, *Marie Jaëll*, 51–53.

39. Jaëll to Saint-Saëns, 7 August 1893, in Laurent Hurpeau, "Correspondance Jaëll—Saint-Saëns," in Hurpeau, *Marie Jaëll*, 121–22. Also (though it erroneously omits the emphatic underlining of *très neuves*) in Sébastien Troester, "La passion de composer," in the small book accompanying the 3-CD set *Marie Jaëll: Musique symphonique, musique pour piano* (Palazzetto Bru Zane / Ediciones Singulares ES 1022), 21–37 (here 25). The set is volume 3 in the series of "[Composer] Portraits." Troester's essay also appears in a translation by Sue Rose ("A Passion for Composing") on pp. 73–88 of the book; Jaëll's letter quoted is on p. 77. My translation incorporates some phrases from the rendering of the same passage in Florence Launay and Jann Pasler, "*Le Maître* and the 'Strange Woman,' Marie Jaëll: Two Virtuoso-Composers in Resonance," in *Camille Saint-Saëns and His World*, ed. Jann Pasler (Princeton, NJ: Princeton University Press, 2012), 85–101 (here 95). A previous letter from Jaëll to Saint-Saëns (August 2, 1893) makes clear that Jaëll is referring specifically to her three Dante-inspired sets: *Ce qu'on entend dans l'Enfer / le Purgatoire / le Paradis* ("Correspondance Jaëll—Saint-Saëns," 121). But the "very new" compositional procedures in the "Dante" pieces are also central to the two sets

of short pieces *Les beaux jours* and *Les jours pluvieux*, likewise composed (or at least completed) in 1893. All five sets—which Jaëll would probably have described as "scientific" (see n. 49)—were published in 1894, the year after this letter, by Heugel. On October 8, 1894, Jaëll apparently relented and sent the works in question (presumably now published, rather than in manuscript) to Saint-Saëns; see the letter she wrote to him on that date, in Hurpeau, "Correspondance Jaëll—Saint-Saëns," 122.

40. Letter from Liszt to Jaëll, July 18, 1871 (i.e., very early in her compositional career), in Jean Chantavoine, "Lettres inédites de Liszt à Alfred et Marie Jaëll," *Revue internationale de musique* 12 (1952): 31–47, here 34. Liszt concludes with thanks to Marie for dedicating the sonata to him. The main sentences from this letter are also printed in Marie-Laure Ingelaere, "Marie Jaëll au regard de ses correspondants," in the book to the 3-CD set (see n. 39), 38–49, here 46. (Ingelaere's essay is translated by Mark Wiggins as "Marie Jaëll through the Eyes of Her Correspondents," in the same book to the CD set, 89–100.) The letters published in Hurpeau, "Liszt-Jaëll," are a selection meant to complement those in Chantavoine, "Lettres inédites." The letters published by Chantavoine are all by Liszt, except for two from Alfred Jaëll to Liszt. Marie Jaëll's relationship to Liszt is also treated (with brief quotations from letters) in Kiener, *Marie Jaëll*, 55–64.

41. See the entry for *compagnonne* at *Trésor de la langue française informatisé*: http://atilf.atilf.fr/tlf.htm. Unfortunately, the *TLFi* entry for *compositeur/-trice* does not distinguish between the masculine and female nouns. On prejudices against women composers in nineteenth-century France, see Florence Launay and Jann Pasler, "*Le Maître* and the 'Strange Woman,'"; Florence Launay, *Les compositrices en France au xixe siècle* (Paris: Fayard, 2006); and Florence Launay, "Marie Jaëll and les autres compositrices françaises de la fin du xixe siècle," in the book accompanying the 3-CD set of Jaëll's works (see n. 39), 50–56. Launay's article is translated (and in places mistranslated) by Mark Wiggins: "Marie Jaëll and the Other Women French Composers from the End of the Nineteenth Century" (101–7). Interestingly, Alfred Jaëll likewise referred to his wife in a wording that suggests that "compositeur" was for him a kind of gender-neutral word: he thanks Liszt for encouraging "la jeune compositeur" (letter to Liszt, June 9, 1876), in Hurpeau, "Correspondance Liszt-Jaëll," 94.

42. Letter from Alfred Jaëll to Liszt, September 6, 1876, reporting information that "l'ami Sander" had conveyed to him about the Liszt-Saint-Saëns performance of Jaëll's four-hand waltz set, *Douze valses et finale* (Chantavoine, "Lettres," 36). (Presumably "Sander" was the lawyer Charles Sandherr, whose wife Anna was a pianist and friend of Marie Jaëll; see the entry for Charles Sandherr in Hurpeau, *Marie Jaëll*, 254.) In several letters written by Liszt, around the same time, to Alfred alone or to both Alfred and Marie, he expresses his admiration for Marie's waltz set and proposes making some local changes to them

(Chantavoine, "Lettres," 35–37). The waltz set is sometimes said to have been published in 1874, but the letters make clear that it was still in manuscript in 1876. In addition, the manuscript offered poetic inscriptions above each movement. The work was published by F. E. C. Leuckart, Leipzig; and E. Gérard, Paris. The Gérard edition (which can be downloaded from IMSLP.com) lacks the poetic inscriptions. I have not seen the Leuckart.

43. *Ossiane* contains important parts for solo soprano and chorus (and possibly also a *récitant*) and lasts seventy to seventy-five minutes. It originally carried the German title *Götterlieder*. (Jaëll wrote the words in German and then had them translated into French by Charles Grandmougin.) The work remains unpublished, but portions of it were performed in Paris on May 13, 1879, and favorably reviewed by the composer-critic Ernest Reyer in the *Journal des débats*. Further, see Sébastien Troester, "*Ossiane* ou les *Götterlieder* de Marie Jaëll: Une oeuvre musicale hors du commun," *Association Marie Jaëll-Alsace, Lettre d'information* no. 9 (April, 2014): 2–4, and no. 10 (November, 2014): 3–5, viewable at: http://www.mariejaell-alsace.com/pdf/infos2014_05.pdf and http://www.mariejaell-alsace.com/pdf/infos2014_11.pdf. Perhaps Jaëll found the precedent of Liszt's symphonic poems—he had largely invented the genre—a little too overwhelming. But, of course, it was also easier, in general, to publish piano-solo works than ones for large ensemble. (Other Jaëll works with orchestra, even the superb cello concerto, likewise went unpublished.)

44. See n. 72 below.

45. See n. 42.

46. Remarks made by Brahms to Richard Heuberger and [Josef?] Gänsbacher (December 18, 1888). Brahms's remarks read, in full, "Es ist doch fad, wenn die Klavierspielerinnen immer dieselben Lisztschen Stücke spielen! Da lob ich mir die Jaëll! Ist eine intelligente, geistreiche Person und macht sich die Klaviersachen, die eben so schlecht sind wie die Lisztschen, selbst!" (That is: she manages to compose piano pieces on her own that are just as bad as those by Liszt.) Heuberger reports that Brahms had teased Jaëll the day before, after a solo recital of hers that he had attended in Vienna and that had consisted almost entirely of pieces by her. The first piece had been an unpublished one by Liszt: "Brahms fragte sie ganz lustig, ob der erste 'Schmarrn,' den sie gespielt habe, auch von ihr sei!" (That is, he asked her—"cheerily," which I take to mean teasingly yet not without admiration—whether the first bit of "rubbish" that she had played was by her as well.) Richard Heuberger, *Erinnerungen an Johannes Brahms, Tagebuchnotizen aus den Jahren 1875 bis 1897, erstmals vollständig herausgegeben von Kurt Hofmann*, 2nd expanded edition (Tutzing: Hans Schneider, 1975), 40.

47. The two *Jours* sets were dedicated to Kitty, Duddie, Flibbie, Ruy, and Jimmy Spalding, five children of an American family that was living in Paris; they were among Marie Jaëll's earliest piano students. (See the Spalding entry

in Hurpeau, *Marie Jaëll*, 255.) But the two sets are far more challenging in musical style than what one normally gave children to play, especially in the nineteenth century. Sketches for an orchestral version of *Les jours pluvieux* survive in the Jaëll collection at the University of Strasbourg. See a list of Jaëll's works (published and in manuscript) at http://www.mariejaell-alsace.net/pdf/catalogue.pdf.

48. There is apparently, though, no evidence that Jaëll or anybody else at the time performed all twenty-four pieces as one continuous mega-work. Nor perhaps did anybody perform all twelve pieces from one set or the other. For this reason, I give the titles of the individual movements in italics rather than between quotation marks. I think of them mainly as individual short works, not as limbs in a carefully structured whole. I would be happy to be disproven.

49. Letter from Marie Jaëll to Marie Kiener, probably c. 1904–5, as quoted in Christiane de Turckheim, "Correspondances," in Hurpeau, *Marie Jaëll*, 57–73, here 69. (Kiener, a cousin's daughter, was herself a pianist and someone to whom Jaëll wrote with particular affection and directness. Kiener gathered much of the surviving documentation about Jaëll with the aim of writing a biography of Jaëll, a project that her sister Hélène carried out—see n. 29.) The word in question, "scientifique," occurs in a passage in which Jaëll (Turckheim explains) is speaking of her own works and (I would add) sees them as related to a tradition of serious composition: "cette merveilluse musique scientifique qui est la vraie musique" ("that marvelous scientific music, which is [the only] true music"). One might at first be tempted to think that Jaëll was referring to "scientific" in the modern academic sense of that word, e.g., "scholarly" (as in the *comité scientifique* of a journal or conference) and thus referring to music that showed a rich awareness of past styles (e.g., Bach) or of scholarly approaches to musical works. But surely the phrase that she would have used in that case was *musique savante*. Jaëll's method of piano playing and pedagogy was, of course, scientific in yet another sense, the everyday one, meaning something like "based on current-day research experiments (in such fields as, here, physiology and psychology)." A contemporary (Jacques Vincent) probably had this latter sense in mind, because of Jaëll's writings and pedagogical principles, when describing her as a *pianiste scientifique*: Hurpeau, "Correspondance Jaëll—Saint-Saëns," 121.

50. In ibid. (See the excerpt quoted above in the main text, to which n. 38 is attached.)

51. Satie likewise uses grace notes as essential melodic notes (indeed, in conjunct motion) in *Gnossienne* no. 1 (published 1893—i.e., the same year as his *Vexations* and her piece under discussion here, *On rêve au mauvais temps*). Jaëll, living in Paris, may well have known Satie's published pieces, though presumably not *Vexations* (first published in 1969).

52. The clash will recur in measure 34, at the end of the nearly complete restatement of the opening melody. Pianist Dana Ciorlie (in the 3-CD set—see n. 39) downplays the clash in measure 13, emphasizes it in measure 34.
53. I think I also hear some Schumann in this piece but cannot identify one particular piece of his that resembles it closely. The pianist Alexandre Sorel likewise finds Schumannesque features in various of Jaëll's works ("L'œuvre").
54. "Souvent ses fins coupent brusquement le morceau sans le conclure; d'autres fois, surtout dans la dernière période de son activité, les œuvres se terminent par des phrases qui s'éteignent comme *si le souffle de Dieu se retirait d'elles*" (Jaëll, Liszt program booklet, 29, emphasis added). The words that Jaëll italicized seem indebted to various passages from the Bible about death, e.g., Ecclesiastes 12:7 and Job 34:14–15.
55. See above, at the passage to which n. 46 is attached.
56. See Amy Bauer's discussion of how Ligeti reworked the trope of heroic virtuosity: "From Pulsation to Sensation: Virtuosity and Modernism in Ligeti's First and Ninth Piano Etudes," *Contemporary Music Review* 38, nos. 3–4 (2019): 344–65.
57. Kregor discusses, but distances himself from, a tendency among certain writers—whom he does not name—that sees in Liszt's experimental late style an anticipation of late twentieth-century minimalist works by, say, Reich and Glass (*Liszt as Transcriber* [Cambridge: Cambridge University Press, 2010, 191). Shay Loya, a few years later, invoked minimalism in regard to Liszt's late works (*Liszt's Transcultural Modernism*, 41; see also 33–34, 41, 258n9, and the chapter on late style: 225–51). [Ed.] See also Loya's contribution to this volume.
58. Troester, "Passion," 25–26 (and, in the English translation, 77). Troester specifically draws comparisons between the three *Ce qu'on entend* collections (with their intense and varied repetition of short motives), Satie's *Vexations*, and also (as others have done regarding Liszt) later-era repetition-based and minimalist works. He presumably has in mind such composers as Cage, Glass, and Reich. (See also Launay and Pasler, "*Le Maître* and the 'Strange Woman,'" 94.) *Vexations* consists of four statements of a bass melody, either alone or with startling material over it, and carries a puzzling inscription that seems to suggest that what Satie calls the *motif* (the bass line? the whole little piece?) be repeated 804 times, a feat that takes many hours and has sometimes been carried out in recent decades.
59. Jaëll perhaps knew a somewhat similar piece by another didactically inclined composer: Antoine Reicha's *Fantaisie sur un seul accord*, which is no. 4 in his *Practische Beispiele* (1803). The fantasy has been recorded by pianist Ivan Ilić on *Reicha Rediscovered*, vol. 1 (Chandos CD 10950). Unlike Jaëll's piece, Reicha's does at times suggest a second (unstated) chord—the dominant—by pausing on the fifth degree by itself. Of course, there are also extended passages on a

single chord (heard, inevitably, as tonic) at the beginning or end of various lengthy works (e.g., the opening of Wagner's *Das Rheingold* and the opening and closing of Schoenberg's *Gurrelieder*). But to base an entire short piece on one chord is to make a different kind of aesthetic statement.

60. André Gide, *Notes on Chopin* (1948), trans. Bernard Frechtman (New York: Philosophical Library, 1949), 46: "One should not seek to diminish the effect of the discord [in mm. 10–15], whether by the pedal or by a timid *pianissimo*. . . . Oh! no, indeed, this is not a concert piece. . . . But played in a whisper for oneself alone, its indefinable emotion cannot be exhausted, nor that kind of almost physical terror, as if one were before a world glimpsed in passing, of a world hostile to tenderness, from which human affection is excluded."

61. See Lawrence Kramer, *Music as Cultural Practice, 1800–1900* (Berkeley: University of California Press, 1990), 72–101, beginning with a discussion of Gide's remark. Further on the A-Minor Prelude, see Zbigniew Granat, "Chopin's Tones, Schubert's Words: The Secret Programme of the A[-]Minor Prelude," Kamila Stępień-Kutera, ed., *The Lyric and the Vocal Element in Instrumental Music of the Nineteenth Century* (Warsaw: The Fryderyk Chopin Institute, 2017), 139–53.

62. And yet another is Beethoven. Some of the Bagatelles, and portions of the Phantasie, op. 77, are not difficult to execute but borderline bizarre in their sequence of ideas. See, for example, Hugh Macdonald, "Beethoven's Game of Cat and Mouse," in his *Beethoven's Century: Essays on Composers and Themes* (Rochester, NY: University of Rochester Press, 2008), 3–15.

63. "Easy to sing" includes the fact that the range in many Schubert songs is conveniently narrow. "Die liebe Farbe" requires exactly an octave, whereas numerous opera arias of the day require something closer to two octaves. Another practical advantage for use in home or school: a narrow-ranged song can be sung simultaneously by many singers regardless of their vocal category (soprano, alto, tenor, or bass). Or it can be sung solo successively by several different singers without the pianist's having to transpose the keyboard part.

64. I should mention that certain works of another highly cosmopolitan composer, Charles Martin Loeffler (1861–1935), show parallels to the religious-reflective side of Liszt's output, e.g., Loeffler's *By the Rivers of Babylon*, op. 3, for chorus, two flutes, solo cello, harp, and organ (1901), a work that—in its instrumentation and in other respects—may, I propose, have been partly modeled on Liszt's Elegy no. 1 just mentioned. The importance of Liszt for Loeffler has not been much noted. Most strikingly, Loeffler uses Gregorian chants in several of his works: for example, the "Dies Irae" appears (to disparate expressive purposes) in the first of the Two Rhapsodies for Oboe, Viola, and Piano (1901) and in the colorful, if highly episodic orchestral work *La villanelle du diable*, op. 9 (1901). (The Two Rhapsodies and the *Villanelle*—though they are purely instrumental—are freely based on songs that Loeffler wrote to poems by Maurice

Rollinat.) Most of all, the final movement of the Divertissement in A Minor for Violin and Orchestra ends with a movement that is entitled "Carnaval des morts" and consists of a long set of variations on, again, the "Dies Irae." (The divertissement received its premiere in Berlin in 1905, with Karl Halir as soloist and Richard Strauss conducting.) Several other Gregorian chants are used extensively in the *Music for Four Stringed Instruments*. Loeffler, though born in Berlin, identified strongly with France and even misled friends and writers into thinking that he had been born in Alsace. He had a strong attraction to Catholicism. Though he may never have converted (much less taken priestly orders, as Liszt did), he spent some months, in midlife, at a largely silent retreat at a Benedictine abbey in Austria. Loeffler presumably knew at least some of Liszt's religion-tinted pieces: almost surely *Totentanz* (which, like the lengthy finale of Loeffler's divertissement, is essentially a set of variations on the "Dies Irae" chant) and perhaps also, as I just posited, the Elegy no. 1. For a reliable, basic account of Loeffler's life and work, see Ellen Knight, *Charles Martin Loeffler: A Life Apart in American Music* (Urbana: University of Illinois Press, 1993).

65. Jonathan Kregor, *Liszt as Transcriber*, 186–219. On *Pensée des morts*, see n. 67.
66. Still, there is, as I hope I have helped make clear, something special and disconcerting about pieces by Liszt that fulfill all four of those criteria, pieces largely written (or revised for the last time) in his final decade.
67. These phrases are from Lamartine's preface to his poetry collection *Harmonies poétiques et religieuses*, as reprinted by Liszt at the head of his eponymous piano piece published in 1835 (see translation in Kregor, *Liszt as Transcriber*, 195). Liszt reused most of these quotations again in 1853, placing them at the head of his ten-piece set bearing the same four-word title that the single piece had had in 1835. See Andrew Haringer, "Liszt and the Legacy of Lamartine," in Deaville and Saffle, *Liszt's Legacies*, 72–91.
68. Jaëll, Liszt program booklet, 4–5.
69. "En m'addressant à quelques-uns plutôt qu'à la foule" (Jaëll, Liszt program booklet, 4–5; the full preface to the *Album* is reproduced widely in the Liszt literature).
70. On the importance of getting to know music that no longer survives in the active performance and classroom repertoires, see Jim Samson, "The Musical Work and Nineteenth-Century History," in Jim Samson, ed., *Cambridge History of Nineteenth-Century Music* (Cambridge: Cambridge University Press, 2001), 3–28; and my "Nineteenth-Century Music: Quantity, Quality, Qualities," *Nineteenth-Century Music Review* 1 (2004): 3–41.
71. See Alan Walker, *Franz Liszt, Volume 3*, 440 (Friedheim), 444–46 (Mansfeldt).
72. Jaëll, for example, had plentiful time alone with Liszt in residence in the Weimar Altenburg, so perhaps was shown certain pieces that he normally

kept to himself. In May 1884, Lina Ramann and others came to Liszt's house where "we found Mme Jaëll. She frequently reads and composes at his residence [*bei ihm*]" (Lina Ramann, *Lisztiana: Erinnerungen an Franz Liszt in Tagebuchblättern, Briefen und Dokumenten aus den Jahren 1873–1886/87*, ed. Arthur Seidl, rev. Friedrich Schnapp [Mainz: Schott, 1983], 228–29). There are numerous references in the recollections of Liszt's pupils to Marie Jaëll's attending concerts with Liszt and a few others, or dining out in similar small company, or playing pieces of hers for Liszt and the assembled students: e.g., Carl Lachmund, *Living with Liszt, from the Diary of Carl Lachmund, an American Pupil of Liszt, 1882–1884*, ed. Alan Walker (Stuyvesant, NY: Pendragon Press, 1995), 45–46, 184, 185, 221, 276. Lachmund also reports (206) (events of July 2, 1883) that Jaëll's four-hand waltzes were played by Alfred Reisenauer and Liszt, with Henryk van Zeyl taking over when Liszt's eyesight forced him to stop.

73. Might Bartók, for example, have had some of Liszt's technically modest yet musically questing works in mind when he penned the first fifty or so pieces in his six-volume *Mikrokosmos* (1926–39)?

74. One last thought: I am tempted to propose that, in such "easy yet complex pieces" as this article has explored, the composers have stumbled upon a musical equivalent of what cultural critic Elizabeth Janeway calls the "powers of the weak," that is, the ability of people who are seemingly not in positions of great effectiveness to turn their supposed weakness into a tool that can help them resist domination or, more generally, help them make things happen (overtly or covertly) that benefit themselves, their family members, or some group to which they belong or have been societally assigned. The "weak," in Janeway's understanding, have included, in various places and times, such massive population categories as women, children, the elderly, and the disabled, as well as certain ethnic, racial, and religious groups. Janeway's book title *The Powers of the Weak* (New York: Albert A. Knopf, 1980) is, of course, purposefully paradoxical.

Chapter Eleven

Virtuosity in Liszt's Late Piano Works

Shay Loya

Liszt's so-called late style is famous for sparse textures, compact and repetitive phrases, dissonance, borderline post-tonality, and general oddness. It is largely a small group of miniature piano works—works in the mold of the iconic *Nuages gris*—that have sealed the reputation of this music for enigmatic, intransigent, and prophetic "lateness." The smallness and stylistic narrowness of this repertoire, however, misrepresents Liszt's wider oeuvre from the 1870s and 1880s, a problem that has occasionally been raised and addressed in recent Liszt literature. James M. Baker, for example, has noted that works depicting "death, premonition, and mourning" have attracted disproportionate attention "thanks primarily to their daringly experimental harmony," which has marginalized "other equally important pieces." His more equitable survey of piano works from 1869 to 1886 serves as a partial redress.[1] In her monograph *Liszt's Final Decade*, Dolores Pesce has similarly explored neglected repertoire, especially sacred works by Liszt, revealing a greater plurality of styles and affects in the composer's late oeuvre.[2] And in my own research I have tried to counter a tendency to homogenize a "late style" through post-tonal analysis.[3]

A general fascination with the aesthetic extremity of a single, overarching late style persists, nevertheless, and one important aspect of this aesthetic extremity seems to be defined by what Ralph P. Locke has conceptualized in this volume as "anti-virtuosity" (see chapter 10). This presents a special challenge for a study of virtuosity in the late solo piano works. The problem is not solved by merely pointing to the well-known fact that virtuosity can be found in many of these works, but to a lesser extent (none of the late solo-piano works is quite as technically demanding as the virtuoso works from c. 1830–63). We cannot get away from the predictable, generic context of virtuosity, which brings the whole issue of implicit incompatibility between Lisztian virtuosity and late style into sharp relief. To take only a few examples from the original works (table 11.1, below; transcriptions will be discussed later in this chapter), virtuosity is often aligned with genre, as in earlier decades of the nineteenth century. The waltzes, marches, and national dances all relate to virtuoso salon pieces, and it is equally predictable to find brilliant passages in a character piece that tone-paints "water play" (*jeux d'eau*). This ostensibly demonstrates that it is not virtuosity that distinguishes these highly original Lisztian pieces from the more commonplace salon fare but other elements more commonly associated with the "late style," of which harmony is probably the most important. It logically follows that virtuosity is coincidental with rather than integral to the late style, an unreflective habit that persisted in Liszt's playing and writing—in contradistinction to his daring harmonic experiments.

Conversely, the further we get from the late style and period, the more virtuosity once more assumes its place as the most widely recognized aspect of Liszt and his music, and this is especially true once we get further back, beyond the year 1848. Considering the historical importance of the pianistic innovations of the 1830s, the so-called *Glanzzeit*, or *Glanzperiode*, of 1838–47, and more broadly the cult of virtuosity in the 1820s, 1830s, and 1840s, the intense scholarly interest in Liszt's virtuosity in this earlier era seems only logical.

Table 11.1: Select original works, ordered according to genre, featuring virtuosity

Fast march genre: *Ungarischer Geschwindmarsch* (1870–71), *Revive Szegedin!* (1879)

Stately march genre: *Bülow-Marsch* (1883), *László Teleki* (1885)

[4] *Valses oubliées* (1881–85)

Mephisto Waltzes nos. 2–4, *Mephisto Polka* and *Bagatelle sans tonalité* (1879–85)

Csárdás macabre (1881), *Csárdás no. 1* + *Csárdás obstinée* (1884–85)

Rhapsodies hongroises nos. 16–19 (1882–85)

Toccata (?1879)

Character piece: "Jeux d'eau à la villa d'Este" (composed 1877) from the *Années de pèlerinage: Troisième année* (1883).

There is a reason why studies of Liszt's virtuosity (rather than, say, harmony or form) look for and find rich picking primarily in this earlier period of his creativity.[4] Liszt's very public transformation in 1848 from a touring virtuoso to Kapellmeister and composer has created a tangible dividing line in scholarly interests, despite the equally palpable persistence of virtuosity in his works. It is as if virtuosity suddenly became less important or otherwise subsumed within something greater. Carl Dahlhaus memorably associated Liszt's career change with deeper cultural shifts, arguing it was emblematic of a wider transition from an age of improvised virtuosity to a post-1848 age of valorized large-scale, logically constructed "musical works."[5]

One has to wonder whether musicological periodization tendencies have overdetermined a tripartite split into interests in Liszt's virtuosity (early years), innovative forms (mainly Weimar period), and post-tonal harmony (mainly in works from the 1870s and, even more so, the 1880s).[6] It is inevitable that intensive research interests in abstract aspects of music such as harmony and form mostly preclude the kind of formal, historical, and reception studies that the phenomenon of virtuosity (as music, spectacle, and business) attracts. Yet it is hard to ignore progressive changes in Liszt's compositional style that lend substantive, technical reasons for the loss of scholarly focus on virtuosity from 1848 onward. Liszt's many revisions of previous works during the Weimar period evince a conscious decision to reduce the virtuoso "excesses" of previous versions, partly in response to changes in pianos, partly to make them more accessible to other virtuoso pianists, and partly to remove virtuosity as a distraction from the value of the works as compositions—and the value of Liszt as a composer (the revision history of the piano études being a famous case).[7] If anything, this trend continued in Liszt's composition in subsequent decades and ended with those final works from the 1880s related to dance genres. We already noted that in such generic contexts, it is not obvious why virtuosity should command much attention when it seems like an unremarkable remnant of the past, in contrast to the avant-garde harmony.

But could there be another story about virtuosity in the late works that requires other criteria of interest? In an essay from 1980, Alfred Brendel made two observations that represent, respectively, two different ways of seeing this phenomenon. The first is the more commonplace story that posits late works as the austere, modernist antithesis to the exuberance of Liszt's virtuoso years:

> Only recently, almost a hundred years after they were written, have they emerged as music that can be played and conveyed to a listening public. It is not, however, from the nineteenth-century concert stage, from the pomp and

intoxication of virtuosity, that these works grow. They do not seek to be persuasive; they hardly even seek to convince. In Liszt's own words, "exuberance of heart" gave way to "bitterness of heart," a bitterness that had various sources [a list of biographical tragedies follows]. . . . "Infirmary music" was his own term for much of what he then composed.[8]

Here "virtuosity" is narrowly understood to be of the *Glanzzeit* type: seductive, charming, bombastic, and musically insubstantial. But elsewhere in the same essay, Brendel warns against imposing "a paralyzing slowness and pallor" on the performance of the late works, shrewdly observing that "Liszt's entire range of pianistic refinement, acquired over long years of experience, has a part to play even in the most awkward sounds this music makes. An enormous stock of nuances should be felt to be available in the background, even when they seem to remain unused."[9] Brendel is surely on to something here, but equally, quite a lot remains unsaid. If late works are not a product of "the nineteenth-century concert stage" and "the pomp and intoxication of virtuosity," then what exactly are the assumptions underpinning the implicit contrast between bad (*Glanzzeit*-like) and good (late) virtuosity?

It is the *quality* of "late" virtuosity that demands an analysis of genre: a context for where virtuosity is expected and then how it is realized, or conversely how and why it is downplayed or even thwarted. Of course, such an analysis cannot and should not escape influential discourses of lateness and modernism that have shaped scholarly thinking about Liszt's late works, particularly in the latter half of the twentieth century. We therefore begin with a brief look at these discourses in relation to virtuosity, and then turn to a few representative compositions, giving equal attention to original works and arrangements, and some attention to select recordings. The discussion here is limited to Liszt's solo piano works, although it can be applied to his wider repertoire.

Liszt's Modernist Rehabilitation and the Lateness Discourse

The late works played an important role in proclaiming Liszt as a precursor of twentieth-century musical modernism, and writings in that vein can be traced back to influential arguments made in the 1930s by Béla Bartók and the Liszt scholar (then at the beginning of his career) Zoltán Gárdonyi.[10] Liszt's "modernist rehabilitation," as I have referred to it elsewhere, was an unabashedly elitist project that pitted "serious" aspects of Liszt's composition—and aspects associated with modernism in particular—against anything deemed to be populist and flashy.[11] A good example of this selectiveness can be gleaned from a concert for the fiftieth anniversary of Liszt's death the young Humphrey Searle (then a student) mounted in Oxford on November 8, 1936. An unusually high proportion of it featured what then were rarely heard, or never-before heard late works like the *Csárdás macabre* (S. 224 / LW A313, 1881–82) the Third Mephisto Waltz (S. 216 / LW A325, 1883), *La lugubre gondola* (S. 200/2 / LW A319b, 1885), and *Schlaflos! Frage und Antwort* (S. 203 LW / A322, 1883) and earlier, equally rare and historically avant-garde works such as *Der Traurige Mönch* (S. 348 / LW P3, 1860) and *Malédiction* for piano and string orchestra (S. 121 / LW H1, 1833–40).[12] With the exception of the *Grand galop chromatique* (though in an unusual version for two pianos, eight hands, arranged by János Végh), more popular works by Liszt, and especially those that have given him a reputation as a composer of show pieces, were left out of this anniversary concert. It was not virtuosity per se that had been rejected: rather, Liszt's virtuosity had to be aligned with a kind of modernist *Werktreue* against the *culture* of nineteenth-century virtuosity that placed performer over composer.[13] The same bias toward Liszt's oeuvre can be observed in Bartók's "Liszt Problems" article (also from 1936), where technically brilliant works such as *Totentanz* (for piano and orchestra, 1847–64, arranged by Liszt for piano solo, 1865) and *Les jeux d'eaux à la Villa d'Este* (S. 163/4 / LW A283/4, 1877) are valorized for their modernism, whereas works such as the operatic paraphrases and Hungarian Rhapsodies are treated as a regrettable concession to the debased public taste of Liszt's time.[14]

After the Second World War, Liszt's modernist rehabilitation gathered steam through historic publications of the late piano works by the British Liszt Society in the early 1950s and by pioneering recordings by Louis Kentner (1951), Alfred Brendel (1958), and Sergio Fiorentino (1963). Scholarly publications in the 1950s and 1960s began to focus on post-tonal aspects of Liszt's harmony, supplying plenty of short-scale yet tantalizing examples, whereas the last quarter of the twentieth century saw the rise of a more systematic approach led by US theorists employing modified Schenkerian analysis and pitch-class-set analysis.[15] This discourse in particular narrowed down the issue of Liszt's modernism—and the valorization of Liszt as a modernist—to the litmus test of post-tonality. Underlying it was an evolutionist view of tonality that posits post-tonality as a logical end goal of musical modernity.[16] Virtuosity was irrelevant to this march of progress, and incompatible with the mode of analysis offered to describe it. It remained even more disassociated from that metaphorical spear Liszt famously wished to hurl "into the undefinable void of the future."[17]

The most important and broadest aspect of Liszt's rehabilitation—the idea that had conferred on his last works metaphysical grandeur—was the notion that they are "late works" that reside outside the normal course of music history. Liszt, of course, fits the mold effortlessly: the "prophetic" post-tonality combined with old age and deteriorating health; the notable stylistic differences between the music of his youth and the music of his old age; the fact that several of these works remained unpublished; and the expressive oddities of some of these unpublished works that reinforce the image of intransigence and "writing against the grain," as articulated by Edward Said after Theodor Adorno.[18] All of this is at odds with the virtuosity associated with the younger Liszt, particularly its sensual, crowd-pleasing, and conquering aspects, which—as mentioned—exists in the context of a completely different kind of reception and scholarship.

It might be useful to think, therefore, of the scholarly discourses on late style and virtuosity as two mutually repelling force fields of ideas and practices. The forces of repulsion have only increased as the modernist rehabilitation of Liszt embraced the late repertoire, while new and more systemic studies of Liszt's virtuosity continued to focus on the 1830s and 1840s (leaving a gap of two or three decades in between). The "*Glanzzeit* bias" of the virtuosity discourse could be said to be the flip side of the modernist rehabilitation, and together they might account for the (admittedly) crude, if clear, set of binary oppositions in table 11.2.

It should be clear from the above that if "lateness" pulls to aesthetic extremes, then in some works the quality of "lateness" is more extreme than in others. And if we can speak of a degree or quality of lateness, then is it possible virtuosity may have functioned as an antithetical quality, somehow reducing or moderating the "modernism" and "latenessness" of some of Liszt works from the 1870s and 1880s, while making them appealing in other ways. But abandon this dichotomous thinking and a more interesting question emerges. If lateness is indeed a quality, is it possible that it had touched and transformed Liszt's virtuosity of old? Is there such a thing as "late virtuosity"?

Lateness Tropes and the Case of the Late Hungarian Rhapsodies

We have already seen that Alfred Brendel has grappled with something like a lateness quality of virtuosity when he warned pianists on the one hand to avoid interpreting it in a way that results in "paralyzing slowness" and on the

Table 11.2: Binary oppositions between the early and late period of Liszt's life

Early period and timeliness	Late period and lateness
Youth, health, athleticism, optimism	Old age, infirmity, resignation, pessimism
Public, extrovert, outgoing	Private, introvert, retiring
Earthly, physical	Transcendent, metaphysical
Musically insubstantial	Musically profound
Emphasis on performance event	Work concept (*Werktreue*)
Morally suspect	Morally elevated
Popular, accessible, generic	Modernist, difficult, anti-generic
Tonal, mostly simple harmony	Post-tonal, strange surface chromaticism
Flamboyant, colorful, full textures	Ascetic, grey, spare textures
Of its time, epoch making	Outside and ahead of its time.

other to be sensitive to "an enormous stock of nuances" that somehow exists "in the background, even when they seem to remain unused." This defines the quality of late virtuosity as being *latent* or apparitional, an unrealized (but felt) potential, or a disembodied visitation from the past rather than the full-bodied phenomenon, which is why performers ought to develop a sixth sense for it (how they might do that remains a mystery). A somewhat similar description of this quality comes from Zoltán Gárdonyi and István Szelényi in their preface to the 1973 *Neue Liszt Ausgabe* (*NLA*) publication of the Hungarian Rhapsodies: "Only the formal scheme of slow-fast [*lassú-friss*] is taken from [the previous fifteen rhapsodies]. In place of the earlier richness in part-writing, near orchestral colorfulness and luxuriant ornamentation, there emerges a strange, new, concise piano style, the content of which is frequently contained within a single voice-part. The cadenza-like moments have also become rarer and now form, as it were, symbolic memories of the once overflowing richness of fantasy."[19] Here we have once more the suggestion of a visitation from the past ("symbolic memories") and of a skeletal virtuosity, stripped down to the bone. There is only a hint here that the shriveling of sound is somehow comparable to the physical decline of the artist. But more explicit forms of this discourse are abundant enough, and the many examples provided by Sam Smiles in his recent genealogical inquiry into the lateness discourse shows how a particularly positive, even valorizing, critical view of late art produced by "great" artists in physical decline came into its own in the early twentieth century. Among several examples, he quotes from an essay by Georg Simmel (1905):

> In some of the greatest artists, extreme old age can bring about a development which seems to reveal the purest and most essential of their art precisely through the actual and natural decline of their vital powers. Forcefulness of form and shape, allure of sensual presentation, and unconstrained abandonment of the immediacy of the world fall away, leaving only the really bold lines—the most profound and personal signs of their creativity.... [Nature] uses destruction [of the artist's body] to extract the eternal out of the extraneous and disingenuous.[20]

The two quotations above both assume artistic greatness as a given and then compare in similar terms the stylistic transformation occurring at the end of such an uncommon creative life, even though the first does this in more neutral, less laudatory terms. Both also map easily unto some of the binaries of table 11.2, beyond the specific situation of any artist or artwork. In fact, the second quotation is not about Liszt or even about the nineteenth century or music; yet its enthusiastic endorsement of how a late style reveals the "purest and most essential" aspects of Leonardo da Vinci's artistry could be applied to Liszt verbatim. The problem for late Liszt, then, is that the glamorizing tropes of late style are implicitly inimical to his virtuosity. Certainly *Glanzzeit* virtuosity would fit Simmel's descriptions of "the extraneous and disingenuous" in a work of art. But the bigger problem may be the limits placed on repertoire exploration by a late-style perspective. According to Gordon McMullan, Smiles's coeditor of *Late Style and Its Discontents*, the metaphysical and ahistorical aesthetic categories of lateness seriously limit art criticism, for despite generating intensely personal stories about artists and their work, they are, in fact, completely generic: readily applicable without being specific to a particular life, a work of art, or a historical period.[21] McMullan's solution is not to abolish a late-style perspective but to develop a keener critical awareness of its shortcomings and work this awareness back into the appraisal of a late work of art.[22]

Coming back to virtuosity in Liszt's late Hungarian Rhapsodies, we can understand the issues outlined above in two ways. First, and most obviously, a characterization of lateness such as the one offered by Gárdonyi and Szelényi in relation to the last four rhapsodies (composed 1881–85), should be scrutinized for the way it may distort the role of virtuosity in these works. Second, one has to decide how to work an awareness of late-style discourse into such scrutiny: what aspects of lateness, if any, are still useful despite the self-evident problems of this discourse? A simple beginning would be to point out that not all four of these rhapsodies match Gárdonyi's and Szelényi's description equally well. Of the four, Rhapsody no. 17 is the best fit, after which numbers 18, 16, and 19 are increasingly less so, certainly if one compares their fast sections.

As I have shown in some detail in an article dedicated to number 17, that rhapsody is not only the shortest and most condensed but also the most antigeneric of the four in its denial, or distortion, of multiple expectations.[23] Most flagrantly, the expected virtuoso finale with a major-mode ending is replaced by a conclusion that makes use of purely monodic passagework with a tonally ambiguous ending (none of the other rhapsodies does that). I agree with the founding editors of *NLA* that at least in this work there are plenty of "symbolic memories of the once overflowing richness of fantasy" in the form of idiomatic textures and figures that can thus be read as gnomic signs for something once familiar.

Number 18 is only a little longer, and shares with number 17 the "strange, new, concise piano style," but it also conforms to the norms of parallel-major conclusion and virtuoso final section.[24] In the *friss* (fast-paced) section, the virtuoso introduction to the main theme in measures 40–56 is generic, even if the harmony leading to the stable A-major theme is not. If there is any symbolic, abstract, and therefore "late" virtuosity, it is found in the anti-generic manner that the main theme itself is denied a virtuoso textural development, which is partly dictated by the brevity of this section and the extremely condensed proportions of the piece as a whole (compare with the virtuoso variations in the F-sharp major section that ends Rhapsody no. 8, m. 139ff.). By contrast, the *friss* section of Rhapsody no. 16 allows the main theme to develop virtuoso figuration, and despite a certain concision in some passages (arpeggios rarely span more than an octave, and figurations often fall within a fixed hand position), overall the textures of this piece are not that far from the "near orchestral colorfulness and luxuriant ornamentation" of previous rhapsodies.[25]

Rhapsody no. 19 takes us even closer to that more familiar world, despite the occasional "late" harmonic idiom and few figurative abstractions, notably at the lassù (slow-tempo) opening and the end.[26] Much of that movement, and even more so the concluding *friss*, feature lush, virtuoso pianistic textures, and the harmony of many measures could have been written in the 1850s. At a much greater remove than Rhapsody no. 16, number 19 makes untenable the idea that a "late" virtuoso genre is defined by the absence or negation of virtuosity. But, no matter. Lateness is a resilient discourse that can offer many different explications and adapt itself flexibly to the musical material. Here is Alan Walker's take on the style of Liszt's final rhapsody: "The piece attracts our attention because it goes against the general trend of his late compositions, with their sparse textures and experimental harmonies. Based on themes from Kornél Ábranyi's *Csárdás nobles*, this rhapsody blazes with color and demands exceptional virtuosity; it is almost as if Liszt was seized with nostalgia and were trying to recapture the days of his youth."[27] And below are two examples reproduced in Walker, one demonstrating, in his words, "cascading cimbalom effects based on the 'Gypsy' scale" (my ex. 11.1 quotes two extra measures for a later purpose); the other, a passage from the *friss* (vivace) section, showing the most virtuoso variant of theme (ex. 11.2; I quote only four measures). Here, Walker writes, "the music reaches a real paroxysm of excitement, and exhibits a level of delirium rare in the compositions of Liszt's old age; it has the pianist's hands racing back and forth across the keyboard with abandon, as if in emulation of the Gypsy bands itself."[28] These exoticizing references to pianistic emulation of Gypsy-band virtuosity, a familiar association with the older rhapsodies, would become increasingly less applicable to numbers 16, 18 and 17, in this order, which happens to be the reverse of the order in which we have so far proceeded. Evidently, a nostalgic, quasi-exotic evocation of virtuosity from a younger age is not the same thing as abstracted/negated virtuosity; more than that, two categories of lateness applied to the same repertoire can be diametrically opposed.

Yes, it is slightly unfair to make this point on the back of a short preface to the Hungarian Rhapsodies and a biography (Walker's) that invariably focuses on the life rather than the works, and it does not invalidate the points these authors have made. It does, however, highlight a problematic relationship between the lateness discourse, with its readily used stock categories, and the quality of virtuosity in Liszt's late works that may bring such categories into conflict. A closer examination of musical detail makes this point even better. Example 11.1 is, on the one hand, emblematic of the lush figurations of old and, on the other, demonstrates some abstraction in its two-voice schematic repetition and intervallic content. A good point of comparison is the more "topically correct" way Liszt presents a classical *verbunkos*-minor scale in the slow section of number 13 (in A minor: A–B–C–D♯–E–F–G♯). The more topical intervallic content is complemented by an impression of freely improvised, luxurious, oriental ornamentation. The quality of example 11.1 is different in several ways. The harmonic-major scale (in A: A–B–C♯–D–E–F–G♯) gives it a bright color, further enhanced by the descending parallel sixths, where major-sixth intervals predominate—a somewhat unusual sonority

Example 11.1. Hungarian Rhapsody no. 19, S. 244/19 (1885), mm. 24–28

Example 11.2. Hungarian Rhapsody no. 19, S. 244/19 (1885), mm. 260–63

for an otherwise familiar topos. The schematic patterning creates a further alienating effect. The way the lower voice joins the first, then the completely synchronous sequences up to the equally schematic rhythmic augmentation in measure 28 (quadrupling of note values) seem almost mechanical or oddly "neoclassical" in comparison with earlier, more varied and therefore seemingly spontaneous passagework.

Of course this does not mean a performance of the passage in example 11.1 needs to sound mechanical. It exists in relation to previous generic equivalents and to an oral performance practice of both Gypsy-band musicians and classical piano performers, which suggests some tempo flexibility. One can readily understand the *crescendo* in Liszt's score to also mean "accelerando" and the augmentation in measure 28 to suggest a gradual slowing down before. Recording artists seem to follow this general understanding, to judge by a short but instructive samples from Szidon (1972, 01:19–01:38), Campanella (1974, 01:08–01:24), Howard (1999, 01:10–01:24), Jandó (1999, 00:59–01:13), and Pizarro (2006, 01:02–01:19).[29] If there are any notable differences, apart from pedaling and global tempo decisions, it is in the way the rhythmic augmentation in measure 28 is interpreted. Of the five, Campanella provides the most literal reading, reverting to the slow note values abruptly and without any "softening" ritenuto and enhancing this rhythmic rigor by giving the slow (sixteenth) notes a sharp staccato articulation. Quasi-mathematical, rhythmic literalism in this context can be understood as a neoclassical aesthetic that negates virtuoso traditions associated with the Hungarian Rhapsodies. Equally, a modernist negation of traditional virtuosity is not inherent in the score but is entirely in the mind and hands of the performing artist. It becomes a question of how much artists know or care about generic traditions or the extent to which they believe "late" Liszt ought to receive a modernist (explicitly anti-Romantic) interpretation as a mark of respect.[30]

The right-hand figuration and technique in example 11.2 arguably gives a more straightforward impression of old-fashioned virtuosity and may indeed be a throwback to the pianism of the 1830s (there are many famous examples of such figurations from Chopin as well as Liszt).[31] Nevertheless, a comparison with appearances of this technique in the older rhapsodies will make the general remarks of the *NLA* editors surprisingly relevant again. The nearest equivalent to this passage is the concluding presto section of number 1 (composed in 1851). This presto exhibits a much richer, quasi-orchestral texture, and in the manner of a typical virtuoso culmination, it is sustained and intensified all the way to the closing chords. The passage in number 19, by contrast, is a rather short-lived, texturally sparser, twelve-measure virtuoso variant of *part* of the main theme. It flares up suddenly (in two places: mm. 260–71 and mm. 374–85) and stops just as abruptly in the middle of the work. It does not constitute any culminating point or climax.

Both categories of nostalgia and abstraction seem to exist in tension here, but between them they leave quite a lot unexplained. A relatively more concise and disjointed virtuoso style does not *necessarily* point to the lateness trope of limited physical stamina or stripping down excess to the essential truth, or at least we should also consider first some other possibilities in this specific generic context. Again, a comparison with the presto of number 1 is useful, because both reference to some extent the sound and technique of the cimbalom (a type of Gypsy-band zither), but the passage in measures 260–71 of number 19 does this more successfully because of the thinner texture, the avoidance of additional orchestral associations, and the impression given of a short instrumental solo within a band. Likewise, the way the left-hand part mostly follows the melody in parallel sixths emulates the parallel motion of the Gypsy bass, albeit in a more abstract fashion.[32] This is not to deny the qualities of concision, disjointedness, (relative) textural sparseness, and schematic counterpoint but to argue that observing such qualities should not end with a facile reconfirmation of lateness. Rather, it should lead to the examination of how they operate within the world of piano virtuosity, how they interact with traditions and generic expectations at a specific point in history.

Worldly Paraphrases and the Case of *Aida*

We have seen how retrospection and nostalgia provide one context for the virtuosity of Rhapsody no. 19. This is the part of the late-style narrative I am quite suspicious of, not because it is necessarily false, but because on its own it is too incomplete and creates an exaggerated image of inwardness and withdrawal, as if Liszt were writing for himself. In fact, what explains such virtuosity is *engagement* with the world and current musical trends within it, an aspect of Liszt's old age much highlighted in Dolores Pesce's *Liszt's Final Decade* (2014). Again, genre provides the most straightforward reason for the different place number 19 occupies within the group of the last four rhapsodies. Numbers 16–18 are all, unusually, works not based on previous material, and the elemental thematic material easily lends itself to the kind of fragmentary treatment and various levels of abstractions we see in those works. Number 19 is, by contrast, a transcription of a *csárdás* composed in a popular style, and there Liszt's expansion of the form and insertions of more modern-sounding harmony certainly engaged with the musical scene in Budapest.[33]

Liszt's persistent virtuosity was a marker of worldly engagement that stood for certain cultural values. If we look more broadly at virtuoso transcriptions from the 1870s and 1880s, some are dedicated to opera (principally Wagner and Verdi) as expected, but there are also many transcriptions dedicated to works in a dance style, mostly by composers outside the German tradition (see table 11.3). What Liszt typically does there is expand the work both in compositional proportion, weighty ideas, and pianistic virtuosity.

Table 11.3: Select virtuoso transcriptions for piano solo from 1870–86

Related to dance genres
Der Schwur am Rütli (F. Draeseke), 1870 *Danse macabre* (after Saint-Saens), 1876–77 *Valse d'Adèle* (Zichy), 1877 *Valse de Concert* (Végh) 1877 *Polonaise aus der Opera Jewgeny Onegin* (Tchaikovsky), 1879 *Tarantelle, transcrite et amplifiée pour le piano à deux mains* (Dargomïzhsky), 1879 *Tarantelle* (Cui), 1885–86
Operatic
"Am stillen Herd" aus den Meistersingern (Wagner), 1871 *Ballade aus dem fliegenden Holländer* (Wagner), 1872 *Walhalla aus Der Ring des Nibelungen* (Wagner), 1875 *Aida, danza sacra e duetto final* (Verdi), 1876 (pub. 1879) *Réminiscences de Boccanegra* (Verdi), 1882
Related to other genres
Frühlingsnacht (Schumann), 1872 *Liebesszene und Fortunas Kugel aus Die sieben Todsünden* (based on Goldschmidt's oratorio), 1880

Good examples of this are his transcriptions of the Russian composers: the Tchaikovsky Polonaise and the two tarantellas after Dargomizhsky and Cui. Here Liszt uses virtuosity to promote national schools as well as individuals, while also inserting in moderate quantity and intensity some of his newer idioms—thus promoting himself, as noted by Kregor in relation to Cui.[34] The transformation of two of Kornél Ábrányi's *Csárdás nobles* into Rhapsody no. 19 is most probably a similar case.

Virtuosity in the operatic paraphrases serves a different cultural function. The opera paraphrases of 1824–47 were the embodiment of Liszt's maturing virtuosity in the way they were designed to promote the pianist through exciting keyboard reenactments of popular contemporary (with very few exceptions) operas and the way they reflected important changes in the pianism of that era. But as their form, content, and pianism matured in the 1840s, they increasingly came to represent a more serious attempt to convey the main dramatic concept of a given opera.[35] Liszt was already thinking of his place as a composer rather than pianist, a consideration that completely took over after he settled in Weimar. From that point on, what he chose to transcribe or "paraphrase" was designed to promote himself as a composer and Kapellmeister, declare his compositional lineage, and advance the careers of allies and students. This was certainly true of the late transcriptions; if anything, by turning into a feted "elderly statesman" of the musical world (as Pesce refers to him in her book), and as the artistic leader of the Allgemeiner Deutscher Musikverein (increasingly active from 1864 onward), Liszt's seal of approval, whether any composer asked for it or not, carried with it even greater weight.[36] One could say in the broadest terms that that proverbial seal was in the first instance a virtuoso piano style that was recognizably Liszt's. But did virtuosity, or possibly its absence, play a more specific role in the late paraphrases?

Once again, there is a danger of falling into binary thinking by formulating the question in these terms. Although I broadly agree with Charles Suttoni that these late works could "alternate, as needed, between Liszt's earlier concert-based style and the spare, harmonically daring mood of his other late piano works," I also recognize in this formulation (and my own question above), the same old dichotomy that has kept discussion of virtuosity and late style apart.[37] But note also Suttoni's interesting (and unexplained) "as needed." The Tchaikovsky Polonaise *needed* a more homogenous and traditional virtuoso style, because its function was to introduce a relatively upcoming composer in a more straightforwardly promotional way (Liszt was responding to a publisher's request), while reminding the world that the composer of the celebrated Hungarian Rhapsodies was also actively encouraging burgeoning national schools around Europe. In generic terms, it did not matter that the music originated in an opera: it was a single dance movement.

Liszt's paraphrases of Verdi's *Aida* (S. 436 / LW A276) and *Simone Boccanegra* (S. 438 / LW A314) are a different kind of work altogether. As fully developed operatic paraphrases (though on a smaller scale than those of Liszt's younger years), they are formally more complex, with varied and contrasting sections that try to capture something of the opera's dramatic essence. As in older paraphrases, virtuosity is harnessed for dramatic purposes (especially in *Boccanegra*) or due to an association with an exotic dance (*Aida*). The *Danza sacra e duetto finale d'Aida* concentrates on one of the most exotic-sounding moments in the opera, the Dance of the Priestesses, from act 1. The quasi-Phrygian harmony, quasi-oriental melisma, and Verdi's original exoticist orchestration are not only sensitively transcribed but elicit a scalar flourish at measures 11–15 that is entirely Liszt's and that references the virtuoso idiom through which much "exotic" harmonic material is sounded in his Hungarian Rhapsodies. The second, major-mode theme from the *Danza sacra*, beginning in measure 66, is the most fully fledged virtuoso idiom in this work: colorful sparkling arpeggios and broken octaves that enrich the melody in the left hand create a texture that could easily date back to the early Weimar period, when Liszt was refining his virtuoso writing for the piano.

A telling change of pianistic style occurs where the exotic music of those alluring priestesses from act 1 gives way to the somber music of the grave and the transcendent final duet between Radamès and Aida, as they bid farewell to earthly existence (mm. 99–118). This extraordinary transition passage presents a special challenge for the interpretation of virtuosity in a late work. An immediate impression is that of complete contrast between the exuberant music before measure 99 (the arpeggiated second theme) and the immobile blocks of chords against tremolando that come next, whose harmony and textures are not far removed from the world of *Nuages gris*. This leads to the sparely textured first evocation of the love duet in measure 111, in counterpoint to the *Possente possente Ftha* (O mighty Ptah) melody that was heard before in the *Danza sacra* (ex. 11.3).

The reason for the two-stage style change is programmatic. The transition music is a topical evocation of a tomb, a recurring musical trope in Liszt's music dating back at least to *Il penseroso* of 1839 (S. 157b / LW A55/2, later revised and collected in the second book of the *Années de pèlerinage*). Here, specifically, the sharp transition into the final tomb scene puts a break on the exuberant virtuosity, and just as suddenly we enter the sound world of harmonic idioms specific to the final years. The new harmonic language may also have a programmatic meaning: perhaps Liszt reimagining the lovers in the tomb "searching" in the dark before they meet at measure 119 (from which point we hear the tune in its proper diatonic version, as Verdi wrote it), against the priests' singing above, which evokes the split-floor scene in the original opera. Be that as it may, the sharp change of style seems to confirm lateness (post-tonal harmony, spare textures) through anti-virtuosity, or to put it differently, it gives grounds for perceiving virtuosity as the early/middle-style antithesis of Liszt's late style. Even the critically conscious analyst, all too aware of predetermined lateness tropes, will be hard pressed to deny a break in style that can easily be formulated in terms of creative periods.

Even so, it would be a mistake to align virtuosity so clearly and cleanly with past creativity. Liszt makes a point about relating apparently contrasting styles through a subtle associative process. I would argue that measures 99–110 provide an uncanny *déjà entendu*, not only because of a strange thematic transformation of the "O Mighty Ptah" melody already heard, but also because we half expect a change to a quivering tremolando texture, albeit not in this terrifying form. The previous appearance of the second (arpeggiated)

Example 11.3. *Danza sacra e duetto finale d'Aida*, S. 436 (1876/79), mm. 105–13

theme in B major continued into a third theme replete with trills, which then led to the first *Danza sacra* theme, now written over a continuous trill, the music as a whole sounding delicately in the treble register of the piano in measures 83–85, and continuing the key of B major (ex. 11.4). This *almost* happens again in a similar order of thematic rotation, when the second theme, now in E-flat major, continues into another theme in that key (at least initially) which sounds in chords over a rapid tremolando texture. Of course, this is a *different* earlier theme, and the whole texture is transposed to the bass, in order to evoke the grave topos. Nevertheless, despite this shift in sonority and harmonic language (preparing for the quasi-post-tonal passage that will follow), measures 99–110 continue the same virtuoso idiom and mirror measures 83–85. One may hear it this way as a stylistic transposition rather than as a break. If the music from measure 99 is heard as "late," then this lateness has been incipient in everything heard before.

Why Liszt chose to interfere with Verdi's music in this specific fashion is another question. To add another hypothesis to Kregor's idea about Liszt promoting his late style through popular arrangements, my view is that these more widely disseminated scores allowed him another way of taking a public position in cultural matters.[38] I think Liszt shrewdly perceived that, in *Aida*, Verdi was taking note of Wagner's operas and possibly other developments in the music world Liszt approved of. It is with this transcription, and even more so with *Simone Boccanegra*, that Liszt tacitly welcomed Verdi into the fold of a new music, while making it clear that this new music was not only "New German." Virtuosity in both transcriptions served, once again, both expressive and propagandist functions.

Endings

In this chapter I have not sought to provide a grand survey of virtuosity in Liszt's late works as much as ponder how we may theorize its putative "late" aspects against a lateness discourse that all but ignores this creative side of Liszt's final years. Some solutions are easy enough, like observing the comparative brevity of a virtuoso passage or (in some cases) the reduced level of technical difficulty. A more complex approach to this problem involves noting a deliberate, radical curtailment of virtuosity against generic expectations (see the "fast" section of Hungarian Rhapsody no. 17) and questioning the relationship of what appears to be an older type of virtuoso writing to a more stereotypical "late" piano style (the case of the *Aida* transcription).

Example 11.4. *Danza sacra e duetto finale d'Aida*, S. 436 (1876/79), mm. 83–85

Finally, we should consider whether there are instances where the virtuoso aspects of Liszt's late piano works could have belonged only to a late era, that is, whether they possess a quality we might describe as "late." I have already offered some preliminary thoughts about this in relation to Hungarian Rhapsody no. 19. It is fitting to return to some of these questions at the end by dealing with one of the most consistent features of Liszt's late virtuoso writing that *can* be easily theorized within a late style, namely, curious antigeneric endings within virtuoso genres outside the high-classical tradition (namely, the operatic paraphrases, Hungarian Rhapsodies, and various dance genres). We need to look at Liszt's uncompromising insistence on snubbing the cult of virtuosity by robbing it of its most precious moment: the gratifying bravura conclusion of the showpiece.

The lack of proper cadences, the melodic lines that seem to wander into oblivion are familiar markers of Liszt's late style and an oft-repeated point of discussion. Within the context of virtuosity such endings seem to me to be the most extreme instance of "anti-virtuosity," to borrow again Locke's term. Liszt's old contract with his audience was more or less an extension of the Rossini *crescendo*, and it can be described like this: toward the end, repeated material will continue to intensify in texture and dynamics, the performance will become increasingly athletic and frenzied yet exhilaratingly under control, even unto a breaking point, and (whether or not a quieter moment is interpolated just before the end) this momentum will eventually lead to the obligatory thunderous cadences, followed by a tremendous applause. I would like to suggest, tentatively, that none of Liszt's late virtuoso works does exactly that.[39] The Rossini-*crescendo* type of ending (or its "Gypsy" *friss* equivalent) is either complicated or frustrated, forcing those who know and expect it to develop as critical listeners, or else perceive such endings to be in some way bizarre or unsatisfying.[40]

The *Toccata* of 1879 (S. 197a / LW A295) presents a prime example of this challenge. Its suggestion of a proto-Debussian piano style (and occasionally harmony too: see mm. 57–62) immediately activates the lateness trope of a work dislocated from its time. Once again, as in the *Aida* transcription, it is the gothic sonorities of chromatically descending chords against tremolos (mm. 63–78) that halt the freely flowing arpeggios and lead to a thinly textured, fragmented passage. Except that this is not a little respite within the prestissimo perpetuum mobile but rather its unexpected end (ex. 11.5, from m. 71). It is not only the rhythmic augmentation that completely halts the flow. The abrupt turn to prolonged sixth chords in measure 63 is just as arbitrarily prolonged in those hushed chords that end the piece (mm. 84–90). There is no syntactical logic that leads to such a conclusion and certainly no hammer-blow, dominant-tonic chords in root position.

A more complex case is where such a disruption is preceded by a semblance of the Rossini *crescendo*, yet somehow the effect of a grand ending is undercut by something going wrong. The *Csardas obstinée* (S. 225/2 / LW A333/2, 1884–85) is a prime example of this. It intensifies throughout, almost like a proper *friss* movement. The final variation in the parallel major (a mode switch from the minor that entirely conforms to a traditional *verbunkos* idiom), imitates the cimbalom and recalls the technique and sound used in the finale of Hungarian Rhapsody no. 6. So far, so reassuring. And yet something goes wrong in the way this passage ends (ex. 11.6). Whereas the finale of the older rhapsody keeps building up until it explodes in a climax of octaves running in contrary motion toward a resonant, tonic-affirming, cadential ending, this cimbalom variation ends not long after it has begun, never really realizing its full virtuoso potential.

Both expectation and frustration are set up by harmonic means. After a great deal of chromatic shifting, this variation offers, initially, a perfectly regular I–iii progression in B major, and the appearance of what initially sounds as a secondary dominant (V^7/V, the C-sharp dominant seventh chord in ex. 11.6) creates an expectation for a coming dominant-tonic closure. But the progression gets stuck on the secondary dominant at the insistence of the bass. It is a very obstinate *csárdás*, after all, and previously it was the dominant note (F♯) the bass clung to, with an "obstinacy" that matched the perpetually

Example 11.5. *Toccata*, S. 197a (1879), mm. 71–94

repeating four-note motif in the melody. That repeating bass on the dominant may well be a humorous exaggeration of a real feature of *verbunkos* I have termed the "*verbunkos* I $^6_4$ chord," and likewise, the E♯ in the bass (mm. 279–82) sounds like a wrong-note caricature of Gypsy-band bass playing, missing the much-needed F♯ by a semitone.[41] But these artfully grotesque gestures also prevent a V/V–V–I functional closure, and the resulting syntactical impasse leads to another breakdown. The texture of rapid percussive octaves gives way to more ponderous parallel octaves, starting at half speed and then accelerating as if determined to reach that exhilarating *friss* conclusion at all cost. The problem is that the harmonic engine and full sound that might drive such an ending to a heroic conclusion are completely absent. The chromatic climb of the monodic tetrachords prevents any sense of a proper progression back to the tonic or even a proper expectation of its return. This progression settles arbitrarily on D-sharp minor, before that tetrachord smoothly transforms itself to B major. We do not even realize we have arrived, before B major brings the unruly *csárdás* to a full stop with a rude slap.

Example 11.6. *Csárdás obstinée*, S. 225/2 (1884–85), mm. 275–90

One cannot possibly take seriously or be "disappointed" by an ending that sends up the cult of virtuosity with such relish. Nor can one easily explain or valorize it through a lateness discourse. It is neither a transcendental reflection on art nor part of what Liszt self-deprecatingly referred to as his "infirmary music" (recall Brendel's comments at the beginning of this chapter). If this ending is humorous, or even satirical, as I think it is, then the object of the satire requires further investigation into both biography and genre; a wry, knowing joke about the banality or impossibility of a satisfying conclusion from the grand master of virtuoso genres seems to be inwardly about Liszt himself, as well as more publicly about the artistic boundaries of the popular Hungarian music of the day. This may well bring us back to the lateness discourse but in terms that are more historically grounded and less prone to myth-making, predetermined tropes, and decontextualized quotations.

But then we should consider the wider world of Liszt reception beyond score-based analysis and aesthetics, and acknowledge that there are other ways of responding to his late virtuosity, including, to some extent, misreading or even rejecting it in contemporary performance. Cyprien Katsaris's hyper-virtuoso version of the of the *Csárdás obstinée* includes exaggerated tempo fluctuations, note repetitions, and a capricious, over-the-top-cascade-of-octaves ending that brings back the cult of virtuosity with a vengeance.[42] This irreverently reclaims and recreates the work for the performative moment, rather than carefully reproducing it for the benefit of a story about late Liszt. And yet an interventionist performance does not invalidate the quality of virtuosity we find in the score or other interpretations that seek to understand and reproduce it.

For me, placing Liszt's music back in the time it was written is an equally important task that requires more systematic analysis of different formal and contextual aspects of this phenomenon: figuration and textures, genres and techniques, image and self-image, reports about Liszt's playing and Liszt's reported and written sayings on the subject. In this chapter I was only able to provide a taste of some formal aspects of late virtuosity, including an exploration of a few pianistic figures in Hungarian Rhapsody no. 19, the mixing of old and new pianistic styles in *Aida*, and the bravura-thwarting conclusion. These tasters point to wider possibilities: a taxonomy of late virtuoso figuration (related to and compared with an older Lisztian style), the "late" role of virtuosity in communicating Liszt's promotional, critical or other views on the music of his day, in both original and paraphrased music; all the reasons for which expected, generic moments of virtuosity are uncomfortably, strangely transformed or denied; and the way any understanding of "late" virtuosity has been mediated by recordings and contemporary performances. Beyond these specific test cases of virtuosity there is the whole world of performance in Liszt's time, reports of Liszt's continued (albeit rarer) appearances as a performer, Liszt as teacher and performer in his master classes, and the numerous scores prepared for students. The relationship of Liszt's late virtuoso writing to these has yet to be clarified. Finally, any further study in this area needs to be aware of how the lateness discourse and modernist rehabilitation of Liszt shaped the performance, reception of, and scholarship on Liszt's late piano works. For these reasons and more, this chapter is just the beginning.

Notes

1. James M. Baker, "Liszt's Late Piano Works: A Survey," in *The Cambridge Companion to Liszt*, ed. Kenneth Hamilton (Cambridge: Cambridge University Press, 2005), 90.
2. Dolores Pesce, *Liszt's Final Decade* (Rochester, NY: University of Rochester Press, 2014), 171–257; [Ed.] See Dolores Pesce's contribution to this volume for a further expansion of this point.
3. Shay Loya, *Liszt's Transcultural Modernism and the Hungarian-Gypsy Tradition* (Rochester, NY: University of Rochester Press, 2006), 225–51. In this study, I have countered a mythologizing tendency to view late works as standing outside normal music history by locating many of them within a longer, continuous transcultural process of fusing the *verbunkos* idiom ("Hungarian-Gypsy

style") with a modernist aesthetic (and vice versa), from c. 1839 to Liszt's death in 1886.

4. Important publications include James Deaville, "The Politics of Liszt's Virtuosity: New Light on the Dialectics of a Cultural Phenomenon," in *Liszt and the Birth of Modern Europe*, ed. Michael Saffle and Rossana Dalmonte (Hillsdale, NY: Pendragon Press, 2003), 115–42; Jim Samson, *Virtuosity and the Musical Work: The "Transcendental Studies" of Liszt* (Cambridge: Cambridge University Press, 2003); Dana Gooley, *The Virtuoso Liszt* (Cambridge: Cambridge University Press, 2004); Bruno Moysan, *Liszt: virtuose subversive* (Lyon: Symétrie, 2009). An earlier, widely read publication that brought to attention the connection between Liszt's pianistic and compositional innovations is Charles Rosen, *The Romantic Generation* (Cambridge, MA: Harvard University Press, 1995), 471–541.

5. Carl Dahlhaus, *Nineteenth-Century Music* (Berkeley: University of California Press, 1989), 134–42.

6. This is not the place to provide an overlong bibliography. However, I would add that the tradition of three-part periodization is perhaps part of the reason works from the so-called Roman period of 1861–69 have received the least musical-analytical attention, an issue that deserves a separate study.

7. See Samson, *Virtuosity and the Musical Work*.

8. Alfred Brendel, "Liszt's Bitterness of Heart" (1980), in *Music, Sense and Nonsense* (London: Biteback Publishing, 2017), 478–79.

9. Ibid., 484.

10. Zoltán Gárdonyi, *Le Style hongroise de François Liszt* (1936, orig. 1931), *Liszt Ferenc magyar stílusa/Le Style hongrois de François Liszt* [Joint Hungarian/French edition] (Budapest: Orsz. Széchényi Könyvtár, 1936), 99–120. Originally published as *Die ungarischen Stileigentü mlichkeiten in den musikalischen Werken Franz Liszts* (Berlin: Walter de Gruyter, 1931). Béla Bartók, "Liszt Problems" (1936), in Bartók, *Essays*, ed. Benjamin Suchoff (Lincoln: University of Nebraska Press, 1993), 502–5. Bartók had already written in 1911 a polemical essay condemning the Hungarian public for lacking the capacity to understand Liszt's artistry, "Liszt's Music and the Public of Today" (ibid., 451–54), but the 1936 essay celebrates Liszt more pointedly as a proto-modernist.

11. Loya, *Liszt's Transcultural Modernism*, 17–19.

12. [Ed.] For a compositional history of *Malédiction*, see Kenneth Hamilton's contribution to this volume.

13. Humphrey Searle, *Quadrille with a Raven: Memoirs by Humphrey Searle* (MusicWeb International), http://www.musicweb-international.com/searle/you.htm, accessed September 21, 2019. (The memoirs, completed in 1982, have so far only been published online.) *Malédiction* has some virtuoso moments, but the work itself is not designed to please crowds or be easily understood. Even the *Grand galop chromatique*, the concert's only properly *Glanzzietisch* work, was given in a new version for two pianos that, arguably,

does not celebrate a "heroic" virtuoso in the same way the more familiar solo version does.

14. The same operative principle of this modernist elitism dates back to the invention of "bad taste" in the nineteenth century, in which—as Richard Taruskin has argued—stage virtuosity was deeply implicated. Citing Gillan D'Arcy Wood's concept of "virtuosophobia" and Jonas Barish's "antitheatrical prejudice," Taruskin maintains such sentiments were an important aspect of both Liszt bashing and Liszt rehabilitation. See Richard Taruskin, "Liszt and Bad Taste," *Studia Musicologica* 54, no. 1 (2013): 96.

15. Early publications that set the templates for future studies along the former lines include Humphrey Searle, "Liszt," in *New Grove Dictionary of Music and Musicians* (1954); Bence Szabolcsi, *The Twilight of Ferenc Liszt*, trans. András Deák (Budapest: Hungarian Academy of Sciences, 1959); originally published as *Liszt Ferenc Estéje* (Budapest: Zeneműkiadó Vállalat, 1956); István Szelényi, "Der unbekannte Liszt," *Studia Musicologica Academiae Scientiarum Hungaricae* 5 (1963): 311–31; Alan Walker, "Liszt and the Twentieth Century," in *Franz Liszt: The Man and his Music*, ed. Alan Walker (London: Barrie & Jenkins, 1970), 350–64; Lajos Bárdos, "Ferenc Liszt, the Innovator," *Studia Musicologica Academiae Scientiarum Hungaricae* 17 (1975): 3–38; and Serge Gut, *Franz Liszt: Les éléments du langage musicale* (Paris: Klincksieck, 1975; Bourg-la-Reine: Zurfluh, 2009).

   Important studies of the latter include Robert P. Morgan, "Dissonant Prolongations: Theoretical and Compositional Precedents," *Journal of Music Theory* 20, no. 1 (1976): 49–91; Allen Forte, "Liszt's Experimental Idiom and Music of the Early Twentieth Century," *Nineteenth-Century Music* 10, no. 3 (1987): 209–28; James M. Baker, "The Limits of Tonality in the Late Music of Franz Liszt," *Journal of Music Theory* 34, no. 2 (1990): 145–74; and Ramon Satyendra, "Conceptualizing Expressive Chromaticism in Liszt's Music," *Music Analysis* 16, no. 2 (1997): 219–52.

16. Much of Liszt's modernist rehabilitation has rested in this way on what I nickname "the grand tonal narrative." See Loya, *Liszt's Transcultural Modernism*, 154–57, 229–33.

17. "Ma seule ambition de musicien était et serait de lancer mon javelot dans les espaces indéfinis de l'avenir," Letter from February 9, 1974, in *Franz Liszts Briefe*, vol. 7, ed. La Mara (Leipzig: Breitkopf & Härtel, 1902), 57–58.

18. Theodore W. Adorno, "Late Style in Beethoven" (1937), in *Essays on Music*, ed. Richard Leppert (Berkeley: University of California Press, 2002), 564–68; Edward W. Said, *Late Style: Music and Literature against the Grain* (London: Bloomsbury, 2006).

19. Zoltán Gárdonyi and István Szelényi, "Preface," in *Ungarische Rhapsodien* II, *Neue Liszt Ausgabe* vol. 1, no. 4 (Budapest: Editio Musica Budapest, 1973), xii–xiii.

20. Sam Smiles, "From Titian to Impressionism: The Genealogy of Late Style," in *Late Style and its Discontents: Essays in Art, Literature and Music*, ed. Gordon McMullen and Sam Smiles (Oxford: Oxford University Press, 2016), 19–20. Smiles quotes from Georg Simmel, "Leonardo da Vinci's Last Supper," trans. Brigitte Kueppers and Alfred Willis, *Achademia Leonardo Vinci* 10 (1997): 142.
21. Gordon McMullen, "The 'Strangeness' of George Oppen: Criticism, Modernity, and the Conditions of the Late Style," in *Late Style and its Discontents*, 31–47.
22. Ibid, 46.
23. Shay Loya, "The Mystery of the Seventeenth Hungarian Rhapsody," *Quaderni dell'Instituto Liszt* 15 (2015): 107–46. This work's abstracted virtuosity is especially notable toward the end, and I shall discuss virtuoso endings at the close of this chapter.
24. I am not comparing these rhapsodies to the slow-movement Rhapsodies nos. 3 and 5, which obviously diverge from the slow-fast pairing, although they conform to the *verbunkos* genre in other ways.
25. My observations here are specifically about virtuosity in relation to technique and texture, and do not address the harmonic idiom. Gárdonyi and Szelényi do bring up harmony when, a sentence later, they refer to the "Klangwelt" of these works (confusingly translated—presumably by the writers—as "tonal world" in the English version of the preface, xiii). However, this needs more qualification, since local harmony and tonal structure relate differently to the perception of virtuosity; see the concluding section of this chapter.
26. In this case, mostly to do with harmonic stasis and a penchant for octatonic sonorities. See also previous footnote.
27. Alan Walker, *Franz Liszt, Volume 3: The Final Years, 1861–1886* (London: Faber and Faber, 1997), 467.
28. Ibid.
29. Roberto Szidon (Munich, 1972), *The 19 Hungarian Rhapsodies*, Deutsche Grammophon 453 034-2, 1997. Maurizio Pollini. *Sonata in B Minor*, Deutsche Gramophone, 1988. Michele Campanella, *Liszt: Complete Hungarian Rhapsodies*, Philips 6998 015, 1974. Leslie Howard, *The Complete Music for Solo Piano, Vol. 57—Hungarian Rhapsodies*, Hyperion CDA67418/9, 1999.
30. One of the pianists who established a modernist approach to Liszt is the aforementioned Alfred Brendel. One could also mention in this vein Maurizio Pollini's influential "Sonata in B Minor" album (Deutsche Grammophon, 1988), which celebrated the late style and Liszt as a revered composer by programming *Nuages gris, Unstern!, La Lugubre Gondola I*, and *R.W.-Venezia* on side B of an LP that featured his most celebrated work. Although Louis Kentner (1905–87) pioneered recordings of late Liszt, it was Brendel's legacy that has ultimately been more influential. Their respective recordings of the *Csárdás macabre* in Brendel (1958) and Kentner (1951) provide an instructive contrast. Brendel's playing adheres to the work concept: crisp and technically

brilliant, played in strict tempo and without a note added. Kentner, a generation older than Brendel, plays with expressive rubato and thinks nothing of adding improvised figurations to the more virtuoso passages of the *csárdás*, all of which might be thought to belong to a Lisztian tradition. This is not a tradition that has been much associated with the composer's late works after Brendel's 1958 recordings made their mark, but there has also been a competing, albeit less widespread tradition of augmenting the virtuoso element in late Liszt: see recordings of Hungarian Rhapsody no. 19 by Cziffra (1954–56) and Horowitz (1962) and the brief discussion of Cyprien Katsaris (2005) in the closing paragraph of this chapter.

31. An early example can be found in several passages from Liszt's *Grande Fantaisie sur La Tyrolienne de l'opéra "La fiancée" d'Auber* (S. 385/1 / LW A12a/1, first version, 1829: see for example m. 144ff.). My thanks to Kenneth Hamilton for pointing this out to me. From Chopin, the most paradigmatic example is Étude no. 12 in C Minor from op. 25.
32. On this type of parallelism and its adaptation in Liszt's music see, Loya, *Liszt's Transcultural Modernism*, 53.
33. Liszt had a considerable circle of followers in Hungary. By virtue of his influential position, much of his national composition served to demonstrate to them what more could be done with the popular national idiom. See also Shay Loya, "Liszt's Legacy and the Paradoxes of Hungarian Musical Modernism," in *Liszt's Legacies: A Collection of Essays*, ed. James Deaville and Michael Saffle (Hillsdale, NY: Pendragon Press, 2014), 17–42. For the sources of this rhapsody, see Leslie Howard's liner notes in *The Complete Music for Solo Piano, Vol. 57—Hungarian Rhapsodies*, Hyperion CDA67418/9 (1999); also available online: https://www.hyperion-records.co.uk/dc.asp?dc=D_CDA67418/9, accessed June 4th, 2018.
34. Jonathan Kregor, *Liszt as Transcriber* (Cambridge: Cambridge University Press, 2010), 208–11, 218–19.
35. Charles Suttoni, "Opera Paraphrases," in *The Liszt Companion*, ed. Ben Arnolds (Westport, CT: Greenwood Press, 2002), 179–91.
36. Liszt's tortured relationship with Wagner is a special case, but suffice it to say here that on the whole his Wagner pieces moved steadily from transcription to an increasingly free and personalized paraphrase that often amounted to compositional intervention. See Kregor, *Liszt as Transcriber*, 180–85.
37. Suttoni, "Opera Paraphrases," 188. This dichotomy is echoed in Suttoni's closing sentence: "Finally, at the close [of his life], with *Aida* and *Boccanegra*, the virtuoso is long gone, and the aged Liszt confines himself to his ever-personal interpretation of the music alone" (ibid., 189).
38. See Kregor, *Liszt as Transcriber*, 180–85.
39. Even in a work like *Tarantelle de César Cui* (S. 482 / LW A327, 1885), which almost ends as the genre demands, Liszt interrupts the momentum with a

forlorn, tonally ambiguous monody, shortly before the end (mm. 618–45); and the concluding chords lack deep bass support (mm. 688–95).

40. Scholars are not necessarily immune from the latter perception. See Baker, "A Survey," 110.
41. Loya, *Liszt's Transcultural Modernism*, 46–48.
42. Cyprien Katsaris, "*Csárdás obstinée*" (live recording, 2005). Available also on https://www.youtube.com/watch?v=JDxA_FiEv7w, accessed June 6, 2018.

Contributors

ROBERT DORAN is professor of French and comparative literature at the University of Rochester and an affiliate faculty member of the Music Theory Department at the Eastman School of Music. He is the author of two monographs, *The Theory of the Sublime from Longinus to Kant* and *The Ethics of Theory: Philosophy, History, Literature* and has edited several books and journal issues.

NICOLAS DUFETEL is a researcher at the CNRS (Centre national de la recherche scientifique) and vice director of the IReMus (Institut de recherche en musicologie), Paris. He is the author of numerous articles on Liszt, nineteenth-century music, and the Westernization of music in the Ottoman Empire, and is the editor or coeditor of ten books, including *Liszt et le son Érard* and, with Malou Haine, Dana Gooley, and Jonathan Kregor, *Liszt et la France*.

JONATHAN DUNSBY is professor of music theory at the Eastman School of Music and is founding editor of the UK journal *Music Analysis* (1982–86) and founding president of the Society for Music Analysis. He has published widely on music analysis and performance studies, including the monographs *Making Words Sing: Nineteenth- and Twentieth-Century Song* and *Performing Music: Shared Concerns*, and he has edited, with Jonathan Goldman, the collection *The Dawn of Music Semiology*, published by University of Rochester Press.

KENNETH HAMILTON is head of the School of Music at Cardiff University. He is the editor of *The Cambridge Companion to Liszt* and has authored two monographs: *Liszt: Sonata in B Minor* and *After the Golden Age: Romantic Pianism and Modern Performance*. His recordings include the solo piano CD *Liszt, Rachmaninov, Busoni: Back to Bach—Tributes and Transcriptions*, released in 2017 by Prima Facie.

DAVID KEEP is assistant professor of music theory and piano at Hope College, where his research focuses on musical meaning in Brahms, performance and analysis, and nineteenth-century music. He received his PhD in music theory at the Eastman School of Music (University of Rochester) in 2020, with a dissertation entitled "Re-Creativity in Brahms's Opp. 80–90." He also holds degrees in piano performance from the Jacobs School of Music (Indiana University) and Lawrence

University and is currently engaged in a performance cycle of Brahms's complete works for solo piano.

JONATHAN KREGOR is professor of musicology at the College-Conservatory of Music, University of Cincinnati and, since 2012, is the editor of the *Journal of the American Liszt Society*. He is the author of *Liszt as Transcriber*, which won the Alan Walker Book Award from the American Liszt Society, and *Program Music*, which includes several chapters on Liszt.

RALPH P. LOCKE is professor emeritus of musicology at the Eastman School of Music and research affiliate at the University of Maryland. He is the founding, and continuing, editor of the University of Rochester Press's Eastman Studies in Music and is the author of the monographs *Musical Exoticism: Images and Reflections*; *Music and the Exotic from the Renaissance to Mozart*; and *Music, Musicians, and the Saint-Simonians*.

SHAY LOYA is senior lecturer in the Department of Music at City, University of London, a trustee of the Society for Music Analysis, and a board member of the journal *Music Analysis*. His book, *Liszt's Transcultural Modernism and the Hungarian-Gypsy Tradition*, published by the University of Rochester Press, won the Alan Walker Book Award from the American Liszt Society; he is currently working on a book project entitled *Liszt's Late Styles*.

DOLORES PESCE is Avis Blewett Professor of Music in Arts & Sciences at Washington University in St. Louis. In addition to *Liszt's Final Decade*, published by the University of Rochester Press and winner of the 2017 Alan Walker Book Award from the American Liszt Society, she has published numerous essays on Liszt's music, as well as monographs and essays on medieval theory and music.

JIM SAMSON is professor of music, emeritus, at Royal Holloway, University of London, and Distinguished Visiting Professor of Humanities at the Chinese University of Hong Kong. He has published widely on the music of Chopin, on analytical and aesthetic topics in nineteenth- and twentieth-century music, and on the social histories of music in east-central and southeastern Europe. His monograph, *Virtuosity and the Musical Work: The "Transcendental Studies" of Liszt*, was awarded the Royal Philharmonic Book Prize.

OLIVIA SHAM is a concert pianist and honorary research fellow at the Royal Academy of Music. She received her PhD from the Royal Academy of Music with a dissertation entitled "Performing the Unperformable: Notions of Virtuosity in Liszt's Solo Piano Music," and her debut album, *Liszt: The Art of Remembering*, was released in 2015 by Avie Records.

Index of Liszt's Musical Works

(S.) numbering by Humphrey Searle in *Grove's Dictionary*, later revised by Sharon Winklhofer, Michael Short, and Leslie Howard

(LW) numbering by Mária Eckhardt and Rena Charnin Mueller, used in *Grove Music Online*

All works are for piano solo, unless otherwise indicated.

Arrangements and Transcriptions

Beethoven-Liszt, *Grand septuor de Beethoven* (S. 465 / LW A69, 1840), 183n30

Beethoven-Liszt, Symphony no. 6 ("Pastoral") (S. 463b / LW A37b/2, 1837), 50, 165, 170

Berlioz-Liszt, *Symphonie fantastique* (*Episode de la vie d'un artiste: Grande symphonie fantastique par Hector Berlioz*) (S. 470 / LW 16a, 1833), 71, 83, 154–58, 162

Cui-Liszt, *Tarentelle* (S. 482 / LW A327, 1885–86), 400

Dargomïzhsky-Liszt, *Tarantelle, transcrite et amplifiée pour le piano à deux mains* (S. 483 / LW, A291, 1879), 400

Draeseke-Liszt, *Der Schwur am Rütli* (S. 485a / LW A251, 1870), 400

Goldschmidt-Liszt, *Liebesszene und Fortunas* (S. 490 / LW A298, 1880), 400

Rossini-Liszt, *William Tell* Overture (S. 552 / LW A54, 1838), 50, 179, 282

Schubert-Liszt, "Ave Maria" (S. 558/12 / LW A42/12, 1837–38), 361

Schubert-Liszt, *Franz Schuberts Grosse Fantasie*, for piano and orchestra (S. 366 / LW H13, 1851), 239, 241–66

Schubert-Liszt, *Franz Schuberts Grosse Fantasie*, for two pianos (S. 653 / LW C5, 1851–62), 262n6

Schubert-Liszt, *Le roi des aulnes* (*Erlkönig*) (S. 558/4 / LW A42/4, 1837–38), 3, 24, 224, 243–48, 265n27

Schumann-Liszt, *Frühlingsnacht* (S. 568 / LW A257, 1872), 400

Szabady-Liszt, *Revive Szegedin! (Marche hongroise de Szabady)* (S. 572 / LW A292, 1879), 388

Tchaikovsky-Liszt, *Polonaise aus der Opera Jewgeny Onegin* (S. 429 LW / A293, 1879), 400

Végh-Liszt, *Valse de Concert* (S. 430 / LW A318, 1877), 400

Wagner-Liszt, *"Am stillen Herd" aus den Meistersingern* (S. 448 / LW A254 1871), 400

Wagner-Liszt, *Ballade aus dem fliegenden Holländer* (S. 441 / LW A259, 1872), 400

Wagner-Liszt, *Ouvertüre zu Tannhäuser* (S. 442 / LW A146, 1848), 101

Wagner-Liszt, *Walhalla aus Der Ring des Nibelungen* (S. 449 / LW A269 1875), 400

Zichy-Liszt, *Valse d'Adèle (Transcription brillante)* (S. 456 LW / A281, 1877), 400

Original Compositions, Fantasies, Free Arrangements, Paraphrases, and Variations

Album d'un voyageur, volume 1: *Impressions et poésies* (S. 156 / LW A40a, 1834–36), 41–42, 61, 124, 140n6, 153, 373, 376n21
no. 1, *Lyon*, 22, 376n21
no. 2, *Le lac de Wallenstadt (The Lake of Wallenstadt)*, 41, 61
no. 3, *Au bord d'une source*, 360–61
no. 4, *Les cloches de G***** (The Bells of Geneva)*, 61
no. 5, *Vallée d'Obermann*, 42, 61–65, 72, 89n44, 101–3
no. 6. *La chapelle de Guillaume Tell (The Chapel of William Tell)*, 61
Allegro di bravura (S. 151 / LW A6, 1824–25), 288
Années de pèlerinage: Première année: Suisse (S. 160 / LW A159, 1836–55), 3, 42, 124, 148, 153, 165, 350, 355, 361–62, 372, 376–77n21
no. 2, *Au lac de Wallenstadt*, 41
no. 4, *Au bord d'une source*, 41, 360–61
no. 5, *Orage*, 68

no. 6, *Vallée d'Obermann*, 42, 89n44, 179, 183n27, 279, 281, 305n63, Horowitz's; version of, 4, 29n19, ossia passages in, 148–53, 167, period instruments and, 101–4, Weber's Piano Sonata no. 4 and, 61–65, 72
no. 8, *Le mal du pays*, 350, 372
Années de pèlerinage: Deuxième année: Italie (S. 161 / LW A55, 1846–49), 54, 61, 165, 350, 355, 362, 402
no. 3, *Il penseroso*, 350, 372, 402
no. 7, *Après une lecture du Dante (Fantasia quasi Sonata)* (*Dante* Sonata), 42, 53–61, 72, 81, 83, 84n1, 269, 299, 304n52, 305n63, see also *Fragment nach Dante*, *Paralipomènes à la "Divina Commedia,"* and *Prologomènes à la "Divina Commedia"*
Années de pèlerinage: Deuxième année: Italie Supplément: Venezia e Napoli (S. 162 / LW A197, 1859), 98
no. 3, *Tarantella*, 98

Années de pèlerinage: Troisième année (S. 163 / LW A283, 1883), 165, 311, 343n2, 355, 361–62, 416
  no. 2, *Aux cyprès de la Villa d'Este (Thrénodie I)*, 311–45
  no. 3, *Aux cyprès de la Villa d'Este (Thrénodie II)*, 311–45
  no. 4, *Jeux d'eau à la villa d'Este*, 105–6, 343, 374n2, 388, 391
Apparitions (S. 155 / LW A19, 1834), 22, 156, 182n13
  no. 1, 372
  no. 3, *Fantaisie sur une valse de François Schubert*, 66
Ave maris stella (S. 669/2 / LW E27/2b, 1877), 361

Bagatelle sans tonalité (S. 216a / LW A338, 1885), 373, 388
Ballade no. 1 in D-flat Major (S. 170/ LW A117, 1845–48), 32n38, 165
Ballade no. 2 in B Minor (S. 171 / LW A181, 1853), 32n38, 152, 165, 176, 184n37
Bülow-Marsch (S. 230 / LW A326, 1883), 388

Caprices-Valses (S. 214 / LW A32, 1850–52), 362
  no. 1, *Valse de bravoure*, 288, 362
Consolations (S. 172 / LW A111b, 1849–50) no. 3 (*Lento placido*), 139
Csárdás obstinée (S. 225/2 / LW A333/2, 1884), 388, 406–9, 414n42
Csárdás macabre (S. 224 / LW A313, 1881–82), 105–6, 388, 391, 412–13n30

Danse macabre (after Saint-Saens) (S. 555 / LW A273, 1876–77), 400
Dante Symphony (S. 109 / LW G14, 1839), 54, 83

Danza sacra e duetto finale d'Aida (S. 436 / LW A276, 1876), 399–406, 409, 413n37
Der Traurige Mönch (S. 348 / LW P3, 1860), 391
Deux légendes (*Two Legends*) (S. 175 / LW A219, 1862–63), 25
  no. 1, *St François d'Assise: la prédication aux oiseaux*, 25
  no. 2, *St François de Paule: marchant sur les flots*, 25, 29n17, 81, 282
Die Zelle in Nonnenwerth for violin and piano (S. 274ii / LW N6, 1858–60), 354

Elegy no. 1 *(Première Élégie)* for piano, harp, and harmonium (S. 130a / LW D13a, 1874), 372, 385n64
En rêve (*Notturno*) (S. 207 / LW A336, 1885), 354
Étude en douze exercices (S. 136 / LW A8, 1826), 23, 44, 56, 94–95, 97, 130, 134, 274, 284–85, 306n77

Fantaisie sur des motifs favoris de l'opéra "La sonnambula" de Bellini (S. 393ii / LW A56/2, 1839), 280
Faust Symphony (S. 108 / LW G12, 1857–61), 49, 54, 68, 73–74, 77, 82–83, 355, 360, 362
Fragment nach Dante (S. 701e, c. 1837), 53–56, 72, 89n43

Gaudeamus igitur (S. 509 / LW A246, 1869–70), 184n37
Grande fantaisie de bravoure sur "La clochette" de Paganini (S. 420 / LW A15, 1832), 13, 23–24, 34n56, 154, 158–60, 167, 182n16, 182n17, 288

Grande fantaisie sur la tyrolienne de "La fiancé" d'Auber (S. 385i / LW A12a/1, 1829), 48, 128, 413n31
Grand galop chromatique (S. 219 / A43, 1838), 3, 24, 37n102, 271–75, 289, 299, 302n25, 391, 410–11n13
Grande valse di bravura (Le bal de Berne) (S. 209 / LW A32a, 1836), 123, 288, 362
Grosses Konzertsolo (S. 176 / A167, 1849–50), 14, 81

Harmonies poétiques et religieuses (single work) (S. 154 / LW A18, 1833–34), 49, 61, 122, 125, 130, 143n34, 145n47, 156, 182n13, 372–73. See also *Pensée des morts*
Harmonies poétiques et religieuses (collection, intermediate version) (S. 172c / LW A61, 1847–48)
  no. 1, *Invocation*, 168
Harmonies poétiques et religieuses (collection, revised version) (S. 173 / LW A158, 1840–53), 49, 355, 385n67
  no. 1, *Invocation*, 74, 81–82
  no. 4, *Pensée des morts*, 49, 372–73, 385n67
  no. 7, *Funérailles*, 17, 71–72, 83, 90n56, 279, 299
Hexaméron: Grandes variations de bravoure sur la marche des Puritains de Bellini (S. 392 / A41, 1839), 43–53, 87n25–n27, 125, 276, 288

Il penseroso (S. 157b / LW A55/2, 1839), 402
Impromptu brillant sur des thèmes de Rossini et Spontini (S. 150 / LW A5, 1824), 287

Introduction des variations sur une marche du "Siège de Corinthe" (S. 421a / LW A13, 1830), 124–26

La lugubre gondola (S. 200/1 and 2 / LW A319a and b, 1883–85), 391, 412n30
Leyer und Schwerdt (Heroide nach Carl Maria von Weber) (S. 452 / LW A151, 1848), 123–24
Liebesszene und Fortunas Kugel aus dem Oratorium Die sieben Todsünden (Fantasiestück nach Adalbert von Goldschmidt) (S. 490 / LW A298, 1880), 400

Hungarian Rhapsodies (S. 244 / LW 132, 1846–85), 98, 165, 181n9, 194, 280, 287, 350, 378n30, 391–99
  no. 2, 29n17, 272, 376n16
  no. 6, 279
  no. 10, 279
  no. 14, 184n31
  no. 15, 167–68
  no. 16, 388, 395–99
  no. 17, 388, 395–99, 404
  no. 18, 388, 395–99
  no. 19, 388, 395–400, 405, 409, 413n30

Klavierstück in F major (S. 695 / LW A100, 1843), 91n68

Malédiction (Sextet for Piano and Strings) (S. 121 / LW H1, 1833), 42, 65–71, 83, 89n50, 119, 391, 410
Mazeppa (piano solo, separately published) (S. 138 / LW A172/4, 1840), 290
Mazurka brillante (S. 221 / LW A168, 1850), 167, 228

Mephisto Polka (S. 217 / LW A317, 1883), 179, 388
Mephisto Waltz no. 1 (S. 514 / LW A189/1, 1859–61) 2, 25, 33n42, 49, 171, 272, 299, 376n16
Mephisto Waltz no. 2 (S. 515 / LW A288, 1878-81), 288
Mephisto Waltz no. 3 (S. 216 / LW A325, 1883), 288, 347, 362, 388, 391
Mephisto Waltz no. 4 (S. 696 / LW A337, 1885), 288

Nuages gris (*Trübe Wolken*) (S. 199 / LW A305, 1881), 350–56, 360–61, 365–66, 376n19, 377n22, 377n23, 387, 402, 412n30

Paralipomènes à la "Divina Commedia": Fantaisie Symphonique (S. 158a / LW A55/7, 1839), 54–60, 88n39
Paganini Etudes (*Études d'exécution transcendante d'après Paganini*) (S. 140 / LW A52, 1838), 23, 159, 169, 183n22, 194, 284–87
 no. 1 (Tremolo), 160–61, 280, 283
 no. 2 (Octave), 305n69
 no. 3, *Campanella*, 305n66
 no. 4 (versions I and II), 284–85
 no. 5 ("La chasse"), 286–87, 305n68, 306n78
Paganini Etudes (*Grandes études de Paganini*) (S. 141 / LW A173, 1851), 10, 16, 194, 284–87, 306n69
 no. 1 (Tremolo), 280, 283, 305n66
 no. 2 (Octave), 305n68–69
 no. 3, *La campanella*, 14, 305n66
 no. 4 (Arpeggios), 284–85
 no. 5 ("La chasse"), 286–87
 no. 6 in A Minor, 18, 198
Paraphrase de concert sur Rigoletto (S. 434 / LW A187, 1855–59), 25

Piano Concerto no. 1 in E-flat Major (S. 124 / LW H4, 1856), 86–87n24, 263n14, 293, 376n16
Piano Concerto no. 2 in A Major (S. 125 / LW H6, 1861), 86–87n24, 293–96, 376n16
Piano Concerto in E-flat Major (posthumous, S. 125a / LW Q6, 1836–39), 86–87n24
Prolégomènes à la "Divina Commedia" (S. 158b / LW A55/7, c. 1840), 54
Prometheus (Symphonic Poem no. 5) (S. 99 / LW G6, 1850–55), 68

Réminiscences de Boccanegra (S. 438 / LW A314, 1882), 400–401, 404, 413n37
Réminiscences de Don Juan (*Don Juan Fantasy*) (S. 418 / LW A80, 1841), 22–23, 27n3, 37n105, 178–79, 185n47, 280, 295–99, 304n52, 304n56, 307n87
Réminiscences de "La juive" (*Fantaisie brillante sur des motifs de l'opéra de Halévy*) (S 409a / LW A20, 1835), 287–88
Réminiscences de Norma (*Norma Fantasy*) (S. 394 / LW A77, 1841), 14, 24, 99, 197, 280
Réminiscences de Robert le diable: Valse infernale (S. 413 / LW A78, 1841), 3, 24, 90n58, 170
Réminiscences de Lucrezia Borgia (S. 400 / LW A71b, 1848), 181n6
Réminiscences des Puritains de Bellini (S. 390ii / LW34/2, 1836–37), 45
Rondo di bravura (S. 152 / LW A 7, 1824–25), 288

Scherzo und Marsch (S. 177 / LW A174, 1851), 14

Schlaflos! Frage und Antwort (S. 203 / LW A322, 1883), 171–79, 185n45, 354, 377n23, 391
Sonata in B Minor (S. 178 / LW A179, 1853), 2, 8, 13, 21, 32n38, 42, 72–83, 84n3, 165, 241–42, 247, 299, 305n63, 371, 412n29–n30
Sonata in F Minor (lost fragment, S. 692b / LW S22, 1825, copied from memory by Liszt in 1880), 44, 85n10
St. Elisabeth (*Die Legende von der Heiligen Elisabeth*), for voices and orchestra (S. 2 / LW I4, 1857–62), 74

Tarantelle di bravura d'après la tarantelle de "La muette" de Portici (S. 386 / LW A125, 1846/1869), 288
Technische Studien (S. 146 / LW A242, 1868–71), 130, 134, 137, 145n48, 146n62
Totentanz for piano and orchestra (S. 126ii / LW H8, 1852–59), 18, 55, 68, 98, 304n52, 355, 377n23, 385n64, 391
Trois études de concert (*Three Concert Études*) (S. 144 / LW A118, 1845–49), 16, 25
 no. 2, *La leggierezza*, 17, 152, 167
 no. 3, *Un sospiro*, 170, 184n35–n36, 197, 280
Toccata (S. 197a / LW A295, 1879), 388, 406–7
Transcendental Études (*Grandes études*, S. 137 / LW A39, 1837), 23–24, 26, 34n57, 56, 94, 125, 129–30, 145n47, 274, 284–87, 305n64
 no. 1 (*Preludio*), 9, 284, 290
 no. 4 (*Mazeppa*), 37n99, 290
 no. 5 (*Feux follets*), 290
 no. 6 (*Vision*), 37n99
 no. 8 (*Wilde Jagd*), 11, 33n43, 94–95, 122, 305n65
 no. 11 (*Harmonies du Soir*), 37n99, 280
Transcendental Études (*Études d'exécution transcendante*) (S. 139 / LW A172, 1851), 26, 171, 195, 284–87
 no. 1, *Preludio*, 32n38, 284, 290
 no. 4, *Mazeppa*, 17–18, 26, 32n38, 171, 226, 284, 290, 304n52, 376n16
 no. 5, *Feux follets*, 11, 26, 226, 290
 no. 6, *Vision*, 171–72, 185n40, 282
 no. 7, *Eroica*, 226, 291–92
 no. 8, *Wilde Jagd*, 11, 32n38, 94–95
 no. 10 in F Minor, 11
 no. 11, *Harmonies du soir*, 226, 280
 no. 12, *Chasse-neige*, 283–84

Un soir dans les montagnes (S. 156/18 / LW A40c/2, 1837–38), 50, 62, 68
Ungarischer Geschwindmarsch (S. 233 / LW A252, 1870–71), 388
Ungarische Volkslieder (1–5) (S. 245 / LW A263, 1872), 170
Unstern (S. 208 / LW A312, 1881), 377n23, 412n30

Valse de l'opéra Faust (S. 407 / LW A208, 1861), 25, 179
Valse-impromptu (S. 213 / LW A84c, 1842–52), 170
Valses oubliées, 1–4 (S. 215 / LW, A311 1881–85), 388
Variations brillantes sur un thème de Rossini (S. 149 / LW A4, 1824), 287
Vexilla regis prodeunt (S. 185 / LW A226, 1864), 167

Weihnachtsbaum (S. 185a / LW A267, 1873–74), 361
Weinen, Klagen, Sorgen, Zagen (S. 179 / LW A198, 1859), 25

Zwei Konzertetüden (*Two Concert Études*) (S. 145 / LW A218, 1862), 25

General Index

Ábranyi, Kornél, 396, 400
Adam, Louis, 282
Adami, Heinrich, 45–47, 55–61
Adler, Martin, 73, 91n64
Adorno, Theodor, 240, 261, 262n9, 263n12, 265n34, 265n42, 392, 411n18
affect, 344n8, 344n16, 345n25
Agoult, Marie d' (Countess), 24, 87n24, 98, 107n8, 111, 123, 182n13, 298; evolution of Liszt's *Dante* Sonata and, 53–54, 88n35, 88n37; evolution of Liszt's *Malédiction* Concerto (Sextet for Piano and Strings) and, 66–67
Albrechsberger, Johann, 223
Alkan, Charles-Valentin: *Grande Sonate: Les quatre âges*, 42, 72–77, 80–83, 90n63; Twelve Studies in the Major Keys, 16
Aristotle, 19, 229
Arrau, Claudio, 225–27, 235n23, 236n30
Auerbach, Brent, 204–6, 216n49, 216n53

Bach, Johann Sebastian, 4, 6, 30n26, 33n45, 71, 81, 152, 191, 227, 231, 233, 263n12; Chaconne, 194; *Goldberg Variations*, 13, 31n34; Liszt's early notebooks and, 126, 128; Prelude in D Major (BWV 850), 302n28; Toccatas, 180n5; *Well-Tempered Clavier*, 11

Badiou, Alain, 237n43
Badura-Skoda, Eva, 30n22, 30n28
Badura-Skoda, Paul, 30n28
Baker, James, 377n23, 387, 409n1, 411n15, 414n40
Balakireff, Mily Alexeyevich, 72
Bartók, Béla, 21, 72, 90n62, 263n14, 355, 377n23, 390–91, 410n10; *Mikrokosmos*, 386n73
Bauer, Amy, 383n56
Baumann, Richard, 224, 235n18
beautiful (the), aesthetic concept of, 249, 278–79, 303n45. *See also* sublime (the), aesthetic concept of
Bechstein piano, 101, 105
Beethoven, Ludwig van, 6–8, 12, 15, 19, 27n7, 35, 43, 84n9, 193, 224; Bagatelles, 384n62; Brahms and, 190, 193, 195; bravura virtuosity and, 275–76; cadenzas for Piano Concertos, 28n13; *Coriolan* Overture, op. 62, 81, 91n70; Alfred Cortot's editions of, 242; "Diabelli" Variations for Piano, op. 120, 13; influence on Liszt, 43–46, 195, 312; Marie Jaëll and, 362; late piano works of, 269; legato playing of, 30n28; *Leonora* Overture no. 3, op. 72b, 83, 92n72; Liszt's performances of, 61, 90n60, 128; Liszt's transcriptions of, 4, 50, 155, 165, 170, 183n30, 184n37, 185n41, 195, 249, 280; *Phantasie*, op. 77, 384n62; Piano

Beethoven, Ludwig van—*(cont'd)* Concerto no. 1 in C Major, op. 15, 152–53, 169, 180n5, 304n51; Piano Concerto no. 3 in C Minor, op. 37, 61; Piano Concerto no. 4 in G Major, op. 58, 8, 249, 300n1; Piano Concerto no. 5 in E-flat Major ("Emperor"), op. 73, 27n5, 151, 249, 267–68; Piano Sonata in A-flat Major ("Funeral March"), op. 26, 46, 282; Piano Sonata in A-flat Major, op. 110, 276; Piano Sonata in B-flat Major, op. 22, 276; Piano Sonata in B-flat Major ("Hammerklavier"), op. 106, 8, 13, 14, 193, 238, 258, 276, 301n10; Piano Sonata in C Major ("Waldstein"), op. 53, 8, 14, 264n25, 279, 304n51; Piano Sonata in C Minor, op. 13 ("Pathétique"), 276, 282; Piano Sonata in C minor, op. 111, 81; Piano Sonata in C-sharp Minor ("Moonlight"), op. 27, no. 2; Piano Sonata in D Major ("Pastoral"), op. 28; Piano Sonata in D Minor ("Tempest"), op. 31, no. 2, 8; Piano Sonata in E-flat Major, op. 7, 276; Piano Sonata in E-flat Major ("The Hunt"), op. 31, no. 3, 276, 280, 304n53; Piano Sonata in F Minor ("Appassionata"), op. 57, 2, 8, 14, 28n7; pianos of, 6–8, 94; Schubert and, 261, 262n9; Symphony no. 5 in C Minor, op. 67, 313, 315

Beissinger, Margaret, 228, 236n35

Belgiojoso, Princess Cristina, 47

Beller-McKenna, Daniel, 210, 217n63

Bent, Ian, 235n13

Berezovsky, Boris, 26

Berio, Luciano, 211, 217n65, 231

Berlioz, Louis-Hector, 48, 165, 237n46; *Harold in Italy*, 313; relation to Liszt, 122, 231–32, 236n42, 263n14, 298, 301n10, 343n6; *Symphonie Fantastique* (and Liszt's transcription of), 71, 83, 154–58, 182n13, 182n14, 232, 236n44

Bernsdorf, Eduard, 213n11

Bernstein, Susan, 215n34

Bertini, Henri, 128

Bigot, Marie, 14, 35n61

Bilson, Malcolm, 264n24

Boissier, Valérie and Madame Auguste, 54, 88n36; lessons with Liszt, 110–12, 116, 120, 127–39, 141n9, 141n16, 143n28, 144n40, 144n41, 145n56, 147n69

Bolet, Jorge, 4, 26, 38n106, 183n27

Bomberger, Douglas, 36n88, 375n11

Borodin, Alexander, 72, 90n61

Bösendorfer piano, 101, 105

Botstein, Leon, 196, 215n36

Botticelli, Andrea, 31n31, 31n32, 32n37

Bourdieu, Pierre, 229–30, 236n36

Brahms, Johannes, xn7, 2, 24, 186–217; *51 Übungen*, 201; Bach Chaconne (left-hand study), 194–95; Double Concerto for Violin and Cello in A Minor, op. 102, 194; *Ein deutsches Requiem*, op. 45, 191; G-Minor Bach study, 194; Intermezzi, op. 118, 196; Intermezzi, op. 119, 196; Intermezzo in E Minor, op. 116, no. 5, 196, 207; Intermezzo in F Minor, op. 118, no. 4, 189, 207–9; left-hand study of the Bach Chaconne, 194; Piano Concerto no. 1 in D Minor, op. 15, 27n5, 190, 192, 195; Piano Concerto no. 2 in B-flat Major, op. 83, 27n5, 191; Piano Quartet no. 1 in G Minor, op. 25, 194; Piano Quintet in F minor, op. 34, 195; Piano Sonata no. 1 in C Major, op. 1, 151, 193; Piano Sonata no. 2 in F-sharp Minor, op. 2, 193; Rhapsody in B minor, op. 79, no. 1,

189, 204–7; Scherzo in E-flat Minor, op. 4, 193; Variations and Fugue on a Theme by Handel, op. 24, 13, 193, 201; Variations for Piano on a Theme by Paganini, op. 35, 189, 191, 193–94, 199–203; Variations on a Hungarian Song, op. 21, no. 2, 201; Variations on a Theme by Schumann, op. 9, 201; Variations on an Original Theme, op. 21, no. 1, 216n47; Violin Concerto in D Major, op. 77, 194; Waltzes, op. 39, 216n47
bravura style, 18, 20–22, 48, 194, 228, 232, 405, 409; comparison with brilliant style, 24, 254, 267–307
Brendel, Alfred, 4, 20–22, 29n18, 226, 235n29, 242, 264n22, 302n30; late Liszt and, 21, 389–92, 408, 410n8, 412n30
brilliant style (*stile brillante*), 6, 9, 44, 50, 254, 267–307
Broadwood piano, 6–8, 31n32, 97, 314
Brown, Matthew, 377n25
Brüstle, Christa, 228, 236n32
Bülow, Hans von, 16, 35n65, 73, 101, 107n12, 191
Bunyan, John, 61
Burkholder, J. Peter, 211, 217n64
Busoni, Ferruccio, 16–17, 26, 27n5, 29n17, 35n68, 38n108, 90n59, 179n1, 226, 305n61; edition of Liszt's complete études, 287; edition of Liszt's *Don Juan* Fantasy, 179, 185n47, 307n87
Butini, Caroline, 128, 143n38
Byron, Lord, 62, 119

Campanella, Michele, 398, 412n29
Campos, Rémy, 144n45
Carl Alexander, Grand Duke of Saxe-Weimar-Eisenach, 110, 139, 140n7, 147n71

Carter, Gerard, 73, 91n64
Chantavoine, Jean, 348, 375n9, 380n40
Chechlińska, Zofia, 90n56, 231, 236n39
Chickering piano, 105
Chissell, Joan, 28n7
Cho, Hye-Won Jennifer, 243, 264n23
Chopin, Fryderyk, 2, 18, 66, 362; aesthetic concept of beautiful and, 278–79; Ballade no. 1 in G Minor, op. 23, 205; Ballade no. 2 in F Major, op. 38, 227; Ballade no. 4 in F Minor, op. 52; Ballades (1–4), 12, 227; Brahms and, 191, 193; counterpoint in, 227; early ("brilliant") style of, 271, 287–90, 300n3, 301n15; editions of, 152, 179n2, 230–31, 242; Étude in A Minor, op. 10, no. 2, 10–11, 272–73, 290, 302n28; Étude in A Minor ("Winter Wind"), op. 25, no. 11, 11, 206; Étude in A-flat Major ("Aeolian Harp"), op. 25, no. 1, 283–84; Étude in B Minor ("Octave"), op. 25, no. 10, 279; Étude in C Major, op. 10, no. 1, 9; Étude in C Minor ("Ocean"), op. 25, no. 12, 302n27, 413n31; Étude in C Minor ("Revolutionary"), op. 10, no. 12, 11, 27n6, 126; Étude in C-sharp Minor, op. 10, no. 4, 28n11; Étude in E Major, op. 10, no. 3, 28n11, 289, 306n75; Étude in G-flat Major ("Black Key"), op. 10, no. 5, 28n13, 264n25, 289–90; Étude in G-sharp Minor ("Thirds"), op. 25, no. 6, 11–12; Études (op. 10 and op. 25), 6, 10, 16, 279, 298, 306n76; Fantasy in F Minor, op. 49, 9, 37n105; fingering and, 17; *Grande polonaise brillante* in E-flat Major, op. 22, 271, 287; *Hexaméron* contribution, 47–48, 50, 87n27, 90n56; improvisation and, 307n83; Liszt and, 154,

426   GENERAL INDEX

Chopin, Fryderyk—*(cont'd)*
162, 231–32, 261, 271, 280–81, 296–99, 305n64, 398; Mendelssohn and, 231–32; Nocturne in G Minor, op. 37, no. 1, 17; Paris debut, 111; Piano Concerti (1–2), 271, 304n56; piano method of, 129, 144n46, 236n41; *Polonaise brillante*, op. 3, for cello and piano, 271, 287; Polonaise in A-flat Major (relation to Liszt's *Funérailles*), op. 53, 71, 83; Prelude in A Minor, op. 28, no. 2, 371–72, 384n60, 384n61; Preludes, op. 28, 122; question of difficulty and, 11–13, 16–17; question of piano and, 9, 30n22, 33n44, 37n105; question of superficial virtuosity and, 20; Scherzi (1–4), 193; Scherzo in B Minor, op. 20, 35n74, 278; Sonata no. 2 in B-flat Minor, op. 35, 32n39, 224; Sonata no. 3 in B Minor, op. 58, 81; variants and, 28n13, 181n8; Variations for Piano and Orchestra on Mozart's "Là ci darem la mano," op. 2, 27n3; Waltz in E-flat Major (*Grande valse brillante*), op. 18, 127, 272–73, 302n29
Clarke, Christopher, 31n32
Clementi, Muzio, 6–7, 120–21, 128; *Gradus ad Parnassum*, 16, 134–37, 146n59; Piano Sonata in C Major, op. 2, no. 2, 282
Cohen, H. Robert, 375n13
Cone, Edward, 208, 217n59
Cook, Nicholas, 221, 228, 233n2, 236n32, 236n33
Cooper, Barry, 84n9
Cortot, Alfred, 91n71, 160, 183n22, 242, 264n19, 264n20
Cramer, Johann Baptist, 6, 16, 120–21, 335n14
Cubero, Diego, 217n60

Cvejić, Žarko, viii, 230, 236n38
Czerny, Carl, 7, 14, 16, 112, 128, 300n1, 300n5; *The Art of Finger Dexterity*, op. 740, 276–77; brilliant style and, 271, 274–76, 290; cadenza improvisation theories of, 179n2; *Hexaméron* contribution, 47–48, 50, 276; influence on Brahms, 192; influence on Liszt, 41–92, 117–18, 120–21, 238, 284, 305n64; *On the Proper Performance of All Beethoven's Works for Piano*, 31n29, 275–76, 303n34; Piano Concerto in F Major, op. 28, 44; Piano Sonata in A-flat Major, op. 7, 42, 44–46, 53, 55–59, 72, 269; *Pianoforte-Schule*, op. 500, 147n67, 147n68; *Reichstadt Waltz with Brilliant Variations*, op. 14, 44; *School of the Virtuoso*, op. 365, 242–43; *School of Velocity*, op. 299, 43; as teacher of Liszt, 96–97, 113, 116, 139, 142n21, 154, 213n15, 241, 267; Variations on a Theme by Rode "La Ricordanza," op. 33, 44
Cziffra, György, 4, 413n30

Dante Alighieri, 19, 56, 88n37, *Divine Comedy*, 54, 88n36, 110–11, 116, 363, 379n39
Dahlhaus, Carl, viii, ixn615, 28n10, 269, 275, 299, 389
Daverio, John, 192, 194, 213n9, 214n26
Davies, James Q., 140n4, 142n18, 374n1
Deaville, James, 213, 375n12, 377n23, 410n4
Debussy, Claude, 22, 227, 233, 246–47, 377n28, 379n35; *Des pas sur la neige*, 256–62
Derrida, Jacques, 156, 182n15
Döhler, Theodor, 112, 142n17

Domokos, Zsuzsanna, 84n1
Donin, Nicolas, 223
double-escapement action, 8–9, 97, 100, 280
Dreyschock, Alexander, 1, 27n6
Dryden, John, 42
Dufetel, Nicolas, 86n21, 142n19, 143n27
Dunsby, Jonathan, 15, 262n8, 265n34, 277
Dussek, Jan Ladislav, *Sufferings of the Queen of France*, 83

Eckhardt, Maria, 181n13
Edin, Martin, 179n2
Eigeldinger, Jean-Jacques, 29n13, 35n69, 129–30, 144n45, 144n46, 152
Einstein, Alfred, 1, 27n1
Ella, John, 84n5
Ellis, Katharine, 48–49, 87n29, 377n21
Epstein, Julius, 112, 142n17
Érard, Pierre, 99–100, 107n9, 107n10
Érard, Sebastian, 280
Érard Piano, 8–10, 31n32, 33n44, 97–101, 269, 280
Erdener, Yıldıray, 234n10
Erkel, Ferenc, 83

Fay, Amy, 50, 88n34
Ferrière le Vayer, Marquise de, 111
Field, John, 122–23, 126–27, 162, 180n5, 301n13
Finlow, Simon, 289–90, 306n76
Fiorentino, Sergio, 391
Fischer, Edwin, 225
Forte, Allen, 411n15
fortepiano, 5–6, 8, 10, 30n22, 34n50, 37n105, 93–94, 96, 98–99, 304n55
French New Romantic School, 61
Friedheim, Arthur, 24–25, 35n76, 90n63, 385n71

Friedheim, Philip, 181n9, 240, 263n9, 373
Fuller-Maitland, J. A., 181n10

Ganz, Peter, 234n14
Gárdonyi, Zoltán, 169, 390, 393–95, 410n10, 411n19, 412n25
Gasparin, Valérie de, 128, 141n10, 144n39
Gerstein, Kirill, 26, 171, 347–48, 374n7
Gessele, Cynthia, 235n15
Gibbs, Christopher, 86n18
Gide, André, 371–72, 384n60, 384n61
Gilels, Emil, 201, 216n45
Gill, Denise, 344n8
Giltburg, Boris, 26
Gjerdingen, Robert O., 223–24, 234n11, 234n12
Glass, Phillip, 371, 383n57, 383n58
Gobbi, Henrik, 184
Goehr, Alexander, 222, 234n7
Goethe, Johann Wolfgang von, 73, 81, 91n71, 113, 115
Godowsky, Leopold, 16, 27n4
Göllerich, August, 32n34, 48, 73, 87n28, 116, 135, 170
Gooley, Dana, 35n78, 84n1, 121, 142n18, 259–60, 265n32, 270, 277, 279
Gould, Glenn, 9
Grabócz, Márta, 314, 343n4
Gramit, David, 84n1
Granat, Zbigniew, 384n61
Grieg, Edvard, 2
Grillparzer, Franz, 27
Groth, Klaus, 192
Guichard, Catherine, 378n29
Gut, Serge, 411n15

Habets, Alfred, 90n61
Halfyard, Janet, 211, 217n65
Hallé, Charles, 304n53

Halliwell, Stephen, 36n79, 84n1, 84n3
Hamelin, Marc-André, 16
Hamilton, Kenneth, 32n39, 38n108, 86n21, 88n32, 90n56, 170, 184n33, 215n41, 225
Hatten, Robert, 313, 343–44n7
Halévy, Fromental, 86n20, 287
Hanslick, Eduard, 192, 196, 213n22, 215n35
Haydn, Joseph, 6, 20, 35n61, 44, 84n9, 128; Piano Sonata in C Major, Hob. XVI: 50 (1794), 30n27; Piano Sonata in E-flat Major, Hob. XVI: 52 (1794), 13, 30n27; Variations in F Minor, Hob. XVII: 6 (1793), 30n27
Helbig, Nadine, 112, 117, 141n15
Heller, Stephen, 16
Henschel, George, 213n16
Henselt, Adolf von, 2, 14, 16, 152, 179n2; *Études caractéristiques*, op. 2, no. 6, "Si oiseau j'étais, à toi je volerais," 27n4; Piano Concerto in F Minor, op. 16, 27n4
Herz, Henri, 1, 44, 47–50, 87n28, 87n29, 120–21, 128, 146n59, 361; contribution to *Hexaméron*, 47–50, 87n27
Heuberger, Richard, 212n8, 381n46
Hiller, Ferdinand, 100, 123, 126–28, 290
Hofmann, Josef, 27n5, 27n23
Hofmann, Kurt, 212n7
Holtmeier, Ludwig, 223–24
Honko, Lauri, 222–23, 234n5
Hoppe, Christiane, 30–31n21
Horowitz, Joseph, 235n23
Horowitz, Vladimir, 20, 26, 27n5, 29n16, 38n107, 44, 286, 305n68, 413n30; reworkings of Liszt's works, 4, 29n17, 29n19
Horton, Julian, 301n13

Hough, Stephen, 30n23, 35n70, 302n22, 374n5
Hovland, Erlend, 237n44
Howard, Leslie, 26, 87n25, 171, 398, 412n29, 413n33
Hughes, Edwin, 181n9
Hugo, Victor, 81, 128, 364
Hummel, Nepomuk, 97, 107n7, 112, 128, 142n17, 154, 290; *A Complete Theoretical and Practical Course of Instructions on the Art of Playing the Pianoforte*, 7, 9, 31n30; Piano Concerto in A Minor, op. 85, 267–69, 271–72, 300n4; Piano Concerto in B Minor, op. 89, 267–69, 271–72, 300n4, 300n7; Piano Sonata no. 5 in F-sharp Minor, op. 81, 81, 271
Hurpeau, Laurent, 378n30, 378n31

Jaëll, Alfred, 361, 364, 380n40, 380n41, 380n42
Jaëll, Marie, 346–47, 361–71, 373, 378–83n29–54, 383n59, 385–86n72; *Douze valses et finale*, 380n42; *Incendie de broussailes*, 371; *Les beaux jours*, 365, 367–70; *Les jours pluvieux*, 365, 380n39, 382n47; *On rêve au mauvais temps*, 365–70
Jakobson, Roman, 222, 234n6
Jankélévitch, Vladimir, 30n26
Jeffery, Peter, 234n4
Joachim, Joseph, 214n25

Kabisch, Thomas, 242, 247–50, 263n15
Kaczmarczyk, Adrienne, 54, 85n10, 85n39, 122, 143n31, 143n33, 143n34, 182n13, 183n28
Kalbeck, Max, 213n17
Kalkbrenner, Friedrich, 1, 4, 8, 32n35, 128, 146n59, 271, 290

GENERAL INDEX 429

Kallberg, Jeffrey, 181n8
Kammertöns, Christopher, 87n29
Katsaris, Cyprien, 185n41, 408, 413n30, 414n42
Kawabata, Mai, viii
Keep, David, 2, 10
Kentner, Louis, 21, 391, 412–13n30
Kessler, J. C., 54–55, 88n36, 113, 116, 128
Kiener, Hélène, 378n29, 382n49
Kildea, Paul, 30n22
Kim, Hyun Joo, vii, 37n98
Kirby, F. E., 214
Kirnberger, Johann, 223, 234n13
Klimo, Peter, 306n69
Knight, Ellen, 385n64
Knop, Ernest, 50
Knyt, Erinn E., 179n1
Kobrin, Alexander, 264
Körner, Theodor, 122–24
Kovács, Mária, 345n19
Kramer, Lawrence, 372, 384n61
Krause, Martin, 18, 184n31
Kregor, Jonathan, 13, 29n15, 182n17, 240, 242, 263n10, 349, 372, 383n57, 400
Kroó, György, 140n6
Kullak, Theodore, 14, 152–53, 169, 180n4, 180n5

Lachmund, Carl, 386n72
Lamartine, Alphonse de, 49, 373, 385n67
Lang, Lang, 2
Larson, Levi Keith, 84n17
Legány, Dezsö, 86
Lesure, François, 377n27
Levin, Robert, 28n13, 30n23
Ligeti, György Sándor, 16, 371, 383n56
Liszt, Franz. *See* separate index of Liszt's musical works
Littlewood, Julian, 216n44

Locke, Ralph P., 20, 36n80, 36n82, 387, 405
Loeffler, Charles Martin, 384–85n64
Loesch, Heinz von, viii, ixn6
Lord, Albert, 234n9
Loya, Shay, 21, 214n28, 350, 383n57

Macdonald, Hugh, 384n62
MacDonald, Malcolm, 195, 215n33
MacIntyre, Alasdair, 229–30, 236n37
Madsen, Charles, 262n7
Mansfeldt, Hugo, 373, 385n71
Mason, William, 92n73
May, Florence, 212
Mayer, Carl, 128
McMullan, Gordon, 394
Mechetti, Pietro, 46, 54–55
Mendelssohn, Felix, 21, 23, 36n88, 66, 231–32, 240, 271, 300n1; *Capriccio Brillant*, op. 22, 271; Piano Concerto no. 1, op. 25, 271; *Rondo Brillant*, op. 29, 271; "Songs without Words," 66; *Variations sérieuses*, op. 54, 13
Mérimée, Prosper, 139, 147n71
Meyerbeer, Giacomo, 3, 24, 90n58
Michałowski, Kornel, 271, 301n15
Michelangeli, Arturo Benedetti, 201, 216n45
Michelangelo, 19, 111, 249
Micznik, Vera, 343n6
Minder-Jeanneret, Irène, 143–44n38
Mollo, Tranquillo, 152
Montgolfier, Jenny, 129–30
Montgomery, David, 244, 246, 265n28
Morgan, Robert P., 411n15
Moscheles, Charlotte, 85n11
Moscheles, Isaac Ignaz, 16, 44, 112, 120–21, 128, 142, 271, 300n7, 361
Moseley, Roger, 190–91, 197, 210, 213n10

Moysan, Bruno, 130, 134, 145n48, 146n58, 410n4
Mozart, Wolfgang Amadeus, 12, 32n36, 33n48, 44, 84n9, 112, 127–128, 250, 264n25, 268, 304n56; bravura style and, 270; cadenzas and, 15, 28n13, 31n28; *Die Entführung aus dem Serail*, 270; *Don Giovanni* (*Don Juan*), 3, 23–24, 27n3, 55, 185, 307n87; editions of, 152; fortepiano of, 6–7, 10, 30n23, 34n50, 37n105, 96; non-legato style and, 7, 30n28; Piano Concerto no. 9 in E-flat Major, K. 271, 249; Piano Concerto no. 17 in G major, K. 453, 34n51; Piano Concerto no. 24 in C Minor, K. 491, 300n1; Piano Sonata in A Major, K. 331, 34n51; Piano Sonata in C Major, K. 330, 33n41; Piano Sonata in C Minor, K. 457, 282; Piano Sonata in D Major, K. 576, 34n48; Piano Sonata in F Major, K. 332, 28n13; *Requiem*, 122–26, 143n34
Mueller, Rena Charnin, 113, 117, 142n20, 142n21, 143n25, 181n13
Mussorgsky, Modest, 28n12

Notley, Margaret, 207, 210, 216–17n56
Novack, Saul, 222, 234n7

Paganini, Niccolò, 1, 138, 165; *24 Caprices*, op. 1, Brahms's transformation of, 189, 191, 193, 197–203, 216n46; *24 Caprices*, op. 1, Liszt's transformation of, 10, 16, 18, 23, 159, 160–62, 165, 169, 183n22, 183n24, 194, 198, 280, 283–87, 305n68, 306n69, 306n78; *24 Caprices*, op. 1, Schumann's transformation of, 160–61, 194; 1832 concert in Paris, 23, 111, 141n11, 154, 182n13; aesthetic concept of sublimity and, 278–79; "Clochette" theme and Liszt, 13–14, 23, 154, 158–59, 182n17, 288, 305n66; virtuosity of, 1, 13, 19, 27n6, 188, 191, 194, 197, 212n5, 238, 275, 314
Parry, John Orlando, 50
Parry, Milman, 223–24, 234n9
Pascal, Blaise, 128
Perl, Alfredo, 170–71, 185n40
Pesce, Dolores, 21, 185n45, 343n1, 354, 376n19, 387, 399, 401, 409n2
Pierce, J. Mackenzie, 346, 374n1
Pixis, Johann Peter, 47–50, 87n27, 290
Plaskin, Glenn, 27n1, 29n19
Plato, Platonic, 3, 33n45, 226
Pleyel, Marie, 14
Pleyel piano, 9, 33n44, 97
Ployer, Barbara, 28n13
Poulenc, Francis, 377n26
Prellmechanik action, 96–97
Prokofiev, Sergei Sergeyevich, 2, 269
Pruckner, Dionys, 45

Raab, Antonia ("Toni"), 170–71
Rachmaninoff, Sergei, 2, 8, 27n4, 226, 268–69; Second Piano Sonata, op. 36, 29n17; Third Piano Concerto, op. 30, 151, 268–69
Ramann, Lina, 43–44, 71, 84n8, 85n10, 89n53, 109, 111–12, 139, 140n2, 141, 145n54, 169–70
Ratner, Leonard, 271, 302n21, 343n3
Ravel, Maurice, 227, 233, 284, 371, 377n26
Reich, Nancy B., 182n20
Reich, Steve, 371, 383n57, 383n58
Reicha, Antoine, 55, 236n42, 383n59
Reisenauer, Alfred, 386n72
Reynaud, Cécile, ixn3
Riemann, Hugo, 147n67

Ries, Ferdinand, 120–21, 300n1, 305n59
Rings, Steven, 207–8, 215n35, 217n58, 281–82
Rink, John, 29n13, 65, 89n45, 128–30, 144n40, 195, 215n32
Rogé, Pascal, 181n7
Rosen, Charles: debate with Alfred Brendel, 22–23; views on Berlioz, 237n42; views on Chopin, 16, 206, 216n54, 227, 278–79; views on Liszt, 18, 21–24, 35n67, 35n72, 215n34, 278–79, 299, 307n85, 410n4
Rosenblatt, Jay, 65–66, 86n24, 89n47, 263n13
Rossini, Gioachino Antonio, 122–24, 127, 154, 287, 405–6
Rowland, David, 32n35, 215n41
Rubinstein, Anton, 2, 16, 272, 302n26, 302n27, 304n55, Étude in C Major, op. 23, no. 2, 35n66
Rubinstein, Arthur, 26, 305–6n68

Saffle, Michael, 28n8, 28n9, 37n99, 84n1, 183n29, 376n20
Salieri, Antonio, 232
Samaroff, Olga, 241, 260, 263n12
Samarotto, Frank, 204–5, 216n51
Samson, Jim, 3, 236n34, 267; on Chopin, 236n41, 237n47, 271, 300n3, 301n15, 302n24, 305n70, 307n83; on Liszt, 27n2, 212n5, 270, 279, 284, 305n64, 305n67; on virtuosity, 1, 5, 13, 18, 29n21, 30n26, 121, 160, 186–89, 212n2, 275, 301–2n16
Saint-Saëns, Camille, 2, 14, 302n22, 361–64, 366, 379n38, 379n39, 380n42, 400
Saint-Simonians, 20, 36n82
Sanguinetti, Giorgio, 224, 325n17
Satie, Erik, *Vexations*, 371, 382n51, 383n58

Satyendra, Ramon, 411n15
Sauer, Emil von, 14, 18, 35n70, 35n71, 35n72, 178–79, 185n46
Scarlatti, Antonio, 22, 30n22, 30n26
Schmidt, Christian Martin, 207, 216n56
Schmidt, Georg Philipp, 65
Schmitt, Alois, 134–35, 146n58
Schnabel, Artur, 20, 225, 242, 264n19
Schnapper, Laure, 87n29
Schoenberg, Arnold, 212n3, 226, 247, 355, 375n8, 376n20, 384n59; *Drei Klavierstücke* (Three Piano Pieces), op. 11, no. 2, 226; *Verklärte Nacht* (Transfigured Night), for string sextet, op. 4, 247
Schonberg, Harold, 29n19
Schopenhauer, Arthur, 36n81
Schubert, Franz, 94, 165, 180n3, 191, 198, 213n9, 224, 238–66, 271; "Ave Maria," D. 839, 361; "Das Fischermädchen," D. 957, 162; "Der Atlas," D. 957, 162; "Der Wanderer," D. 489, 65, 250, 254, 262n3; "Der Doppelgänger," D. 957, 162, 372; "Der Leiermann," D. 911, 372; "Die liebe Farbe," D. 795, 372, 384n63; "Die Taubenpost," D. 965a, 162; "Du bist die Ruh," D. 776, 42, 65–72, 83, 89n51;"Erlkönig," D. 328, 3, 24, 241, 244, 247–48, 265n27; "Liebesbotschaft," D. 957, 62; Liszt's editions of, 152; "Lützows wilde Jagd," D. 205, 122; *Moment Musical* in F minor, op. 94, no. 5, D. 780, 261; Piano Sonata in A minor, D. 748, 244–46; Piano Sonata in C Minor, D. 958, 227, 261; Piano Sonata in D major, D. 850, 261; "Ständchen," D. 957, 162–65, 184n31; *Wanderer* Fantasy in C Major, D. 760, 13, 238–66, 277

Schumann, Clara, 2, 140n6, 182n20, 240, 261, 263n11; Beethoven's "Appassionata" and, 2, 27–28n7; Brahms and, 196, 201, 215n39; Liszt and, 160, 225, 235n25, 279

Schumann, Robert, 24, 43, 89n52, 140n6, 165, 214n31; *Carnaval*, op. 9, 160, 227; Études after Paganini Caprices, op. 3 and op. 10, 160–61, 169, 182n19, 183n23–24, 194; *Fantasiestücke*, op. 12, 160; Fantasy in C major, op. 17, 13, 72, 83; *Humoreske*, op. 20, 208; Marie Jaëll and, 362, 383n53; relation to Brahms, 194–95, 201, 212n8, 213n9; review of Liszt's Berlioz-Liszt *Symphonie fantastique*, 71, 155, 182n14; review of Liszt's *Études d'exécution transcendante d'après Paganini*, 161, 183n24; review of Liszt's *Grandes études*, 24; *Symphonic Études*, op. 13, 295–96; virtuosity and, 20–21, 191–92, 213n14, 261, 348, 375n8

Searle, Humphrey, 21, 391, 410n13, 411n15

Senancour, Étienne Pivert de, *Obermann* (novel), 41, 61

Shakespeare, William, 41, 249

Sham, Olivia, 10, 11, 33n44, 33n47, 87n26, 347, 374n5

Smiles, Sam, 393–94, 412n20

Smith, Peter H., 214n24

Somfai, Laszlo, 91n66

Stradal, August, 81, 88n41, 91n69, 91n70, 92n72

Staël, Germaine (Madame) de, 115, 119, 133

Stavenhagen, Bernhard, 65–66

Stefaniak, Alexander, ix, 182n20, 191–92, 213n14, 214n22, 304n50, 348

Steibelt, Daniel, "Storm Rondo" (from Piano Concerto no. 3, op. 33), 281–83, 305n58

Stein, Johann Andreas, 96
Stein piano, 96
Steinway piano, 30n23, 93, 105, 244
Stoepel, François, 49, 61
Stradal, August, 81, 88n41, 91n69, 91n70, 92n72
Stradivari, Antonio, 5
Stravinsky, Igor, 27n6, 226
Strohm, Reinhard, 224, 235n19
Strunck, Oliver, 225, 235n21
sublime (the), aesthetic concept of, 61, 63, 278–79, 303n44, 303–4n45, 304n50, 344n1. *See also* beautiful, aesthetic concept of
Suttoni, Charles, 401, 413n35, 413n37
Szabolcsi, Bence, 411n15
Szelenyi, István, 169, 393–95, 411n15, 411n19, 412n25
Szendy, Peter, 170, 184n38
Szidon, Roberto, 412n29

Talbot, Michael, 260, 266
Tappolet, Claude, 144n45
Taruskin, Richard, 6, 22, 36n90, 344n16, 411n14
Tausenau, Karl, 61, 89n43
Tausig, Carl, 16, 35n65
Taylor, Philip S., 302
Tchaikovsky, Peter Ilich, 2, 212n3, 400–401; Piano Concerto no. 1 in B-flat Minor, op. 23, 2, 27n5, 348, 374–75n7
Thalberg, Sigismond, 2–3, 21, 47, 112, 154, 160, 269, 272; *Andante final de Lucie de Lammermoor varié*, op. 44, 190; contribution to *Hexaméron*, 47; *Fantaisie sur l'opéra "Moïse" de Rossini*, op. 33, 3, 197; *Grande fantaisie et variations sur "Don Juan,"* op. 14, 190; *Grandes Valses brillantes*, op. 47, 306n73; Piano Concerto in F Minor, op. 5, 3; relation to Brahms, 190; relation to Liszt, 2, 25, 160, 278–79;

Souvenirs d'Amérique, 306n73; "three-hand" technique of, 14, 186, 197, 280; *Valse mélodique*, op. 62; virtuosity of, 13–14, 269, 272, 276, 278, 288
Thym, Jürgen, 376n15
Tischer, Gerhard, 140n6
Todd, R. Larry, 23, 36n94, 236n41
Torbianelli, Edoardo, 144
Trifonov, Daniil, 26, 27n6
Trippett, David, 84n1
Troester, Sébastien, 371, 379n39, 381n43, 383n58
Tubeuf, André, 227

Uchida, Mitsuko, 244, 265n26

Verdi, Giuseppe, 25, 28n12, 399–404
Vianna da Motta, José, 31–32n34, 171–73, 377n23

Wagner, Richard, 212n8; *Das Rheingold*, 384n59; *Ein Brief über Franz Liszt's Symphonische Dichtungen*, 90n60; Liszt's transcriptions of, 37n103, 280, 399–400, 404; *Parsifal*, 61, 63, 89n44; relation to Liszt, 72–74, 82–83, 91n67, 138, 140n6, 188, 298, 413n36
Walker, Alan, 35n65, 87n24, 89n54, 147n64, 411n15; views on Chopin, 281, 304n53; views on Hans von Bülow, 35n65; views on Liszt, 33n45, 71, 87, 185n45, 242, 262n5, 306n71, 354, 396, 411n15
Walker, Bettina, 138, 147n66
Warren, Jeff R., 181n12
Watkins, Holly, 375
Weber, Carl Maria Friedrich Ernst von, 33n45, 128, 143n35; *Der Freischütz*, op. 77, 49; *Invitation to the Dance*, op. 65, 90n58, 127; *Konzertstück*, op. 79, 37n101, 267, 277, 300n4, 302n20; Liszt's editions of, 152, 239, 277; "Lützows wilde Jagd," op. 42, no. 2, 122–24; Piano Sonata no. 2 in A-flat Major, op. 39, 56, 60, 269, 282; Piano Sonata no. 4 in E Minor, op. 70, 42, 62–64, 72, 81, 269; Piano Sonatas (1–4), 271; virtuosity of, 271, 277, 290
Wild, Earl, 4, 29n17
Williams, Adrian, 107n1
Wittgenstein, Fürstin Carolyne (Princess), 85
Wolff, Pierre, 111, 138, 141n11, 160, 182n18
Wolkowicz, Vera, 264n21
Wright, Andrew, 378n29
Wright, James K., 376n20
Wright, William, 85n13

www.ingramcontent.com/pod-product-compliance
Lightning Source LLC
Jackson TN
JSHW061114250625
86703JS00004B/38